The Sokoto Caliphate

IBADAN HISTORY SERIES
Editor K. O. Dike Ph.D.

Published by Northwestern University Press

CHRISTIAN MISSIONS IN NIGERIA 1841–1891
by J. F. A. Ajayi
Professor of History, University of Ibadan

THE ZULU AFTERMATH
by J. D. Omer-Cooper
Professor of History, University of Zambia

Published by Humanities Press

THE MISSIONARY IMPACT ON MODERN NIGERIA 1842–1914
by E. A. Ayandele
Department of History, University of Ibadan

THE INTERNATIONAL BOUNDARIES OF NIGERIA
by J. C. Anene
Professor of History, University of Biafra

THE SOKOTO CALIPHATE
by Murray Last
Research Fellow, Ahmadu Bello University, Zaria

In preparation (to be published by Humanities Press)

BRITAIN AND THE CONGO QUESTION
by S. J. S. Cookey
Department of History, University of Ibadan

THE LAGOS PROTECTORATE
by A. B. Aderibigbe
Professor of History, University of Lagos

NIGER DELTA RIVALRY
Itsekiri-Urhobo Relations and European Enterprise 1884–1936
by O. Ikime
Department of History, University of Ibadan

1. al-haji Junaidu, Wazirin Sokoto

Ibadan History Series

The Sokoto Caliphate

Murray Last Ph.D.
Research Fellow, Northern History Research Scheme, Ahmadu Bello University, Zaria

HUMANITIES PRESS

First published
in the United States of America 1967
by Humanities Press Inc.
303 Park Avenue South
New York, N.Y. 10010

Library of Congress Catalog Card No. 67–16974

Printed in Great Britain by
Western Printing Services Ltd, Bristol

For the Waziri

Introduction to the Ibadan History Series

The 'Ibadan History Series' grew out of the efforts of some members of the Department of History, Ibadan University, Nigeria, to evolve a balanced and scholarly study of the history of African peoples south of the Sahara. In the years before the Second World War, the study of African history was retarded, and to some extent vitiated, by the assumption of many scholars that lack of written records in some areas of Africa meant also the absence of history. Documentary evidence had become so overwhelmingly important for the European scholar that he tended to equate written documents with history, and to take the absence of documents to mean the absence of events worthy of historical study. As a result in the nineteenth century, when Europe occupied Africa, her scholars did not attempt to understand or to build on the historical traditions in existence there; they sought instead to challenge and to supplant them. The history of European traders, missionaries, explorers, conquerors and rulers constituted, in their view, the sum total of African history.

Fortunately for the historian of today, African historical consciousness remained alive throughout the period of colonial rule: that tradition was too much a part of the African way of life to succumb to the attacks of the European scholar. Even in the heyday of white supremacy some educated Africans of the period were sufficiently dominated by their past to feel impelled to commit to writing the laws, customs, proverbs, sayings and historical traditions of their own communities. Notable among these may be mentioned James Africanus Horton of Sierra Leone, Reindorf and Sarbah of Ghana, Otomba Payne and Samuel Johnson of Nigeria, Apolo Kagwa of Uganda, to name but a few. The published works they left behind have become important sources of African history today; but they were swimming against the current of their time and made little impression on contemporaries. Historians continued to write as if Africans were not active participants in the great events that shaped their continent.

The decided change towards a new African historiography came with the movement towards independence. African nationalists rejected the European appraisal of their past. They demanded a new orientation and improved educational facilities to effect this reappraisal. With the establishment of new universities in Africa, it was inevitable that the teaching of history and the training of African historians would receive a new impetus. For obvious reasons the change-over was slow in coming. Even in the new universities the old theories for a time prevailed: besides European history, there were courses only on 'European activities in Africa' at the undergraduate level, and at the postgraduate level research was generally on British and French policy towards their African territories.

By the late 1940's, however, African research students were insisting that African history must be the history of Africans, not of Europeans *per se* in Africa; that local records and historical traditions must be used to supplement European metropolitan archives; in short, that oral tradition must be accepted as valid material for historical reconstruction. No doubt the validity of non-written sources for historical research had been pointed out before, but it was new for university departments of history to accept it, especially in relation to African oral tradition. Even then not everyone was happy about it. Anthropologists replied cautiously that oral tradition, even when seemingly factual, was not history and could only be interpreted in terms of its functions in society and within the particular culture. But this did not destroy its validity as material for history; it only argued for a return to the link between history and sociology advocated in the fourteenth century by the famous North African historian, Ibn Khaldūn.

Even in studies of European impact on African societies and cultures, where European archival material still remains our major source, this source should be checked and supplemented by oral tradition, material artefacts and other sources of history in Africa. The achievement of the present position in the study of African history has been the result of individual and co-operative efforts of many scholars in different parts of the world, but I think it is fair to say that the universities in Africa, and Ibadan in particular, have played and are playing their part in this pioneering work.

K. ONWUKA DIKE

Acknowledgements

This work was originally done for a Ph.D. degree at the University of Ibadan, with the financial support of, first, the Leverhulme Trust and, later, the Nigerian Federal Ministry of Education. Without the welcome given me by the University and without the kindliness of those who administered the scholarship grants, my three years as a student of Ibadan would not have been the great pleasure that they were.

Although many acknowledgements are made in the course of the book, I would especially like to thank al-haji Junaidu, Wazirin Sokoto, for his kind help both in my work and during my year in Sokoto. In Ibadan, I received the greatest assistance and encouragement from Professor H. F. C. Smith (now of Ahmadu Bello University, Zaria), from J. O. Hunwick, who helped me learn Arabic, and from F. H. El-Masri and M. A. al-Hajj, both of whom not only discussed my work and made suggestions but also read the original thesis in manuscript. I am grateful to Dr. C. F. Hoffmann for his help in translating some passages in German, and I should also like to thank the staff of the University Library, Ibadan, for their patience, to thank G. I. Okolo and E. A. Ṣoręmi for their help in drawing the originals of the maps and genealogies, and Mrs Trudi Mittelmann for compiling the Index. I wish also to thank Messrs. John Murray (Publishers) Ltd. for permission to quote from *Bornu, Sahara and Sudan* by H. R. Palmer, and M. Hiskett and Ibadan University Press for permission to quote from the translation of *Tazyīn al-Waraqāt*. Finally, I am greatly indebted to Elizabeth Hopkins for all her work and perseverance in making the typescript fit for presentation.

Contents

Illustrations

For No. 2 acknowledgement is made to the Surveyor-General, Northern Nigerian Survey; for Nos. 10 and 11 to the National Archives, Kaduna. The other illustrations are from photographs by the author.

Maps

Genealogies (in pocket)

Abbreviations

A.M.	*Anīs al-mufīd.*
B.C.A.F.	*Bulletin, Comité de l'Afrique Française.*
B.S.O.A.S.	*Bulletin, School of Oriental and African Studies.*
Bull., Com. Et. Hist. Sc. de l'A.O.F.	*Bulletin, Comité d'Etudes Historiques et Scientifiques de l'Afrique Occidentale Française.*
D.M.	*Ḍabṭ al-multaqaṭāt.*
E.I.	*Encyclopedia of Islam.*
G.A.L. (*S*)	*Geschichte der Arabischen Litteratur* (*Supplementband*).
I.F.A.N.	*Institut Français d'Afrique Noire* (*Bulletin*).
I.M.	*Infāq al-maisūr.*
I.N.	*'Īdā' al-nusūkh.*
J.A.H.	*Journal of African History.*
J.A.S.	*Journal of the African Society* (*African Affairs*).
J.H.S.N.	*Journal, Historical Society of Nigeria.*
J.R.G.S.	*Journal, Royal Geographical Society.*
K.B.	*al-Kashf wa 'l-bayān.*
K.F.	*Kitāb al-farq.*
M.I.O.	*Mitteilungen des Instituts für Orient-Forschung.*
M.S.O.S.	*Mitteilungen des Seminars für Orientalische Sprachen zu Berlin.*
R.A.	*Rauḍāt al-afkār.*

Abbreviations

R.J.	*Rauḍ al-jinān.*
R.M.M.	*Revue du Monde Musulman.*
T.W.	*Tazyīn al-waraqāt.*

Glossary

A'jamī	non-Arabic language written in Arabic script.
Asānīd	academic genealogies.
Baraka	numinous authority; blessing.
Bay'a	act of homage (to a new Caliph).
Dār al-Islām	land in which Islamic rule is established.
Ḥadīth	tradition about the Prophet.
Hijra	emigration for the Faith.
Ijtihād	reinterpretation of the Law.
Jihād	action, war for the Faith.
Jinn	elemental spirit.
Jizya	poll-tax.
Karāmāt	miracles.
Kharāj	land-tax.
Laqab	nickname.
Malam (mu'allim)	learned man, teacher.
Muhājirūn	participants in a hijra.
Mujāhidūn	participants in a jihād.
Muqaddam	leader.
Murābiṭūn	garrison of a ribāṭ.
Ribāṭ	frontier stronghold.
Salāsil	genealogies.

Sharīʿa	Islamic Law.
Ṣūfī	Islamic mystic.
Sunna	the practice of the Prophet.
Ṭarīqa	path in Islamic mysticism, brotherhood.
Waqf	property dedicated to Islam.
Wird	recitation following prayer.
Zakāt	canonical alms required of all Muslims.

Arabic words have been given diacritical marks, even though they sometimes occur in the form of an English plural. But certain words, like Quran and sufi, which are used in various forms, are so well known that the diacritical marks have been omitted.

Preface

The purpose of this work is threefold. First, I try to show what sources are available for a description of the development of the Sokoto Community. The Arabic manuscripts in several cases required collection and collation, and some critique is made of the texts used. Similarly, primary material, whether travellers' journals or oral tradition preserved in written form in Hausa, English or French, required a critical examination of its origins and its relation to other sources.

Second, from the sources examined and collated, I try to reconstruct the way the Community of the Shaikh developed through the nineteenth century and the physical means used to maintain a framework in which there could continue both the practice of Islam and the Islamic scholarship for which Sokoto is distinguished. No detailed discussion of the literature arising from that scholarship is attempted except in relation to the vizierate. Since the sources are too uneven to produce a comprehensive history of consistent depth throughout the period, my aim is not to give an annalistic account, but to provide the groundwork of details which illustrate certain facets crucial to the history of Sokoto. Thus I describe the background and the growth of the Community before the jihād, as a framework on which Sokoto of the nineteenth century developed. This is followed by a brief interpretation of the jihād and the pattern of movements in it. The period, which coincides with the life of the Shaikh, closes with the administration he set up and the divisions already incipient within it. In the second period, from the death of the Shaikh in 1817 to the arrival of the British in 1903, I trace the growth of the caliphate in Sokoto geographically and politically, and carry the account in outline through the nineteenth century to show both the consistency in Sokoto and the developments. The coming of the British is discussed only in so far as it impinged on life in general in Sokoto and closed the period of the independent caliphate.

The third purpose of this book is to use the same sources to reconstruct a history in outline of a leading family of Sokoto and to give a brief account of their work. In this I try to show another aspect of the nature of the Sokoto caliphate through the nineteenth century and the way an Islamic society was maintained. The vizierate was chosen because it is the best documented of the offices: the Viziers were themselves historians of Sokoto, and the present Vizier, al-haji Junaidu, is the modern authority on Sokoto history and possesses the best historical library in Sokoto.

The reason for the threefold aim of this book is the sketchiness of the work done previously in this field. The Arabic material previously had only been partially recovered (and much, it is suspected, remains to be recovered): consequently earlier accounts were found to be inadequate, not least since those that drew on Arabic material failed to collate or criticise their sources. Therefore before a history of Sokoto could be written, some critique of the sources was necessary. Similarly, no account of the vizierate in Sokoto could be written without an outline of the caliphate in which the Viziers served. Therefore, in order to make this study, it has been necessary to undertake both a history and a historiography of Sokoto and to use them to illustrate each other.

Sokoto, July 1966 — MURRAY LAST

The Sources

The sources for nineteenth-century Sokoto history fall into two groups: those written in the nineteenth century, and those compiled after the arrival of the British in 1903. In the first group are (*a*) the Arabic books written mostly in Sokoto by eyewitnesses or contemporaries of eyewitnesses; (*b*) the files of the correspondence of the Viziers and others; (*c*) the journals of European travellers. The second, post-British group includes material which is usually a written version of oral tradition: the histories written in Hausa, the District notebooks and Provincial gazetteers, and, finally, my own field notes. The twentieth-century Arabic sources, while written after the arrival of the British, have been included in the pre-British group of sources since the data given in them are accumulated from earlier Arabic works and comparatively little is derived from strictly oral sources.

I

(a) *Nineteenth-century Arabic manuscripts.* The genuineness of most of these manuscripts is not doubted. Due to the cross-references within the works of the Shaikh, his brother 'Abdullāh, his son Muḥammad Bello and the Viziers Gidado and 'Abd al-Qādir b. Gidado, a successful forger would have had to compose several dozen works with a consistency and scholarship that would make him famous. The only forgeries identified so far are three short works aimed at establishing the credentials of one new scholastic family: apart from contemporary evidence, their style and purpose make the books clearly spurious.

Where works have no author's name but are attributed to a possible author, a note is given. Copies, especially of the important works, are widely distributed in private collections. Public libraries of manuscripts are an innovation, since a scholar could borrow a book and make his own copy. Copyists' errors have thus crept into most of the texts used: I have, therefore, usually referred to more than one text, preferring the oldest copies to those made for public collections.

The public libraries used were:

Sokoto Divisional Library (SDL), containing some 270 books (*c.* 4,800 folios), many of which are new or duplicate copies. A large number, however, derive from the collection of the present Sarkin Dogarai, Shehu Adili. The library was started *c.* 1961. Those books not already in the library of the University of Ibadan (according to the catalogue of W. E. N. Kensdale, 1955–8) were sent there for microfilming. Catalogues of the books in the SDL are now held in Sokoto, Zaria and Ibadan.

Sokoto Town Council Library (STL), containing some 85 books, which are generally older than those in SDL. The library was started *c.* 1955. Books neither in Ibadan nor in SDL were sent for microfilming.

Nizamiyya School Library, Sokoto (Niz.), containing over a hundred books belonging to the Marafa of Sokoto. The Marafa belongs to the distinguished family holding the title of Magajin gari and his collection contains generally old, and sometimes rare, books. Those not found elsewhere were sent for microfilming.

Shahuci Judicial School, Kano (Ko). The library contains a large number of both classical and Nigerian works, including over 150 of the latter. A list of 90 Nigerian books was published by J. O. Hunwick in the *Supplement to the Bulletin of News of the Historical Society of Nigeria* (VII, 2, 1962); some of these books were microfilmed for Ibadan and Zaria. The library has some rare copies, probably from the collection of the Emirs of Kano, on whose library this collection is based.

National Archives, Kaduna (NAK), containing some 160 different works by the Shaikh, 'Abdullāh and Muḥammad Bello, as well as a very large number of obscure and miscellaneous works: the collection contains over 3,000 pieces. The books from Sokoto ('Sokprof') include the collection of M. Umaru Nagwamatse, whose father, M. Akali, was a noted scholar. The 'Kadcap' boxes contain the papers and manuscripts collected by J. A. Burdon, first British Resident in Sokoto, who obtained copies and translations into English or Hausa of most of the major texts of Sokoto history. The papers of F. Edgar, an administrator interested in Hausa material, are also in 'Kadcap'.

Department of Antiquities, Jos (Jos). *A Descriptive Catalogue* (Luzac, 1965) has been published by Dr. A. S. Arif and A. M. Abū Hakima. Some 1,100 manuscripts are listed, but only a small proportion of these are by the Shaikh, 'Abdullāh and Muḥammad Bello. A few of the manuscripts listed are only microfilm copies. The collection, started in 1958 and based on the work of Dr. A. D. H. Bivar and Malam Muntaka Coomassie, contains many of the manuscripts collected by H. R. Palmer, including the new books written at his request.

University of Ibadan. A catalogue of the holdings of the library both in manuscript and on microfilm was published by W. E. N. Kensdale (1955–8). Since 1958, much material has been brought for microfilming; most of it is in the process of being catalogued. In the bibliography, books in the Kensdale Catalogue are marked (K.), but most of the other books should be in the library on microfilm or xerox-prints.

Bibliothèque Nationale (BN), *Institut de France* (IF), *Paris.* BN contains several volumes of manuscripts from Segu, taken or copied by the French. A brief note on the collection was published by Professor H. F. C. Smith in *Supplement to the Bulletin of News of the Historical Society of Nigeria* (IV, 2, 1959). An *Index Général des Manuscrits Arabes Musulmans de la Bibliothèque Nationale de Paris* was published by G. Vajda (Paris, 1953); earlier he had contributed an article on Arabic literature in West Africa to *Journal de la Société des Africanistes* (1950, pp. 229–38). Some of the Segu manuscripts have relevance to Sokoto. My references are to the volume and page numbering of the BN. The IF possesses the de Gironcourt collection, containing both books and documents. The books were generally copied for the collection in Zinder or Say from texts originating in Sokoto. The documents are concerned particularly with Masina. Short notes on the collection are given by D. P. de Pedrals in *Archéologie de l'Afrique Noire* (Paris, 1950) and by Professor H. F. C. Smith in the *Journal of the Historical Society of Nigeria* (I, 3, 1958, pp. 240–1).

The main private collection used was that of al-haji Junaidu, Wazirin Sokoto. His collection is one of the oldest and largest in Sokoto and contains rare copies of several early poems. The collection has texts reputedly in the handwriting of the first Vizier, the great-grandfather of al-haji Junaidu, who started the collection. Other rare books were lent to me by M. Yahaya, Alkalin Lardin Sokoto, who is a son of the Vizier 'Abd al-Qādir Machido: some of these books were from his own collection, some from the collection of the Sarkin Musulmi, al-haji Sir Abubakar. Some texts from these private collections have already been microfilmed in Zaria: a catalogue of manuscripts on microfilm in Zaria has been published in the *First Interim Report* of the Northern History Research Scheme (Zaria, 1966).

The main Arabic sources used for the period up to 1855 are:

al-SHAIKH 'UTHMĀN B. MUḤAMMAD FODIYE (died 1817/1232)

The Shaikh did not write strictly historical works, but some of his books on law or religion contain incidental historical data. Of these, published texts are:

Kitāb al-farq (*K.F.*) (6 pages), in a text and translation by M. Hiskett (*B.S.O.A.S.*, 1960), in which data on Hausa political practice is given. The source for the Shaikh's description in *Kitāb al-farq* may be his own experiences when preaching in Kebbi. The titles to which he objected occur in Kebbi, while one of the titles, Kokani, is found neither in Gobir nor in Hausa Katsina/Maradi.[1]

[1] Contrast Hiskett (*B.S.O.A.S.*, 1960), p. 573. I assume, with Hiskett (p. 576), that the titles are not later additions.

Wathīqat ahl al-Sūdān (4 pages), in a translation by Dr. A. D. H. Bivar (*J.A.H.*, 1961).

Nour el-Eulbabe (i.e. *Nūr al-albāb*) (13 pages), in a text and translation by I. Hamet (*Revue Africaine*, Algiers 41 and 42, 1897–8).

Tanbīh al-ikhwān, in a translation by H. R. Palmer (*J.A.S.*, 52, 53, 54, 1914–15).

Iḥyā' al-sunna (226 pages), printed in Cairo in 1962.

Numerous other texts have been printed privately or by the Gaskiya Corporation, but these copies are usually unedited and thus have the status of manuscripts. Where texts exist in the Ibadan library, reference is made to those copies. One important legal text, *Bayān wujūb al-hijra 'alā 'l-'ibād*, is being edited and translated by F. H. El-Masri of the University of Ibadan, and I quote from his translation.

'ABDULLĀH B. MUḤAMMAD FODIYE (died 1829/1245)

(i) *'Īdā' al-nusūkh* (I.N.) (8 pages): a text and translation has been published by M. Hiskett (*B.S.O.A.S.*, 1957), and I refer to that text. The Northern Region Literature Agency published the same text in Zaria in 1958: it derives from one seemingly good manuscript. The work, dated October 1812 (1227), gives details of the Shaikhs who taught 'Abdullāh and his brother, and the books they read. I have taken the genealogies of some of the Shaikhs as correct, except that both here and in *Tazyīn al-waraqāt* (*v. infra*) 'Abdullāh makes Ayyuba the son, instead of the father, of Masirana: cf. Muḥammad Bello: *Ishāra wa-i'lām* (*v. infra*).
(ii) *Tazyīn al-waraqāt* (T.W.) (58 pages): an edited text and translation has been published by M. Hiskett (Ibadan, 1963). I refer to the text established by him. A text has also been published in Kano in 1963. The manuscript in Ibadan is incomplete; I used a copy kindly lent to me by Mr. F. H. El-Masri of Ibadan. M. Hiskett has a useful short introduction on the career and poetry of 'Abdullāh, but his map incorrectly sites some towns (Gimbana, for example). *Tazyīn al-waraqāt*, dated October 1813(1228), is valuable for the poems

which 'Abdullāh wrote before the jihād and for the history that accompanies the poems. The chronology of the period before the jihād is based on this work.
(iii) *Nasab* (3 fols.): this manuscript is undated, and is only attributed to 'Abdullāh. Copies are in NAK (Sokprof 1:15), Niz., and SDL. It contains lists of the Shaikh's relatives and companions; the three texts vary slightly in omitting or misspelling some names, and they contain names not found in the lists of Gidado dan Laima (*v. infra*).
(iv) A history of the origins and course of the jihād is given as an appendix by the Shaikh in *Tanbīh al-ikhwān* (1226) and in a letter of the Shaikh's in *Infāq al-maisūr* (1228), pp. 167 ff. Copies of *Tanbīh al-ikhwān* are in SDL and Niz., and photocopies in Ibadan (No. 212) and in Jos; a translation by H. G. Harris is in NAK (Kadcap 1:20) and H. R. Palmer published another translation in *J.A.S.*, 1915.[2] The account was probably written as a reply to al-Kanemi's criticisms of the jihād and is taken, therefore, as one of the orthodox versions. His account in T.W. is more detailed, and differs slightly in emphasis.

Where legal or political works by 'Abdullāh are quoted, folio references are made to the Ibadan copies. An important legal work, however, *Ḍiyā' al-ḥukkām*, has been photographed and published by the Northern Region Literature Agency (Zaria, 1956), and use has been made both of that text, and of the copies in Ibadan (Nos. 4, 5, 6).

MUḤAMMAD BELLO B. AL-SHAIKH 'UTHMĀN (died 1837/1253)

(i) *Infāq al-maisūr* (I.M.) (212 pages): a text has been published by C. E. J. Whitting (London, 1951); it was collated from three manuscripts but errors in the text are not uncom-

---

[2] Palmer's translation is sometimes misleading. For example, on p. 189, he translates 'al-jamā'a' as 'The People' ('the people' is also used on p. 190 to translate 'al-nās'); 'jamā'a' has rather the meaning of 'Community', or, in modern usage, 'party'. Also on p. 189 Palmer translates 'some from the armies of the sultans' (ba'ḍ man kāna min (or fī) junūd al-salāṭīn) as 'Of the ruling classes some ...' (cf. Ibadan MS. 212, pp. 24 f.; *Infāq al-maisūr*, p. 168).

mon.[3] It is, for example, undated, but a copy in SDL gives the date, in words, as Tuesday 5 Dhū'l-qa'da 1227 (Tuesday 10 November 1812): another copy, in the possession of al-haji Junaidu, gives the date as above, except for the year, here 1228 written in figures. In 1964 a text based on copies from the Moroccan Archives, Rabat, and from Sokoto was printed in Cairo: though more easy to use than Whitting's edition, it is only in private circulation, and therefore no references have been made to it.[4] A new text is being prepared by Muhammad al-Hajj of Abdullahi Bayero College, Kano. A 'paraphrase and in some parts a translation' of *Infāq al-maisūr* was published by E. J. Arnett in the *Rise of the Sokoto Fulani* (Kano, 1922). As a translation, it is unreliable, adding, omitting, paraphrasing or mistranslating.[5] Therefore, despite the unsatisfactory text, references are made to the edition of Whitting.

Infāq al-maisūr is the most detailed and factual account of the jihād, and its chronology is usually preferred to that in the T.W., which is more vague. Some of the poems of 'Abdullāh quoted in I.M. are incomplete when compared with the text of T.W. (for example, I.M., p. 119, and T.W., pp. 76–7). The letters of al-Kanemi quoted in I.M. differ only slightly

[3] One of the three manuscripts used is a copy dated October 1935 (Rajab 1354), and is preserved in the University Library, Cambridge. A photo-copy was shown to me by Professor H. F. C. Smith.

[4] The Rabat text has the date of its copying as October 1820 (Muḥarram 1236), but its new appearance and the elegant Maghribi script (not found in Sokoto) suggests that it has been copied, together with its date, more recently in Morocco.

[5] For example: Whitting, p. 5, l. 19: Arnett, p. 4, § 5.
" p. 79, ll. 24–5: " p. 60, § 4.
" p. 119, ll. 13–17: " p. 97 fin.
" pp. 181–2 (16 lines): Arnett, p. 122 (omitted).

On pp. 97 (line 10), 98 (line 13), Arnett translates 'rabī'' as summer, whereas elsewhere he translates it as spring. In a close examination of the first twelves pages of Arnett's translation, Professor H. F. C. Smith has found thirty inaccuracies or omissions, with considerable variations from the other texts on p. 12. Extracts from I.M. dealing with points of geographical interest were also translated by A. V. Salame and published as an appendix in Denham and Clapperton, *Travels* (London, 1826), pp. 158–70.

from some separate texts found in Bornu.[6] Some of Muḥammad Bello's data on Gobir may be derived from a Gobir king-list, since it is similar to some of the material in 'Abd al-Qādir b. al-Muṣṭafā: *Rauḍāt al-afkār* (*v. infra*). The Sultan of Agades Muḥammad al-Bāqirī was an acknowledged source on Hausaland (I.M., p. 18). The book is far from homogeneous, suggesting that it was compiled over a long period, perhaps with the help of various visitors and informants. I have found only one important case of textual corruption, and it is common to all the copies I have seen. It may prove to be due to an original confusion of facts (*v. infra*, p. 38 n. 94).

The honesty of Muḥammad Bello, in quoting criticisms of the Sokoto Community by al-Kanemi and others and in recounting the defeats and the difficulties in the jihād, suggests the book is a reliable source; the miraculous element is played down and the account is detailed wherever Bello was an eyewitness. I have therefore used it as the basis for the history of the jihād.

(ii) *Sard al-kalām* (7 fols.): the text referred to is a photo-copy (No. 122) in the Ibadan library; another copy used is in SDL. A translation was made by H. G. Harris and copies are found in Ibadan and NAK (Kadcap 1:8). The text is not dated, but the subject of the book is the dispute with the Arewa scholar 'Abd al-Salām and his subsequent rebellion in 1817–18. Some letters from 'Abd al-Salām, highly critical of trends in Sokoto, are quoted, it seems, in full and thus give the book a tone of authenticity. Further details of the dispute are given by al-ḥājj Sa'īd (*v. infra*).

(iii) *Ishāra wa-i 'lām* (80 fols.): I have seen only one text and a copy made from it in the collection of al-haji Junaidu. The work is ascribed to Bello: the ascription is justified for the opening by internal evidence, but the work as a whole, it seems, is by several hands: the style changes more than once, though there is an overall scheme to the book. There is, however, no formal ending on the copy used. The text is difficult, being lists of largely unvowelled Fulani names of the Shaikh's

[6] Copies of these texts, collected by Muḥammad al-Hajj, are in Ibadan (MS. 231).

relatives and ancestors, probably totalling about 10,000 names, many of which are repeated; in the section on the descendants of Sa'd b. Muḥammad Ladan, the copyist has omitted some families, but a reconstruction from other references has been made. The amount of detail varies, making only limited identification of notable men possible. For want of other texts, this copy is accepted as accurate: when the data can be checked with I.N., T.W., or *Rauḍ al-jinān* (*v. infra*), it has been found correct, except on the question of Ayyuba.

(iv) *Nasab* (4 fols.): the manuscript was found in Timbuktu and deposited (under a different title) with the de Gironcourt papers (no. 74) in the IF. A partial translation has been published by M. Delafosse in *Revue du Monde Musulman* (XX, 1912, pp. 257 ff.). It was written after I.M. and gives further details on the origins of the Fulani. Although only summarised by Delafosse, the passage on the teachers of Muḥammad Bello is useful as a supplement to the lists in Gidado: *Majmū' aṣḥāb Muḥammad Bello*. The *Nasab* was written as a parallel to the works of 'Abdullāh b. Fodiye and al-Muṣṭafā b. Muḥammad on their teachers.

There are a number of minor manuscripts, often of only a few folios and lacking titles, authors or dates, which are attributed to Muḥammad Bello. For those that I have used, the age and source of the text as well as the subject-matter has made the ascription probable. The owners or copyists sometimes write the author's name on the outside page, and on old copies this ascription is likely to be correct. But till a complete study is made of all Bello's works, numbering probably over a hundred, the authenticity of this minor material is not established. For other major works of Muḥammad Bello to which reference is made, the bibliography indicates the texts used.

'ABD AL-QĀDIR B. AL-MUṢṬAFĀ (died 1864/1280)

(i) *Rauḍāt al-afkār* or *Akhbār al-bilād al-ḥausiyya* (R.A.) (11 fols.): the book has no proper title, and, in some copies, no author is mentioned. The text referred to is the Ibadan copy (No.

18). A translation was published in *J.A.S.* (XV, 1916) by H. R. Palmer, who ascribed the work to Muḥammad Bello. Palmer's translation is unreliable and his terminology sometimes misleading; his text is corrupt and has some minor lacunae.[7] The book is the most detailed early source for eighteenth-century Gobir history, and it may derive from a work used by Muḥammad Bello in *Infāq al-maisūr*. In the account of Kebbi history, the parallels with I.M. include identical phrases: e.g. I.M., p. 19, last line: R.A., f. 3; cf. I.M., p. 20, ll. 18–21; R.A., f. 4. The last event in R. A. is *c.* 1824, some ten years after the writing of I.M., and the closing paragraph of the book suggests it was written soon after the last event mentioned. 'Abd al-Qādir's next book, on his maternal uncle Muḥammad Sambo, is dated December 1825, but his only other history was written in 1864 (*v. infra*). There is only one personal reference, to a visit to Katsina. The ascription to Bello is impossible, since Bello is referred to in the third person. 'Abd al-Qādir was within the group of Sokoto scholars, although he was young at the time of writing *Rauḍāt al-afkār*. His mother was a daughter of the Shaikh, and his father a scribe, if not the chief scribe, in the Shaikh's Community.

The book is valuable not only for its Gobir history, but also for its brief annalistic account of the first twenty-one years of the jihād. I have accepted the order of events given in this account as correct.

(ii) *Mauṣūfat al-sūdān* (9 fols.): I refer to the Ibadan text (No. 19), but a copy was also used from the SDL. The date of the Ibadan text, overlooked by Kensdale, is 1280/1863–4. A poem on the author's death by Asmā' bint al-Shaikh is also dated 1280. The book gives, in verse, the history of the hijra and the jihād to 1842. It is based on a poem in Fulfulde by Asmā' bint al-Shaikh: the original, composed in 1256/1840–1841, consists of 135 lines rhyming in nā.

---

[7] For example: Palmer, p. 266, § 8: Ibadan text, f. 8
„ p. 269, § 3: „ „ f. 7b–8.
„ p. 270, § 2, 3: „ „ f. 8b.

ʿABDULLĀH B. MUḤAMMAD AL-KANĀWĪ
(*Thirty-five dāʾira*) (13 fols.).

Copies are in the collections of M. Boyi Sokoto (also on film at Ibadan) and al-haji Junaidu. Another copy is in NAK (Bauprof 6:10) but dawāʾir 23–32 are missing. The book describes the Shaikh's preaching at Sifawa in 1814/1229 and the author says he wrote the book later that year.

GIDADO DAN LAIMA (died 1851)

(i) *Rauḍ al-jinān* (R.J.) (14 fols.). The text referred to is in Ibadan (No. 28). An early but mutilated copy of *Rauḍ al-jinān* is referred to by M. Hiskett (T.W., p. 132) as *Karāmāt al-Shaikh*: other copies of this corrupt text are found deriving from one of al-haji Junaidu's two copies. The corruption occurred within the lifetime of Gidado as a note by the copyist of the *Karāmāt* indicates. ʿAbd al-Qādir b. Gidado quotes from the 'Karāmāt al-Shaikh' in *Anīs al-mufīd* (p. 8; *v. infra*). The texts of *Rauḍ al-jinān* and *Karāmāt al-Shaikh* are the same except that the latter lacks both title and author's name. Both texts, that in Ibadan and the *Karāmāt al-Shaikh*, are somewhat deficient, and I therefore collated them for my use. A translation was made by H. G. Harris (in NAK, Kadcap 1:23), but I have not checked its accuracy. Both ʿĪsa b. al-Shaikh (in NAK, Kadcap 1:11) and al-haji Junaidu (*rawāʾ iḥ al-azhār min rauḍ al-jinān*) have put the contents of *Rauḍ al-jinān* into verse. The lists at the end of R.J. are the main source for the personnel of the Community, while the karāmāt ('miracles') are important for the biography of the Shaikh. A brief analysis of the date and content of this work is made below, p. 210.
(ii) *al-Kashf waʾl-bayān* (K.B.) (24 pages): I refer to the Ibadan microfilm copy (No. 179) of one of the copies in the collection of al-haji Junaidu. This copy is incomplete; another incomplete copy is in SDL. The sections omitted are on Bello's aḥzāb (SDL), raids (SDL; Ibadan) and places where he stayed (SDL; Ibadan): the last section is recopied in Gidado's *Majmūʿ aṣḥāb Muḥammad Bello* (*v. infra*). A complete text is found in the collection of al-haji Junaidu and in NAK (Kadcap 1:7). A translation which omits some 220

lines (over a quarter of the book) was made of the complete text by H. G. Harris: I have not checked the accuracy of this translation.

The book is dated December 1838 (1254), a year after the death of Muḥammad Bello, about whom the book is written. A brief analysis of its contents is given below, p. 210.

(iii) *Majmūʿ aṣḥāb Muḥammad Bello* (4 fols.): no title or author is given in the text, but the copy in the possession of al-haji Junaidu is said to be in Gidado's handwriting. Another copy is in NAK (Sokprof 8:2), but this is less complete than al-haji Junaidu's text. The book supplements K.B. with lists of Bello's friends and household such as Gidado also gave for the Shaikh in R.J.

(iv) *Majmūʿ khiṣāl al-Shaikh* (4 fols.): no proper title or author is given, but the text is dated January 1839 (1254). The copies used were in the collection of al-haji Junaidu and in the library of the Department of Antiquities, Jos (microfilm 565/G2): the former copy is the more complete, but both texts are illegible where the edges of the paper are torn. This is important in the plan showing the Shaikh's neighbours at Degel. Part of this book (on the character of the Shaikh) is copied in ʿAbd al-Qādir b. Gidado: *Anīs al-mufīd.*

(v) *Kashf al-ḥijāb* (4 fols.): the outside page has the title 'Kashf al-niqāb' but the phrase occurs in the text as 'Kashf al-ḥijāb'. No author is given in the text, but the work is ascribed on the outside page to Gidado and this is confirmed by al-haji Junaidu. I have used two copies, one in SDL and the other in Niz.; lacunae in the SDL copy were filled from the Niz. copy, which is now on microfilm at Ibadan and Zaria. The contents of the book, which refutes claims that Bello was a Tijānī, are given on pp. 216 ff.

(vi) *Risāla fī 'l-nisba* (1 fol.): the text used is in the collection of al-haji Junaidu. It is dated 1840 (1256), and gives details of Gidado's ancestors and his children.

ʿABD AL-QĀDIR B. GIDADO (died 1859)

(i) *Anīs al-mufīd* (38 pages): references are made to the Ibadan text (No. 173), a photocopy of a text in NAK (Kadcap 2:13) which derives from Sokoto, *c.* 1903. Comparison was made in Ibadan with a photo-copy (No. 174) of a text from the collection of al-haji Junaidu. The book was written after the death of Gidado in 1851 (p. 8), and gives biographical details of the Shaikh, 'Abdullāh and Muḥammad Bello: *v. infra* p. 214.

(ii) *Majmū' manāqib Amīr al-mu'minīn 'Alī* (14 fols.): the text used was from the collection of al-haji Junaidu. A partial translation by H. G. Harris is in NAK (Kadcap 1:19) and a copy is now in Ibadan, but I have not checked its accuracy. Slightly abbreviated versions of the Hadejia crisis are found in al-haji Junaidu: *Ḍabṭ al-multaqaṭāt* and *Tarihin Fulani* (*v. infra*). The last event in the work is datable to *c.* 1853. As the author was Vizier under 'Alī, the basic facts on the history of the caliphate of 'Alī are accepted as accurate.

(iii) *Basṭ al-fawā'id* (12 fols.): the text used was from the collection of al-haji Junaidu. No date is given but from internal evidence a date *c.* 1848–50 is probable. The book contains three lists in alphabetical order, roughly corresponding to generations, of men who fought in the jihād in Sokoto and elsewhere. In all some 450 names are given.

Of the other works of 'Abd al-Qādir b. Gidado,
al-Mawāhib al-rabbāniyya (8 fols.) was borrowed from Muhammad al-Hajj (now of Abdullahi Bayero College), who obtained it in Bida (a photo-copy is in Ibadan, MS. No. 243);
al-Lawāmi' al-nūrāniyya (95 fols.) was borrowed from M. Yahaya, Alkalin Lardin Sokoto;
al-Iktifā' (85 fols.) was borrowed from the Nizamiyya School Library, and is on microfilm at Ibadan and Zaria. For their contents, *v. infra*, pp. 217 f.

'UMAR B. MUḤAMMAD BUKHARI B. AL-SHAIKH (died *c.* 1881)

(i) *Tanbīh al-ikhwān* (9 fols.): the text used was from the collection of al-haji Junaidu; another copy is in NAK (Kadcap 1:5). The last event is datable to *c.* 1845. Since the author was not yet 15 years old by the time the Shaikh died, the data on the life of the Shaikh are probably traditional. The account only becomes detailed with the campaigns of Abū Bakr

(1837–42) and 'Alī (1842–59), in which he is likely to have been involved.

(ii) *Nubdha li-iẓhār ba'ḍ manāqib Shaikhinā Khalīl* (12 fols.): there are two texts in SDL and a third in NAK (Sokprof 4:16). The last event is datable to *c.* 1849–50. The work gives annalistically the campaigns of the Emir of Gwandu Khalilu b. 'Abdullāh: these reappear in the history of Gwandu by the Alkalin Gwandu Aḥmad quoted by Arnett (*op. cit.*, pp. 38–40). The author's father was brought up by Khalilu's father, and both families continued to have close ties. The author's town, Tambawel, was seven miles from Gwandu.

SA'D B. 'ABD AL-RAḤMĀN

Tartīb al-aṣḥāb wa-tajmī' al-arbāb min aṣḥāb al-Shaikh 'Abdullāh b. Fodiye (7 fols.): there are texts in the collection of al-haji Junaidu and in NAK (Sokprof 23:7). The author had been a companion of 'Abdullāh b. Fodiye, and wrote this book under the Emir of Gwandu Khalilu (1835–60). It contains lists of 'Abdullāh's companions and students, and gives their ethnic origins; it also has a discussion on the length of 'Abdullāh's term of office as Emir and on his dispute with Muḥammad Bello.

Poetry: a considerable amount of poetry in Arabic, Fulfulde and Hausa is extant, some of it containing useful historical data. The Shaikh 'Uthmān is credited with over fifty poems written in what is now somewhat archaic Fulfulde: a thorough study of this material has yet to be made. I have read forty of these, but only in Hausa translations. Thirty-nine poems in Arabic by Muḥammad Bello are collected in al-haji Junaidu: *Ifādat al-ṭālibīn*; fourteen poems (179 lines) of Muḥammad Bukhari b. al-Shaikh (died 1255 (1839–40)) are collected in a manuscript in the library of the Shahuci School, Kano; some nine poems (270 lines) by 'Abd al-Qādir b. al-Muṣṭafā are in the collection of al-haji Junaidu, who also has a large number of poems by the Shaikh. He also has at least seven poems in Arabic by Asmā' bint al-Shaikh (died 1280/1864), collected in *al-Durrat al-'aṣmā'*. The most voluminous poet of the jihād was 'Abdullāh b. Muḥammad Fodiye; some of his poems are in T.W. and I.M., but no complete collection has been made that I have seen. Minor poets were numerous in Sokoto: al-haji Junaidu has several poems dating from the nineteenth century, including seventeen by 'Uthmān b. Isḥāq (*fl.* 1868), while the National Archives, Kaduna, is also strong in this field.

AL-ḤĀJJ SA'ĪD

Taqāyīd mimmā waṣala ilainā min aḥwāl umarā' al-muslimīn salāṭīn ḥausa (2 fols. and 31 pp.). The printed text used is the one published as *Ta'rīkh Sokoto* by O. Houdas in the volume containing *Tedzkiret en-nisian* (Paris, 1899); the volume includes a French translation, which has since been translated into English (NAK, Kadcap 1:9). A translation of the Arabic text was published by C. E. J. Whitting (Kano, 1949). Both French and English translations are misleading and sometimes inaccurate, and the names are very confused.[8]

The published text, however, is only part of the original work which, though copied as a whole, was divided and bound in separate volumes of manuscripts. The published text, covering the period 1817 to *c.* 1845, derives from volume 5422 in the Bibliothèque Nationale; the first part, covering the period 1803–17, is to be found in volume 5484, and no text or translation of it has been published. For this part, therefore, I refer to the manuscript in the Bibliothèque Nationale. The manuscript is poorly written and was probably copied for the French administration. The text is corrupt in several places.

The author does not give his name at the beginning of the book, but on p. 218 he is referred to as al-ḥājj Sa'īd. In a note to the translation in NAK, al-ḥājj Sa'īd is said, on the authority of the Vizier Muḥammad Bukhari (died 1910), to have been the tutor to the sons of Amīr al-mu'minīn 'Alī b. Bello and to have come from Gworgol, near Timbuktu. From the text (pp. 214–15), however, it is clear he was not from the

[8] For example, the name Mudegel is printed in C. E. J. Whitting's translation as Butifl (e.g. p. 17); other inaccuracies, in Whitting, e.g. p. 9, l. 3, or in Houdas, e.g. p. 200 (fin).

area of Timbuktu. Gworgol only means west in Fulani, and it is possible that no specific place is meant. Whatever his origin, it is clear that he was a Fulani, a Tijānī and a follower of al-ḥājj 'Umar.[9]

Al-ḥājj 'Umar, after visiting Mecca and Medina where he was appointed muqaddam of the Tijāniyya in the western Sudan, stayed in Sokoto for some eight years, 1830–8.[10] He married a daughter of Muḥammad Bello, Mariam, who died in February 1838 (1254).[11] He also married another Sokoto girl, 'Ā'isha, who bore him a son in Sokoto *c.* 1833: the son was Aḥmad b. 'Umar, for whom al-ḥājj Sa'īd wrote this book.[12] Al-ḥājj Sa'īd was in Sokoto in the 1830's, before Bello's death, and stayed till *c.* 1854.[13] He seems to have been familiar with court circles, and became a reader of the Quran for Amīr al-mu'minīn 'Alī.[14] He wrote his history after leaving Sokoto. At the beginning, he says he wrote it for his 'sayyid' and 'maulā' Aḥmad al-Madanī. 'Umar's eldest son is called, in Segu documents, Aḥmad al-kabīr al-Madanī; and in some manuscripts dated 1288 (1872) he is given the titles Amīr al-mu'minīn and Sulṭān.[15] It is probable that al-ḥājj Sa'īd wrote this history before Aḥmad was commonly styled Amīr al-mu'minīn, and after his appointment by his

---

[9] It is possible that he is the Sa'īd Hann mentioned by Hampate Ba and Cardaire in *Le Sage de Bandiagara* (Présence Africaine, Paris, 1957, pp. 14–21); Hampate Ba says that he is of Sokoto origin (emphatically denied in Sokoto) and that he died in 1890. My attention was drawn to this by Mr. W. A Brown.

[10] Clapperton (2nd journey), p. 202; Sa'īd, pp. 191, 202; cf. H. F. C. Smith (*J.H.S.N.*, II, 2; 1961), pp. 181 ff. 'Umar is known to have been in Medina in April 1829: he wrote *Tadhkirat al-mustarshidīn* there.

[11] Sa'īd, p. 191; al-ḥājj 'Umar, *Rimāḥ*, p. 210 (1345 edition).

[12] Sa'īd, p. 194; M. E. Mage, *Voyage dans le Soudan Occidental* (Paris, 1868), pp. 233, 667. Mage, mistakenly, it seems, gives 'Ā'isha as the name of Bello's daughter. Aḥmad's mother was said to have been the daughter of a slave (A. de Loppinot, 'Souvenirs d'Aguibou', *Bull., Com. Et. Hist. Sc. de l'A.O.F.*, 1919, p. 38). Aḥmad was 'Umar's eldest son.

[13] Sa'īd, pp. 191, 193–5, 197, 217. No mention is made of the time of al-ḥājj Sa'īd's pilgrimage, and it is not known whether he first met al-ḥājj 'Umar on the pilgrimage or in Sokoto.

[14] Sa'īd, pp. 218, 219.

[15] BN 5689, f. 97; BN 5640, ff. 25–38.

father as governor of Segu *c.* 1862.[16] Al-ḥājj Sa'īd nowhere implies that al-ḥājj 'Umar was dead at the time of writing, but it seems there was an attempt to conceal or minimise his death in 1864, and Aḥmad did not take the title of Amīr al-mu'minīn immediately.[17] The date of this book, therefore, is possibly early in the 1860's, not long after al-ḥājj Sa'īd returned from Sokoto.[18]

The book, in giving an account of the first four caliphates in Sokoto, is very detailed, but only in a few places does al-ḥājj Sa'īd mention his sources, for example, the followers of 'Alī Jedo (p. 199), or 'Alī Hāshim (pp. 193–7). But some of his factual material can be checked against other sources; for example, his quotation from a poem of 'Abd al-Qādir b. al-Shaikh is correct.[19] His chronology of 'Alī's caliphate, however, differs somewhat from that in 'Abd al-Qādir b. Gidado, *Majmū' manāqib 'Alī*, and Barth (e.g. IV, 183–4). Some bias in the book is due to the fact that he was a follower of al-ḥājj 'Umar and a Tijānī, writing for the son of al-ḥājj 'Umar and the Tijānī Community. For this reason, I believe, the role of al-ḥājj 'Umar in Sokoto politics is exaggerated. Similarly his persistent hostility towards the Viziers Gidado and 'Abd al-Qādir may be accounted for by their championing the Qādiriyya and refuting all Tijānī claims that Bello was a Tijānī.[20] The hostility of al-ḥājj Sa'īd to the Viziers is emphasised by the praise he gives to others.

This book of al-ḥājj Sa'īd is poorly regarded by al-haji Junaidu as a source for Sokoto history. But given the fact that al-ḥājj Sa'īd was writing some years after leaving Sokoto with little means of checking his data, and that he was a foreigner

[16] Mage, *op. cit.*, p. 264.

[17] e.g. Sa'īd, p. 202; Mage, who was in Segu 1864–6, seems not to have heard of 'Umar's death till April 1866 (pp. 600 ff.).

[18] If Hampate Ba's Sa'īd Hann is the author, then it is possible he wrote the book for a son of Aḥmad b. 'Umar, also called Aḥmad al-Madanī, who in his father's absence was left in charge of Segu where Sa'īd Hann was the presiding scholar: in which case the book may have been written as late as 1889–90.

[19] The whole poem is quoted in 'Abd al-Qādir b. Gidado: *Anīs al-mufīd*, p. 32. Cf. Sa'īd, p. 195.

[20] *v. infra*, p. 215. Cf. Sa'īd, pp. 200–1, 206, 208, 211–12.

and a Tijānī (albeit a Fulani), his book is useful as both a corroboration and a commentary for the texts mentioned above.

Material of any sort for the period 1855–80 is meagre, and the Arabic sources for 1880–1903 are of a different kind from what has been described above. The main texts are:

MUḤAMMAD BUKHARI B. AḤMAD (died 1910)

(i) *Rauḍ al-rayāḥīn* (4 fols.): the text used is in the collection of al-haji Junaidu, who reproduces much of the material in his *Ḍabṭ al-multaqaṭāt* (fols. 74–84) and *Tarihin Fulani* (pp. 59–61; *v. infra*): in the *Tarihin Fulani* there are a number of misprints. The text is undated, but from internal evidence it appears it was written late in 1891: the subject is the Mafara revolt (*v. infra*, pp. 131 ff.), for which it is useful as the official account.
(ii) *Kitāb fī-mā jarā bainī wa-bain Amīr Hadijia wa-Yūsuf* (8 fols.): the text used is in NAK (Sokprof 2:30). The book is undated, but was probably written *c.* 1895, from internal evidence. It is the Vizier's account of his part in the Kano crisis (*v. infra*, pp. 134 ff.).[21]
(iii) *Risāla ilā ahl al-'ilm wa 'l-tadabbur* (5 fols.): the text used is in the collection of al-haji Junaidu. Undated, it was probably written soon after 1903: it describes the Vizier's action after the battle at Sokoto against the British, and quotes a learned justification of his position by Aḥmad b. Sa'd, the Alkalin Gwandu.
(iv) *Ta'nīs al-ikhwān* (16 fols.): the text used is in NAK (Kadcap. 1:3), where there is also a translation by H. G. Harris. The work is a general history of Sokoto till 1903. According to a note on the front of the text, it was dictated by Muḥammad Bukhari to his son 'Abd al-Qādir Machido in September 1905, evidently at the request of the Resident, J. A.

---

[21] It is possible that both this book and *Rauḍ al-rayāḥīn* were written after the British conquest, at the request of the administration. Both al-haji Junaidu and M. Yahaya, however, believe this was not so.

Burdon. The book, for the later Caliphs, has the structure of a king-list, and some of the material may be drawn from, or share a common source with, the history of Sokoto by the Imam 'Alī (*v. infra*). The dates for the caliphates after 1842 are derived from this work, and have been checked with those given in the history by Imam 'Alī. The notes to the translation are useful, being based on the replies of the author and representing oral tradition *c.* 1905.

'ALĪ B. ABĪ BAKR

Majmū' al-khulafā': the book, a general history of Sokoto, ends in the caliphate of Abū Bakr b. Bello (1873–7) and is continued by Muḥammad, Alkalin Waziri, till 1903, when he left Sokoto with the Caliph Muḥammad Attahiru b. Aḥmad. I have only seen an incomplete Hausa copy and a translation, possibly of that Hausa copy, by W. F. Gowers (NAK, Kadcap 1:12). The data for the later caliphates is similar to and as brief as that given in *Ta'nīs al-ikhwān*. The author was Imam of the Shaikh 'Uthmān mosque in Sokoto.

AḤMAD B. SA'D

Ta'rīkh Gwandu: the author was Alkalin Gwandu and wrote this history of Gwandu for the British administration; for the early period he draws heavily on 'Umar b. Bukhari's *Nubdha li-iẓhār ba'ḍ manāqib Shaikhinā Khalīl* (*v. supra*). It was translated by McAllister in 1909; I have not seen the original. Though he was a Tijānī, it has not influenced his work.

Relevant to the history of Sokoto are the following two Kano manuscripts in the library of the Antiquities Department, Jos.

MUḤAMMAD B. ṢĀLIḤ

Taqyīd al-akhbār (32 fols.): the book is dated 1284 (1868); the author was al-qāḍī under the Emir of Kano 'Abdullāh, and he gives the history of Kano from the start of the jihād (Jos: 365, M 97).

(ANON)

Faiḍ al-qadīr fī auṣāf al-malik al-khaṭīr (28 fols.): it was written, together with an abbreviated version (8 fols.), for H. R. Palmer when in Katsina, *c.* 1908. The author, whose name is possibly (Dan) Muḥammad al-Amīn, was scribe to the Emir of Kano Muḥammad Bello (died 1893) and his son Tukur (died 1895).[22] The book gives the Tukur version of the Kano crisis of 1893–5, as well as a history of Kano under the Emir Muḥammad Bello (Jos: 372 X 51, 52).

'ABD AL-QĀDIR MACHIDO B. MUḤAMMAD BUKHARI (died 1933)

Tabshīr al-ikhwān (26 fols.): the text used is in the collection of al-haji Junaidu; another copy is in NAK (Sokprof 22:7), and a photo-copy is in Ibadan (No. 212). The book, written in 1913, gives a fuller account of the history of Sokoto than *Ta'nīs al-ikhwān*, and draws on many of the sources listed above. It also contains the text of Abū Bakr Atiku's fifteen secrets, of which there is a separate anonymous copy in the Shahuci School Library, and a microfilm copy in Jos (5A). The dates of the Caliphs given here show some divergences from those in *Ta'nīs al-ikhwān* and *Majmū' al-khulafā'*: cf. J. A. Burdon ('Sokoto History', *J.A.S.*, 1907, pp. 367–74), whose dates, drawn, sometimes indirectly, from these books, seem to be correct.

AL-HAJI JUNAIDU

Ḍabṭ al-multaqaṭāt (99 fols.): the text used was given by the author to the Ibadan library (No. 31). A Hausa translation (*Tarihin Fulani*) was published by the Northern Region Literature Agency in 1957. The book is based on the works in the author's collection, many of which are listed above. It also draws on his own voluminous writings. As the author is the most learned historian in Sokoto, the work is valuable as

[22] Folio 11b.

the major modern work on Sokoto history, carrying the account through from the origins of the Fulani to Sokoto in the 1950's. For his other historical books, see the bibliography.

(b) *Correspondence.* The major collections are:

(i) 598 letters in the possession of al-haji Junaidu. Photographed copies are in NAK (Sokprof letters, 1) and in the Department of Antiquities, Jos: neither set is complete. I used the original texts, but in the references I follow the numbering of Dr. A. D. H. Bivar who sorted and arranged the letters for the Department of Antiquities;
(ii) 131 letters taken from the Vizier's house and published by H. F. Backwell in *The Occupation of Hausaland* (Lagos, 1927). His translations, with some exceptions (e.g. No. 125), are fairly accurate. The originals are in NAK (Sokprof letters, 3);
(iii) 227 letters collected from Gombe, now in NAK (Bauprof letters, 1).

Most of the correspondence was written between 1880 and 1903. The 730 letters (Nos. i and ii) are from the files of the Vizier Muḥammad Bukhari (1886–1910) and form a disjointed series of letters received in Sokoto. For a description of the Sokoto Chancery, see below. The Gombe letters cover a period *c.* 1898–1902, and are especially detailed on the Ako incident.

On microfilm at Ibadan are ninety letters from Bauchi, mostly only in a translation by A. N. Skinner. Also at Ibadan are a number of microfilm copies of originals from Bauchi and elsewhere; there are also some at Ahmadu Bello University, the University of Ife, the Department of Antiquities, Jos, and NAK. In NAK (Kadcap 11:26) is the *Arabic Letter Book* of the Royal Niger Company and the British administration from 1899. It contains copies of a few letters from Sokoto, with often inaccurate translations. Some of the letters at Jos were collected in Sokoto by Dr. A. D. H. Bivar, who published five letters, with an introduction, in *B.S.O.A.S.* (1959). Other letters, copied from originals since lost, are found as separate works or in 'Abd al-Qādir b. Gidado: *Majmū'* (38 fols.). The

Majmū' was made in 1849 by the then Vizier, and contains thirteen letters from Muḥammad Bello, four from Abū Bakr Atiku and twelve from 'Alī b. Bello: some of them are found separately elsewhere. No serious attempt has been made to collect letters from emirates other than Gombe and Bauchi. Further letters of advice, of which Bello wrote several, are known to exist in the possession of the descendants of the Tuareg Muḥammad Jailani, while the archives in Tripoli are expected to contain documents from Sokoto.[23]

(c) *Travellers' Journals*

Those who visited Sokoto and published journals are Clapperton in 1824 and, with Lander, in 1826–7; Barth in 1853 and 1854; Flegel in 1880–1; Thomson in 1885; Staudinger in 1886; Monteil in 1891; Wallace in 1894. Cazemajou in 1898 was not allowed to enter Sokoto.[24]

Clapperton stayed in Sokoto some eight months in all, and on both his visits he was the guest of the Vizier Gidado. Clapperton was either uninterested in, or not very well informed on, the politics or history of Sokoto, and it is unlikely that he discussed them with the Vizier or the Vizier's brother, Mudi. In incidental observations, however, Clapperton can sometimes be corroborated from manuscript sources, while his description of the agricultural year is true today.[25] Barth is more detailed on the workings of the caliphate, but he stayed only two months in all in Sokoto.[26] His visit coincided with the period of revolt in Kebbi, Zamfara and Hadejia, and therefore is useful for fixing the chronology of events described in the Arabic sources. In many details he corrobor-

---

[23] Cf. A. D. H. Bivar, 'Arabic Documents of Northern Nigeria' (*B.S.O.A.S.*, 1959), pp. 345–8; B. G. Martin, 'Five Letters from the Tripoli Archives' (*J.H.S.N.*, II, 3, 1962), p. 350.

[24] For full references, see bibliography.

[25] Clapperton (2nd journey), pp. 216 ff.

[26] His early letters, however, in *J.R.G.S.* (XXI, e.g. pp. 191 ff.) are misinformed on the Sokoto court; they were written before he visited Sokoto.

ates both 'Abd al-Qādir b. Gidado and al-ḥājj Sa'īd. His maps and itineraries are valuable for checking local histories in the District notebooks, though I have found occasional inaccuracies.[27] The names of Barth's informants are seldom given: his host in Wurno was the Galadima, but he mentions talking with 'Abd al-Qādir b. al-Muṣṭafā, the historian whose books are listed above.[28]

Of the later travellers, Flegel has left only a meagre account of his visit to Sokoto, while Thomson, who lost his papers on the return journey, remembered enough to write three articles. His remarks, being from memory, are somewhat general, but I have assumed that his description of the Vizier is substantially correct.[29] Staudinger, who visited Sokoto with Hartert six months later, gives a more detailed account than Thomson, and the accuracy of his observations has been borne out from my field work. He is, however, poorly informed on names and occasionally confuses relationships and titles: this has made identification of the men he met very difficult.[30]

Monteil is remarkably inaccurate; in his data on the Sokoto titles and offices, he was seriously misinformed.[31] It is probable that he was not welcome in Sokoto, having a large escort of soldiers and coming from Argungu. His interpreters seem to have been western Fulani, a fact which may also have limited the number of his informants. Wallace, on the other hand, who visited Sokoto in 1894 in the company of the Vizier and stayed a short time, has published only a brief address on his journey. His account affords an example of the hazards of using travellers' journals. He remarked that Fulfulde was scarcely spoken at the caliphal court; Staudinger, however, some eight years earlier had found Fulfulde the

---

[27] e.g. compare accounts of the Kotorkoshi campaign in Barth, *Travels*, IV, 183–4; Sa'īd, pp. 213–14; 'Abd al-Qādir, *Majmū' manāqib 'Alī*; or the Agades succession dispute in Barth, IV, 185–6; V, 342, and Sa'īd, pp. 214, 220. A topographical error: Barth, IV, 523.

[28] Barth, IV, 183.

[29] Thomson, *Good Words* (1886), p. 327.

[30] Staudinger, *Im Herzen der Haussa Länder*, e.g. pp. 243, 323, 374.

[31] Monteil, *De Saint-Louis à Tripoli*, e.g. pp. 254–5; cf. p. 248.

main language.[32] Although the disagreement may be due to the change in Caliphs, it is clear that Fulfulde was widely spoken, as Cazemajou found in 1898.[33] Cazemajou, by travelling round the north of Sokoto, entered territory new to European visitors and for this reason his account is useful, if brief.

In general, travellers' observations are more reliable than their information, which seems to have usually reached them by way of their servants or men of low rank. This information, then, is useful as oral evidence, but, unless the informant is known, must be treated as of doubtful authority. Travellers' observations, though factually reliable, depend on so many variables that it is difficult either to generalise, or to accept a traveller's generalisation, on, for example, the state of insecurity in Sokoto. But granted that the circumstances of a traveller's visit are unique, the incidental information in the journals can help in reconstructing the history of Sokoto. A large number of other travellers have passed through various emirates of the Sokoto caliphate, particularly on the Niger and Benue rivers. A selection of published travellers' accounts is given in the bibliography, but the list is far from exhaustive: there are, for example, several French and German travellers whose papers I have not traced. Further, there is material gleaned from Hausa and Arab traders in North Africa, as well as the accounts of slaves released in Sierra Leone.[34] Although much of this information is peripheral, it cannot be neglected.

---

[32] Wallace (*Geographical Journal*, 1896, p. 217): 'the court language at Wurno is not Fulah, but Hausa'; 'Fulah is the court language in provincial capitals, such as Zaria and Yola' (June 1894). Staudinger (*op. cit.*, pp. 365–6) said that the Amīr al-mu'minīn ('Umar) used Fulfulde in all but salutation but that the Fulani in the proper Hausa lands had almost forgotten their language (February 1886).

[33] Cazemajou ('Journal'): *B.C.A.F.*, 1900, p. 90.

[34] e.g. Muḥammad al-Tūnisī (*Voyage au Ouaday*, trans. Perron, 1851), whose information on the jihād seems largely inaccurate, or the accounts of Hausaland in the journals of Hornemann (1802) or Lyon (1821); *v.* bibliography. Historical material from freed slaves was published by Koelle in *African Native Literature* (London, 1854), pp. 212 ff.

II

Sources of oral tradition. Much of the early oral tradition was written down by or for European administrators. Some of this material was written in Hausa—in a'jamī or Roman script; some was oral history collected to form the basis of District notebooks, assessment reports and Provincial gazetteers. The main Hausa sources written outside Sokoto are the manuscripts written at the end of the nineteenth century for G. A. Krause and A. Mischlich in Salaga and Kete-Krachi in Togo. Some of the Krause manuscripts were published, with a note, by M. Heepe, in *M.S.O.S.* (Berlin, 1928).[35] Some of the Mischlich papers have also been published: a history of the Hausa states published by Lippert and Mischlich in *M.S.O.S.* (Berlin, 1903), ethnographic material also published by Mischlich in *M.S.O.S.* (1907–9), and two manuscripts on Kebbi published by H. Sölken in *M.I.O.* (Berlin, 1959 and 1963).[36] The last two were written by Imam 'Umar, who came from Kano to Salaga, where his brother was working for Krause.[37] Their father was of Kebbi origin. No mention is made of the author either of the history of the Hausa states in *M.S.O.S.* (1903) or of the Krause manuscripts: much of the data, however, in the history of the jihād in the Krause collection is similar to the history in *M.S.O.S.*, and they may share a common origin.

---

[35] They had been deposited with Preussische Staatsbibliothek, Berlin, in 1896. Some of the manuscripts have recently been republished, with a translation, by D. A. Olderogge in *Zapadnyi Sudan* (Moscow, 1960), pp. 141–243.

[36] See bibliography. The German translation of the history in *M.S.O.S.* (1903) was translated into English and published in J. A. Burdon, *Northern Nigeria* (London, 1909), pp. 91 ff. The references below are to the Hausa text.

[37] H. Sölken (1959), pp. 123–4. Imam 'Umar is probably the al-ḥājj 'Umar b. Abī Bakr b. 'Uthmān al-Kabbawī al-Kanāwī al-Salagawī, several of whose works have been collected by the Institute of African Studies, University of Ghana (*Check List of Arabic Works from Ghana*, December 1962) and who is the author of *al-Sarḥa al-warīqa fī 'ilm al-wathīqa*, a manual on letter-writing in circulation in Northern Nigeria, dated 1877 (Ṣafar, 1294): *v. G.A.L.*, S., I, 483 (an alternative reading found in a copy in Jos is al-sirriyya for al-sarḥa).

The main Hausa collections deriving from within Sokoto are those of J. A. Burdon, the first British Resident in Sokoto. Much of his material was transliterated and published by F. Edgar in *Litafi na Tatsuniyoyi na Hausa* (Belfast: 3 vols., 1911–1913). In addition, Edgar himself collected histories in Hausa, and his notebooks and papers are in NAK (Kadcap 2). Other works in Hausa were published by R. M. East in *Labarun Hausawa da Makwabtansu* (Zaria, 1932), but many are translations from well-known Arabic manuscripts.[38] The origin of the histories given to Burdon and Edgar is not stated, but it is probable that the Hausa material derives from a level in society below that of the Emirs and officials who wrote the main Arabic histories. The fact, however, that the stories are in Hausa does not guarantee that they reflect a non-Fulani view.

The oral tradition collected by the British administrators reflects their interests and needs: it is therefore less diffuse than the material written in Hausa. The Sokoto administrative records fall into two periods, divided roughly by the 1939–45 war. The first period, 1903–39, includes the Residents' reports, the District notebooks with their historical sections, and the tax assessment reports, most of which were written before 1920.[39] These were used by the Resident E. J. Arnett, in his *Provincial Gazetteer* (1920) and his *Rise of the Sokoto Fulani* (Kano, 1922), along with translations of Arabic manuscripts. S. J. Hogben also used both this administrative material and Arnett's work for his chapter on Sokoto in *Muhammadan Emirates of Northern Nigeria* (Oxford, 1930).[40] Later, another Resident, P. G. Harris, rearranged the material from these files and used his own touring notes to

---

[38] e.g. the *Kano Chronicle*, Arabic texts of which are in NAK (Sokprof 1:25) and Ibadan (Nos. 165, 166, 167, 212).

[39] This material is largely in the National Archives, Kaduna, and catalogues for it have been published. Most of the early reports are contained in SNP. 15; some, however, have been recatalogued under Sokprof, and a few files remain still in Sokoto.

[40] A revised edition of this work has been published by S. J. Hogben and A. H. M. Kirk-Greene under the title *The Emirates of Northern Nigeria* (Oxford, 1966).

make his *Sokoto Provincial Gazetteer* (1939). In the Niger Republic, similar material is provided by the histories gathered by the Mission Tilho and published in 1911. Later, Urvoy used the French administrative files for his *Histoire des Populations du Soudan Central* (Paris, 1956), and Perié made a detailed study of Maradi (*I.F.A.N.*, 1939).

In the second period, the Sokoto District notebooks were revised in 1953, and the histories largely rewritten, by the acting Resident, H. A. S. Johnston.[41] The notebooks include genealogies, and these are sometimes referred to by District Heads. In my own field work, therefore, I tried to have points elucidated or confirmed, using data from other Districts to cross-check the information given. I found that informants tended to confirm the 1953 histories: as these differ, sometimes quite considerably, from the histories in the early District notebooks, the oral tradition of two generations is now represented in the administrative files. My criterion in judging the accuracy of these histories has been, if possible, to see whether they corroborate either the Arabic documentation or the travellers' accounts: thus in many cases, the chronology given in the notebooks has been found to be wrong. I have also taken into account a possible bias in the early notebooks in favour of Amīr al-mu'minīn Aḥmad b. Abī Bakr Atiku; the descendants of Aḥmad were Sultans of Sokoto for half of the period during which the notebooks were compiled, and the Sultan's representative who accompanied the District Officers on tour may have influenced the histories taken down in his presence.[42]

In this period, also, detailed studies have been made by K. Krieger on Zamfara (1959), F. Nicolas on the Eastern Ulemiden and Adar (1950) and by two anthropologists, C. E. Hopen on the Gwandu Fulani (1958) and M. Dupire on the Fulani in the Niger Republic (1962).[43] The study of D. J. Stenning, *Savannah Nomads* (Oxford, 1959), although on the

[41] It is to these notebooks, kept in the Divisional Office, Sokoto, that I refer below.

[42] A son of 'Alī b. Bello was Sultan, 1903–15, while Aḥmad's son and grandson held the sultanate from 1915 to 1931.

[43] See bibliography.

Bornu Fulani, has data relevant to Sokoto. Similarly the work of Dr. M. G. Smith on Zaria is very useful in showing the workings of a major emirate under Sokoto. On Kano, a history written in Hausa has been published by al-haji Abubakar Dokaji (Zaria, 1958): it appears to be based mainly on oral tradition, which contradicts some of the written sources listed above.

My own work in the Sokoto area was from September 1962 to September 1963, with a break of six weeks in June and July.[44] The Sultan of Sokoto graciously allowed me the use of the Native Authority rest-house, north-east of the Waziri's house in the centre of the old town. I received the greatest help from al-haji Junaidu, Wazirin Sokoto, who not only has the finest historical library, but is also the most learned historian, in Sokoto. It was due to his kindness that I could work in his library and ask him to explain points and answer questions throughout the year. My dependence on al-haji Junaidu was difficult to avoid, since everyone referred me back to him. His position as the leading historian in Sokoto partly depends on a detailed knowledge of the material—books, poetry in both Arabic and Fulfulde, correspondence—in his library and in the libraries of other scholars. It is also the result of having been interested in Sokoto history as a young man and having heard then the traditions of his family. Where this information could be checked against accounts by European travellers or other later sources, it was found to be largely accurate.

Others who helped me were the Marafa, who kindly allowed me to borrow some of his books; the Waziri's nephew, M. Yahaya, Alkalin Lardin Sokoto, who both gave me advice on points of law and lent me books; the Waziri's cousin, M. Abd al-Qadiri Machido, Reader in the Qadi School in Sokoto, who told me about his grandfather, the Vizier Ibrāhīm Khalilu; the late M. Umaru Nagwamatse, who told me of Sokoto in his youth before the British came; and many others in the Waziri's household and elsewhere in

[44] Between 1963 and 1966, after the main field-work was completed, I have made several visits of varying length to Sokoto to check and amplify on the material originally collected.

Sokoto with whom I was acquainted. Within the Sokoto area, I visited the following towns and villages: Achida, Hamma Ali, Chacha, Marnona, Wurno, Goronyo, Sabon Birni, Isa, Katuru, Zurmi, Kaura Namoda, Moriki, Maradun, Faru, Talata Mafara, Maru, Kanoma, Bungudu, Gusau, Kotorkoshi, Yandoto, Anka, Bukkwiyum, Gummi, Jega, Birnin Kebbi, Tambawel, Gwandu, Jabo, Yabo, Kilgori, Sanyinna, Argungu, Sifawa, Bodinga, Dingyadi, Silame, Wamako, Kasarawa, Shuni, Denge, Danchadi, Durbawa, Raba, Gandi, Bakura, Dundaye, Kware, Gwadabawa, Chimola, Tangaza, Binji; and I visited the sites of Alkalawa, Degel, Gudu, Gwongono, Tabkin Kwotto, Alwassa, and in the Niger Republic, Konya, Tsohon Birni, and Dakorawa (?). The site of Gawakuke was described to me by some Kel Geres from Madaoua. In the Niger Republic, I also visited Maradi, Tsibiri, Madaoua, Arzarori, Illela (Washr), Tahaoua, Birnin Konni and Dogondoutchi. Except in the Niger Republic, I was usually accompanied, if I had much data to check, by M. Abbas Yahaya, M. Ibrahim Mukoshy or M. Ibrahim Maru: they were of great assistance whenever my Hausa failed me.[45]

In the study that follows I have relied primarily on the Arabic sources, and to a lesser extent on the journals of travellers. The later oral tradition has been used particularly where the contemporary sources fail—for example, in the traditions of small towns or hostile peoples. The accuracy of the chronology on particular details in the contemporary sources is seldom questioned by these traditions. A very large quantity of documentation, including Arabic material running into several hundred thousand folios, still remains to be analysed in detail for the history of Northern Nigeria. My bibliography, and the history based on it, covers, therefore, only a part of that documentation.

---

[45] M. Ibrahim Mukoshy is a great-grandson of Amīr al-mu'minīn Attahiru b. Aḥmad and was brought up in the emigrant Fulani community in the Sudan; M. Abbas Yahaya is a great-grandson of the Vizier Bukhari and was brought up in Gidadawa, Sokoto; M. Ibrahim Maru is a relation of the Banaga of Maru.

The Sources

Modern histories of Sokoto have used very little of this documentation, relying, often uncritically, on material already published. Consequently, the omissions and errors in these works are so many that I have not made references to where I agree or differ; instead, references are given to the original sources on which I have worked.

Dates

For the conversion of dates from A.H. to A.D., I have used the *Tables de Concordance des Eres Chrétienne et Hégirienne* by H.-G. Cattenoz (third edition, Rabat, 1961). He assumes that the months of the lunar year have alternately 29 and 30 days. This assumption can be misleading, since the first day of the month depends on the sighting of the new moon, which in Sokoto can vary according to weather conditions. However, when both days and dates are given, they have been found to correspond sufficiently often with the conversion in Cattenoz that I have followed the conversion even when no day is given. Where there is a discrepancy, I have assumed that the day given in a manuscript is more likely to be correct than the date, since days are more easily remembered and the succession of days is invariable. Although the tables contain some misprints, for example in the conversion of 1 Muḥarram 1220 and 1 Muḥarram 1250, more drastic errors seem to have been avoided.

Names

Personal names have been divided into two categories; standard Muslim names, like Muḥammad or 'Uthmān, have been kept in their Arabic form, while nicknames have been written in their colloquial form, even if they have an Arabic origin. Thus Atiku and Bukhari are written instead of al-'Atīq and al-Bukhārī. Similarly I have not used the Arabic spelling for Fulani nicknames, like Sambo (Arabic: Thanbu) or Bello (Arabic: Ballu). Certain nicknames have been used in preference to the proper names: for example, 'Uthmān b. Abī Bakr is better known as Gidado dan Laima, and 'Uthmān b. 'Umar as Mudegel. But both proper names and nicknames are given at least once in the text. Finally, names of living people are spelt as people spell them today.

Titles have been kept in the English or Arabic form: thus I use 'Shaikh' for the Hausa 'Shehu', and 'Vizier' for 'Waziri', 'Emir' for 'Sarki', and 'Amīr al-mu'minīn' for the Hausa 'Sarkin Musulmi', Fulfulde 'Lamido Julbe' and the English 'Sultan'. I have, however, retained the title 'Sultan' for rulers of major, specifically Hausa states like Gobir, Kebbi, or Zamfara. 'Sarki' is retained both for minor Hausa rulers, and for the titles of Sokoto princes, whose title, in form but not in fact, implied territorial power; for example, the Sokoto prince, Sarkin Kebbi, had in fact no power over Kebbi beyond the area around his town of Silame. Since other Hausa titles, like Magajin gari or Sarkin galma, were in use in Sokoto at the time princely titles like Sarkin Kebbi were adopted, I have kept such titles in their Hausa form. But to distinguish the Sarkin Kebbi from the leader of the Kebbi Fulani at Yabo, I use the title Amīr Kebbi (Yabo) for the latter, since the use of this title probably antedated the introduction of Hausa titles. Where confusion is likely to arise, the name of the town with which the title is associated is also given.

Genealogies

The genealogy of the ancestors and relations of the Shaikh is based primarily on Muḥammad Bello, *Ishāra wa-i'lām* (*v. supra*) and 'Abdullāh b. Fodiye, *'Īdā' al-nusūkh* (*v. supra*); supplementary data have been taken from the works of Gidado dan Laima and Muḥammad Bello, *Infāq al-maisūr*. The genealogy is not complete. There are likely to be inaccuracies in the vowelling of Fulani names: though the names have been checked by several Fulfulde-speakers, my informants were not unanimous on the pronunciation of a few of the names.

The genealogy of the descendants of the Shaikh derives largely from District notebooks and information given me by al-haji Junaidu and the relevant District Heads. The genealogy is not complete: the Shaikh, for example, had thirty-seven children, and Muḥammad Bello seventy-three while the number of children of the other sons and daughters of the Shaikh is not known. The selection of descendants given in the genealogy is arbitrary, but I have attempted to include the major figures in the nineteenth century.

The genealogy of the family and connections of Gidado is based on information given me by al-haji Junaidu, who is a son of the Vizier Bukhari. Again, the genealogy is not complete; Gidado had forty-eight children, but their careers are not all known. Similarly, the marriage connections of the family are not given in full. The genealogies of some of the leading officials in Sokoto are drawn from the District note-books and checked with al-haji Junaidu and some members of the families of these officials. I have not made a particular study of these families; and the genealogies given do not pretend to be complete.

Maps

The maps are traced from the 1 : 1,000,000 Administrative Map of Nigeria (third edition, 1956; sheet 1), the 1 : 1,000,000 War Office maps of Niamey (second edition, 1941) and Zinder (second edition, 1942), and the 1 : 5,000,000 map of Africa published by the Ministère des Travaux Publics et des Transports (Paris, 1930; sheets 1 and 3). Data were also taken from the War Office 1 : 2,000,000 map of Nigeria (1910) and the 1 : 500,000 map of Nigeria (third edition, 1953; sheets 1 and 2) published by the Survey Department, Lagos. Maps in *Documents Scientifiques de la Mission Tilho* and in the journals of Clapperton, Barth, and Staudinger were also used. The spelling of place-names follows the practice of the Survey Department, for example in using 'ch' for the Hausa 'c'.

No boundaries are shown on the maps: since the area which leading towns controlled was frequently changing, it would be necessary to specify the year for which the boundaries were valid; information for the nineteenth century is insufficient to do this. Instead, only the leading towns are shown.

The sites of several towns are known to have changed: I have tried to show towns in their nineteenth-century sites, but I do not have exact data for all the towns shown. For the sites of towns which have been abandoned I have relied on the District notebooks and my own field notes. The map of Sokoto town in the nineteenth century is an approximate reconstruction and the line of the roads is only tentative: it has been compiled largely from information given by al-haji Junaidu, Wazirin Sokoto, and the late M. Umaru Nagwamatse; from the map by Barth (*Travels*, IV, 182); from the aerial photographs and the map of Sokoto derived from them (1 : 4,800; Federal Surveys, Lagos, 1960).

Introduction

(i) *North-western Hausaland, or 'Sokoto'*

In the common phrases 'Sokoto jihād', 'Sokoto empire', the term 'Sokoto' is an anachronism. Founded as a camp late in 1809—over five years after the jihād began—the town of Sokoto for most of the nineteenth century was not the residence of the Caliph or his court. It did, however, have the houses of the Shaikh, of his sons and their councillors; it was the largest town in the area. It thus became in 1903 the headquarters of a province named after it. But the term is alien: the 'Sokoto jihād' is the jihād of the Shaikh, the 'Sokoto empire' is the Shaikh's Community; the 'Sultan of Sokoto' is the Commander of the Believers and the Sokoto townspeople are Kadirawa. Only the town is Sokoto.[1]

Nonetheless the term 'Sokoto' is now used both for the town and its hinterland, differentiating it from Katsina or Zaria. It is also used to refer to the hegemony that the Commander of the Believers exercised over the rest of Hausaland and beyond. I will confine myself largely to the town and its hinterland.

[1] 'Jihād' is the campaign which Muslims should wage against Unbelief (and Unbelievers). 'Community' is a translation of 'jamā'a', the usual Arabic and Hausa term for the followers of the Shaikh. 'Sultan' is the English term for 'Amīr al-mu'minīn' (Arabic), 'Sarkin Musulmi' (Hausa), and 'Lamido Julbe' (Fulfulde), meaning 'Commander of the Believers' (Arabic) or 'of the Muslims' (Hausa).

'Kadirawa' are those who follow the Qādiriyya ṭarīqa or way, and, by extension, are the followers of the Shaikh, who was himself a Qādirī: the term is still in use; for the period of the jihād, cf. 'Abdullāh b. Fodiye, *Tazyīn al-waraqāt* (T.W.), pp. 81, 82.

The hinterland, as I use it, is more of a historical than a geographical unit: it is the imprecise area of activity of the Shaikh and his people in north-western Hausaland. The northern boundary, which geographically should stop at the limit of cultivation near Tahoua, is extended north to include Agades and its northern springs (Tafadek, for example); the eastern boundary runs through the scrub land, the 'desert' ('daji') that divides Zamfara from Katsina province; the southern boundary takes in the states of the Zamfara river valley and excludes the pagan communities farther south;[2] the boundary on the west is the plateau of rough scrub beyond the Dallol Mauri.[3] To call the whole area a part of Hausaland is not a misnomer, in that the language of the peasant is still Hausa.

The crucial feature of the area are the rivers.[4] The Rima and the Sokoto rise in the same rough land, the hilly 'desert' between Zamfara and Katsina. A short way to the south are the headwaters of the Zamfara river. The Rima river, drawing a great arc through Gobir and accumulating tributaries from the north, joins the Sokoto river near Sokoto town and then curves through Kebbi to the Niger, having already been joined by the river Zamfara. The Zamfara river valley is the frontier to the south, fertile but underpopulated. The valleys of these rivers are broad, sometimes more than three miles, and usually bounded by hills or an escarpment over a hundred feet high. While water may not be perennially flowing, there are pools of water close beneath the surface. In the past the valleys were thickly wooded, but even by the time of

---

[2] That is, including Gummi and Zauma (west and south-west of Gummi, cf. T.W., p. 39) and excluding Birnin Gwari and Kotonkoro (between B. Gwari and B. Yauri), which owed allegiance to Katsina before the jihād (Clapperton, 2nd journey, pp. 154–5). See map 1.

[3] That is, including the Arewa, but excluding Zaberma (see map 1).

[4] Although the following account is largely drawn from my own observations and those of recent anthropologists it is, I believe, generally true of the eighteenth and nineteenth centuries: from the descriptions of peasant life and surroundings given by Clapperton in 1824 and 1826 and by Barth in 1853–4, conditions do not appear to have greatly changed. Nonetheless, I use the present tense to indicate the contemporary nature of the data.

Clapperton's second journey (1826) cultivation had cleared much of the ground near the towns.[5]

There are other sources of perennial water; on the otherwise dry plateaux the springs and pools are invaluable to cattle-herders. Though some of the pools now dry up after the middle of the hot season, the water table is close enough for wells. Outside the valleys and their tributaries the land is relatively flat, covered in scrub and trees. The plains are occasionally broken by ridges and isolated hills: the latter are rare and striking enough to have become the home of spirits, the villages lying at their feet; but at Kanoma, for example, where the hill is large enough and has water, the high ground itself is inhabited.

The long dry season makes life outside the river valleys difficult towards April. The rains begin in late May or early June, reach their peak in August (with *c.* 9·3 in.) and are virtually over by the end of September. Freak storms in April and October give about half an inch for each month, but it is not enough to bring up fresh pasture and no farming can begin till at least weekly rain is assured. Just before and after the rainy season are the Sokoto dog-days: the temperature reaches its maximum in April, and with the shortage of food and water illness seems to be, and to have been, more common. In September–October, when the harvest is virtually over and the new grain is being eaten, the temperature and humidity are both still high; a periodic migraine (popularly attributed to the new corn) and ill-health are prevalent.[6]

---

[5] Clapperton (2nd journey), p. 246. Clearly not only the growth in population and settlement, but also the increasing demand for the cash crops, groundnuts and cotton, has greatly reduced the forests, especially in the valleys.

[6] Data for rainfall, temperatures and humidity are taken from K. M. Buchanan and J. C. Pugh, *Land and People in Nigeria* (London, 1955), pp. 243–5. The harvest migraine is called masassarar kaka (Hausa) or paboje (Fulfulde). Bello speaks of a spring fever (ḥummat al-rabīʿ) in *Infāq al-maisūr* (I.M.), p. 95. Of the eleven Caliphs in Sokoto, six died within a perod of six weeks in September–November, and four within a similar period in March–April; one, the only Caliph who died of wounds, died in late November, after Ramaḍān. None of the Caliphs died in Ramaḍān.

The dry season affects the cattle nomad worst.[7] Dependent on his cows for food, and his cows dependent on pasture, he is close to starvation as pasture and water become scarce. Though he is down in the valleys near pools, it is a lonely season—pasture is not sufficient for many herds together. The peasant at least can store his grain and supplement his diet with fish and the game that is attracted like the cattle to the water. For the peasant the dry season is comparatively leisurely: with the harvest all in after December, there is the craftwork and maintenance which uses the stalks and grasses from the harvest. So long as the grain store remains, he is independent. But that store itself depends on the rains: if he mistakes a storm for the beginning of the rains, his seed is lost; if there is drought in mid-season for a fortnight, communal prayers are said. Though the planting, hoeing, cutting and harvesting are strenuous labour, the harvest of bulrush millet ('gero') is over by early September, and that of guinea-corn ('dawa') and rice by December; the stalks and grasses are gathered for firewood and craftwork, and the fields are bare. The leaves of trees as they come into season are gathered for the gravy that is eaten with the staple, a porridge or pudding made of guinea-corn or rice.

By contrast the rainy season, despite the hardships of rain and cold, is festive for the cattle nomad. His cattle recoup on the good pasture, and he joins his fellow clansmen in celebrating clan events and ceremonies and picking up the news of relatives and information on grazing conditions. As the rains end and pasture deteriorates, the herds have to be returned to the valleys. At this period arises the conflict between peasant and pastoralist: if the harvest is not in—as the dawa will not be—the cattle may cause great damage. The tracks to the water may pass through farmland, or the cattle may break into fields by night. For this reason, rights of way to the pools and rivers are kept open, the drifts being delineated by aguwa

---

[7] Data for the cattle Fulani from C. E. Hopen, *The Pastoral Fulbe Family in Gwandu* (Oxford, 1958); D. J. Stenning, *Savannah Nomads* (Oxford, 1959); M. Dupire, *Peuls Nomades* (Paris, 1962); my own field-work in Sokoto, 1962–3. For the peasant, cf. Clapperton (2nd journey), pp. 216 ff.

bushes.[8] Otherwise, the peasant needs the pastoralist for the manure: his fields, starved of the decaying leaves and stalks, depend on the cattle dung for their continued fertility. Thus, although the cattle may use and foul the water pool, they are to be tolerated for their dung.

The other nomads in the area, the Tuareg, are less dominated by the needs of their livestock.[9] In the dry season, there is the salt caravan to Bilma in October and a lesser one in the spring; for the rest, they are mainly confined to the wells in the desert or go south for pasture to the Gobir valleys or the pools of Adar. Just before the rains, they start returning north to reach the fresh pastures necessary for the herds. This is the season for the desert raids, when pasture is ample and moist.

The Tuareg comes into less conflict with the peasant, since most of his movements are north of the line of cultivation. However, in the eighteenth and nineteenth centuries a constant pressure from more northerly tribes and the lure of easier pasture were driving the southern Tuareg against the Gobir marches.[10] In addition, the peasant villages offered opportunities of raiding against which there could be little retaliation.

While the Tuareg in the past were both outside the sphere of the peasant states and aggressive, the cattle Fulani were peaceable, and by the demands of their cattle for dry-season pasture and so long as the peasants controlled the river valleys, were open to peasant pressure. Both groups, Tuareg and Fulani, kept aloof from the peasants, speaking different languages and seldom intermarrying. On the other hand, no group was cut off: communications are adequate, since,

---

[8] The planting of aguwa to mark the rights of way is attributed to the Shaikh. Compare the route from Bakura to Jega, said to have been similarly marked as a reminder of the revolt of ʻAbd al-Salām, whose son took that road (*v. infra*, p. 69). The legal requirements for rights of way are given in the Shaikh's *Bayān wujūb al-hijra ʻalā 'l-ʻibād*, ch. 10.

[9] Data for the Tuareg from F. R. Rodd, *People of the Veil* (London, 1926), and F. Nicolas, *Tamesna* (Paris, 1950); my own field-work, 1962–3.

[10] Cf. the migration of the Gobirawa from Agades, and their continued fighting against the Tuareg (ʻAbd al-Qādir b. al-Muṣṭafā, *Rauḍāt al-afkār* (R.A.), ff. 5b, 7).

where there are no roads, any direction can become a path and, once time ceases to be so valuable, distance is no delay. Routes tended to follow the valleys, where villages were staging-posts and water was obtainable; hazards of robbers and beasts made group travel preferable. While the nomad was kept from isolation by his clan cohesion and transhumance, the peasant societies depended on the merchant and pilgrim traffic: so long as there was a powerful state on the Rima river system, this traffic was ensured, bringing kola-nuts from the south and salt from the north; receiving luxury goods from the market towns of the east, Katsina and Kano, and forwarding pilgrims from the west. Though the trade was mainly in Hausa hands, the Tuaregs brought in the salt, and a great number of the pilgrims were Fulani.

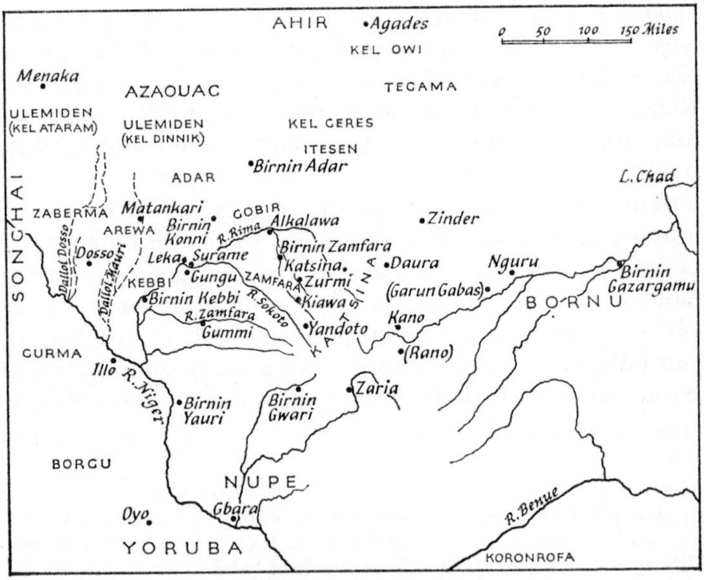

1. Hausaland, pre-1800

(ii) *The Hausa States*

Since the early sixteenth century there had been a powerful state on the Rima river system. The state of Kanta or Kebbi had been a province in the Songhai 'empire' until its ruler, the Kanta Kotal, after building up his own local power on the Kebbi river near Silame, rebelled against the Askia. Under the Kanta, Kebbi was powerful enough to withstand and counter-attack Bornu whose ruler, Mai 'Alī, was alarmed by the Kanta's control of the Agades region on his north-west frontier.[11] The importance of Kebbi is shown by its three towns, Gungu, Leka and Surame: the circuit of the walls of Surame is some six miles long. Bello says the state survived the Kanta by some hundred years; it was not however superseded by Zamfara till the early eighteenth century. Then Surame was destroyed and the refugees moved about sixty miles downstream to Birnin Kebbi.

There was, it seems, a division between Kebbi and Zamfara which was more than political: Kebbi consistently looked west to the Niger river, whereas Zamfara and Gobir looked east. Possibly this reflects a dichotomy between a fishing people and an agricultural people: whereas the rivers Rima and Sokoto above their junction are not very good for fish, the united river is and there is a considerable fishing tradition on the lower river (at Argungu, for example). Thus, Surame is on the frontier of the fishing zone.[12] The difference is also expressed in the myths of origin. The Zamfarawa are said to be descended from a Katsina father and a Gobir mother, while the Kebbawa are ascribed a Songhai father and a Katsina mother.[13] But by the eighteenth century the political division between the 'empires' of Songhai and Bornu, which may have reflected ethnic differences, had disappeared. Although Zamfara continued to pay tribute to Bornu, the authority of Bornu had been much reduced by the Koronrofa invasions of both Kano and Bornu itself, while the imperial power of Songhai had been destroyed by the Moroccan invasion at the end of the sixteenth century.[14]

---

[11] Kebbi: *Tarikh es-Soudan*, p. 78; *Tarikh el-Fettach*, p. 189; *ibid.*, Appendix II, p. 339; I.M., pp. 19–21; R.A., ff. 3, 4; E. J. Arnett, *Rise of the Sokoto Fulani*, p. 14 n.; P. G. Harris, *Sokoto Provincial Gazetteer*, pp. 32 ff.

[12] Cf. P. G. Harris, *op. cit.*, pp. 22, 230, 266.

[13] I.M., p. 19.

[14] Bornu tribute: Hornemann (*Journal*, London, 1802), p. 112; R.A., f. 6b. Koronrofa: I.M., p. 19. By the nineteenth century, Kebbi had been

The Zamfarawa seem to have moved gradually westwards from the borders of Katsina to the upper tributaries of the Rima river. Although conquered by Songhai and Kebbi in the sixteenth century, in the seventeenth century Zamfara was fighting wars against Kano and Katsina, and by the end of the eighteenth century, with Kebbi conquered, Zamfara became the leading state on the Rima river system.[15] But the supremacy was short-lived; for Zamfara in turn was overshadowed by the Gobirawa who had been pushing south—under Tuareg pressure—from Ahir.[16] Though ascribed an Egyptian origin, the Gobirawa are also claimed as part of the Hausa, while the Zamfarawa are 'banza'—worthless, that is non-Hausa—and so linked with Kebbi.[17] This distinction is perhaps part of Gobir propaganda to justify their defeat of Zamfara: the lists of Hausa and 'banza' peoples which are given by Bello and 'Abd al-Qādir b. al-Muṣṭafā are probably derived from a source written under Gobir ascendancy.[18] Similarly the genealogical myth that gives a Gobir mother to the Zamfarawa and thus implies Gobir seniority may also be propaganda. The myth conflicts with the story of the Gobirawa immigration, which suggests that the state of Gobir was ruled by an alien aristocracy: in that case the indigenous people were Zamfarawa.

The rise of Gobir involved the eclipse of Zamfara. In the wars of the second half of the eighteenth century, the Gobirawa sacked Birnin Zamfara and pursued the refugees to Kiawa and Maradun. But by attacking Kiawa the Gobirawa menaced Katsina, then a major state controlling regions to the south of Zamfara, such as Yandoto, Birnin Gwari and

---

much influenced by the states to the east; the titles in use in Kebbi, while some are confined to Kebbi, also include common Zamfara or Gobir titles: *v.* H. Sölken (*M.I.O.*, 1959), pp. 138–50.

15 K. Krieger, *Geschichte von Zamfara* (Berlin, 1959), pp. 37 ff.; he quotes the *Tarihin Zamfara* and other sources.

16 R.A., f. 5b.

17 I.M., p. 18; R.A., f. 5.

18 I.M., pp. 17–22; R.A., ff. 2–5. Muḥammad Bello (I.M., p. 18) says he heard it from the Sultan of Agades, Muḥammad al-Bāqirī, who visited Sokoto and Gwandu in 1808–9.

Kotonkoro.[19] In addition, the wars which had forced the Gobirawa to move south were continued against the Tuaregs of Agades.[20] Only in the west, after the early capture of Birnin Konni, and the submission of Kebbi, was there no threat to Gobir.[21]

The new capital of Gobir, Alkalawa, was established strategically in the north-east some twenty-five miles downstream from the old Birnin Zamfara, at the confluence of a tributary draining northern Katsina.[22] The Gobirawa were probably immigrants forming an aristocracy over the Zamfarawa peasantry; their Sultans, equipped with a formidable army whose main weapon was heavy cavalry, seem to have been always on the offensive. But frequent campaigning, unless consistently successful, is a drain on the state; and Gobir by the late eighteenth century was not consistently successful, suffering defeats in Katsina and Zamfara. Under Nafata (*c.* 1796–1802), the state was said to be in disorder and its power weakened: Zamfara was in revolt, Katsina could not be prevented from raiding, and Kebbi no longer asked Gobir to appoint its new Sarki.[23]

In addition to the main centres, Kebbi, Zamfara, Gobir, there were dependent peoples who proved important in the history of the area. To the west of Kebbi in the Dallol Mauri, mention has been made of the Arewa, a predominantly non-Muslim but Hausa-speaking group which remained loyal to Kebbi for most of the nineteenth century in the face of Sokoto pressure. At least one scholar noted in the jihād, Mikaila or ʻAbd al-Salām, came from this group. West of Zamfara on the middle Sokoto valley round Bakura were the Burmawa, who are said to have moved there from Bornu.[24] They proved consistently awkward for Sokoto to govern. West of Gobir

---

[19] R.A., ff. 7 seqq.; Clapperton (2nd journey), pp. 149 f., 154 f.

[20] R.A., f. 7b.

[21] R.A., f. 6; Sölken, *op. cit.*, p. 150; cf. Mischlich (*M.S.O.S.*, 1903), pp. 210 f.

[22] The previous capital, Tsohon Birni, was some five miles east of Konya (see map 7).

[23] R.A., f. 8b; Sölken, *op. cit.*, p. 150.

[24] P. G. Harris, *op. cit.*, p. 118; cf. p. 182.

were the Adarawa. Though their ruling house was a branch of the family of the Sultan of Agades and their aristocracy was Tuareg, the peasantry maintained themselves in virtually independent (and, later, impregnable) villages. A jihād in the early nineteenth century against them was not successful.[25]

Conditions in these eighteenth-century Sultanates are described only in sources committed to Islam and the jihād. Despite this, the charges of non-Islamic government laid against the Hausa states by the Shaikh in *Kitāb al-farq* are likely to be substantially true: the illegalities are familiar.[26] The question is the extent to which these illegalities were practised. The question is unanswerable, and did not need an answer: illegalities are the way of the unbelievers. Clearly local practice overruled the Sharī'a in several spheres, such as taxation, music and women, methods of justice, conscription and appointments of officials. Likewise, the Sultan and his subjects undoubtedly made or allowed sacrifices in a manner that was polytheistic. Nonetheless the Sultan was regarded primarily as a Muslim, and Gobir as a Muslim state.[27]

In *Kitāb al-farq*, the Shaikh is not attacking Gobir specifically. For example, the titles he criticises are not apposite for Gobir;[28] and as the Shaikh, according to Sokoto sources, was unacquainted with life in a Hausa city, his charges are probably based on second-hand reports and complaints. Apart from those that reflect common Hausa society, the charges are against the tyrannies of the Sultan and injustice. For Gobir, we know the Sultan Bawa imposed a fence-tax, and the Shaikh made the fifth of his demands to the Sultan the abolition of excessive taxes.[29] The fourth demand, the release of all those in gaol, reflects the complaint of injustice.

---

[25] *v. infra*, p. 109.

[26] 'Uthmān b. Fodiye, *Kitāb al-farq* (K.F.), *B.S.O.A.S.*, 1960, pp. 560–3.

[27] Cf. T.W., p. 58 (I.M., p. 77), where the Sultan of Gobir Yunfa is mocked for saying his prayers in a hurry.

[28] *v. supra*, p. xxviiii.

[29] R.A., f. 8; Gidado dan Laima, *Rauḍ al-jinān* (R.J.), f. 7.

Another illegality the Sultan enforced was the prohibition on wearing a cap and turban. The Sultan Nafata extended it to the wearing of veils by women. The prohibition was regarded as important by the Muslims, since the turban was the mark of a member of the Muslim Community, and a symbol of Muslim solidarity.[30] The prohibition became one of the issues of the jihād.

But this prohibition, like the limitations imposed on preaching and conversions, was aimed specifically at the threat the Shaikh and his followers posed for the Sultan. There had long been Muslims in Gobir, but in the past they were few or followed the Sultan. Now, at the end of the eighteenth century, they followed the Shaikh, in opposition to the Sultan.

The Shaikh, in *Tanbīh al-ikhwān*, claims that Islam was widespread among the people, if not among the rulers, of Hausaland.[31] Certainly the demand and respect for Islamic learning must have been widespread and strong enough to support the large class of wandering scholars and preachers. Nonetheless although Islam was common by the end of the eighteenth century compared to the days of Aḥmad Baba—the sixteenth-century Timbuktu scholar whom the Shaikh quotes as an authority on the state of Islam in the Sudan—non-Muslim cults were still strong. From twentieth-century accounts and from collections of folk-tales, it appears that the main characteristic of non-Muslim belief was a reverence for a large number of spirits localised particularly in trees; stones, wells and rivers are also mentioned. Although these spirits become identified with jinns, practices connected with them, such as possession ceremonies and sacrifices, are still polytheistic.[32]

---

[30] R.J., ff. 6b, 7; T.W., p. 54; I.M., pp. 67, 130, 125; K.F., p. 562. Though the wearing of a turban is not a duty (farḍ), it is sunna and recommended: *v. Encyclopedia of Islam*, IV, 885.

[31] 'Uthmān b. Fodiye, *Tanbīh al-ikhwān* (translated, H. R. Palmer, *J.A.S.*, XIV, pp. 53 f.).

[32] 'Uthmān b. Fodiye, *Ta'līm al-ikhwān*. Cf. J. H. Greenberg, *The Influence of Islam on a Sudanese Religion* (New York, 1946), pp. 27 ff.; A. J. N. Tremearne, *The Ban of the Bori* (London, 1914); I.M., pp. 143, 173.

As a major state Gobir was integrated in Hausa trade, and doubtless shared the tastes of other courts. The gifts, for example, which the Sultan of Gobir Bawa gave the Sultan of Zamfara were valuable as luxuries, probably imported: apart from the many slave boys and girls, and 100 horses, twelve of which were of Bornuan breed, there were chrysolite and silks.[33] In *Kitāb al-farq*, decorated carpets are mentioned.[34] Paper must also have been imported for the copyists of Alkalawa and Kadaye. A crucial import was salt, which was brought in by the Tuareg; it is possible that the wars of Gobir against Agades were attempts at the control of this trade. A further, probably major, item of trade was the kola-nut, which reached the Sokoto area from Gonja (in modern Ghana).[35] But precise details of the pattern of eighteenth-century trade are rare, since most of the documentary sources are nineteenth century, and it cannot be assumed that eighteenth- and nineteenth-century trade was similar: the jihād was partly aimed at the corrupt luxuries of Gobir.

(iii) *The Fulani and Tuareg*

I have suggested that there was a cultural watershed between Kebbi and Zamfara/Gobir, and that that watershed had political expression in the boundaries of Bornu and Songhai, of Zamfara and Kebbi. Although there were peasants and hunters all along the valleys and many of the village sites in the border lands were occupied before the jihād, they were out of the reach of the centres of power—four or five days away. In this area were Fulani. They found there the high plateaux in the rains, the river valleys and pools in the dry season. Should trouble arise, there were time and room to move away. But, as has been said, the pattern of campaigns left the area comparatively quiet: the Fulani were no enemy, opting out of society and too elusive.[36]

---

[33] R.A., f. 8.

[34] K.F., p. 561.

[35] R.J., f. 2. Though the book was written in the nineteenth century, the incident referred to was before the jihād (1804).

[36] Cf. the proverb quoted by C. E. Hopen, *op. cit.* (p. 162): 'Running that is its defence' ('dogal kam woni magani majum').

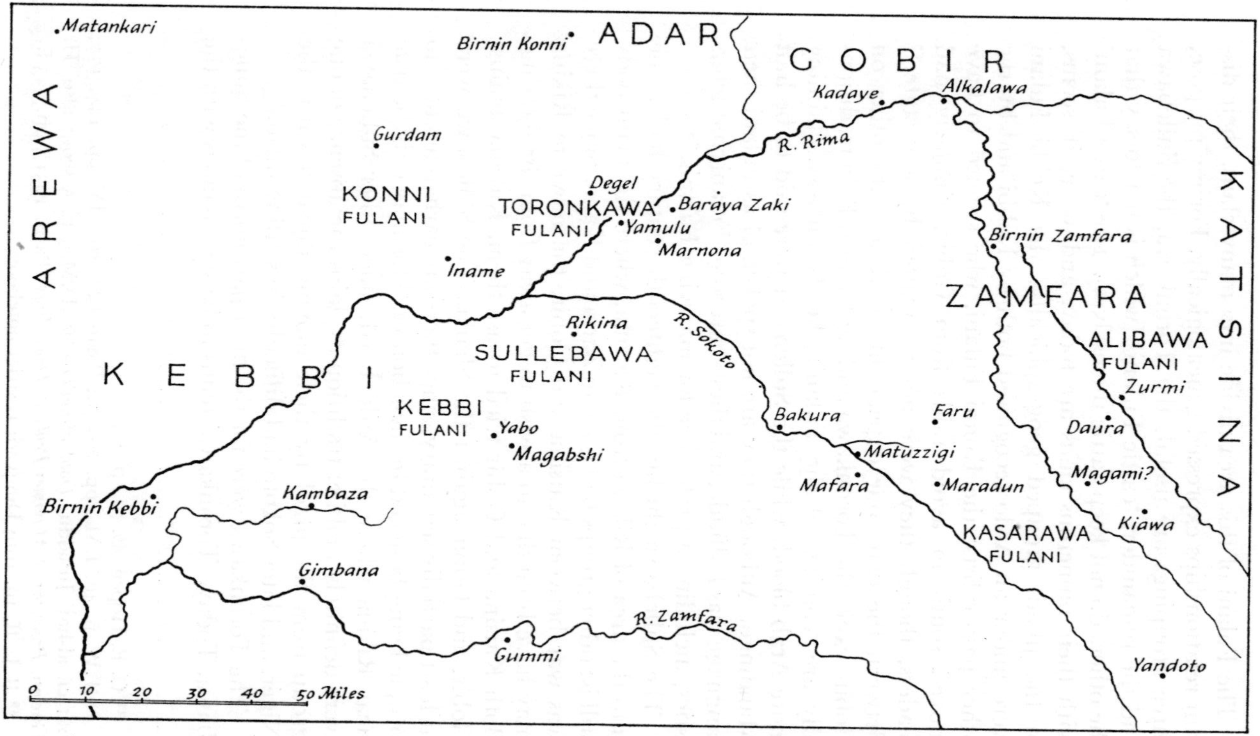

2. The Sokoto Area, *c.* 1800

The Fulani of this area divide into many clans, their distant relationships expressed genealogically. For my purpose, three groupings are useful: the Toronkawa, the Sullebawa and the remainder, 'cattle Fulani' (which is not to say that the others do not keep cattle themselves). The 'cattle Fulani' with their numerous clans are today, and were, it seems, in the jihād, grouped geographically: the Kebbi Fulani were under an Ardo recognised both by Kebbi and by the other pastoralists; the Konni Fulani, who seemed to have moved south to avoid raids from Gobir, similarly had leaders, though they were not recognised by any state.[37] Between the two—one dependent on Kebbi, the other on Gobir—were the Toronkawa and Sullebawa. Both traditionally are 'cousins' of the Fulani: the Toronkawa claiming more Arab blood, while the Sullebawa were said to be half Mandingo. Although they are not spoken of as Fulani their language was Fulfulde, and they share some Fulani characteristics, including a preference for marrying Fulanis.[38]

The Sullebawa during the eighteenth century had come into the area of Rikina from Katsina, where the main body still is; other groups had gone to Zaria and Kano. Since there was war between Katsina and Gobir, the move to Rikina may have been due to a wish to get away from the fighting. Both Katsina and Gobir tried to use them, Katsina against Gobir, and Gobir against the Shaikh. The Sullebawa were at least partially sedentary, since there are early references to people being besieged in their houses. This may only be true near Rikina where the Ardo lived, since other Sullebawa were definitely mobile: tradition explains the absence of one group from the jihād by their moving down towards the Niger, and later Sokoto had difficulty in settling them.[39]

The Toronkawa were for the most part north of the Sullebawa. Today, 'Toronkawa' tends to be synonymous with the

---

[37] C. E. Hopen, *op. cit.*, p. 10.

[38] T.W. p. 40; I.M., pp. 207 ff.; Barth (*Travels*), IV, pp. 144, 177; but cf. al-haji Junaidu, *Ḍabṭ al-multaqaṭāt* (D.M.), ff. 5 seqq; also, H. Gaden, *Proverbes et Maximes Peuls et Toucouleurs* (Paris, 1931), pp. 325 f.

[39] R.J., ff. 10, 10b; Dingyadi District notebook.

Shaikh's family; in the past, they comprised the descendants of the group, divided into four houses, led by Mūsā Jokollo from the west. Their home, as the name 'Toronkawa' may imply, was originally in Futa Toro.[40] The date of the immigration to Konni can be roughly deduced from the genealogies: Mūsā Jokollo is the eleventh generation from the Shaikh, and so possibly fifteenth century. The immigrants were probably Muslim, a suggestion partly supported by the common use of Muslim names. The Toronkawa are famous as Islamic scholars throughout West Africa, becoming almost a caste in areas where caste-consciousness exists.[41]

The Shaikh's ancestors settled in Konni on the borders of Bornu and Songhai, till persecution drove some out to Maratta about the beginning of the eighteenth century under Muḥammad Sa'd, the Shaikh's great-grandfather; others moved to Qoloba. A further move by the Shaikh's father after 1754 brought them from Maratta to Degel, but several of their relations stayed in the area of Konni.[42] Other Toronkawa, such as Gidado's family, were farther south in Kebbi.

Outside this area of the Kebbi–Gobir borders, indeed spread throughout Hausaland and Bornu, were other cattle

---

[40] D.M., ff. 5–8. In Nigeria, 'Toronkawa', 'Torobe' are usually taken to mean 'men from Toro', but farther west, following Gaden (*op. cit.*, pp. 316 f.), the preferred meaning is 'those who go round begging together'.

[41] Caste in Senegal and the modern Mali: C. Tauxier, *Mœurs et Histoire des Peuls* (Paris, 1937), pp. 142 f. Castes were not found, it seems, in Sokoto. The Zoromawa, though distinguished from other Fulani and having a separate quarter, were not part of an organised system in Sokoto. They are said to be descended from a servant of 'Uqba b. Nāfi' (the ancestor of the Toronkawa Fulani) and Bajomango, who was previously the wife of 'Uqba. Their trade in Sokoto was mainly blacksmithing, though Barth speaks of them as merchants or leather-workers. The head of the Zoromawa community in Sokoto in 1853 had been one of the closest friends of the Caliph Atiku; another Zoromawa family, that of Muḥammad Shibi, were friends or servants of the Shaikh and Bello. (Barth, IV, 146–7, 175, 190; Sa'īd, p. 201; genealogical details were given by al-haji Junaidu. Cf. Trimingham, *History of Islam in West Africa*, p. 145 n.)

[42] D.M., f. 8.

Fulani. In Zamfara, for example, on the upper Rima were the Alibawa Fulani whose leader is identified as the 'Alī al-Fāris killed by the Sultan of Gobir.[43] Farther south were the Kasarawa Fulani and the clans of the upper Sokoto valleys. From such groups many of the Shaikh's followers were drawn.

While the Toronkawa and some clans were Muslim, many of the cattle Fulani and Sullebawa were not. There is evidence for some reverence of their cattle and for the practice of rites round bonfires and trees. But Stenning, who made the closest study of a cattle Fulani community, could not obtain a description of their beliefs.[44] Cattle, however, dominate their life, as both Hopen in Gwandu and Stenning in Bornu show. Although in the small cattle Fulani family there was little place for the non-productive member, and the needs of pasture and water prevented a tight political structure, nonetheless there were Fulani leaders, Ardo'en and Dikko'en, who were recognised by the Sultans as being able to command some following. In as mobile a people as the Fulani, it is difficult to trace movements in the eighteenth century with any precision: local conditions determine areas of grazing and shortages prevent the congregation of herds. Consequently, I have taken, with other supplementary evidence, the area with which the Ardo is associated as the approximate area of his fellow clansmen. Even the Toronkawa—so-called 'town-Fulani' (in reality, 'house-Fulani'; and thus not necessarily living in a town)—moved as the calling of a scholar required.[45] Though the name of a great scholar is usually linked to one place, it is little guide to his origin.

Similar reservations apply to the Tuareg. In their case there was also the constant pressure to move from the desert to the better pastures of the south. In addition to the Tuareg–

---

[43] R.A., f. 8b; H. R. Palmer, *J.A.S.*, XVI, p. 270, n. 1.

[44] D. J. Stenning, *op. cit.*, p. 20. For the Fulani of Senegal, see the brief account by G. Dieterlen, in *African Systems of Thought* (ed. Fortes and Dieterlen, London, 1965).

[45] The term is 'Fulanin gida' (Hausa), 'Fulbe sāre (*or* siire)' (Fulfulde); 'gida, sāre' means a compound or house. A semi-permanent cattle camp could contain such a house.

Hausa towns of Agades and Adar, four major Tuareg groups affected the Sokoto area: the eastern Ulemiden (Kel Dinnik), the Kel Geres, the Itesen and the Kel Owi. Some smaller groups were noted for their leaders or their hostility: the Tamesgida, for example, under their leader, Ibra.

The eastern Ulemiden who dominated the desert north and west of Tahoua had split from the other Ulemiden (Kel Ataram) and were still pressing south and east: consequently they clashed with the Tuareg groups from the east, all being interested in the lands of Adar and Gobir.[46] The latter, from the east, were the Kel Geres and Itesen in particular: they had been pushed from north Ahir to the south-west of Agades by the Kel Owi from the northern deserts. Due south of Agades and east of the Kel Geres and Itesen were the other smaller groupings, of which the Tamesgida seem to have been the most formidable. The towns of Agades and Adar were under a dynasty nominated by the local Tuareg groups, that of Adar being a junior branch of the Agades house. The Sultans' influence was largely confined to the town and its immediate hinterland, the people of which were largely Hausa-speaking.[47]

Tuareg society was highly fragmented into caste and clan, but only the Imazegen ('nobles') with their Imgad ('vassals') and the Ineslemen ('Muslims') stand out in Sokoto history. While the 'nobles' were a kind of military aristocracy, the Muslims were the only non-vassal, non-servile group; they paid tribute, but through their profession in the spheres of religion, education and justice they had an independent status and were consulted in elections and assemblies. This status was increased when the Ineslemen of the eastern Ulemiden after the split with the main body were allowed to carry arms.[48] Nonetheless the Muslims were not strong enough to carry through a jihād, as Jibrīl b. 'Umar and Muḥammad Jailani both found.

---

[46] F. Nicolas, *op. cit.* p. 55; cf. Clapperton (2nd journey), pp. 228–9.

[47] Barth, I, pp. 469, 464, 411. Barth found what he thought was a dialect of Songhai also spoken there.

[48] F. Nicolas, *op. cit.*, p. 56; *v. infra*, p. 109.

(iv) *The Scholars*

The Fulani considered all those neither Tuareg nor Fulani as Sudanese, as 'Blacks': the term 'land of the Blacks' (bilād al-sūdān) had classical authority, being used in travellers' accounts and discussions on the state of Islam.[49] Although Bello and 'Abd al-Qādir b. al-Muṣṭafā repeat the division into seven Hausa and seven 'worthless' states, both groups were Sudanese and thus included in the general charge of heathenism. When the Shaikh called on the Hausa Sultans to declare for Islam, only the Sultan of Zaria obeyed, and it some two years later was revoked.[50] But there were undoubtedly a large number of Hausa malams or scholars within these states which had had a Muslim tradition for several centuries already. Being, however, within the framework of their society, they had ties which prejudiced their assessment of it; they knew the limits of their position and were prepared to accept the *status quo*.[51] Since the argument on what constitutes a Muslim was inconclusive in a Sudanese context, the Hausa malams could condone the pre-Islamic practices without compromising themselves. Even in towns famous for their learning, like Yandoto where the Shaikh's ancestor went to study, opposition to Islamic reform persisted.[52]

The scholars were quite numerous: tradition says that the Shaikh had over a thousand behind him at the meeting with the Sultan of Gobir Bawa ạt Magami.[53] They were a formidable community, but in an energetic state like Gobir lacked either the will or the power to reform. According to *Infāq al-maisūr*, the malams of Gobir supported the Sultan Yunfa as much out of conviction as from necessity: the Shaikh used to attack the false malams on his preaching tours, and his position doubtless antagonised them.[54] Not surprisingly,

[49] The term 'Hausa', and its variations (e.g. Kado, Habe), are rarely used in the literature of the jihād.

[50] I.M., p. 83.

[51] The work of a malam could be very lucrative; it is possible, as Muhammad al-Hajj suggests, that the Hausa malams feared both competition from the Fulani scholars and any reform that might curtail their income.

[52] I.M., p. 105. [53] R.J., f. 6b. [54] I.M., pp. 65 f., 69.

Bello could say that after the disaster at Alwassa none of the Kebbi Sudanese were on their side.[55] Some of the Hausa malams had found martyrdom in the defeat at Tsuntsua, while others stayed aloof. Nonetheless others like 'Abd al-Salām, an Arewa, stayed with the Community till the Shaikh died, though not without misgivings. It is difficult to trace other Hausa scholars. In a list of the companions of 'Abdullāh b. Fodiye, some 20 per cent are neither Fulani nor Tuareg. The other lists of those who fought in the jihād mention only a few men specifically as 'the Hausa' or 'the Sudanese', and, apart from a special list of Bello's Tuareg supporters, rarely if ever use the terms 'the Falāta' or 'the Tārikī'.[56]

The lists do not reflect, I believe, a Fulani bias by deliberately omitting Hausa malams, since the emphasis is consistently Muslim: national and ethnic origins are not usually mentioned in any of the literature. Rather, those at Degel were bound to be the more mobile scholars, and it was they who became the leaders. It is likely that many Hausa scholars in Gobir were tacitly favouring the Muslims; outside of Alkalawa, the residence of the Sultan of Gobir, there was little resistance, and although it is arguable that the peasant was basically non-political, much help must have come to the Shaikh from all classes of Hausa in the negative form of apathy.

The Tuareg malams listed are more numerous than the Hausa in the jihād. Owing to the fragmented authority in Tuareg society, a malam could join the Shaikh without great recrimination. Conversely, though the Sultan of Agades could pay allegiance to Sokoto, those who appointed him were free to fight Sokoto. The list of Tuareg who helped Bello is long; equally, Bello's wars against the Tuareg were chronic. Alliances were ephemeral, not least because they were seldom a matter of survival.

---

[55] I.M., p. 103.

[56] List of 'Abdullāh's companions: Sa'd b. 'Abd al-Raḥmān, *Tartīb al-aṣḥāb*. List of Tuareg: Gidado dan Laima, *Majmū' aṣḥāb Bello*. Other lists in Gidado, R.J., *Majmū' khiṣāl al-Shaikh*; and 'Abd al-Qādir b. Gidado, *Basṭ al-fawā' id*. For the use of Tārikī, cf. R.J., f. 14b; I.M., pp. 68, 88.

Undoubtedly some of the friendship between Tuareg and Fulani scholars will have been based on pre-jihād contact. The Shaikh's family came from Adar, which borders on the Tuareg grazing grounds; several of his family had been to Agades, as had the Shaikh himself; some of his distant relations had married scholars from the Azaouac. There was friendship between the Shaikh and Shaikh al-Mukhtār and the Kunta scholars near Timbuktu, as well as contact with the Imam of the Kel es-Souk of the western Ulemiden.[57]

There were Tuareg scholars with the Shaikh from the start. Agali tried to win support for the Shaikh from other Tuareg, and he seems to have been successful. The Emir of Adar recognised the Shaikh early in the jihād and left his sons with him.[58]

The Tuareg malam, if a member of an Ineslemen clan, had a defined role in his society. Though he would move with the herds in the rains, he was comparatively settled; but by this degree of mobility he avoided the rigidity and restraints of a peasant society. Like other scholars they travelled and received students; the common language between Tuareg and Fulani was Arabic. Agades itself was a centre of learning, and being a gateway to the western Sudan on the pilgrims' road, it was cosmopolitan.[59] Though some Tuareg malams could recognise the Shaikh as a scholar and their master, others opposed him. Ibra, for example, the leader of the noble Tamesgida and a consistent antagonist of Sokoto and her allies, was evidently a noted malam. The Ineslemen had no monopoly on learning: there were noble families with a tradition of great learning—for example the ahl al-Shaikh among the Kel Geres, mentioned by Barth.[60] Caste interests may have played a greater part in selecting the allies of the Shaikh than we can detect from the lists. The jihād of Muḥammad Jailani derived its strength from the appeal to the Ineslemen against the nobles; in general, it would not be surprising that in a rivalry between castes, the Sokoto

---

[57] I.M., pp. 200 ff.; R.J., f. 9b.

[58] R.J., f. 9; I.M., p. 68.

[59] I.M., p. 182.

[60] Barth, I, p. 357.

Community would attract the Muslims and alarm the dominant aristocracy.

There seems to have been an affinity between the Tuareg and Fulani malams, which the Hausa did not share. Both were less a hostage to their society, both led a more mobile and austere life, both despised the peasant society. But the Fulani malam was outside both the nomad and the peasant societies. As a Fulani, he spoke the language, followed the marriage preferences, probably ate the food and kept a few of the cattle of the nomad Fulani. His interests and pattern of life, however, were different: his centred on Islam, the nomad's on the herd. Nonetheless contact between nomad and settled Fulani was maintained. A Fulani scholar like the Shaikh at Degel lived outside the towns in a permanent camp or small village. Equally the Fulani malam was outside peasant society. If he taught or held office in a town, as did Galadima Doshero, he may have curtailed his freedom; but Galadima Doshero, when the conflict came, joined the Shaikh.[61] Unlike the Hausa malam, he had few ties in the town—his relatives and people were outside.

Almost constituting a clan themselves, the Fulani malams were self-supporting: they tended to intermarry either with their own clansmen, following Fulani practice, or with other scholar families, though doubtless they also took wives from their kin, the cattle Fulani, as Fulani sayings suggest. For their basic education they could pass from cousin to cousin and to other Fulani scholars. The wandering life began early: a student earned his claim to scholarship by travelling to famous scholars and reading with them the classical texts in which they specialised; he then received a licence to teach that book. Once they had received the basic education, many of the malams began an itinerant life of preaching, teaching and learning.[62]

The insecurity and hardness of this life seems to have encouraged mysticism and religious rigour. For the only values

---

[61] *v. infra*, p. 30.

[62] For the education of the Shaikh and 'Abdullāh, *v.* 'Abdullāh b. Fodiye: T.W., and *'Īdā' al-nusūkh.*

the malam held were those of Islam: it was his career, and his reward, if necessary, was to be had in Paradise. He belonged to the Community of Islam, rather than to any particular state; his allegiance was to an ideal, not to a Sultan. The lingua franca of the community was Arabic, and thus it transcended national divisions; and having a common body of beliefs, aims and rules, Islam gave the malam the security he otherwise lacked.

(v) *Conclusion*

In short, the Muslim Community divided into two: those based primarily in the society of the town, and those based outside. The former were involved in society as teachers and officials. The latter generally went on preaching tours or taught in a base camp. The former tended to be Hausa or at least of that sedentary society—for there were doubtless many minor malams of no great distinction in the small towns—while the latter were predominantly Fulani or Tuareg.

While the two main cultures, peasant and nomad, were far from being Islamically orthodox, the fundamental lack of authority among nomads allowed the nomad malams greater freedom to develop, whereas the town malams were bound into the obligations of their society. Again, nomad malams, divorced from the culture of most of their kin, depended on Islam for their values, ambitions and sense of security, which the town malams would largely adopt, according to the strength of their convictions, from their own society.

What made the Fulani malams particularly formidable were:

(i) they maintained contact with each other over long distances in the ordinary course of either their own movements or those of their relatives with their herds;

(ii) they were a consistently coherent group, not only within their own clans but also outwardly, *vis-à-vis* the peasants around them;

(iii) unlike the Tuareg, they were seldom engaged in feuds. Consequently, the Shaikh could encourage similar movements throughout Hausaland and beyond; the non-Muslim or lightly Muslim Fulani like the Sullebawa would support the Shaikh against Gobir for seemingly no other reason than national loyalty; lastly, the Shaikh was able to have the support of the Sullebawa, the Konni Fulani and the Kebbi Fulani without splitting the movement.

It is possible, now, to see some of the factors that favoured a jihād at this particular place and time.

(i) The interests of a peasant are fundamentally different from those of a nomad; while for the most part relations were peaceable, there was always a possibility of a dispute over grazing and water. The nomad was outside the peasant society and despised it; he felt himself of a different and superior race. On this contempt the Fulani and Tuareg were agreed and, as nomads, shared a pattern of life. Though there was bound to be some competition over water, the grazing areas of both were generally separate.

(ii) Geographically, the Fulani involved in the jihād were away from the centres of peasant power. They appear to have moved into the area of the Kebbi–Gobir marches within the last fifty years before the jihād to avoid the pressures of war; here, in comparative peace, they built up their resources and followers.

(iii) These followers were mainly found in Kebbi and Zamfara, both of which were weak states containing many Muslims. At the time of the clash with Gobir, Gobir was itself weaker than it had been twenty years before. The Sultan was new, and there may have been rival claimants to his throne. His support was diminished by oppression, which affected both peasant and nomad in spheres in which Islam is particularly precise, justice and taxation. At the same time there was unrest among the Tuareg Ineslemen—the scholar caste—especially among the Ulemiden, who had lately been allowed weapons. Further, with the beginning of the thirteenth Islamic century, there were expectations of a Mujaddid (reformer) and after him the Mahdi and the subsequent end of the world.[63]

[63] Prophecies foretold the coming of the Shaikh (I.M., pp. 29, 30) and the Shaikh himself believed he was this last Mujaddid. But it is not clear

(iv) Psychologically, the Fulani malam was well prepared for the jihād. Outside both Fulani and Hausa societies, his only ideal was Islam: preaching and teaching was his career, and he was under pressure to put his teachings into practice. Previously he had been too weak, like a prophet in the wilderness, or he had lost his independence in some Sultan's court. The Shaikh, however, was able to attract enough students and followers to form a community out of the wider community of Islam, including Tuareg, Hausa and Fulani.

(v) Lastly, although the jihād represented different interests for different groups, the ideal of Islam appealed to all. Knowledge of Islam was widespread enough, and the Hausa states corrupt enough, to make Islamic reform welcome. Thus when a reformer of the calibre and personality of the Shaikh appeared, the Muslim protest against the Hausa states found the leadership necessary for the jihād.

---

at what point millennialist prophecies became important in Sokoto: references are found in both pre- and post-jihād literature. For the Mujaddid, cf. R.J., f. 11, where reference is made to the ḥadīth in Abū Dāwūd: 'Surely Allah will raise up for this Community [of Muslims], at the commencement of every century, one who will reform their religion.' (36:1. Quoted from Muhammad Ali, *Religion of Islam*, Lahore, 1950, p. 263.)

Part I:

The Establishment of Dār al-Islām in Sokoto, 1754–1817: 1168–1232

I
The Community

(i) *The Shaikh and the Growth of his Community*

The Shaikh 'Uthmān b. Muḥammad b. 'Uthmān b. Ṣāliḥ was born in Gobir at a place called Maratta in the land of Galmi on Sunday 15 December 1754.[1] He was known as bi Fodiye, dan Fodio or Ibn Fudiyi, 'the son of the Fodiye'. His father had earned the Fulani name of Fodiye, 'the learned', by his teaching, but, apart from his instructing his sons in the Quran, his work as a scholar has not survived.[2]

The family moved some thirty miles south of Birnin Konni to Degel, leaving several of their relatives in the north.[3] Degel

---

[1] Gidado dan Laima, *al-Kashf wa'l-bayān* (K.B.), p. 4: 'Sunday, the last day of Ṣafar, 1168'. The site of Maratta is not known in Sokoto now. There is a Galmi thirty miles north-east of Birnin Konni. Cf. Muḥammad Bello, *Infāq al-maisūr* (I.M.), p. 72. Gidado dan Laima, *Rauḍ al-jinān* (R.J.), f. 6.

[2] For his teaching of the Quran, *v.* 'Abdullāh b. Muḥammad Fodiye, *'Īdā' al-nusūkh* (I.N.), p. 554. 'Fodiye' (or 'Foduye') is translated in Arabic as 'faqīh'.

[3] It is possible that Muḥammad Fodiye was already at Degel at the time of the birth of the Shaikh. Maratta was the home of his wife's lineage, and she may have gone there to have the Shaikh, though he was her second child. Alternatively, Muḥammad Fodiye may have been living at Maratta at the time, though his own lineage, the Banū 'Alī of the Banū Mūsā, were living at Qoloba (in the same general area?); Qoloba is the third possible home of Muḥammad Fodiye (cf. I.M., p. 72; al-haji Junaidu, *Ḍabṭ al-multaqaṭāt* (D.M.), f. 8). He was, however, at Degel by the time the Shaikh was a youth (ḥadath): R.J., f. 1b. For his relatives in the north cf. 'Abdullāh b. Muḥammad Fodiye, *Tazyīn al-waraqāt* (T.W.), p. 45, and R.J., f. 6.

is about three miles from the river Rima valley on the plateau to the west: the plateau is roughly flat but for a low hill less than a mile to the north of Degel.[4] In some traditional accounts collected by early British administrators, Degel is equated with Rugar Fako, 'ruga' being a Fulani cattle encampment.[5] The country is good for cattle, with both dry and wet season pasture easily accessible. Being near the Rima valley, it is on the edge of the main route between Birnin Kebbi and the Gobir towns of Alkalawa and Kadaye.[6] A few miles west was another north–south route to Birnin Konni and Adar. A market was near by.[7]

Muḥammad Fodiye died in Degel and is buried there.[8] Though his side of the family up to his great-grandfather is unexceptional with few names of note that can be precisely identified, his wife Ḥawwā' bint Muḥammad, especially through her mother Ruqayya, was linked to the branch of the family most noted for its learning.[9] Ḥawwā', the mother of the

[4] Kwomkwombilo. On this hill, the Shaikh showed jinns to some students (R.J., f. 1b).

[5] For example, Edgar, II, 397–9; notes on the translation of Muḥammad Bukhari, *Ta'nīs al-ikhwān*; cf. Barth, IV, 168.

[6] Alkalawa, written al-qāḍāwa, the capital of Gobir at this time, is so called because it was built on the estates of the Alkalin (al-qāḍī) Zamfara.

[7] R.J., f. 2.

[8] al-haji Junaidu, *Idrāk al-amal* (1382: 1962–3).

[9] The Shaikh's descent from the Prophet is through Ḥawwā' bint Muḥammad b. Fāṭima bint Muḥammad b. al-Sharīf 'Abd al-Ṣamad (see genealogy); 'Abd al-Ṣamad derives his claim to being a Sharīf through Moulay Idrīs of Morocco (I.M., pp. 181–2). Although this would be known to the Shaikh and 'Abdullāh, neither mentions it; instead the Shaikh refutes those who say he is the Mahdi on the grounds that he is not a descendant of the Prophet (*Taḥdhīr al-ikhwān*, p. 2). 'Abd al-Qādir b. Gidado (*al-Iktifā'*, 1265/1848–9) gives the descent: Ḥawwā' bint Muḥammad b. Aḥmad al-Sharīf b. 'Alī al-Yanbū'ī b. 'Abd al-Razzāq b. al-Ṣalīḥ b. al-Mubārak b. Aḥmad b. Abī'l-Ḥasan al-Shādhalī b. 'Abdullāh b. 'Abd al-Jabbār b. Hurmuz b. Ḥātim b. Quṣay b. Yūsha' b. Ward b. Baṭṭāl b. Aḥmad b. Tamīm b. Muḥammad b. 'Īsa b. Muḥammad b. al-Ḥasan b. Fāṭima, daughter of the Prophet. This genealogy, together with a shorter one, was put into verse by Muḥammad Bukhari and is quoted in Sir Ahmadu Bello, *My Life* (Cambridge, 1962), p. 239. Muḥammad Bukhari, *Salsalar Toronkawa* (Zaria, 1961; recorded, H.M.V. 45 NHJ 11).

Shaikh, was the third cousin of her husband. Her family lived by Baraya Zaki and Marnona, a day's journey east of Degel across the Rima valley, where Toronkawa and other learned Fulani seem to have been settled for some time already.[10] Here the land is a high plateau between the two rivers, the Sokoto and Rima, whose tributaries cut sharply into it. The plateau ceases abruptly at the edge of the Gundumi 'desert', a wild, dry scrubland stretching across to Alkalawa and Birnin Zamfara.

After studying the Quran with his father, the Shaikh moved to other teachers. They included his relations, 'Uthmān Binduri and Muḥammad Sambo: the Shaikh accompanied Binduri for some two years and 'moulded himself to his pattern of piety, enjoining the right and forbidding the wrong'.[11] Muḥammad Sambo, during this time, it seems, left for the pilgrimage on which he spent between thirteen and nineteen years in Mecca and Medina. As he reached Agades on his way back in Ramaḍān 1207 (1793), his pilgrimage probably began *c.* 1190 (*c.* 1776), that is, when the Shaikh was about 22.[12]

After being taught by 'Uthmān Binduri, the Shaikh joined Jibrīl b. 'Umar. Jibrīl was a learned and controversial figure. He had gone on the pilgrimage early and returned to preach and teach among the Tuaregs. His preaching was rigorous, defining a Muslim by the strictest standards, which became the subject of disagreement between him and the Shaikh.[13] His call to jihād on these rigorous terms so angered the Tuaregs that Jibrīl had to leave for a second pilgrimage. The Shaikh was with Jibril a year before he went on his second

---

[10] I.M., pp. 26, 29; K.B., p. 6. Ḥawwā' is buried at Marnona; near by at Marnona is the tomb of Muḥammad Magori, mentioned in I.M., p. 29. The Shaikh married the daughter of one of these local scholars who had himself married a girl from the Toronkawa: the Shaikh's sons by her were Muḥammad Bello and Abū Bakr Atiku.

[11] I.N., p. 554.

[12] T.W., p. 39; I.N., p. 554.

[13] 'Uthmān b. Fodiye, *Shifā' al-ghalīl*; cf. I.M., p. 184. Cf. Hiskett, 'An Islamic tradition of reform in the Western Sudan', *B.S.O.A.S.*, 1962, pp. 589 ff. Jibrīl was, it seems, a Berber (or North African) by origin, but in his ijāza he is given the laqab, al-Aqdasī; he was not a Hausa or a Fulani. The genealogy shows him married to a distant relation of the Shaikh, though this is now disputed.

pilgrimage. As the Shaikh had not his father's permission to go to Mecca, he was sent back to his father from Agades. Jibrīl did not stay long at Mecca.[14] He was back in Adar by about 1200 (1786), when the Shaikh and his younger brother 'Abdullāh visited him. It was, therefore, a short journey, less than ten years, compared to the thirteen to nineteen years of Muḥammad Sambo who left a year before Jibrīl and returned in 1207 (1793) to Agades.[15] On his return, Jibrīl seems to have stayed in Adar; he died near Madaoua, and his son, Muḥammadān, was in Adar before joining the Shaikh at the beginning of the jihād.[16]

Jibrīl, it seems, contributed as much by his being a stimulus as by his scholarship. By his uncompromising attitude and attacks on local practices, he prepared the way for the Shaikh. Though he taught the Shaikh only for a year, he also had 'Abdullāh and the Shaikh's cousins Muḥammad Firabri and al-Muṣṭafā b. 'Uthmān as his students, and his views and writings were probably widely known. This accounts for his place as the dominant influence in the Shaikh's life, as Muḥammad Bello suggests.[17]

The date the Shaikh had begun his preaching was about 1188 (1774–5) when he was 20: he was, therefore, studying and preaching at the same time, and in this was following the

---

[14] The account Muḥammad Bello gives of the scholars Jibrīl met is brief, compared to his account of Jibrīl's first pilgrimage. The Hausa Chronicle allows twelve years in Mecca for the first, and only two years for the second pilgrimage (I.M., p. 27; *M.S.O.S.*, 1903, p. 171).

[15] The chronology for Jibrīl is based on 'Abdullāh b. Muḥammad: I.N., p. 555; T.W., p. 31; on Muḥammad Bello: I.M., p. 27; cf. Hausa Chronicle (*M.S.O.S.*, 1903), p. 171. The vague length, thirteen to nineteen years, is based on "*ashr wa-bid*" (T.W., p. 39; cf. I.N., p. 554).

[16] I.M., p. 74. Another son of Jibrīl, who accompanied him to Egypt, seems to have died before the jihād.

[17] I.M., pp. 28, 31–2. 'Uthmān b. Fodiye, *Shifā' al-ghalīl*. Jibrīl is said to have been the first to salute the Shaikh as leader before the jihād and to have given him the flag of victory (D.M., f. 20). The Shaikh derived many of his salāsil in the Qādiriyya, Shādhiliyya, and Khalwatiyya as well as several academic licences from Jibrīl on Jibrīl's return from Egypt: there, in 1198, he had been given them by Muḥammad Murtaḍā b. Muḥammad al-Ḥusainī al-Wāsiṭī (Muḥammad Bello, *al-Durar al-zāhiriyya*; 'Uthmān b. Fodiye, *Asānīd al-faqīr*).

traditional practice of Muslim scholarship.[18] Later, *c.* 1193, his younger brother, 'Abdullāh, came to study under him; in 1200 he attended the Maulid assembly at Marnona of his cousin Muḥammad b. Raji, who had returned from the pilgrimage, and he received there further academic asānīd.[19] During this period, 1188–1200 (1774–86), from his base at Degel he preached and taught locally in Kebbi and Gobir, avoiding the courts of kings.[20] When, however, his following had increased, he went to the Sultan of Gobir and expounded Islam there, before returning to Degel: the length of his stay at Alkalawa is not mentioned.[21] He then went to Zamfara, staying on the upper Sokoto river for about five years (1201–1206).[22] At the end of the year 1202 or 1203 (1788–9), he was summoned by the Sultan of Gobir Bawa to go to Magami for the 'Īd al-kabīr.[23] Whatever the plans of the Sultan may have been—and he is said to have been going to kill the Shaikh—he acquiesced to the five points the Shaikh demanded. The Sultan was now old, about 75, and he doubtless recognised he could not prevent the power of the Shaikh from growing. At the 'Īd prayers at Magami, all his scholars had joined the Shaikh's followers, leaving the Sultan: together the malams numbered over a thousand. Later the Sultan said, publicly pointing out the Shaikh, that there would be no more than a local head of Alkalawa after himself.[24] The next year, 1203 or 1204 (1789–90), after the disaster at Dankache in which his son was killed, Bawa died.[25]

---

[18] T.W., p. 27. [19] I.N., p. 553; 'Uthmān b. Fodiye, *Asānīd al-faqīr*.

[20] T.W., p. 27; D.M., f. 11.

[21] D.M., ff. 11b, 12. The Gobir title for the Sultan is Sarkin Gobir.

[22] T.W., p. 27. R.J. (f. 14) has the Shaikh in Daura, east of Bakura, for a whole year, and four years in Faru after 1202. T.W. (*ibid.*) has him in Daura, while a document quoting Abū Bakr Atiku b. al-Shaikh and repeated in 'Abd al-Qādir b. Muḥammad Bukhari, *Tabshīr al-ikhwān*, mentions the Shaikh in Faru. The Shaikh's house in Faru, it is said, is used now by the village head (source: al-haji Junaidu).

[23] T.W., p. 30; R.J., ff. 6b, 7; 'Abd al-Qādir b. Gidado, *Anīs al-mufīd* (A.M.), p. 5. The date, 10 Dhū'l-ḥijja 1202, is 11 September 1788.

[24] R.J., f. 7.

[25] The date is calculated from the years of reigns given by 'Abd al-Qādir b. al-Muṣṭafā, *Rauḍāt al-Afkār* (R.A.) where (f. 7b) Bawa is said

The Shaikh returned to Degel. His position, and that of his people, was established. He had won from the Sultan of Gobir five concessions: to be allowed to call people to God in his country; that none should be stopped from responding to the call; that any man wearing a turban was to be treated with respect; that all prisoners be freed; that his subjects should not be burdened by taxes.[26] Though his position was strong, the Shaikh did not go out of his way to antagonise the rulers: he ignored them as far as possible. He told his sons not to go to the court, and he himself tended to keep away from Alkalawa.[27] But this did not prevent charges of self-seeking and hypocrisy against him.[28] Hausa tradition maintains the Shaikh taught Yunfa, the son of the Sultan of Gobir Nafata, and helped him to get the throne in the absence of the other princes. Similarly, the Sultans are said to have visited Degel to greet the Shaikh, possibly because the number of candidates eligible to succeed after the long reign of Bawa made a new Sultan's position insecure.[29] When Ya'qūb, the successor to Bawa, was heavily defeated and killed in battle *c.* 1209 (dry season, 1794–5), the power of Gobir was on the decline.[30] By contrast, the following of the Shaikh was growing, as his students themselves preached and taught.[31] But although, as 'Abdullāh says, 'most of the country, the common people and the nobles', were coming to the Shaikh, very few of the scholars related to the Shaikh ever visited him or showed any enthusiasm for the Community.[32] 'Abdullāh therefore in this

---

to have died forty days after the news of his son's death. A Hausa history gives the date as Saturday 16 Ṣafar 1201. The year is certainly wrong (cf. T.W., p. 30), but the day and month may be right: either Saturday 15 Ṣafar 1203 (15 November 1788) or Sunday 16 Ṣafar 1203. The day is less liable to error than the date (F. Edgar, *Labarin mafitar Bawa*, p. 4 (notebook)).

[26] R.J., ff. 6b, 7. The prisoners had presumably been gaoled contrary to Islamic Law.

[27] I.M., pp. 65, 66; cf. 'Uthmān b. Fodiye, *Tanbīh al-ikhwān*.

[28] I.M., pp. 34, 35.

[29] R.J., ff. 7, 7b.

[30] R.A., ff. 8, 8b; R.J., f. 7. Ya'qūb had been notably hostile to the Shaikh.

[31] Cf. I.M., p. 65.

[32] T.W., p. 41; the translation is by M. Hiskett (p. 98).

period (*c.* 1207) sent his relatives a poem of advice, which was answered favourably first by his cousin al-Muṣṭafā b. al-ḥājj 'Uthmān in 1208 (1793–4) and again a year later (1209) by his cousin Zaid b. Muḥammad Sa'd: from this time, then, it seems the Shaikh also had the support of his clan.[33]

Meanwhile the Shaikh was writing a number of books in Arabic and composing long poems in Fulfulde. The most famous of the books is *Iḥyā' al-sunna wa-ikhmād al-bid'a*: finished before 1793, it seems to have established the Shaikh's reputation amongst contemporary scholars. Though he was engaged in disputes over scholasticism and wrote over fifty works against the quibbles of local scholars, *Iḥyā' al-sunna* is not a polemical book. Moderate in tone, its purpose is rather to instruct men on the Islamic regulations for daily life. Several of his longer poems in Fulfulde have the same purpose, touching on tafsīr, tauḥīd and fiqh, as well as the more esoteric themes of sufism. The majority of these poems were written before the jihād, and their existence underlines the extent to which the Shaikh's teaching was aimed at the Fulani and at raising their standard of Islam.[34] By contrast, his preaching in Hausa, being essentially oral, has survived only in the academic medium of Arabic.[35]

It is clear the Shaikh at no time confined himself to the more secluded branch of scholarship, the reading of classical texts to a circle of students. This may have been the cause for the slow recognition given to the Shaikh by his family: like

---

[33] T.W., pp. 41–5; al-Muṣṭafā b. al-ḥājj 'Uthmān, *al-Sulāla 'alā 'l-risāla*; Zād b. Muḥammad Sa'd (distinguished by the name Zaid), *Khulāṣat al-qarā 'iḥ 'alā 'l-sulāla wa-risālat al-naṣā'iḥ*. The latter poem is a takhmīs. Cf. R.J., f. 6, where the Shaikh visits his family's town. Al-Muṣṭafā had taught 'Abdullāh; Zaid joined the Community and died at Tsuntsua (I.N., p. 557; I.M., p. 87). He is possibly the same Zaid whom 'Abdullāh later rebukes for not joining the emigration (T.W., p. 59).

[34] For example, the Shaikh banned the games which the Fulani hold on the Prophet's birthday and on the two 'Īds. The legality of the games had already been the subject of controversy among local scholars: cf. I.M., p. 23.

[35] e.g. I.M., pp. 42–62. Several of the Shaikh's books are between five and ten folios long, short enough to have been the basis of sermons or seminars. Many were later incorporated into long works.

his teacher Jibrīl, he forsook quietism for the radical life of preaching, and as the Gobir armies were harassing the Fulani in his family's area, quietism would have been the safer course. In addition, prophecies were current foretelling the coming of the Mahdi from the West in the year 1200 or 1204, and popular imagination identified the Shaikh as the Mahdi.[36] Though the Shaikh was at pains to deny this, the widespread belief in the imminent end of the world (which the Shaikh shared) only added to the force and urgency of his teaching.

It was in this period also, mid-1208 (early 1794), that the Shaikh had the mystic experiences described in his *Wird*. The first had occurred in 1204, when his vision and understanding were made clear; the second occurred in mid-1208. In this, he saw the saints and was invested with the sword of truth to use against the enemies of Allah.[37] In a similar vision of the Shaikh's described in *Rauḍ al-jinān*, it was Muḥammad Bello who was equipped to fight the jihād as an assistant of the Shaikh. Earlier, it is related how the Shaikh got instructions from the saint 'Abd al-Qādir where to make his hijra.[38] The Shaikh seems always to have been familiar with jinns and the supernatural: accounts of this familiarity appear even in as uncoloured a book as *Infāq al-maisūr*.[39] This, together with his asceticism, was a feature of his life at Degel at this time. He avoided property, living without wealth or servants, and occasionally went into retreat, but only for short periods: in a vision once he had been told to fast only a fortnight, instead of forty days.[40]

His main work was teaching. Although, after his return from Faru, he continued to tour, going beyond Kebbi as far as Illo across the Niger, and, in the south, travelling to Zugu,

---

[36] 'Uthmān b. Fodiye: *al-Nabā' al-hādī* (quoting 'Abd al-Wahhāb al-Sha'rānī and al-Qurṭubī).

[37] 'Uthmān b. Fodiye, *Wird*, p. 3.

[38] R.J., f. 6b: cf. f. 3.

[39] I.M., p. 116. His familiarity with jinns is frequently mentioned in R.J.; *v. infra*.

[40] R.J., f. 6. That is, to follow the rule of al-Ash'arī, and not that of al-Junaid.

beyond the Zamfara river valley, he seems thereafter mainly to have preached locally, holding meetings at Degel on Thursday evenings.[41] But those whom he had taught probably returned to their homes to spread the impetus of Islam. The effect of the Shaikh was thus felt beyond the Kebbi–Gobir area before the jihād. The verses from Bornu freely translated by Palmer illustrate an aspect of this impulse as it was felt by groups hostile to the Shaikh, or, at least, to his followers.[42]

Verily a cloud has settled on God's earth
A cloud so dense that escape from it is impossible.
Everywhere between Kordofan and Gobir
And the cities of the Kindin [Tuareg]
Are settlements of the dogs of Fellata [Bi la'ila]
Serving God in all their dwelling places
(I swear by the life of the Prophet and his over-
flowing grace)
In reforming all districts and provinces
Ready for future bliss
So in this year of 1214 they are following their
beneficent theories
As though it were time to set the world in order by
preaching
Alas! that I know all about the tongue of the fox.

This poem was written two years after the crucial decision by the Shaikh that his followers should take arms, since it was 'sunna', the practice of the Prophet. The decision, as related in *Tazyīn al-waraqāt*, was followed by a poem in which the destruction of the unbelievers is expected. The poem is dated 1212 (1797–8).[43] Earlier, *c.* 1209 (1794–5), the Sultan of

[41] T.W., p. 39; I.M., p. 65. The sermons are described in I.M., pp. 42–62. Zugu, the town of the Emir of Zauma, is just south of Gummi.

[42] H. R. Palmer, *Bornu Sahara and Sudan* (London, 1936), p. 52. He writes 'A.H. 1124 (A.D. 1799)': 1124 is clearly a misprint for 1214. I have not yet seen the Arabic original of this poem.

[43] Reading the date as b. sh.y.r., not a.b.sh.r.w.a. F. H. El-Masri ('The Life of Shehu Usuman Dan Fodio before the Jihad', *J.H.S.N.*, II, 4, 1963, p. 444, n. 3) prefers the second date (1210: 1795–6), that is, immediately after Nafata's accession. T.W., pp. 54, 51.

Gobir, Ya'qūb, had been killed in battle, and his brother, Nafata, became Sultan. Nafata's son, Yunfa, had been taught by the Shaikh, or, at the least, had visited Degel.[44] But this contact did not relieve tension. Nafata issued a proclamation forbidding anyone but the Shaikh from preaching, forbidding the conversion of a son away from his father's faith, and ordering those that had been converted to Islam to return to the religion of their fathers. Further, the wearing of turbans and veils, a distinctive mark of a Muslim, was proscribed.[45] The proclamation thus reversed the policy of the Sultan of Gobir Bawa made more than ten years before: previously, the Community had been allowed to become virtually independent of Gobir; now it was to be reintegrated into the state.[46] The date of the proclamation is uncertain: in the *Tazyīn al-waraqāt* it follows the poem dated 1212, yet it is clearly opening a new chapter on the jihād. The proclamation is usually taken in Sokoto histories as the first shot of the jihād. These Sokoto accounts blame the Sultan's scholars and courtiers more than the Sultan for the stronger line against the Muslims.[47] Similarly, no aggressive role is attributed to the Shaikh: it appears that other leading figures in the Community, like the Shaikh's brother 'Abdullāh, were more eager to fight.[48]

As the power of Gobir declined under Nafata, so hostility in Zamfara crystallised.[49] 'Alī al-Fāris, a noted leader in Zurmi, was killed by the Gobirawa: he is said to have been the leader of the Alibawa Fulani, who later gave crucial help to the Shaikh.[50] The Zamfarawa, too, only recently and with difficulty subdued, were again in revolt, which Nafata lacked the power to put down.

When Nafata's son, Yunfa, became Sultan, *c.* 1216–17,

---

[44] R.J., ff. 7, 7b; cf. J. A. Burdon, *Northern Nigeria. Some Notes on Certain Emirates and Tribes* (London, 1909), p. 66.

[45] T.W., p. 54; I.M., pp. 67, 130.

[46] T.W., p. 54.

[47] e.g. I.M., p. 69.

[48] R.J., f. 7b; al-ḥājj Sa'īd, *Ta'rīkh Sokoto*, f. 110a. Muḥammad Bello, as a young boy, predicted the jihād against Gobir (K.B., p. 6).

[49] R.A., f. 8b.

[50] R.A., *ibid.*; H. R. Palmer (*J.A.S.*, 1916), p. 270 n.

there might have been a compromise. Yunfa is said to have received the support of the Shaikh in getting the sultanate over his cousins.[51] In Sokoto sources, it is related how he came as Sultan to visit the Shaikh and walked to greet him.[52] While there were ties between Yunfa and the Shaikh, men like 'Abdullāh were very suspicious of Yunfa's intentions. The following year, Yunfa tried to kill the Shaikh at Alkalawa.[53]

At this time, towards the end of 1217, the Shaikh wrote *Masā'il muhimma*. In it are clearly stated the obligations of emigration and jihād against pagan states. In addition, he mentions specific complaints, such as the illegality of selling the Fulani as slaves, seeing that most of them were Muslims.[54] This insistence on the particular instead of on the general is unusual in the theoretical works of the Shaikh. It clearly shows what sort of questions he was being asked exactly a year before the emigration from Degel took place; and who were interested in the answers.

In his first year as Sultan, Yunfa had to face another enemy, the Sultan of Katsina, who marched through Zamfara and down the Sokoto river till he reached Rikina, the main town of the Sullebawa. These Sullebawa had recently moved from Katsina, where the majority of their kin still lived. From Rikina the Sultan of Katsina sent out raiding parties, and tried to get in touch with the Shaikh, but was snubbed. Yunfa then came down to the Shaikh's place—possibly this is the occasion of his walking to greet the Shaikh—and the Sultan of Katsina retired.[55]

Yunfa at the end of his first year, therefore, faced (i) a rebellious Zamfara, inherited from his father and against which he had campaigned that year; (ii) the Sultan of Katsina, who, having proved fatal to the Sultan of Gobir Bawa

---

[51] Hausa Chronicle (*M.S.O.S.*, 1903), p. 210; cf. the Krause manuscripts, pp. 31, 32.

[52] R.J., f. 7b.

[53] T.W., p. 55; R.J., f. 7b. The story is sometimes attributed to Bawa (Edgar, *ibid.* (notebook)). Yunfa tried to shoot the Shaikh, but the gunpowder backfired and burnt Yunfa.

[54] 'Uthmān b. Fodiye, *Masā'il muhimma*, pp. 2, 12.

[55] R.J., f. 9b; R.A., ff. 8b, 9.

and others, was free to raid right across southern Gobir; (iii) the Sullebawa, who were equivocal so long as the Sultan of Katsina was accessible; (iv) the Muslims of the Community who were increasingly powerful and now probably restive under the moderation of the Shaikh; (v) possible rival claimants to his own throne, who were less compromised by Muslim connections than himself: for he had several cousins by his father's senior brothers. His court was strongly against the Shaikh, and Yunfa may have needed their support. Yunfa's response was his attempt to kill the Shaikh.

The crisis over 'Abd al-Salām finally precipitated the breach. A Gobir expedition returning to Alkalawa with Muslim prisoners was made to free them as it went up the valley past Degel. Yunfa, though not in command of the expedition, could not overlook the challenge.

Accounts of the origin of the expedition differ. The Muslim sources imply that it was a deliberate attack, by Yunfa himself or on his orders, on Gimbana, a town near the Zamfara river where an Arewa disciple of the Shaikh, 'Abd al-Salām, had established himself with his followers.[56] 'Abdullāh adds that 'Abd al-Salām had left Degel for Gimbana because he had feared the threats of the Sultan of Gobir Nafata, and then had refused to obey the order of the next Sultan, Yunfa, to return.[57] The Hausa Chronicle relates how Waru, probably the Sultan of Gummi, was sent by Gobir to quell Dosso for the Sultan of Kebbi and on his way down the Zamfara valley was refused the prayers of 'Abd al-Salām; the refusal was repeated on his return from Dosso.[58] Yunfa, on being told this by the Sultan of Gummi, agreed to the arrest of 'Abd

[56] 'Abdullāh b. Fodiye: T.W., p. 54; in I.M., p. 168; in 'Uthmān b. Fodiye, *Tanbīh al-ikhwān* (1226: 1811). Muḥammad Bello in I.M., pp. 67, 130; *Sard al-kalām*, pp. 2, 3. R.J., f. 7b. The last two references of 'Abdullāh b. Fodiye are the same: they were written at the Shaikh's request in reply to al-Kanemi. I.M., p. 130, is Bello's answer to al-Kanemi. They thus constitute the 'Sokoto version'.

[57] T.W., p. 54; cf. *Sard al-kalām, ibid.* As M.A. al-Hajj suggests, it is possible that Gimbana had become a centre for ex-slaves escaping to the Community from Gobir.

[58] *M.S.O.S.*, pp. 210–11. Sultan of Gummi, I.M., 79. The road to Dosso passes through Arewa country.

al-Salām. Gimbana was sacked and prisoners taken. The Shaikh protested and was allowed by the Sultan of Gobir to free the Muslims as they were brought up the Rima valley to Alkalawa, but Yunfa later denied this permission. The prisoners, however, were freed, though other sources suggest force was used or threatened.[59] Al-ḥājj Sa'īd says the Shaikh was annoyed at this hasty act, being angry especially with 'Abdullāh and telling him to return what was taken.[60] Yunfa responded to the episode by ordering the Shaikh to leave Degel with his family, the implication being that the rest of the Community should disperse or be attacked.[61] The Shaikh refused, and although Yunfa later changed his mind, the Muslims made ready to emigrate in the classical manner of Islam.[62]

Again the impression is given that the hands of both the Shaikh and Yunfa were forced. The Shaikh by the defiance of 'Abd al-Salām and the impetuosity of 'Abdullāh, and Yunfa by the provocation of the Sultan of Gummi Waru were moved closer to conflict than either of them wanted. At the same time, however, there seems to have been considerable persecution of the followers of the Shaikh by local rulers and their malams; and this harassment must have given rise to innumerable minor clashes which were not serious enough to precipitate a crisis. Although the Community had been armed in self-defence at least for the past six years, it is clear that the Muslims were not prepared physically for emigration or war. No advance preparations appear to have been made: horses were too few for an effective cavalry, and although

---

[59] Al-ḥājj Sa'īd, *Ta'rīkh Sokoto*, f. 110a; R.J., f. 8. 'Abd al-Salām was not among the prisoners: he had escaped to a Fulani village, and they had asked the Shaikh if they should grant him asylum.

[60] Al-ḥājj Sa'īd, *Ta'rīkh Sokoto* (*ibid.*). Cf. Muḥammad Bello (*Sard al-kalām*, p. 3) who called the Muslims who freed the prisoners 'hooligans' (sufahā').

[61] I.M., pp. 67, 68.

[62] I.M., p. 69. The emigration (hijra) of the Prophet was consciously imitated and the classical terminology used by the Shaikh and his followers. Such constant reference to the life of the Prophet would not only provide a legal justification for the hijra, but also would be an inspiration to the Community to face the hardship of emigration and war.

donkeys from the peasantry and camels from the Tuaregs doubtless helped, not much food or possessions can have been taken.[63] It was already late in February, two-thirds through the dry season with food and water scarce. Even though a large number of the emigrants were probably Fulani and thus might bring along what cattle they could or be able to ask the local Fulani for help, food always remained the major problem: a surplus of food at this time is rare anywhere.[64]

(ii) *The Composition of the Community*

Diplomatically the Muslims were not fully prepared. Muḥammad Bello, who had been away from Degel at the time of the Gimbana episode, did not return till after he had gone to Kebbi and distributed pamphlets calling the Muslims out for the emigration.[65] It is probable that it is about this time that the *Wathīqat ahl al-sūdān* was circulated, containing brief instructions on what is Islamically lawful and unlawful and what courses of action are compulsory for a Muslim individual or Community.[66] Despite this, the Sullebawa Fulani were equivocal, and the Kebbi Fulani in no position to aid the Muslims at Degel:[67] the lines for or against the Shaikh had not yet been drawn. The Muslims, then, at the time of the emigration had much sympathy but few allies.

The Muslim Community was widely dispersed. Emigrants continued to join the Shaikh for months after the original hijra, some coming with, some without their families and belongings.[68] Others waited, joining the Shaikh or his lieutenants as the jihād continued. While the Muslims not at

---

[63] Cf. 'Abd al-Qādir b. al Muṣṭafā, *Mauṣūfat al-sūdān*, f. 2b. Agali is said to have carried the Shaikh's books on his camel. The shortage of cavalry was acute at Kwotto (I.M., p. 76). The decision to bear arms had been made six to eight years earlier, but it may have affected only the scholars, since most men carried arms of some sort.

[64] For the food problem at this stage of the jihād, *v.* I.M., pp. 80, 82.

[65] I.M., p. 68.

[66] A. D. H. Bivar, *Jnl. of African History*, II, 3 (1961), pp. 235–43.

[67] Manori, the leader of the Sullebawa at Rikina, helped Yunfa: R.J., f. 10. The Kebbi Fulani were over sixty miles away from Degel.

[68] I.M., p. 69.

Degel comprised the majority of the Community, details remain only of those who stayed within the Shaikh's circle at Degel or his later camps.[69] Inevitably the complete picture is lacking.

At Degel with the Shaikh were his father, Muḥammad Fodiye, his elder brother 'Alī and his younger brother 'Abdullāh.[70] One of his sons, Muḥammad Bello, lived half a day's journey away across the valley, in a 'bushy place' at Yamulu.[71] Around the Shaikh's house at Degel also lived his close friends and the scholars and students who had settled there.[72] Of his friends, 'Umar al-Kammu was the closest. The first of the Shaikh's students and usually known as his 'friend' or 'companion' (ṣāḥib), he lived next to the Shaikh's house on the south.[73] He accompanied the Shaikh to Alkalawa on the occasion of Yunfa's attempt to murder the Shaikh.[74] He was third, after 'Abdullāh and Muḥammad Bello, in saluting the Shaikh as Amīr al-mu'minīn, while early in the jihād he was given the task of acting as treasurer of the booty on the capture of Matankari.[75] He was present during the Tsuntsua campaign, but died before the Shaikh at Birnin Fulbe near Zauma.[76] Later, his remains were brought to Sokoto by Bello

---

[69] Lists of participants in the jihād and their contemporaries are given in Gidado dan Laima, *Rauḍ al-jinān*, ff. 11–14; *Majmū' khiṣāl al-Shaikh*; *Majmū' aṣḥāb Bello*; 'Abd al-Qādir b. Gidado, *Basṭ al-fawā'id*; 'Abdullāh b. Fodiye, *Nasab*; Sa'd b. 'Abd al-Raḥman, *Tartīb al-aṣḥāb*. In this last book, ethnic origins are given for the helpers ('anṣār') of 'Abdullāh: 150 Fulani, 10 Zamfarawa, 9 Gobirawa, 6 Kebbawa, 6 Adarawa, 2 Zabermawa, 2 from Bornu, and 1 'Arab'. The Fulani included 7 from Gimbana, the place of the Arewa scholar 'Abd al-Salām, 4 western Fulani, 2 from Kano and 1 each from Adamawa, Katagum and Zaria. His (? later) students included 27 Fulani (2 from Gimbana), 3 Zamfarawa, and a Tuareg from Agades, a ba-Gobiri from Kano, and a student each from Damagaram, Kebbi and Nupe. The percentage of non-Fulani 'helpers' is 19 per cent, of non-Fulani students 23 per cent, but since the lists are not precisely dated and probably incomplete, these figures are unreliable.

[70] Gidado, *Majmū' al-khiṣāl.*

[71] K.B., p. 8.

[72] Gidado, *Majmū' al-khiṣāl.*

[73] R.J., f. 2; *Majmū' al-khiṣāl.*

[74] R.J., f. 7b; T.W., p. 55.

[75] I.M., pp. 70, 73.

[76] R.J., f. 10; K.B., p. 20; al-ḥājj Sa'īd, *Ta'rīkh Sokoto* (f. 112a); D.M., f. 32b.

and buried near the Shaikh.[77] He did not belong to any of the major groups of Fulani who later supported the Muslims but lived some fifteen miles south-east of Degel at al-Kammu. Of his children, one son, 'Uthmān 'Mudegel', married a daughter of the Shaikh, Ḥafṣa; another son, Muḥammad 'Autanjido', married another daughter of the Shaikh, Ṣafiyya, as well as one of the Shaikh's distant relatives, Ramla; a daughter, 'Ā'isha, married the Shaikh's son, Muḥammad Bello.

Scribes were important where books were rare and hand-copied; most copyists were probably scholars whose hand-writing was particularly fine. Seventeen scribes are listed in *Rauḍ al-jinān*: of these only three appear at Degel, one of whom, al-Muṣṭafā, is probably the chief scribe and husband of a sister of the Shaikh, Sauda.[78] The others listed were cos-mopolitan: two are nicknamed 'al-Maghribī' implying a North African origin, while another is called 'Malle' which suggests he came from the Niger bend or beyond.

Also at Degel were imams and muezzins. One, the Imam Muḥammad Sambo, married a distant relative of the Shaikh and died a martyr at Tsuntsua.[79] A muezzin at Degel, Aḥmad, who was martyred near Sarma early in the jihād, was 'al-Sūdānī', the usual term for a Hausa man; the other muezzins bear Fulani names.[80] One, M. Mijji, was an elderly relation of the Shaikh. Another, Muḥammad Shibi, had two sons: Muḥammad Sambo, who became one of the servants of the Shaikh, and Yero, one of Bello's servants. It is possible they came from the west and were Zoromawa, a trading caste of mixed parentage found mainly in the west.[81]

The servants of the Shaikh included his sister's son, Kau-manga, as well as the Sambo just mentioned, who looked after the Shaikh's white mare and was later given charge of

[77] K.B., p. 20.

[78] *Majmū' al-khiṣāl*. al-Muṣṭafā is a common name in the lists; thus the uncertainty. This al-Muṣṭafā is not to be confused with the al-Muṣṭafā who married a daughter of the Shaikh, Khadīja.

[79] I.M., p. 87.

[80] I.M., p. 72.

[81] al-ḥājj Sa'īd, *Ta'rīkh Sokoto* (ed. Houdas), pp. 200, 219. The text at p. 200 is corrupt. *v. supra*, p. lxxiii.

Gidan Kaya in Gwadabawa district. At Degel also was Sulaimān Wodi who was sent with a letter to the Sultan of Gobir at the start of the jihād and returned only after some difficulty. He later acted as treasurer for the Shaikh, being the first to hold the title of Ajia.[82] Another servant, Ibrāhīm, was later given the responsibility of bearing the Shaikh's flag and the post of tax-collector (Sā'ī).[83] He was put in charge of a section of the Argungu–Sokoto border; he was married, at one time, to the Shaikh's youngest daughter. The servant Dembo Hamel is less identifiable—the name is common—but he married, it seems, Ḥafṣa bint al-Shaikh who at another time was married to Mudegel.[84] The servant al-Muṣṭafā, who was also a scholar and a scribe, is probably the husband of Khadīja, the daughter of the Shaikh: their son was the well-known historian 'Abd al-Qādir b. al-Muṣṭafā.[85]

Also at Degel were a group of panegyrists, important scholars who had moved to Degel and wrote in praise of the Shaikh. One was the Shaikh Abū Bakr Sambo Laima, who was brought to Degel by his son 'Uthmān Gidado, later the Vizier to Muḥammad Bello.

Others acted as reciters of the Quran: Ismā'īl, for example, possibly the man whose house is listed as the first on the east of the Shaikh's house at Degel, or Abba Bul, the Shaikh's paternal cousin.

Many scholars and sons of scholars joined the Shaikh, some giving their daughters in marriage, as M. Ādam and M. Aḥmad to the Shaikh, or the Tuareg M. Agali to Bello.[86] Among the Shaikh's students were his own immediate family, wives and daughters included, as well as more distant relations like Maḥmūd Gurdam. But most of the students are unidentifiable, though one is specifically named as a Hausa,

[82] I.M., p. 69. His descendants are in Zaki, near Sokoto (al-haji Junaidu).

[83] Sā'ī was responsible for collecting zakāt in classical times: *v. infra.*

[84] Al-Ḥasan, the son of Dembo by Ḥafṣa, died *c.* 1853 in the campaign against Hadejia (Sa'īd, p. 212).

[85] See bibliography.

[86] Malam Ādam, whose daughter was the mother of Muḥammad Bello and Abū Bakr Atiku, had married a distant relative of the Shaikh.

another, a Fulani, is from Kano, while a third is from Konni near by. The Imams Zangi and Abū Bakr brought their wives, Imam Muḥammad Sambo 'his aunt'; three other women are listed, one of whom, Āmina bint Ade, was famed for her sufism. The wife of the Shaikh, 'Ā'isha, was similarly famous.[87] At least seven other students of the Shaikh were Sufis; one married two jinns and two humans while at Degel.[88] The most famous Sufi, Muḥammad Koiranga, regularly saw visions and acted as intermediary between the Shaikh and the saint 'Abd al-Qādir al-Jailānī.[89]

The Shaikh's Community at Degel was quite large: some sixty-two men are mentioned as his neighbours, and the list excludes many whom we know were there.[90] When the Muslims went to Alkalawa to meet Bawa, there were said to be more than a thousand scholars with the Shaikh.[91] At Tsuntsua, Bello says about 2,000 died, some 200 of whom knew the Quran by heart.[92] Degel was a focus for scholars:[93] it is doubtful that it was the permanent home for many, not least because of the problems of food supply. Degel seems to have been a cluster of houses round the Shaikh's compound. The meeting-place of the council was at the entrance to his compound:[94] the open space that it implies probably explains the larger number of houses on the western side since it is likely that the house faced west following Fulani practice.[95] On that side was the house of his elder brother 'Alī,

---

[87] 'Abd al-Qādir b. al-Muṣṭafā, *Salwat al-aḥzān*. The author is 'Ā'isha's grandson; her son, Muḥammad Sambo, also a noted Sufi, is one of the subjects of the book.

[88] Cf. Muḥammad Bello, *Ishāra wa-i'lām*, where the genealogy of some jinns is given in jinn language.

[89] R.J., f. 3.

[90] A torn text makes the figure approximate.

[91] R.J., f. 5b.

[92] I.M., pp. 87, 88.

[93] I.M., p. 65.

[94] K.B., p. 7.

[95] The map in Gidado, *Majmū' khiṣāl al-Shaikh*, shows the house facing east. But Sokoto practice almost always faces the house to the west; this is the practice also of the cattle Fulani, who, according to M. Dupire (*op. cit.*, p. 157), ascribed it to the advice given them by the Shaikh. Cf. D. J. Stenning, *op. cit.*, p. 39. The west, however, is the one quarter almost always sheltered from the rain. The place at Degel now shown as the Shaikh's house faces south-east.

on the north his junior brother 'Abdullāh, and to the south his close friend 'Umar al-Kammu. There is no pattern discernible in the arrangement of the houses, except that the western quarter has a large number of scribes, muezzins and imams, while the south has three of the servants. The siting of 'Abdullāh's house in the north, and, less probably, of 'Alī's house in the west, may reflect the traditional Fulani camp pattern in which seniority by age and by genealogy is recognised—the south reflecting age, the west genealogy.[96]

Outside Degel, the Shaikh had the wider circle of his relatives. Both the Shaikh and 'Abdullāh wrote to them; and after the Shaikh visited some at Maratta, they were convinced of his ability and supported him.[97] Though 'Abdullāh had been taught by many of them, and though they supported the Shaikh, they seem to have kept somewhat aloof: few appear in the Sokoto lists. The genealogy of the Shaikh's family shows his relationship with his teachers, Muḥammad Sambo, 'Uthmān Binduri, Jibrīl, and al-ḥājj Muḥammad; with the teachers of 'Abdullāh, Muḥammad Firabri, Muḥammad Sambo, 'Abdullāh, Aḥmad b. Muḥammad, al-Muṣṭafā b. 'Uthmān and Muḥammad Batogo; with four scholars not mentioned at Degel and two other returned pilgrims who are otherwise unknown.[98] In all, over thirty scholars are shown as contemporaries and relatives of the Shaikh. But not all the scholars related to the Shaikh are shown: five others are listed in *Rauḍ al-jinān*, and one in *'Īdā' al-nusūkh*. Nor are all those that helped him: a further five are in *Rauḍ al-jinān*, and I have not included women whose identification and place in the genealogy are doubtful. By its incompleteness, therefore, the genealogy can only suggest the cohesion and resources available to the Shaikh from his own clan before the jihād.

Outside the circle of the Shaikh but contemporary with him were the scholars who were neither relatives nor residents at Degel. The names of sixty-nine such are given in *Rauḍ al-jinān*, many of them having connections with the Shaikh or

[96] D. J. Stenning, *op. cit.*, pp. 39 ff.

[97] R.J., f. 6; cf. T.W., pp. 41, 45.

[98] The genealogy is compiled mainly out of lists given in Muḥammad Bello: *Ishāra wa-i'lām fī ba'ḍ umūr ṣilat al-arḥām*.

with the jihād in other parts of the caliphate.[99] Roughly a third are known to be Fulani or have names which suggest a Fulani origin. But the rationale of the list is not evident: most of the first thirty-four are identifiably connected with the Sokoto area, while fifteen of the rest are identifiably unconnected. Though the Shaikh attracted students away from their local teachers, it is clear from this that a large number of scholars, at least before the jihād, remained outside the Shaikh's Community, though having ties to the Muslim Community in general. These ties became manifest in the jihād.

[99] R.J., ff. 13, 14.

2

The Jihād

(i) *The Hijra*

With the threat of attack from Gobir, the Muslims had to move out of reach of Yunfa's army.[1] Degel, situated on the main valley south-west of the capital of Gobir, was exposed, despite the number of relatives and friends in the vicinity. They had to leave the valley, making for the western limits of Gobir. There had been a choice of two places: Iname, where 'Alī Jedo was based beside a lake, and the area of Gurdam, where a relation and student of the Shaikh, Maḥmūd, lived.[2] They chose Gudu, a place beside a pool and dominated by steep ridges, with a village near more water some two miles off. To reach Gudu, thirty miles from Degel direct, the Muslims went up the path to Konni by easy and well-watered stages as far as the pool at Kalmalo. There they turned west before cutting south to Gudu: a journey of four or five days, and a distance of about sixty miles.[3]

[1] In the following account of the jihād, 'Muslims' is used as synonymous with the Shaikh's followers: this is their term for themselves. For some of the problems of defining Muslims, see 'Attempts at defining a Muslim in nineteenth-century Hausaland and Bornu' (M.A. al-Hajj, D. M. Last, *J.H.S.N.*, III, 2, 1965, pp. 231 ff.).

[2] 'Abd al-Qādir b. al-Muṣṭafā, *Mauṣūfat al-sūdān*, f. 2b.

[3] 'Abd al-Qādir b. al-Muṣṭafā, *ibid.*; (Anon), *Tabṣirat al-nuẓẓār*. The date of the hijra as given by Bello (I.M., p. 68) and 'Abdullāh (I.M., p. 169; *Tanbīh al-ikhwān*) is 10 Dhū'l-qa'da 1218 (Tuesday 21 February 1804); but the date given by 'Abd al-Qādir b. al-Muṣṭafā (*op. cit.*) is Thursday 12 Dhū'l-qa'da, and he is followed by al-haji Junaidu (D.M., f. 18b). As the emigration did not take place on a single day, it is likely

Not all the Muslims could make the emigration then. The Tuareg scholar Agali, who is said to have carried the Shaikh's books on his camel, went back with camels and donkeys to help in the evacuation.[4] He had, meanwhile, written to the Tuareg chiefs asking for their support, while Bello was in Kebbi distributing letters.[5]

The Sultan of Gobir, alarmed at the numbers joining the Shaikh, forbade further emigration and started harassing the refugees and confiscating their goods.[6] With negotiations between Gobir and the Muslims broken down and an attack therefore imminent, the Muslims prepared defences and elected a leader.[7] The Shaikh was formally chosen as the Imam of the Community and given the salute of homage, first by 'Abdullāh, and then by Muḥammad Bello.[8] There is a tradition that the Shaikh at first had been reluctant; he did not feel strong enough to bear the burden of jihād.[9] 'Abdullāh's name was put forward, but it was objected that he favoured some over others; alternative candidates were 'Umar al-Kammu and the Imam Muḥammad Sambo, the latter being Bello's choice. But as no one else was acceptable, the Shaikh was forced to accept the leadership. The story may be apocryphal, designed to show the Shaikh's lack of political ambition, which is not, in itself, so implausible: the Shaikh was old—50—and was to take no part in the fighting. But it is hard to see how any of the other candidates could have led the jihād.

The first skirmish occurred when a small punitive expedition from Gobir was beaten back. The Muslims went to capture Matankari and Konni, both important towns on their

---

that Asmā' bint al-Shaikh (on whose poem 'Abd al-Qādir bases his account) left after the Shaikh; alternatively an advance party was sent off two days before the Shaikh left.

[4] 'Abd al-Qādir b. al-Muṣṭafā, *ibid.*; I.M., p. 68; D.M., f. 18b.

[5] I.M., pp. 68, 69.

[6] I.M., p. 69.

[7] I.M., pp. 69, 70–1; I.M., p. 169 ('Abdullāh's account); T.W., p. 55.

[8] I.M., pp. 70, 71; T.W., p. 55. Neither of these eyewitness accounts mentions the precise titles by which the Shaikh was saluted as leader. Al-ḥājj Sa'īd implies the title was only Imam.

[9] Al-ḥājj Sa'īd, *Ta'rīkh Sokoto* (110b).

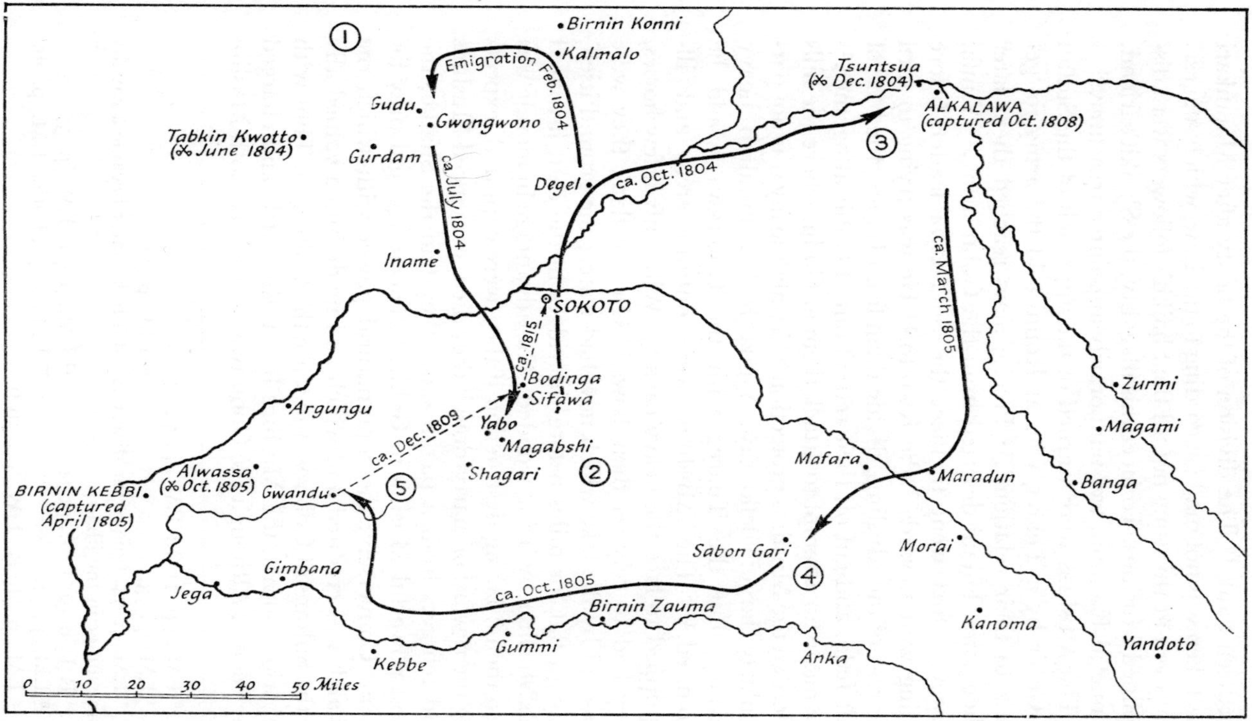

3. Movements of the Shaikh 1804–1817

northern flank.[10] The division of the booty after Matankari was taken was not made according to the Law, which suggests that even at this time not all the Shaikh's followers were disciplined Muslims. To meet this illegality, the Shaikh's friend, 'Umar al-Kammu, was temporarily appointed treasurer.[11]

The Muslims were warned of the approach of the Sultan of Gobir by a Tuareg who at Konni told the army to 'get back to their relations'.[12] Precise news reached them later when some Fulani deserted from the Gobir army.[13] Yunfa, however, first went to meet the Sullebawa leaders before riding west towards Lake Kwotto.[14] He was trying to turn the rear of the Muslims, divide them from Iname, the base of 'Alī Jedo, and cut off their retreat out of Gobir altogether.[15] He made no attempt to attack them at Gudu, where the hills afforded the Muslims protection.[16] Yunfa's army was not particularly large: Bello says Yunfa had a hundred heavy cavalry, but the Tuareg with the Gobirawa would be mounted.[17] The Muslims were outnumbered and ill-equipped to face the heavy cavalry. With only a few horses, they had to rely on their bows.[18] On one flank they were covered by the lake which now had water; the ground itself, though flat for miles before the ridges in the east, favoured the Muslims by being wooded. The advantage in morale was also theirs: facing destruction if they were captured, expecting the reward of martyrdom if they died, convinced Muslims and refugees from a pagan state, they had the Shaikh, the most powerful Muslim in Gobir, to encourage and pray for them. Conversely, the supernatural power with which the Shaikh was credited and which had made him a valued ally of the Sultans of Gobir would scare the Gobirawa. Thus with superior morale, the Muslims began the battle and charged the enemy. Although the Gobirawa overlapped both Muslim

---

[10] I.M., pp. 71 ff.; T.W., p. 55.

[11] I.M., p. 73.

[12] I.M., p. 73.

[13] I.M., p. 74. One of the deserters, Abū Bakr, later became a cavalry commander in the jihād.

[14] R.J., f. 10; I.M., p. 74.

[15] I.M., p. 76; T.W., p. 57.

[16] I.M., p. 74.

[17] I.M., p. 75; but cf. I.M., p. 76.

[18] I.M., p. 76; cf. T.W., pp. 56 ff.

wings and drove them into the centre, the centre held: being bunched together was little hindrance, since each man with his bow could be effective.[19] The Gobirawa were eventually turned back in a rout.[20]

Both armies were mixed racially; the Gobirawa certainly had some Tuareg and Sullebawa, and probably other Fulani than those who had deserted.[21] The Muslims also consisted of Hausa and Fulani:[22] the Konni Fulani rallied by 'Alī Jedo provided local support for the Shaikh.[23] The Tuareg element consisted of Agali and the Adar Muslims, including possibly the sons of the Emir of Adar who had been at Degel with the Shaikh: but no one else of note is mentioned as coming with Agali apart from M. Jibrīl's son, Muḥammadān, and Joda b. Muḥammad.[24] Help had already been received from friendly Tuareg, some of whom may have joined the Muslims but are not mentioned.[25]

The rains of 1804 had already started, but food supplies—before the new harvest—were still low. The local villagers were hostile and unwilling to sell corn;[26] the Muslims' cattle were inadequate to provide enough milk and would not usually be slaughtered. With booty the only source of food, inevitably it was the peasant who suffered. When that source of food was finished, there was no alternative but to move to a new area. The campaigns of the jihād are explicable in these terms: the search for food and, in addition, for pasture and water for the cattle.[27]

---

[19] I.M., p. 76.

[20] 10 Rabī' I, 1219 (19 June 1804) is a Tuesday, but the battle was on a Thursday: therefore 21 June 1804 (T.W., p. 57; I.M., pp. 73, 75).

[21] T.W., p. 55; I.M., p. 74; R.J., f. 10; I.M., p. 78. The Galadima in Gobir, a Fulani, Doshero, had not yet joined the Muslims, though he was known to favour the Shaikh (I.M., p. 84).

[22] I.M., p. 77 (line 17); T.W., p. 58 (line 8).

[23] 'Abd al-Qādir b. al-Muṣṭafā, *Mauṣūfat al-sūdān*, f. 2b.

[24] I.M., p. 74; R.J., f. 9. [25] e.g. I.M., pp. 73, 69. [26] I.M., p. 80.

[27] Food became so scarce during the jihād that Bello speaks of men so weak from hunger and sickness that they were 'shaking violently'; he says it was through death from these causes that the Community lost its best people (*al-Dhikrā; Nuṣḥ kāfi*: the same passage is found in both books).

Support, however, after the success at Tabkin Kwotto, was increasing. Manori, the leader of the Sullebawa Fulani who grazed the area south-east of the junction of the rivers Rima and Sokoto, came to the Shaikh.[28] His brother, according to tradition, had already been to the Shaikh at Degel, and other Sullebawa were known to favour the Muslims before the battle at Kwotto.[29] Identifying now the Sullebawa with the Muslims, the Gobirawa started attacking their villages near Rikina.[30] But though with the aid, or at least the friendship, of the Sullebawa assured the Muslims were much stronger, they were scarcely better off for food. The Emirs of Mafara, Burmi and Donko, however, had also allied themselves to the Shaikh after Kwotto, leaving only the Emir of Gummi in south-western Zamfara to support Gobir.[31] The basis of the friendship with these states began some twenty years previously, when the Shaikh was living and teaching in the area of Mafara and Burmi. As they sent traders with food to the Muslims, their friendship was very useful; but, as Bello says, their friendship was due more to their hostility to Gobir than to their adherence to Islam.[32]

Yet the shortage of food was still not solved. The Shaikh, therefore, sent by Muḥammad Bello a request for hospitality to another leader, Moijo, who with his base at Yabo was responsible for the Kebbi Fulani.[33] In July or August, the Shaikh moved south, through Iname—the Konni Fulani base of 'Alī Jedo—and Kaworuga and Dingyadi—Sullebawa Fulani country, where he is traditionally said to have met other leading Sullebawa—finally reaching Magabshi in the lee of Yabo in Kebbi.[34] While the role of the Sullebawa is

---

[28] R.J., f. 10b. [29] R.J., f. 10. [30] I.M., p. 82.

[31] I.M., pp. 82, 80. The normal Hausa title used by these Hausa rulers is Sarki, not Amīr.

[32] I.M., p. 82.

[33] I.M., p. 82. Moijo is said to have gone to Gudu and saluted the Shaikh (*Mauṣūfat al-sūdān*, f. 3), but no mention of this is made in I.M. or R.J. Moijo had captured the towns neighbouring Yabo before the Shaikh came—Bello implies in preparation for the Shaikh (I.M., p. 82).

[34] July–August 1804: *c.* Rabī' II, 1219. 'Faṣl al-rabī'' (I.M., p. 83) normally extends from 21 March to 21 June, but here it loosely includes the rainy season as well. Muḥammad Bello in I.M. uses only rabī',

somewhat obscure, since few names are mentioned and tradition makes a group of them go towards the Niger for several years, Moijo and the Kebbi Fulani proved active allies.[35]

The Shaikh's identification with the Fulani, necessary now if the Muslims were to survive, probably alienated the non-Fulani in his following. The goodwill of the peasantry seems to have been lost due to the need for food:[36] the piety of the pastoral Fulani had been open to question and the motives of the majority who went on the expeditions were probably more mercenary than Muslim.[37] The division between the Muslim reformers and the Hausa establishment moved on to a wider plane when the Shaikh, while at Magabshi, wrote to the Sultans of the neighbouring states and called them to join in the reform. Although the Sultan of Kano is said to have wavered at first, only the Sulṭan of Zaria replied favourably: his people, however, rebelled after his death two years later.[38] Although the call for jihād was extended to the other Hausa states, communications between the Shaikh and the Muslims in the east were difficult to maintain, and the various communities remained isolated.[39]

(ii) *The Long Campaign*

With the harvest in (October 1804), the first of the aggressive campaigns began. Working on interior lines, with the

---

'spring', and kharīf, 'autumn', for the seasons: the division would fall just before the harvest. Cf. I.M., p. 118, where the Niger is forded in rabī': i.e. April–May (Nedeco, *River Studies*, pp. 26, 27); and I.M., pp. 115–16, where the fall of Alkalawa (3 October 1808) is in kharīf. For the route of the Shaikh, see (Anon), *Tabṣirat al-nuẓẓār*. He had left Gudu for Gwongwono, some two miles south-east, soon after Tabkin Kwotto, and had had his house there till he moved to Magabshi. His route from Dingyadi to Magabshi was through Sifawa, Jaredi and Yabo.

[35] e.g. I.M., pp. 106, 99 (where the name is misspelt).

[36] I.M., p. 80; cf. I.M., p. 90.

[37] Cf. I.M., p. 30; pp. 73, 100.

[38] I.M., p. 83. Cf. D. M. Last, 'A solution to the problems of dynastic chronology in nineteenth-century Zaria and Kano' (*J.H.S.N.*, III, 3, 1966, p. 463).

[39] Muḥammad Bello, *al-Dhikrā*. The copy used derived from the library of the Sultan of Sokoto.

interior being both known and largely friendly, the Muslims had a choice of movement and attack; they were also less hampered by baggage, while their cattle could move with them. Able to retreat out of the valleys into the scrubland, they were safe against cavalry attack. At the same time, their cattle required the dry-season pasture of the wide valleys. They therefore moved to the hinterland of the Gobir capital, Alkalawa.

The Muslims were still undefeated, having followed up the victory at Kwotto by capturing several villages in south and west Gobir.[40] An attempt at mediation by the Sarkin Gummi had broken down: the Muslims were strong enough to dictate terms and to refuse prevarication when the Sultan of Gobir would not come in person to the Shaikh.[41] They were confident, then, in attacking the enemy capital.

Already a group of Muslims under the Tuareg Agali, Muḥammadān b. Jibrīl b. 'Umar from Adar, Joda b. Muḥammad and Muḥammad Tukur had been fighting on the borders of Adar and Gobir.[42] In south-eastern Gobir, in the old Zamfara, the Muslims had further allies: the Alibawa Fulani, grazing in the upper Rima valleys, had suffered at the hands of Gobir.[43] Based at Zurmi, midway between Zamfara and Katsina, they gave great help not only to the Shaikh but also to the Community in Katsina.[44] From Gobir itself, the Galadima in Alkalawa, a Katsina Fulani, deserted to the Shaikh, as did the Sharīf Baba, whom Yunfa, perhaps on account of his descent from the Prophet, was anxious to keep in Alkalawa.[45]

Though the Sultan of Gobir had written to his fellow Sultans warning them against the Muslims, the main allies

---

[40] For example on the campaigns against Mane (I.M., pp. 80, 81) and Dangeda (I.M., pp. 84, 85).

[41] I.M., pp. 84, 85.

[42] I.M., p. 83.

[43] R.A., f. 8b. 'Alī al-Fāris, identified as the Alibawa leader in Zurmi, had been killed by the Gobirawa.

[44] I.M., pp. 86, 94, 96. At I.M., p. 94, the published text reads Zūma for Zurmi; on p. 86, Namōka should be Namoda.

[45] I.M., pp. 84, 85.

of Gobir were the Tuareg: the other Sultans were too preoccupied with local opposition to be able to combine against the Shaikh.[46] The Tuareg nearest Gobir, the Kel Geres, Itesen, Kel Tegama, like the Fulani, were accustomed to come to the valleys for winter grazing: given the choice between the Sultan of Gobir, in whose lands they had long grazed, and the Muslims who both as strict Muslims and as Fulani pastoralists or Hausa peasants had different interests and whose chances of taking the walled town of Alkalawa were small (it was to fall only on the fourth attempt), these Tuareg joined the Gobirawa.[47] The Tuareg were useful in the campaigns. The Gobirawa seldom fought without some Tuareg present: the Tuareg complemented the Gobirawa, being usually mounted and fast, armed with a large shield, a javelin and sword. They were present in force at the two major Muslim reverses, Tsuntsua and Alwassa; while not invincible—they had been present at the defeat of Kwotto, and were badly beaten later at Zurmi—they caused great fear, raiding as much for pleasure as for profit.[48]

With the Muslims camped less than a day's journey away from Alkalawa and probably dispersed in search of food, the Gobirawa were in a good position to counter-attack.[49] With the help of the Tuareg they did so, at Tsuntsua two miles from the capital.[50] The Muslims in the ensuing battle lost, according to Bello, about two thousand.[51] It is possible that since it was the month of Ramaḍān the fast was being kept.[52]

---

[46] I.M., p. 73. The Sultans of Katsina and Daura, however, went to aid Kano (I.M., p. 95), and there is said to have been a Bornu contingent in Alkalawa in 1808 (F. Edgar, notebook: *Labarin mafitar Bawa*, p. 8).

[47] I.M., p. 87.

[48] As often in conflicts between camel- and horse-borne armies, the fear horses have of camels can prove decisive in battle. In Sokoto later they always tried to accustom their horses to camels, but in the confused early days of the jihād this was probably impossible, and the little cavalry the Muslims had may have thus been rendered useless against camel-mounted Tuareg.

[49] The camp was at Bore, half a day away from Alkalawa. I.M., pp. 86, 87.

[50] I.M., p. 88. For other details, cf. T.W., p. 61; R.J., f. 10.

[51] I.M., p. 87.

[52] I.M., p. 88.

Bello, at least, was sick, while 'Abdullāh had a wounded leg;[53] 'Ali Jedo, the Commander of the Army, is not mentioned. The Muslim leader was a cousin of Bello, Muḥammad Sa'd b. al-Ḥasan; among the dead were other relations of his, the Imam Muḥammad Sambo, Zaid b. Muḥammad Sa'd and Maḥmūd Gurdam.[54] Out of the two thousand killed, two hundred knew the Quran by heart. In a community where books were scarce, most serious scholars would have known the Quran by heart: the number illustrates the size of the scholastic movement, since few of the scholars listed elsewhere are mentioned as martyrs at Tsuntsua. It is also interesting that 1,800, or 90 per cent, were not scholars. Thus though the number of scholars is high, the Community depended on the less educated Muslims for military support. The composition of this 90 per cent is not precisely known.

Whatever their accuracy, these figures show that the total number of Muslims on this Gobir campaign was very large: food and pasture would soon run short. After the defeat at Tsuntsua in December, the Muslims stayed the rest of Ramaḍān in the valley, still west of Alkalawa, before starting upriver towards Zamfara in January and February in search of food.[55] By March, they had foregathered at Sabon Gari and made a camp there.[56]

Here again, in south-western Zamfara, the Muslims had established friends. The Emirs of Mafara, Burmi and Donko were to the north and south of Sabon Gari, and though the Zamfarawa were largely pagan, they were more hostile to the Gobirawa than to the Muslims.[57] The Gobirawa some fifty years before had sacked the capital of Zamfara and had been overrunning the country since, driving out the Zamfarawa refugees.[58] The Shaikh was both welcome and well known, after his five years of teaching and preaching some thirty-five miles north-east of Sabon Gari, and was therefore called upon by the Zamfarawa to settle a dispute over the election of a

---

[53] Bello sick, I.M., p. 87; 'Abdullāh's wound, I.M., p. 86.

[54] I.M., p. 87; T.W., p. 61.

[55] I.M., pp. 88, 90. Cf. T.W., p. 62.

[56] I.M., p. 91; T.W., p. 62.

[57] I.M., pp. 82, 90.

[58] R.A., ff. 7–8.

new Sarkin Zamfara.[59] The Shaikh, it seems, installed Abarshi whom the Sultan of Gobir Bawa had released from prison at the Shaikh's request some seventeen years before.[60] A further connection with the area was that the famous Fulani scholar Muḥammad Tukur, who had been fighting in Gobir with Agali, had lived at Matuzzigi, near Mafara, and had Muslim followers there. Finally there were groups of Fulani who supported the Shaikh, like the Kasarawa, grazing both sides of the upper Sokoto river.[61] Their support was important, since the Muslims, very short of food now at the end of the dry season, soon exhausted their welcome among the Zamfarawa; and those who previously were isolated in their hostility to the Muslims, like Banaga in the east, or the Sarkin Gummi in the south, now became more formidable.[62]

At first, the expeditions out of Sabon Gari were against Kebbi and Gobir, then later against local towns in Zamfara. The Kebbi expedition was under the charge of the Vizier 'Abdullāh and 'Alī Jedo, the Commander of the Army;[63] Bello, after staying behind a while, led the expedition against Gobir.[64] The Muslims were evidently still numerous enough to mount two armies simultaneously, as well as leaving a force to guard the camp, where the Shaikh remained.[65]

The Kebbi expedition was crucial: the Kebbi capital was taken and the Kebbawa fled north upriver.[66] The campaign

---

[59] I.M., p. 90.

[60] R.J., f. 7; cf. Krieger, *Geschichte von Zamfara* (Berlin, 1959), pp. 80 ff.

[61] The area of modern Bungudu district. The name, Kasarawa, is presumably taken from the river Kasara, which flows past Gora and joins the Sokoto river.

[62] I.M., pp. 91, 95. Gummi was attacked by the expedition en route for Birnin Kebbi; its Emir made peace with the Muslims, and later received the title of Amīr Mafara (I.M., p. 91; T.W., pp. 62 ff.). Banaga: cf. Bello's poem: I.M., pp. 98, 95; Krieger, *op. cit.*, pp. 82 ff.

[63] I.M., p. 91; T.W., p. 62. [64] I.M., p. 93.

[65] But cf. I.M., p. 91, where neither 'Alī Jedo nor Muḥammad Bello could raise a force for a raid a few weeks before these campaigns.

[66] I.M., p. 91; T.W., pp. 62 ff. The expedition was accompanied by 'Uthmān Massa, a son of the previous Sultan of Kebbi Sulaimān. 'Uthmān had acknowledged the leadership of the Shaikh and was to be installed as Emir of Kebbi in place of the newly-appointed Sultan, his

made the next move, to Gwandu, possible, and allowed a permanent settlement to be founded there, thus ending the Muslims' trek.

Meanwhile during the wet season in Sabon Gari expeditions were sent out, partly to collect food, partly to make the country safe for the Muslims.[67] For example, the pagans were forced out of Kanoma, a stronghold almost impregnable in its cluster of hills and dominating the surrounding country.[68] Following the capture of Kanoma, Bello says that some of the Zamfara towns broke up;[69] shortly after, the oppression admitted by Bello proved too great and the Zamfarawa rebelled.[70] Still short of food and subject now to raids from Zamfara, the Muslims were forced to move out of Sabon Gari to Gwandu after the harvest.[71] The land at Gwandu was fertile, yet out of the main river valley where the refugee Kebbawa still lived. Neighbouring on the north, but not impinging, was the country of Moijo at Yabo; to the west was the old capital of Kebbi, now in Muslim hands. With their base secure, the Muslims could continue the main campaign against Gobir with less risk of repeating the disaster at Tsuntsua.

(iii) *A Permanent Base: Gwandu*

Soon after their arrival in Gwandu, with the harvest largely in and the 'cure salée' of the Tuareg over, the Muslims were faced by a combined attack of Gobirawa, Tuareg and Kebbawa pagans.[72] For several days the fighting continued on the more open ground of the plateau above the Kebbi valley at

---

nephew Hodi. 'Uthmān later rebelled and was killed (I.M., p. 104; Sölken (1959), pp. 150–4). The date of the capture of Birnin Kebbi is Saturday 12 Muḥarram 1220 (13 April 1805): I.M., p. 93.

[67] I.M., p. 91. Although the Zamfarawa were friendly, the local people near Sabon Gari, Bello found, were hostile.

[68] I.M., p. 94.

[69] I.M., p. 95.

[70] I.M., p. 95.

[71] I.M., pp. 97–8; T.W., p. 66.

[72] I.M., pp. 99–100; T.W., pp. 66 ff. Alkalin Gwandu Aḥmad *History of Gwandu* (trans. McAllister, 1909), para. 24, says 'Uthmān Massa, the Emir of Kebbi, called in the Tuareg.

Alwassa: Gwandu itself, protected by a ridge, was some twenty miles to the east. At first leaving the safety of a hill, the Muslims were badly beaten on the flat ground and lost according to Bello about a thousand men; but once the attack was pressed towards Gwandu, the rougher terrain favoured the Muslim bowmen and hindered the camels of the Tuareg.[73] Thereupon the Muslims drove the invaders off in a rout. Nonetheless the country had been despoiled and food again became a problem: the fertile Kebbi valley remained a battle-ground.[74]

Shortly after, a large force of Tuareg, mainly Kel Geres under Agunbulu and Zodi Tambarin Kel Geres, joined up with the Burmawa, the Zamfarawa under their Sarki Abarshi from Kiawa, and the Adarawa of the Emir of Adar Ḥāmid: together they attacked Zurmi, but were heavily defeated by Namoda, the leader of the Alibawa Fulani whose base Zurmi was.[75] Being late in the dry season, food was scarce and the Tuareg were hard pressed: when they came to buy, they were plundered.[76] These two battles effectively stopped Tuareg campaigns against Sokoto for a period; the following year the Tuareg sought peace.[77]

Tuareg policy was unpredictable. At Tsuntsua the Muslims had been deceived in believing the Tuareg favoured them: they were forewarned, however, by another Tuareg, Aḥmad b. Ḥaidara, who later with his followers joined the Shaikh.[78] Before Alwassa peace seems to have been made, but Tuaregs played a part in that battle.[79] At the battle of Zurmi, at Fafara, the leaders were talking of peace while their men made war.[80] The fragmented authority among the Tuaregs

---

[73] I.M., p. 100. Cf. I.M., pp. 102–3. Cf. T.W., pp. 68, 69.

[74] I.M., p. 103.

[75] I.M., pp. 106–11; T.W., p. 74. Namoda had already turned back a Tuareg expedition in search of food (I.M., p. 106).

[76] I.M., pp. 110, 111.

[77] I.M., p. 112.

[78] I.M., pp. 87, 90.

[79] I.M., p. 99. The peace was presumably broken by 'Alī Jedo mistakenly attacking the Tuareg while the Shaikh's messenger was still with them.

[80] I.M., p. 110.

made this inevitable. Policy within Tuareg groups changed: for example, the Itesen, who are praised for their loyalty, deposed the anti-Muslim Ḥāmid as Emir of Adar after Fafara and appointed the pro-Muslim Muḥammad b. al-Muṣṭafā. A little later, they reappointed Ḥāmid, and on his death gave the title to the strongly anti-Muslim Ibrāhīm.[81]

Meanwhile, the Shaikh had sent a scholar from south Katsina, 'Umar Dallaji, to make contact with the Muslim leaders in Katsina, Kano, Daura and Zamfara.[82] Each Community had been isolated, and it was difficult to obtain news and co-operation. A meeting-place, Magami, was chosen, perhaps consciously recalling the meeting of the scholars there under the Sultan of Gobir Bawa.[83] As it happened, Bello met the eastern leaders at Birnin Gada before his Yandoto campaign and read the Shaikh's letter to them; the Shaikh had felt unable to make the journey from Gwandu himself.[84] In the letter he greeted the leaders and asked them to make the bay'a as the Quran and sunna demanded. He told them that Allah had granted the conquest of the land, but that he was afraid to pray for them in case they should be corrupted by the world and become like the Hausa rulers; they should therefore take an oath that they would not be corrupted or changed by power, as were the Israelites in the desert, but they would avoid worldly aspirations, envy, mercilessness, feuds, the pursuit of wealth; that they would avoid falling into the strife that 'makes a man a Muslim in the morning and a pagan by evening'. Bello in the *Infāq al-maisūr* adds that he told them of the Mahdi's coming and that the Shaikh's rule would continue till he came.[85] They took the oaths and dispersed. From this time, then (dry season 1805–1806), the hegemony of Sokoto begins: no longer is the cali-

---

[81] I.M., pp. 117–18; cf. I.M., p. 111.

[82] I.M., p. 95.

[83] I.M., p. 104; T.W., p. 30; R.J., ff. 6b, 7. *v. infra.*

[84] I.M., p. 104. Muḥammad Bello, *al-Dhikrā* (ff. 47, 48), where the oaths are described. In I.M., only the people from Kano are specifically mentioned, but in *al-Dhikrā,* while no one Community is named, it is implied that many groups came. That the Katsinawa came is implied by I.M., p. 96. The Hausa Emir of Zaria was turbannned separately (D.M. Last, *op. cit., J.H.S.N.*, 1966).

[85] I.M., p. 105.

phate recognized only by the Emigrants and those fighting in the Sokoto jihād, but the Muslims in Zamfara, Katsina, Daura and Kano now are formally included in the wider Community. The dry season two years later (1807–8), the Kano Community welcomed 'Abdullāh and were anxious to have his guidance in setting up the proper pattern of government; with his help, they started a mosque and a school 'comparable to al-Azhar'.[86]

Still the expeditions had to continue in all directions. Following the meeting at Birnin Gada Bello led a combined army to Yandoto in an attempt to win over the scholars there.[87] A town on the southern borders of Katsina and Zamfara and famous for its learning, it had been the home of the Shaikh's ancestor, Muḥammad Sa'd, who had married there before returning to Konni.[88] During the jihād some scholars had been forced to leave Yandoto since they favoured the Shaikh: when the other scholars, therefore, refused to come to terms, the town was destroyed.[89]

At the same time, since peace had been established in Kebbi following the battle of Alwassa, expeditions could be sent farther south, to Yauri, the Bauchi and Borgu (mid and late dry season, 1806).[90] The following dry season the Shaikh fell ill in Gwandu.[91] Bello, to give the Shaikh protection while the campaigns were on, built the walls for Gwandu. It is significant that there had been no need for walls till this time: the previous camps had been temporary, protected by ditches or thorns.[92] The building of the Gwandu walls was recognition of Gwandu as a permanent base.

---

[86] T.W., p. 70; 'Abdullāh b. Fodiye, *Ḍiyā' al-ḥukkām* (p. 3); Muḥammad b. Ṣāliḥ, *Taqyīd al-akhbār* (1284/1868).

[87] I.M., pp. 105, 96.

[88] Muḥammad Bello, *Ishāra wa-i'lām*.

[89] I.M., p. 105. The refugee scholars included Muḥammad b. Ashafa (who later fought in Zaria and Sokoto before returning to Wonaka and Gusau), and 'Umar Dallaji, who later became the Emir of Katsina.

[90] I.M., pp. 105, 106, 111. The 'Bauchi' is the area of non-Muslims south of Sokoto, and not the Bauchi of Ya'qūb, the modern Bauchi. A senior title in Kontagora, the area of this Bauchi, is 'Sarkin Bauchi'.

[91] I.M., p. 112.

[92] Before the walls were built, there must have been some defences;

With the walls built, Bello was free to lead an expedition as far west as Dendi; on his return he went out to Zamfara, settling a dispute between the local inhabitants of Zurmi and the members of the Community there.[93] After the campaign in Zamfara he left the Alibawa Fulani under Wauni to take an expedition against Alkalawa; this was followed by similar campaigns under Namoda and 'Umar Dallaji, to 'soften up' the Gobirawa before Bello's major expedition planned for the autumn.

Fighting, however, broke out in Kebbi after a year and a half of peace, and a combined force under 'Abdullāh, 'Alī Jedo and 'Abd al-Salām had to be sent against the Kebbawa towns. But with the situation restored, the planned autumn attack on Alkalawa took place (1807).[94] On the way 'Abdullāh left the army and slipped away with five companions to Kano. There he was detained (he had intended to go to Mecca), and he was persuaded to teach. He delivered the Quranic exegesis during Ramaḍān, led the prayers for the eclipse at the end of the month, and before returning to Gwandu wrote for the Kano Community the standard text-book on government, *Ḍiyā' al-ḥukkām*.[95]

Though the campaign in Gobir had been successful, the Muslims failed to capture Alkalawa. At the beginning of the

---

the town is called ḥiṣn, which means usually a 'birni' or walled town (e.g. twice in I.M., p. 100). Gudu had been protected by a ditch (al-khandaq) while the usual protection for cattle camps was thorn branches (I.M., p. 71; cf. T.W., pp. 56, 108 n.).

[93] I.M., p. 113. The term 'Sūdānī' is used here for the local people, as opposed to the Shaikh's followers, the jamā'a.

[94] The text of I.M. here is out of chronological sequence: the account of the second Alkalawa campaign (p. 112) seems to have been transposed from p. 114 (the date of the campaign is fixed by the Kano eclipse). Wauni's campaign is recounted twice (cf. the repetition of the Yandoto incident, pp. 96, 105), though it is possible that he made two similar expeditions. 'Abdullāh's Argungu campaign is probably before the second Alkalawa expedition, though the time of his return from Kano is not known. His experiences on that campaign may have prompted him to leave the Community: he left, he said, because the attitude of the Muslims was becoming worldly.

[95] Muḥammad b. Ṣāliḥ, *Taqyīd al-akhbār*.

next rains (1808), therefore, the call went out to prepare for another expedition in the autumn.[96] After the first harvest, the Gwandu and local contingents assembled under Bello and the Commander 'Alī Jedo to meet the Zamfara contingent under Namoda and the Katsina contingent under its Emir (presumably 'Umar Dallaji).[97] Surrounded on all sides, Alkalawa fell on 3 October 1808;[98] the Sultan was killed and at least one of his wives captured.[99] The town, however, was not wholly destroyed: the following year, an administrator was appointed; many became Muslims, while the refugees moved off to the north and west to other Gobir towns, like Kadaye.[100] With the fall of Alkalawa, Bello says, resistance to the Muslims was broken everywhere, as the news was spread by travellers.[101]

One of the immediate results was the arrival of the Sultan of Ahir, Muḥammad al-Bāqirī, from Agades.[102] He had already been helping 'Umar Dallaji in Katsina, and backing the pro-Muslim Muḥammad b. al-Muṣṭafā for the emirate

---

[96] I.M., p. 115.

[97] I.M., p. 115. Although Bello was on the expedition, he says 'Alī Jedo was in command of the western, and Namoda of the eastern armies. It is not stated if 'Abdullāh was present, though he had returned from Kano (T.W., p. 75; I.M., p. 115; cf. K.B., pp. 11, 12).

[98] Or 26 September. The day of the capture of Alkalawa was Monday (I.M., p. 115; K.B., p. 12), and the news of its capture reached the Shaikh at Gwandu about midday on Saturday 17 Sha'bān 1223 (Saturday 8 October 1808). The direct distance between Alkalawa and Gwandu is about 135 miles. The Shaikh is said to have been told by jinns (I.M., p. 116), but he makes no mention of it himself ('Uthmān b. Fodiye, *Tanbīh al-fāhim*). While thirty to forty miles a day is possible, it is perhaps too much over a period of five days.

[99] Amongst the captives were Katembale, wife of Yunfa, who later bore for Muḥammad Bello two sons, Fodio and Mualedi; Maitakalmi, the mother of Yunfa (K.B., p. 12) and Iyargurma, a servant (jakadiya) of Yunfa (Clapperton, 2nd journey, p. 249).

[100] Cf. K.B., p. 11. The administrator was probably Modibo Muḥammad b. 'Alī b. Fodiye (I.M., p. 116; Muḥammad Bello, *Sard al-kalām*, p. 8; cf. *M.S.O.S.* (1903), p. 217; Tilho, II, 475). The Gobirawa kept the peace made at this time till 1817–18.

[101] I.M., p. 116. Zaria fell, virtually without resistance, three months later: it was the last of the major Hausa cities.

[102] I.M., p. 117.

of Adar.[103] Now, despite the wishes of some of his cousins in Adar, he persisted in visiting the Shaikh at Gwandu.[104] During his stay, which lasted a month, he received some of the booty taken from the Mai Bornu which had just been brought in to the Shaikh.[105] The Sultan promised to aid in the jihād against Bornu, but he died later that year.[106] On his death his brother Muḥammad Kuma succeeded to the sultanate, and visited the Shaikh at Sifawa, renewing the bonds made by his predecessor.[107]

(iv) *The Division of Responsibilities*

Another result of the fall of Alkalawa was the need to organise an administration. Till now, the Shaikh had 'Abdullāh as his chief minister or Vizier, Muḥammad Bello also as Vizier, but as a kind of minister of defence, and 'Alī Jedo as the Commander of the Army, the Amīr al-jaish.[108] Some of the early leaders were dead. 'Umar al-Kammu, who had acted as temporary treasurer after the capture of Matankari, is said to have died before Alwassa;[109] the Shaikh's elder brother, 'Alī, died soon after Tsuntsua.[110] The Imam Muḥammad Sambo, the Tuareg Agali and Maḥmūd Gurdam, all of whom had been on the hijra with the Shaikh, were now dead.[111] It was decided, therefore, to divide the area to be administered between the two chief helpers of the Shaikh, 'Abdullāh and

---

[103] I.M., pp. 97, 117–18.

[104] I.M., p. 118. Cf. letter of Abū Bakr Atiku to the Tuareg in 'Abd al-Qādir b. Gidado, *Majmū'*.

[105] R.J., f. 8b; I.M., p. 117. Birnin Gazargamu had been captured a few months before.

[106] I.M., p. 117.

[107] I.M., p. 174.

[108] Cf. 'Abd al-Qādir b. al-Muṣṭafā, *Mauṣūfat al-sūdān* (f. 3). 'Abdullāh is referred to by Bello, in I.M., as al-wazīr al-akbar or, simply, as al-wazīr, perhaps out of respect of his age. 'Alī Jedo was called by Bello Qā'id al-jaish, or otherwise Amīr al-jaish.

[109] Al-ḥājj Sa'īd, *Ta'rīkh Sokoto* (112a); D.M., f. 32b. Possibly his death near Zauma occurred while the Shaikh was at Sabon Gari.

[110] I.M., p. 88.

[111] Muḥammad Sambo and Maḥmūd Gurdam at Tsuntsua (I.M., p. 87), and Agali soon after (I.M., p. 88).

Muḥammad Bello. The division was made in 1812 (1227), after the Shaikh had been at Sifawa for some two and a half years.[112] The Shaikh had moved from Gwandu to Sifawa in the dry season of 1809–10.[113] Bello had decided in the autumn of 1809 to make his headquarters at Sokoto, where he had been camped the previous year. About the same time as he moved to Sokoto, Bello built a temporary place for the Shaikh at Sifawa, which he repaired the following rainy season.[114]

Sifawa stands on a tongue of high ground bounded by valleys draining eventually into the Kebbi river. Though still in Kebbi country, it is out of the main valley, standing instead on the route from Sokoto to Yabo and Gwandu; the area is the grazing ground of the Sullebawa, while directly south-west is Yabo, the town of the head of the Kebbi Fulani. About two miles north across rolling, fertile land, 'Abdullāh built his own village, Bodinga; a brother of 'Alī Jedo also had a

---

[112] Sa'd b. 'Abd al-Raḥmān, *Tartīb al-aṣḥāb*, cf. Muḥammad Bello, *Sard al-kalām*, p. 3; I.M., p. 190.

[113] I.M., pp. 119, 121. The date of the Shaikh's move to Sifawa is not precise. The *terminus post quem* is Bello's building of Sifawa in the autumn 1809 (I.M., p. 119); the *terminus ante quem* is probably 'Adbullāh's western expedition in January 1810 (10 Dhū'l-ḥijja; T.W., p. 80), though it is possible this expedition was sent before the Shaikh himself moved. The year was either 1224 or 1225: R.A. (f. 10) puts the move in year 7, while D.M. (ff. 30b, 31) puts it in year 6, but in D.M. one year is mistakenly not counted; further, both R.A. and D.M. have a year between the fall of Alkalawa (1223) and the move. In T.W. (p. 81), 'Abdullāh says the move was 'about a year' after his Tanda campaign (*c.* April 1809: 1224, cf. T.W., p. 75; Nedeco, *River Studies*, pp. 26, 27), but he later says that the Nupe campaign was 'about a year' after the move: the two campaigns were a little over twelve months apart, since Bello in I.M. clearly suggests the Shaikh moved to Sifawa the autumn after the Tanda campaign and before the spring campaign to Nupe. 'Abdullāh implies (T.W., p. 81) that he himself moved to Sifawa early in 1225 (i.e. February–March 1810): the Shaikh probably had already moved before then (i.e. 1224; December 1809 or January 1810). The move would take time to complete and would continue after the harvest: preparatory clearing had already been done (T.W., p. 78). The Shaikh travelled in stages, taking the route Masama, Sala, Kajiji, Shagari, Magabshi, Sifawa (*Tabṣirat al-nuẓẓār*).

[114] I.M., pp. 119–20; 117.

village near by, as did 'Abd al-Salām.[115] At this time, Shagari and Yabo to the south were rebuilt more durably to house the Shaikh's lieutenants and scholars.[116] To the north, Bello built his walled town of Sokoto. Its position was strong: steep escarpments from the east to the north-west and a small valley on the west and south-west protected it against surprise cavalry attacks.[117] The town dominates the broad low land where the two rivers, Rima and Sokoto, meet, being the junction of roads from Gobir in the north, Kebbi in the south and Burmi-Zamfara in the east. It is also where spheres of influence meet: the Sullebawa south-east, the Toronkawa north and the Konni-Adar Fulani north-west.

Though Bello used Sokoto as his headquarters, 'Abdullāh lived at Bodinga, being nearer the Shaikh than Gwandu; Gwandu became his headquarters only after the Shaikh had died.[118]

'Abdullāh was unwilling to take over responsibilities of administration so long as the Shaikh was Caliph, and during the lifetime of the Shaikh, both 'Abdullāh and Bello remained only his Viziers.[119] Thus the division of responsibility between them was not necessarily thought final:[120] 'Abdullāh had hopes of becoming Caliph after the Shaikh, since he was the most senior of the Shaikh's relations and followers. When the dependent emirates outside the hinterland of Sokoto were divided for purposes of supervision, 'Abdullāh took the west and Bello the east. The hinterland was treated separately, since the 'royal' Emirs owed allegiance to the Caliph direct,

---

115 Lukuyawa; Abdalsalame.

116 'Umar b. Bukhari b. al-Shaikh, *Tanbīh al-ikhwān fī amr al-sūdān.*

117 See map p. 183.

118 The move north-east caused a panic among the Muslims living in the west, and they also started moving east to follow the Shaikh. It was to restore confidence in the west that 'Abdullāh was sent on the expedition there in the middle of the dry season (T.W., p. 78). With Gobir now no longer a threat, the aim of the move may well have been to get further away from the hostile Kebbawa, since Sifawa was certainly less exposed in their direction.

119 Sa'd b. 'Abd al-Raḥmān, *op. cit.*

120 Sa'd b. 'Abd al-Raḥmān (*op. cit.*) says the Shaikh made the division 'bi'l-talwīḥ', that is, 'metaphorically'.

having no need of an introduction.[121] The 'royal' Emirs included the powerful local leaders who had helped the Shaikh from the beginning, such as 'Alī Jedo, the Commander of the Army, and the Amīr Kebbi Moijo, as well as the relations of the Shaikh. 'Alī Jedo, for his part, was given the charge of the north in general, as Bello was given the east;[122] a son of the Shaikh, Muḥammad Bukhari shared the south with another son, Abū Bakr Atiku. Both the north and the south came under Sokoto once the caliphate moved there; the position of the west, with its subordinate Emirs, remained more independent, though also finally subordinate to the Caliph.

The west at this time included the Niger valley down to Nupe and extended as far west as Dendi.[123] Later Gwandu, often with Sokoto help, pushed farther in these directions, to include Ilorin in the south and Liptako in the west.[124] It is possible that 'Abdullāh expected to extend farther west still and include the Fulani of Masina. Instead, the Muslims in Masina declared a caliphate of their own; the argument over paying allegiance to the Sokoto Caliph continued till about 1838.[125]

---

[121] 'Non-royal' leaders or sons of 'royal' Emirs had at this time a 'royal' Emir as their introduction to the Caliph. Thus 'Abd al-Salām was first under 'Abdullāh when at Sabuyel, then under Bello when at Sangame (near Sokoto) and Kware.

[122] Muḥammad Bello, *Sard al-kalām*, p. 8. The north here is said to have been given to 'Alī Jedo and Muḥammad Āl or Muḥammadān b. al-Shaikh. The latter may be a mistake for Muḥammad b. 'Alī b. Fodiye (thus a nephew of the Shaikh) whose family had land between Sokoto and Wurno with the title of Ubandoma. He had been appointed administrator at Alkalawa since 1808, and 'Abd al-Salām may be referring to this. Otherwise the existence of a Muḥammad Al b. al-Shaikh is unknown; al-haji Junaidu believes it is an error.

[123] T.W., p. 82; I.M., pp. 121, 112–13, 118–19. The division may not have been fully accepted in Nupe till after the death of the Shaikh: cf. the career of Shaikh 'Abd al-Raḥmān in Maḥmūd b. Muḥammad, *al-Ta'rīkh* (Ibadan MS. 33). The Gwari country came under Bello (I.M., pp. 120 f.; T.W., pp. 81 f.), while Muḥammad b. 'Abdullāh came to Bello for permission to campaign in Nupe in 1826 (Clapperton, 2nd journey, p. 237).

[124] Barth, IV, 203. Tilho, II, 501.

[125] Cf. the letters of Bello and Abū Bakr Atiku to Shaikh Aḥmad of

The southern extension of 'Abdullāh's sphere curtailed the share which fell to Muḥammad Bukhari. Muḥammad Bukhari, however, had been brought up in the house of 'Abdullāh and campaigned with 'Abdullāh's son, Muḥammad. The south-west, his share, never extended beyond the Sokoto area. Nor did the south-east, which was given to Abū Bakr Atiku; when Abū Bakr became Caliph in 1837, the significance of the share was limited to connections with some people and places in the area.[126]

The north under 'Alī Jedo was more extensive, reaching, in theory, as far as Filingue and Adar. On the western boundary of his territory, Gwandu tended to claim the southern Arewa regions, while in the north-west and the Imanan, Sokoto was unable to extend effective control.[127] Konni and Matankari, the former especially, owed allegiance to Sokoto through 'Alī Jedo and his heirs. 'Alī Jedo, as leader of the Konni Fulani, was in effect confirmed in his sphere of influence.[128]

The east at this period included Zamfara, Katsina, Kano, Daura, Bauchi, Bauchi East (i.e. Gombe), Bornu (Katagum) and Bornu East. To this list, given in *Infāq al-maisūr*, should be added Zaria, Hadejia and Adamawa.[129]

Although the boundaries of the eastern half of the caliphate were not yet fixed—Adamawa was to extend as a loosely knit group of emirates far to the east, while in Baghirmi and southern Bornu the situation was still fluid—the future independence of Bornu and the limits of the eastern expansion were probably recognised. By contrast, in the west there were

---

Masina; Hampate Ba, *L'Empire Peul du Macina* (Paris, 1955), p. 41. The Masina documents in the de Gironcourt MSS. regularly refer to Shaikh Aḥmad as Amīr al-mu'minīn.

[126] For example, in Zamfara, the ribāṭ at Bakura; or the Sullebawa generally. The descendants of Abū Bakr kept the title of Sarkin Zamfara and this as their sphere of influence. Conquest of the pagan groups south of the river Zamfara proved difficult and not very rewarding: it later became the sphere of 'Umar Nagwamatse. Because of rivalries in this area relations between the families of Abū Bakr and Muḥammad Bukhari remained strained throughout the century.

[127] Cf. Tilho, II, 497, 502.

[128] Cf. Tilho, II, 492 f.

[129] I.M., p. 190. *v. infra*, p. 53.

possibilities of co-operation both with the Muslim Fulani of Masina and with the Kunta of Timbuktu. As friendly relations were already established, 'Abdullāh's sphere must have seemed diplomatically the more important. Though the area under Gwandu was claimed to be larger than that given to Bello, there is no reason to think that at the time of the division the comparative wealth or size of each was actively considered, nor indeed to think the division was necessarily considered permanent.

3
The Early Caliphate

(i) *The Officials*

The Shaikh had the official titles of Amīr al-mu'minīn and Khalīfa (Caliph).[1] In his *Wathīqat ahl al-sūdān*, he says that the appointment of an Amīr al-mu'minīn is obligatory according to the consensus;[2] in the *Bayān wujūb al-hijra*, however, he uses the term Imam in referring to this obligation.[3] The latter title, Imam, was widely used in the Futa Toro and Futa Jallon; it was later used by Samory.[4] Imam has not the wider implications of Amīr al-mu'minīn, which is one of the defining titles of the Caliph, of the Supreme Imam, of the overall leader of the Faithful.[5] When the Muslim world lost its unity, others outside Baghdad used the title Amīr al-mu'minīn. The theory was developed that there could be two

---

[1] T.W., p. 26; I.M., p. 1. But he was more commonly known as the Shaikh (I.M., *passim*). The form Amīr al-muslimīn, despite the Hausa translation Sarkin Musulmi, does not occur in the Sokoto literature, and its special implications are not relevant.

[2] A. D. H. Bivar (*J.A.H.*, 1961), p. 239. This *Wathīqa* is found widely distributed, as far as Segu. It may date from just before the jihād (Bivar, *op. cit.*, p. 243). Another book, dated 1217 (i.e. pre-jihād), *Masā'il muhimma*, repeats the obligations to an Amīr al-mu'minīn (p. 3, margin).

[3] 'Uthmān b. Fodiye, *Bayān wujūb al-hijra* (November 1806/Ramaḍān 1221), chapter 6.

[4] Although Samory called himself both Imam and Amīr al-mu'minīn, the title al-mamy was most commonly used. He forbade the use of his own name, Samory; *Histoire de Samori*, pp. 151–2, in Delafosse, *Essai de Manuel Pratique de la langue Mandé* (Paris, 1901).

[5] Cf. H. A. R. Gibb, in *E.I.* (1960), I, 445.

Caliphs, so long as they were separated sufficiently in space. These arguments, reproduced in 'Abdullāh's *Ḍiyā' al-ḥukkām*, were used by Shaikh Aḥmad of Masina in his correspondence with Sokoto, in which he refuses to acknowledge the caliphate of Sokoto.[6] He, too, called himself Amīr al-mu'minīn; so, later, did his neighbour Aḥmad b. 'Umar at Segu.[7] For four centuries at least before Sokoto the Sultans of Bornu had styled themselves Amīr al-mu'minīn;[8] so had the Askia of Songhai.[9] They were, in short, the heads of their Muslim Communities. Despite the long-maintained claim of Bornu, there was not, it seems, an argument against the title in the al-Kanemi–Sokoto correspondence.[10] It is possible that the precise classical implications of the title were overlooked at the time. There is an anomaly in the Sultan of Ahir at Agades also bearing the title Amīr al-mu'minīn. The Sultan of Ahir was called Amīr al-mu'minīn by the Shaikh in 1810 when he visited Sokoto and Sifawa:[11] considering the help his brother had given to Katsina and the bay'a he paid to the Shaikh, there can be no doubt that the arguments later used did not apply at this stage.[12]

---

[6] 'Abdullāh b. Fodiye, *Ḍiyā' al-ḥukkām*, bāb 2, faṣl. 2. Shaikh Aḥmad correspondence: Ibadan photocopy, p. 12.

[7] Masina: e.g. de Gironcourt MSS. (IF): 2405, 32. Segu: BN, vol. 5693, f. 14.

[8] Letter from the Sultan of Bornu to the Sultan of Egypt in al-Qalqashandī, *Ṣubḥ al-a'shā* (pt. VIII, pp. 115 ff.), dated 1391/2. Sixteenth century: Aḥmad b. Fartuwa, p. 23.

[9] Al-Sa'dī, *Tarikh es-Soudan*, I, 72, cf. 74; where he is said to have been made Caliph of the Abbasid Caliph for the land of Songhai.

[10] Not, at least, in the correspondence preserved in I.M. The Sultan of Bornu, Aḥmad b. 'Alī, in a letter to the Shaikh, had said he was Amīr al-mu'minīn (I.M., p. 131), but al-Kanemi seems not to have followed up this argument. al-Kanemi, however, did not give the title to the Shaikh, and was probably unimpressed by its use in Bornu; he never used the title himself, since he had connections with the Fezzan and may have owed allegiance to the Ottoman caliphate (letters of al-Kanemi in Dept. of Antiquities, Jos; cf. B. G. Martin, *J.H.S.N.*, 1962, p. 369).

[11] I.M., p. 174.

[12] I.M., pp. 97, 117; arguments on caliphate in 'Abdullāh, *Ḍiyā' al-ḥukkām*, 2, 2. By the time Barth was in Agades (1850), the Sultan had lost much of the independence enjoyed by Muḥammad al-Bāqirī and had

The Caliph in Abbasid theory delegated much of his work to officials: such delegation was a necessary development from the simple caliphate of the early years of Islam. Similarly, when the Shaikh was elected Caliph and he ceased to be merely the head of a scholastic Community, the responsibilities first of the jihād and then of the administration of the caliphate required him to designate some of his followers as his lieutenants and deputies. The Shaikh, who was 50 at the start of the jihād, was not strong enough to campaign; and for this reason, it is said, he wanted to decline the caliphate.[13] But once appointed Caliph, he stayed in the main camp.[14] Consequently he depended on his Viziers: his brother 'Abdullāh, 'Umar al-Kammu, his closest friend, his cousin Sa'd, and his son Muḥammad Bello.[15] 'Umar al-Kammu played no active part in the campaigns, though he was present on the day of the defeat at Tsuntsua, and he died before the Shaikh.[16] The Shaikh's cousin Sa'd b. al-Ḥasan may be the 'brother Sa'd' who commanded at Tsuntsua; otherwise nothing is heard of him.[17] 'Abdullāh, who preferred to live near the Shaikh, was the senior Vizier, but it was Bello who acted for the Shaikh, for example, when the eastern Emirs were sworn in at Birnin Gada.[18] Bello always had his camp away from the Shaikh, usually on the exposed quarter; at

---

ceased to call himself Amīr al-mu'minīn, being 'Emir of Ahir' instead. He did, however, use a seal, which within the Sokoto caliphate was restricted to the Caliph and the Emir of Katsina. Presumably seals had been used in Katsina before the jihād and the new Emirs continued the practice: both Gobir and Katsina (Maradi) continued to use seals. They were all circular. The Shaikhs of Bornu, before the conquest of Rābiḥ, used octagonal seals. Seals are found on letters in NAK (Sokprof letters, 1: 22, 24, 26, 35, 41, 47, 58). Cf. letter reproduced in H. R. Palmer, *Bornu Sahara and Sudan* (London, 1936), facing p. 62.

[13] Al-ḥājj Sa'īd, *Ta'rīkh Sokoto* (110b).

[14] There is no suggestion in I.M. that the Shaikh fought; he encouraged the army, if it was hard pressed. Similarly, he sent out expeditions but did not accompany them.

[15] R.J., f. 12. The office of Vizier is discussed in Part III below.

[16] R.J., f. 10. D.M., f. 32b.

[17] I.M., p. 87; T.W., p. 61. Possibly he was the Sa'd who was killed in that battle.

[18] I.M., p. 104.

Sala, when the Shaikh was in Gwandu;[19] at Sokoto, when the Shaikh was in Sifawa; and, for two years before the jihād, at Yamulu when the Shaikh was at Degel.[20]

Some appointments are likely to have been made by the Shaikh when the Community was at Degel. His Viziers, if not designated by that title, acted as such in the years before the hijra. It is possible, owing to the Islamic obligation to appoint judges and the fundamental importance of the Sharī'a Law, that some of the judges listed also acted in that capacity before the jihād, whether at Degel or in a local village. The judges in Sokoto were numerous, but being drawn from among the scholars of the early Community they formed a closely knit group. Muḥammad Sambo, the chief judge and Imam, a cousin of the Shaikh, had died at Tsuntsua.[21] At Sifawa, the chief judge was Abū Bakr Ladan Rame, but he died there in office; he, too, was a relation of the Shaikh. Bi'ali, another relation of the Shaikh, was a judge and later became chief judge; he died between 1837 and 1842.[22] Other judges include Muḥammad b. Muḥammad Binduwo, of an important Muslim family, but unrelated to the Shaikh: his father had taught the Shaikh, while his brother was a leading helper of Muḥammad Bello.[23] Another judge, Sambo b. Gabinda, was the son of a distinguished scholar. The judges Muḥammad b. Agage, Aḥmad and al-Ḥasan b. Aḥmad are also listed as Shaikhs of Muḥammad Bello, and probably had lived in Kadaye before the jihād; the last two later warned 'Abd al-Salām against rebelling.[24]

The office of Muḥtasib, as the Shaikh says, 'is of later introduction and has the widest scope of all offices—commanding the good and prohibiting the evil, and, as that was

---

[19] About fifteen miles north-east of Gwandu; the birthplace of the two sons of Bello called 'Alī, *c.* 1223–4 (*c.* 1808–9). See Barth (IV, 193–4) for a description of Sala in 1854. Bello is said by the Alkalin Gwandu Aḥmad (*History of Gwandu*, trans. McAllister, 1909, para. 25) to have gone to Sala after the battle of Alwassa.

[20] K.B., pp. 6, 8.

[21] I.M., p. 87; T.W., p. 61. See genealogy.

[22] D.M., f. 46.

[23] R.J., f. 13; *Majmū' aṣḥāb Bello.*

[24] Muḥammad Bello, *Sard al-kalām*, p. 13; K.B., p. 8; *Nasab.* They are possibly referred to in I.M., p. 79.

so frequently needed, the rulers found they had to appoint a man to look into it in the big centres at regular hours'.[25] The Shaikh's appointee was the muezzin Muḥammad Julde, who held the title till he died during the rule of 'Alī b. Bello. Not much is known of him, but his function seems to have been a kind of welfare officer and censor of morals.[26] In the hands of a good man, the office must have given great protection against maladministration and misbehaviour, but in other hands, as possibly at Masina, the office could become an Inquisition.[27]

Some further appointments were made by the Shaikh. Two of the Shaikh's distant relations, al-Ḥusain and Akke, held the title wālī al-shurṭa or chief of police. The family of al-Ḥusain still hold the title of gaoler ('Yari') and the two posts, chief of police and gaoler, are said by al-haji Junaidu to have been kept by one family.[28] The gaoler was an official of rank, with the chief of police as his subordinate: though sometimes concerned with the more important arrests, he was primarily responsible for carrying out the punishments

---

[25] *Bayān wujūb al-hijra 'alā 'l-'ibād*, ch. 10 (translation of F. H. El-Masri).

[26] The present provincial judge of Sokoto says his duties included seeing the judges made appointments for trying cases, so as not to keep everyone waiting; if a beast was ill-fed and the owner too poor, to provide food for the beast; if a farm was under-tilled, and the owner unable to till it, to find a man to share the work and the crop; if a canoe was overloaded, to warn the owner twice before confiscating it. For the classical muḥtasib, cf. Tyan, *Histoire de l'Organisation Judiciaire en pays d'Islam* (2nd ed., Leiden, 1960), pp. 617 ff.

[27] Cf. the opinion of Trimingham, *op. cit.*, p. 181. There was, perhaps, another official of this kind in Sokoto. Bello, in *Sard al-kalām* (p. 5), mentions a 'letter-writer for complainants' (munshi' al-waraqāt li-ajli ahl al-shikāyāt) through whom 'Abd al-Salām's complaint could be handled; I have seen no other references in Sokoto to such an official. Al-haji Junaidu says that Malam Mūsā, an Arab scholar, held such a post under Muḥammad Bello.

[28] The dating of the appointment of al-Ḥusain is not definitely established. He is only mentioned in lists written after the death of the Shaikh, such as in 'Abd al-Qādir b. Gidado, *Basṭ al-fawā'id*, or the genealogy by Bello, *Ishāra wa-i'lām*. Other names of police officials are given by Gidado in his *Majmū' aṣḥāb Bello* for the period of Bello's caliphate; *v. infra.*

prescribed by the courts. The police were for the most part the servants of the leading men or the populace who could be summoned by the Muḥtasib to catch common criminals.

Another early appointment was the imamate. Apart from Muḥammad Sambo already mentioned, who died at Tsuntsua, the other leading Imams were Muḥammad Zangi and Abū Bakr, known as 'Malam'. Muḥammad Zangi died before the Shaikh in Gwandu (the Shaikh had moved from Gwandu by then), after having been a student under the Shaikh at Degel.[29] Abū Bakr, a relation of the Shaikh, was the Imam at Sokoto at the deaths of the Shaikh, Muḥammad Bello and Abū Bakr Atiku, of whom he is said to have been a close friend.[30] The other Imams are not distinguishable.

Another office that may date from this period is that of the Sā'ī. Classically, the Sā'ī was the collector of zakāt.[31] In Sokoto, the Sā'ī was responsible for taxing the cattle Fulani, and the tax, popularly known by its Hausa name jangali, was officially referred to as zakāt, if the Fulani were Muslims, or jizya if they were pagans.[32] The office, however, became honorary as the Fulani settled and zakāt-collection was delegated or surrendered to local officials. Since the holder of the title was also the flag-bearer to the Caliph, the latter office tended to overshadow the post of Sā'ī, but the title remains in the family of Ibrāhīm, the first holder. No Sā'ī is mentioned in any of the early lists of officials in Sokoto, but it is likely that the office was instituted under the Shaikh, since payment of zakāt is one of the major obligations of Islam. The tax, however, remained notoriously difficult to collect.

The Shaikh also appointed a number of Commanders to

---

[29] R.J., ff. 12b, 13.

[30] Sa'īd (ed. Houdas), p. 201.

[31] Cf. al-Dasūqī's commentary on the Mukhtaṣar of Khalīl (Cairo, 1934), vol. II, p. 482. I am indebted to F. H. El-Masri for this reference.

[32] Cf. letter of 'Alī in 'Abd al-Qādir b. Gidado, *Majmū'*. There is no textual, only some oral, evidence for this office in Sokoto. The Sā'ī has a similar function in Zaria (M. G. Smith, *Government in Zazzau*, pp. 93, 142) and in Daura (A. D. H. Bivar, *Jnl. of African History*, 1961, p. 237). The Emir of Bornu (Missau) had extraterritorial rights to collect tax from his Fulani followers, and, by extension, from all Bornu Fulani, after his move from Bornu to Missau.

lead expeditions.[33] Only 'Alī Jedo, however, in Sokoto had the title Qā'id, or Amīr jaish al-Islām: he and his heirs were the official Commanders of the Army. Though the Amīr al-jaish under the Shaikh used to lead out an army by himself, later he more often accompanied the Amīr al-mu'minīn in a subordinate position. The other Commanders listed are 'Abdullāh and Bello; 'Abdullāh's son Muḥammad, whose main sphere of campaigning was Nupe together with his cousin Muḥammad Bukhari and others; Moijo, the leader of the Kebbi Fulani; Muḥammad Namoda, a leader of the Alibawa Fulani of Zamfara who was nicknamed the Victorious; and Muḥammad Wara, one of the Sullebawa (but not, it seems, of the Ardo's family) and based in Gwamatse, near Wamako. Like that of the last three in the list, the importance of 'Alī Jedo lay in his Fulani following, who had undoubtedly been valuable at the first battle of the jihād at Kwotto. His title dates from that campaign;[34] he remained active, however, in leading expeditions throughout the jihād.

The title of Amīr al-jaish was also given to Buba Yero in the lands near Bauchi on the Bornu marches.[35] In Gombe now, it is claimed that he was made Amīr al-jaish before 'Alī Jedo.[36] While 'Ali Jedo is specifically mentioned as Qā'id al-jaish in the Kebbi campaign of the wet season 1805, no mention is ever made of Buba Yero except as the lieutenant for lands in Bauchi.[37] Al-haji Junaidu suggests that all the lieutenants were originally given the title of Qā'id al-jaish, but only Buba Yero retained the title.

It is notable how few of the Shaikh's family led expeditions. Although they led raids, as did Abū Bakr Atiku, they were unable to call upon sufficient following for an expedition: the

---

[33] The office had particular importance under the Shaikh since the Shaikh was a non-combatant.

[34] 'Abd al-Qādir b. al-Muṣṭafā, *Mauṣūfat al-sūdān*, f. 3. Bello, however, is said to have been given charge of the first expedition at Gudu (K.B.).

[35] R.J., f. 13. The title was continued throughout the nineteenth century: *v.* Gombe correspondence (National Archives, Kaduna: Bauprof letters, 1).

[36] Cf. National Archives, K 5031 (biography of Abū Bakr Yero by Idrīs b. Ibrāhīm translated by R. Abraham, 1926).

[37] I.M., pp. 91, 190.

army relied heavily on individuals with their own followers.[38] Such a system made the four clans, Konni, Kebbi, Sullebawa and Alibawa Fulani, the basis of Muslim power in Sokoto and Zamfara.

Every expedition carried a flag.[39] The Shaikh's own flag-bearer was one of his servants, Ibrāhīm, and the office of flag-bearer to the Caliph remained in his family. By extension, when Muslim leaders came in to the Shaikh from other parts of Hausaland, they were sent home to lead a local campaign with a flag blessed by the Shaikh; they were, thus, given the title of Amīr al-jaish like any other leader of an expedition sent out by the Shaikh. However, as the Shaikh divided responsibilities in Sokoto, so the provincial commanders were given spheres of influence. Once established in their regions, they were nuwwāb (lieutenants) or Emirs, with the Viziers 'Abdullāh and Bello only acting as their intermediaries with the Shaikh.[40]

Muḥammad Bello, writing in 1812, gives the following list of nuwwāb:[41]

Abū Ḥāmid	— Zamfara
'Umar Dallaji	— Katsina

[38] A.M., p. 31; Sa'īd (ed. Houdas), p. 194. Even Bello, 'Alī Jedo and 'Abdullāh had trouble in raising armies (I.M., p. 91, T.W., p. 78). Cf. 'Umar b. Bukhari, *Tanbīh al-ikhwān*.

[39] The earliest flag I have seen is said to date from *c.* 1853, and was carried by the Vizier 'Abd al-Qādir b. Gidado. It is white cloth, six feet tall by three feet wide, made of two square pieces and attached to a wooden pole. At the bottom of each piece near the pole is a small inscription in Arabic; otherwise the flag is plain. Other flags I have seen have been smaller; one was blue, while another, dating from *c.* 1860, was made from imported white damask.

[40] The term 'āmil, 'representative', is sometimes used, but mainly for local rulers dependent on a major Emir (e.g. letter of Bello in 'Abd al-Qādir b. Gidado, *Majmū'*; letter of the Emir of Kano in Correspondence, VII, 34, dated *c.* 1883–5). Sambo Lai is referred to as wakīl in Gidado, *Majmū' aṣḥāb Bello* (cf. Dembo, the wakīl in Kazaure). The Shaikh and 'Abdullāh argued about the use of the terms amīr and malik: 'Abdullāh considered the latter pagan, and it is not used in Sokoto ('Abdullāh, *Ḍiyā' al-sulṭān*; 'Uthmān b. Fodiye, *Najm al-ikhwān*).

[41] I.M., p. 190.

Sulaimān b. Aba-Hamma	— Kano
Ya'qūb	— Bauchi
Isḥāq	— Daura
Ibrāhīm	— all Bornu
Muḥammad Manga	— East Bornu
Buba Yero	— land in Bauchi

Gidado, whose work is undated, but may have been written *c.* 1839, has a fuller list:[42]

Moijo	— Kebbi
Abū Ḥāmid	— Zamfara
'Umar Dallaji	— Katsina
Isḥāq	— Daura
Mūsā	— Zaria
Sulaimān	— Kano
Ibrāhīm Zaki	— Bornu (Katagum)
Bi Abdur and his brother Dagimsa	— Bornu (Hadejia)
Lerlima	— Bornu (Marmar)
Muḥammad Manga	— Bornu (Missau)
Muḥammad Nema	— the west[43]
Muḥammad Wabi	— (Jamaari)
Buba Yero	— Amīr al-jaish (Gombe)
Ya'qūb	— Bauchi
Adama	— (Adamawa)
Muḥammad al-ḥājj al-amīn	— Baghirmi[44]

---

[42] R.J., f. 13. Places are only given in brackets if the modern names of the emirates in which the leading families became established differ from those in Gidado's list.

[43] Clapperton (2nd journey, p. 242) in 1827: 'Muhammad Mungo and Muhammad Nema, two of the Fellata chiefs on the frontiers, who were constantly invading Bornou, and carrying off the inhabitants and cattle'. References to Muḥammad Nema are otherwise rare. 'The west' here is al-gharb; an alternative, but less likely, reading is al-'arab.

[44] His son, al-Sayyid, was appointed by Bello to succeed another son, 'Abdullāh, as Emir of his people (? *c.* 1825). Overall responsibility for them was given to M. Adama. Cf. letter from Bello in 'Abd al-Qādir b. Gidado, *Majmū'*; Gidado, *Majmū' aṣḥāb Bello*. A friendly Baghirmi was important to Sokoto owing to the expectation that with the coming of the Mahdi everyone would emigrate to the Nile, and attempts were made to keep the road east always open.

The order of the lists is not particularly significant: both are roughly geographical—west to east—and, seeing that the jihād spread east, both are in approximate chronological order. The omission of Zaria, Hadejia and Adamawa from Bello's list is curious, but not significant: Mūsā was known by Bello to be Emir at the time of writing *Infāq al-maisūr*, while the Hadejia leaders and their campaigns had also been mentioned earlier in the book.[45] In Bornu the emirates had not yet been delineated: Bornu East probably represents Daya, which Muḥammad Manga later evacuated for Missau; similarly M. Adama was only beginning the jihād in what was to become Adamawa.

All the nuwwāb were appointed for established Hausa states except for 'Bornu' and 'Bauchi': both of these were more geographical than political terms. 'Bauchi' implied a fragmented non-Muslim region, in this case that to the east of the Plateau; 'Bornu' referred to that part of the old Bornu state that the Fulani leaders occupied, since, as his correspondence with al-Kanemi suggests, Bello did not presume to rule the state of Bornu itself.[46] This explains the large number of lieutenants in Bornu, all ruling a part of the Bornu marches: two of them, the Emirs in Katagum and Missau, kept the title of Emir of Bornu. A similar geographical title was that later used in Adamawa, where the Emir was called the Emir of the South, though the emirate was known as Adamawa as early as 1823–4.[47]

Of these Emirs, only Ya'qūb was definitely not a Fulani; and he is the only one for whom there are Sokoto traditions about his period of studentship with the Shaikh. Brought by a scholar and introduced into the Community, he was with the Shaikh at Faru and is said to have married a daughter of

[45] I.M., pp. 97, 121 ff. The early Hadejia leaders, Bi Abdur and his son, had died before I.M. was completed.

[46] One of Bello's main arguments was that they were fighting Bornu in self-defence, and only wanted peace.

[47] For the early use of 'Adamawa', see the map in Denham and Clapperton (*Narrative of Travels . . .*, 1826). By the 'South' here was possibly meant the south of Bornu, and not merely south of Sokoto; cf. Muḥammad Nema as Emir of the West, that is west Bornu.

a Zamfara friend of the Shaikh.[48] The other Emirs were primarily scholars in the beginning: 'Umar Dallaji had made the pilgrimage; Gwoni Mukhtār (whose first name means 'learned'), Ibrāhīm Zaki, Adama, Sulaimān and Mūsā were all noted for their learning.[49] But in Bornu, the conflict was also on national lines: Bello recognises this by his frequent references to his 'Fulani brothers'.[50] Some of the leaders, such as Bi Abdur, Lerlima and Muḥammad Wabi, were Ardo'en or the sons of Ardo'en;[51] similarly, in Zamfara, Abū Ḥāmid was an Alibawa Fulani leader under Gobir, and Moijo was the Fulani leader recognized by Kebbi.

The letter of appointment, however, emphasises the Muslim basis of the leadership required by the Shaikh. A letter addressed to Ya'qūb appointing him as Emir of his Community includes seven instructions: (i) to be consistent and stand by what he says and commands; (ii) to be zealous in maintaining mosques; (iii) to be zealous in praying there; (iv) to study the Quran and its teachings; (v) to study the (Islamic) sciences and their teachings; (vi) to maintain the markets and prevent illegalities there; (vii) to wage the jihād.[52] This letter, like the oaths sworn at Birnin Gada by the lieutenants for Kano and Katsina, should be read as only a part of the attempts by the Sokoto leaders to ensure that their own standards of Islam were carried into the provinces: for this purpose, the Shaikh, 'Abdullāh and Muḥammad

---

[48] Maḥmūd b. Muḥammad, *Iḍā'at al-qabas wa'l-miṣbāḥ li'l-a'mash fī ta'rīkh umarā' Bauchi*; al-haji Junaidu, *Tuḥfat al-ikhwān*. Muḥammad Bello seems to have written more to Ya'qūb than to any other Emir in the caliphate, e.g. *al-Ghaith al-shu'būb*; *al-Qaul al-mauhūb*; the letter in Bivar (*B.S.O.A.S.*, 1959), pp. 338 ff. 'Alī b. Bello, though Amīr al-mu'minīn, wrote very politely to Ya'qūb ('Abd al-Qādir b. Gidado, *Majmū'*). Both letters suggest he held a special position *vis-à-vis* Muḥammad Bello.

[49] Gwoni is Fulfulde for al-māhir (I.M., p. 138). Ibrāhīm Zaki was known as al-faqīh (I.M., p. 138), Adama and Mūsā as al-'ālim (R.J., f. 13), and Sulaimān as al-faqīh al-'ādil (I.M., p. 104).

[50] e.g. I.M., p. 123.

[51] A Muḥammad Wabi visited Bello at Alkalawa (i.e. after 1808), K.B., p. 12. For details of the Bornu marches, cf. J. M. Fremantle, *African Affairs*, XXXIX–XLI.

[52] Microfilm M.42, at Ibadan. Also quoted in Maḥmūd b. Muḥammad, *op. cit.*

Bello, as well as Caliphs after them, also wrote books and letters of advice to specific leaders, like Ya'qūb, or to the Community in general, explaining Islamic Law and practice.

Traditionally the Shaikh is said to have had no officials other than the Vizier ('Abdullāh), the Commander of the Army ('Alī Jedo), the judges (Muḥammad Sambo; Abū Bakr Ladan Rame) and a chief of police (al-Ḥusain, Akke). The Shaikh was keeping to the minimum he prescribed in his book *Kitāb al-farq*: there he said a ruler should appoint a Vizier, a judge, a chief of police and an official in charge of the land tax (kharāj).[53] Titles of kings and their officials, he said, were not to be imitated, and rulers in the provinces were only to be called Emir of the place they ruled.[54] Though these instructions were adhered to in principle, what was adequate for the *ad hoc* government of the early caliphate in Sokoto had soon to be developed into an organized administration to govern the vast area under established Muslim control.

(ii) *Two Aspects of the Caliphate*

With the responsibility of government left to his Viziers, the Shaikh was able to teach and write. Eleven books we have are dated during the five years of his stay at Sifawa; and only a small proportion of his work is ever dated.[55] All but the Qādirī genealogy have immediate relevance to the work of the Community, whether answering problems on the Mahdi, giving guidance on fiqh, or replying to the accusations of al-

---

[53] 'Uthmān b. Fodiye, *Kitāb al-farq*, edited and translated by M. Hiskett, *B.S.O.A.S.* (XXIII, 3, 1960), p. 564. Kharāj, it seems, was not collected in Sokoto (*v. infra*), but the Shaikh may be using the term generally. The Shaikh's treasurer ('Ajia') at Sifawa was Sulaimān Wodi.

[54] *Kitāb al-farq* (*B.S.O.A.S.*, 1960), p. 563.

[55] July 1810: 1225, *al-Salāsil al-qādiriyya*; *Ḥiṣn al-afhām*. 1226, *Naṣīḥat ahl al-zamān*; *Sirāj al-ikhwān*; *Tanbīh al-ikhwān*. 1227, *al-Amr bi-muwālāt al-mu'minīn wa'l-nahy 'an muwālāt al-kāfirīn*; *Najm al-ikhwān*. 1228, *Shams al-ikhwān*; *Ta'līm al-ikhwān bi'l-umūr allatī kaffarnā bihā mulūk al-sūdān*; *Tauqīf al-muslimīn 'alā ḥukm madhāhib al-mujtahidīn*. December 1814: 1229, *Taḥdhīr al-ikhwān min iddi'ā' al-mahdiyya al-mau'ūda ākhir al-zamān*.

Kanemi.[56] At his weekly meetings on Thursday night, the Shaikh used to speak against oppression in his district, against extortion from the poor, against allowing roads to be closed between districts and the robbing of markets or mosques, against the condoning of the crimes of sons and slaves.[57] He was also concerned in teaching the religious side of Islam, the doxology of the Qādirī ṭarīqa or sufic subjects like the hidden faith and the seeking of Allah. He was teaching such subjects throughout his stay at Sifawa, giving lessons both by day and night: the *al-Salāsil al-qādiriyya* was written in July 1810 at the beginning of his stay, while some notes taken by a student from Kano on similar topics are dated 1814.[58]

While clearly there was much religious and scholastic activity, not all who were part of the Community attended the seminars and recitations, or went to the mosque. Some of the scholars had remained at Gwandu when the Shaikh left for Sifawa. For example, the noted Sufi Muḥammad Koiranga and the Imam Zangi lived at Gwandu;[59] 'Abd al-Salām, given some towns in Gwandu to supervise, was dissatisfied and had to be moved from Sabuyel to Kware, near Sokoto.[60] Both 'Abdullāh and 'Abd al-Salām, from different motives, had been critical of the way the character of the jihād had changed, and Bello agreed.[61] As early as 1806 it had been necessary for a poet in the jihād to remind his fellow mujāhidūn that servants of Fulani, learned Fulani and pastoral Fulani were all human beings.[62] The Community by

---

[56] Out of this dispute with al-Kanemi arose the definition current in Sokoto that all those who were not with Muslims were against Muslims, and that all those against Muslims were non-Muslims (cf. M. A. al-Hajj, D. M. Last, *op. cit.*, *J.H.S.N.*, 1965).

[57] 'Umar b. Bukhari b. al-Shaikh, *Tanbīh al-ikhwān fī amr al-sūdān*; written *c.* 1845. 'Umar was not an eyewitness: his father was born *c.* 1785–6.

[58] 'Abdullāh b. Muḥammad al-Kanawī (notes of 35 dā'ira of the Shaikh at Sifawa in 1229/1814). The Shaikh's students at Sifawa numbered over three hundred (Muḥammad Raji b. 'Alī, *Risāla*).

[59] Both are also buried there. Cf. R.J., f. 2b.

[60] Muḥammad Bello, *Sard al-kalām*, p. 4.

[61] T.W., pp. 70, 71. Muḥammad Bello, *Sard al-kalām*, pp. 5–7.

[62] Muḥammad Raji b. 'Alī (poem in Fulfulde).

the end of the first jihād was a diverse group: the original Community had been joined by others who did not share the standards which the early reformers expected of Muslims.

In a short pamphlet, Muḥammad Bello describes the new Community.[63] Of the ten types of people in it, nine are not genuine members. There are those who feared the authority of the previous rulers: they are not to be found in the mosque or at seminars, neither reciting nor campaigning when asked, but instead they stay in the garden or the house, in the market or on their land.[64] There are those who are Fulani and think that is a sufficient criterion; they despise the non-Fulani, even if they are learned, pious or mujāhidūn; yet they are better than the previous type as they do go on expeditions, if not to the mosque, seminars or recitations, but they do neglect religion and the theory of jihād. Then there are the learned who are there because it is fashionable, but do not campaign or recite, since they believe their knowledge is enough. A fourth group are the learned whose students have left them for the Shaikh; they criticise the jihād and say it is corrupt. A similar group are those whose children have left them for the Shaikh; they ignore the jihād and make fun of the Community and Islam. There are also those who look only for worldly benefits and support the Community so long as it supports and benefits them. A further group are those who were real members once, but have since been attracted by the world and the devil. The eighth group are those born within the Community; they care only for horses and fighting, and do not attend the mosque, seminars or recitations. The last group are those who were forced to join the Community, as there was no alternative: they are always depressed, for no reason. The real member, by contrast, is guided not by the world but by God, giving up property, power and family for the life to come.

This description of the hangers-on in the Community is probably particularly true of Sokoto—where Muḥammad

[63] Two folios ascribed to Bello but without author or title in the text (fī aqwām al-muhājirīn); from Nizamiyya School Library.

[64] 'Recitations'—majālis al-dhikr; 'seminars'—majālis al-'ilm, throughout.

Bello was living and which had become the centre of activity. The emphasis within the Community had shifted away from scholarship: those who had not been attracted by its practice of Islam were now attracted by its success, and under the conditions of jihād army leaders were as important as scholars. While the Shaikh was alive respect for his authority held any serious divisions in abeyance.[65] The Shaikh had remained at Sifawa till *c.* 1815, when he moved to Sokoto.[66] Muḥammad Bello had built a house for him in a suburb on the western side of the town, with a mosque beyond. The year following the move, the Shaikh fell ill; he died a year later at the age of 62.[67]

---

[65] Muḥammad Bello, *Sard al-kalām*, p. 4. Only in Zamfara in 1816, when the Shaikh was ill, was a punitive campaign found necessary (R.A., f. 10b, where I read Bānāgā for Bābāgā).

[66] R.J., f. 14b; R.A., f. 10b. Sokoto thus became the 'qubbat al-islām', 'the dome of Islam', in the land: it is still the major place of pilgrimage in Hausaland. See map, p. 183.

[67] A.M., p. 15. The exact date is Sunday night 3rd Jumādā II, 1232 (Sunday 20 April 1817). R.J., f. 14b, gives the same date, but says it was on Monday (yaum al-ithnain; cf. A.M.: lailat al-ithnain = Sunday), which would be the 21st April 1817. Note that sixty-four lunar years are equivalent to sixty-two solar years. R.J., A.M., give the length of his life as sixty-three years, but he was born in Ṣafar 1168 (K.B., p. 4). 'Umar b. Bukhari (*Tanbīh al-ikhwān*) gives the date of the Shaikh's death as 1231.

Part II:

The Maintenance of Dār al-Islām in Sokoto, 1817–1903: 1232–1320

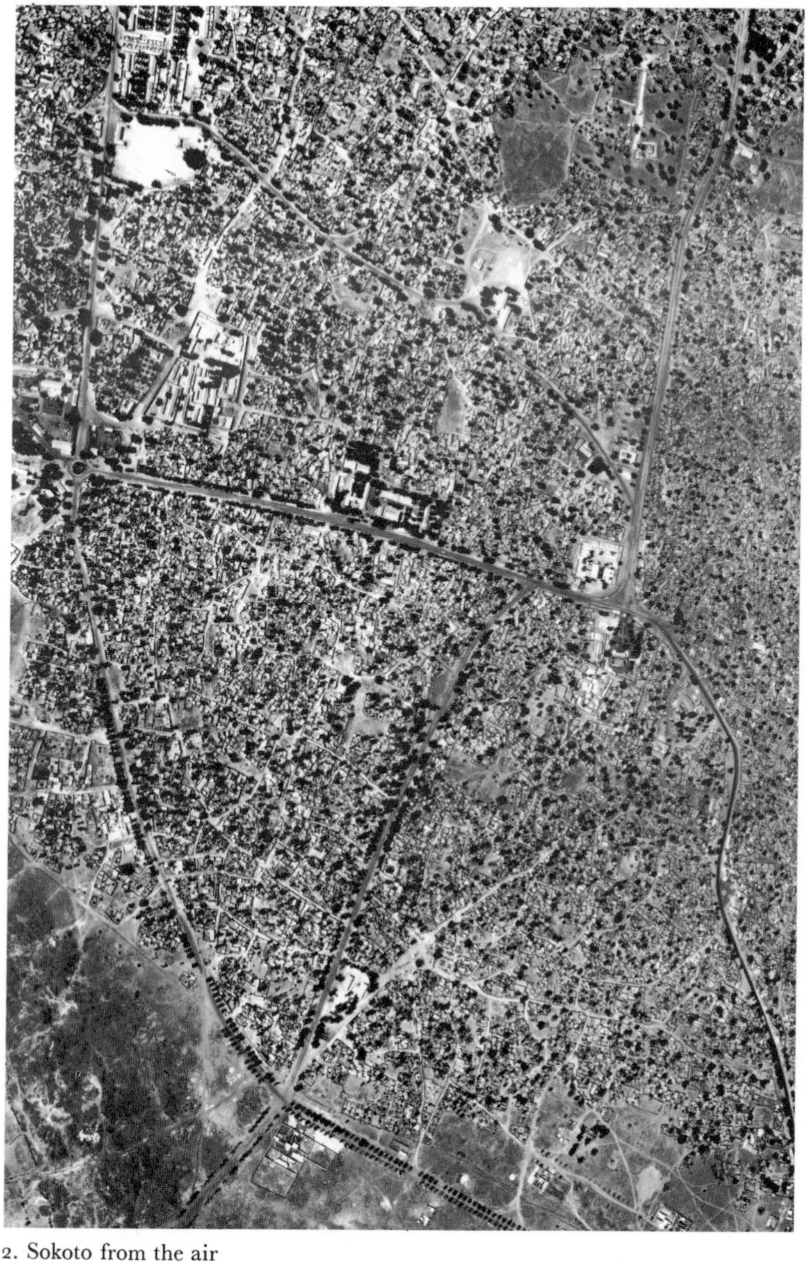

2. Sokoto from the air

3. Inside Sokoto town

4. Inside Wurno town

4
The Consolidation of the Caliphate (1817–1859: 1232–1276)

(i) *The Caliphate of Muḥammad Bello (1817–37: 1232–53)*

Although the jihād was not ended—war continued so long as there was opposition—the caliphate of Muḥammad Bello was a period of consolidation and establishment.[1] The hegemony of Sokoto stretched from Masina to Baghirmi—a four months' journey—and from Yorubaland to the ends of Adar and Agades—a good two months from south to north.[2] The Emirs who had been loyal to the Shaikh remained loyal: they were ruling Communities with enough momentum to continue without aid from Sokoto, as without aid they had started. The history of these emirates is their own, not that of Sokoto: although, as M. G. Smith's studies on Zaria show, Sokoto exercised an increasing influence over appointments in the emirate, daily life both in the capital and the countryside was largely unaffected by Sokoto.[3] I therefore confine myself to the hinterland of Sokoto itself as a self-contained unit, and only touch on the emirates as they shed light on the vizierate in Sokoto.[4]

---

[1] The opposition consisted of pagans (kuffār), apostates (murtaddūn) and Muslims: these last included those failing to recognise an Imam (muhammalūn), outlaws (muḥāribūn) and 'robber barons' (bughāt). Cf. 'Uthmān b. Fodiye, *Sirāj al-ikhwān*, chs. 6, 7; Bivar, *op. cit.*, *J.A.H.*, II, 2, 1961, p. 242. Some of these terms are later used by Abū Bakr Atiku in his letter to the Tuareg ('Abd al-Qādir b. Gidado, *Majmū'*). I am indebted to M. A. al-Hajj for discussions on this point.

[2] The times are given in Sa'īd, f. 111a.

[3] M. G. Smith, *Government in Zazzau* (Oxford, 1960), pp. 74 ff.

[4] Gwandu, although within the hinterland of Sokoto, is excluded

When the Shaikh died, one of his two Viziers, 'Abdullāh, the Shaikh's younger brother and senior Vizier, or Muḥammad Bello, the second-eldest surviving son, was certain to take over the leadership of the Faithful. The Shaikh may have nominated his successor. But while death-bed advice is quoted by al-ḥājj Sa'īd and in tradition recorded by Hampate Ba, none is found in Sokoto literature.[5] 'Abdullāh is said to have hoped for the caliphate and come to Sokoto from Bodinga and found the gates closed.[6] Three weeks later he completed a short book on succession to the imamate, in which he puts forward by implication his claim; but there can have been little doubt about the succession.[7] Bello was in Sokoto, where the Shaikh had lived out his days, his family with him; and Sokoto, as the administrative headquarters for

---

because, having its own subordinate emirates, it formed a semi-independent unit within the caliphate.

[5] Sa'īd, *loc. cit.*; Hampate Ba, *L'Empire Peul du Macina*, p. 242. Al-ḥājj Sa'īd not only reports the Shaikh giving advice to Bello on how to treat the Fulani but also mentions a letter (wathīqa) from the Shaikh on Bello's appointment (p. 189). Sa'īd (p. 198) later quotes the Vizier implying the Shaikh appointed Bello, and Sa'd b. 'Abd al-Raḥmān (*op. cit.*) mentions a will of the Shaikh being produced some two years later at Kalembaina. Clapperton (2nd journey, p. 215) also mentions a will appointing Bello, but elsewhere (e.g. 1st journey, p. 98; 2nd journey, p. 206, on Atiku's bid for the caliphate) implies the will was not used to decide the succession: similarly the silence in the other Sokoto histories and oral tradition (cf. T.W., Introduction, p. 20) might suggest that the will was either an embarrassment or a local rumour.

[6] Burdon, *op. cit.*, p. 68 (followed by M. Hiskett in T.W., Introduction, p. 17); the story is denied in Birnin Kebbi now. The Vizier Bukhari in a note to the translation of *Ta'nīs al-ikhwān* (p. 5, n. 4) is reported as saying that 'Abdullāh was at Gwandu, and that Bello was elected at the insistence of the Sokoto people before 'Abdullāh reached Sokoto; 'Abdullāh then acknowledged Bello as Caliph and returned to Gwandu. However, Sa'd b. 'Abd al-Raḥmān (followed probably by the Alkalin Gwandu in his *History* (translated by McAllister, para. 39) and the Bodinga District notebook) and Sa'īd (p. 190) both mention 'Abdullāh's later move from Bodinga and imply 'Abdullāh was there at the Shaikh's death.

[7] *Sabīl al-salāma fī'l-imāma.* (Mr. John Paden kindly showed me the copy he borrowed from M. Aminu Kano.) Some ten weeks after *Sabīl al-salāma*, Muḥammad Bello put forward, in his *al-Inṣāf fī dhikr mā fī masā'il al-khilāfa*, the claims of the son, as opposed to the brother, to inherit: again, there were no explicit references to the present.

the east, and with the east comprising several established emirates, was clearly the dynamic centre of the caliphate. ʻAbdullāh, who was a scholar and poet of distinction, had been somewhat reclusive since his dissatisfaction with the trends in the Muslim Community had resulted in his leaving for Kano in 1807.[8] Friction between ʻAbdullāh and Bello had evidently been incipient when the Shaikh was at Gwandu, and it had worsened during the last three years when the Shaikh lived at Sifawa and ʻAbdullāh at Bodinga.[9] Lists of those at Gwandu given by al-haji Junaidu suggest that many of the older generation stayed with ʻAbdullāh, while the younger men stayed in Sokoto with Muḥammad Bello.[10]

The bid of Abū Bakr Atiku, Bello's younger brother, for the caliphate is scarcely credible as narrated by Clapperton: Atiku was unpopular and the story is probably exaggerated.[11] Three years younger than Bello and off the centre of the stage, he seems to have been an embittered man. Given only a share of the south together with Muḥammad Bukhari, he was, like his uncle ʻAbdullāh, somewhat reclusive, but without ʻAbdullāh's immense learning. It is possible his movements were restricted after his bid for the caliphate, as Clapperton suggests:[12] his talents were not used, except on expeditions, till the end of Bello's rule, when he was sent to Bakura.[13] The only other rival for the caliphate was ʻAbd al-Salām, some of whose followers recognised him as Amīr al-mu'minīn.[14] However, when called upon to give his recognition of Bello, he went to Sokoto and did so, only to rebel later that year.

---

[8] T.W., pp. 70 f.

[9] (Anon), MS. on the secrets of the Shaikh, quoted also in ʻAbd al-Qādir b. Muḥammad Bukhari b. Aḥmad, *Tabshīr al-ikhwān.*

[10] *Kitāb Saʻd ʻalā ḥurūf abjad* (1380/1961).

[11] Clapperton (1st journey), p. 98; cf. Clapperton (2nd journey), p. 206. A short poem by Muḥammad Bukhari b. al-Shaikh, on Atiku seeking 'mulk', may refer to this incident (manuscript in Shahuci School, Kano).

[12] Clapperton (2nd journey), p. 206.

[13] Letter of Muḥammad Bello to Abū Bakr Atiku in ʻAbd al-Qādir b. Gidado, *Majmūʻ*. He may have had responsibility for Sabon Birni, the new part of Sokoto town in which his, and the Shaikh's, house stood.

[14] *Sard al-kalām*, p. 4.

The election of Bello seems to have gone smoothly. After recognition was given him by the leading Sokoto men, he moved to the house of Sambo b. Ashafa where others from outside the town came to salute him or sent their messengers.[15] Bello did not move into his father's house on taking office: his elder brother, Muḥammad Sambo, lived there, as did his younger brothers and his father's widows. His own house in the old town, instead, became the caliphal palace, and was used as such by Bello's descendants.

Although Bello had become Caliph without any violence, the Community was no longer as cohesive as it had been. Those of the Fulani who had come to provide the military support had different motives from those of the early Community. 'Abdullāh accuses the new Community of being composed of men 'whose purpose is the ruling of countries and their people, in order to obtain delights and acquire rank, according to the custom of the unbelievers, and the titles of their sovereignty. And the appointing of ignorant persons to the highest offices, and the collecting of concubines, and fine clothes and horses that gallop in the towns, not on the battlefields, and the devouring of gifts of sanctity, and booty and bribery, and lutes, and flutes, and the beating of drums. Their activities weaken those charged with managing affairs. And the country people make off from every side; their purpose is fleeing from the judge, the breaking of faith, and the befriending of the unbelievers for fear of the outcome. They were many, but their righteous men were few; they showed the dissimulation of wicked people, the people of the squadrons and of the sellers of free men in the market. Some of them are posing as qāḍīs (judges), in the clothing of foxes!'[16] This is not the charge of one embittered man: the Shaikh also complained of the lawlessness of his followers, and Bello

---

[15] Gidado, K.B., p. 9; Sa'īd, p. 189. Sa'īd says Bello went to the house of (Abū Bakr?) dan Jada. The first to salute Bello was his elder brother, Muḥammad Sambo (D.M., f. 34).

[16] T.W., pp. 121–2; the translation is by M. Hiskett. Muḥammad Jailani, the Tuareg leader, also complained to Bello about a case of injustice: *v.* Bello's reply in 'Abd al-Qādir b. Gidado, *Majmū'*.

joined in the criticism.[17] The brunt of the lawlessness, however, was borne by the Hausa who had submitted to the Shaikh, the dhimmīs.[18] Oral tradition of the injustice of the military persists: for example, there is a story of how 'Alī Jedo killed a man from Kebbi who was bold enough to enter the house of 'Alī Jedo and demand the return of a borrowed horse; for this, the Shaikh is said to have refused to see 'Alī Jedo again.[19] The hostility against the Fulani was such that when after the Shaikh's death 'Abd al-Salām rebelled, the rebels, comprising both Muslims and dhimmīs, attacked the neighbouring Fulani and raided their cattle-camps.[20] On another occasion, 'Abd al-Salām released some prisoners passing by his town: it was reminiscent of the beginning of the Shaikh's jihād, but this time the prisoners were Hausa, dhimmīs who had revolted, and the captors were Muslims; 'Abd al-Salām, who was a Hausa-speaking Arewa, identified himself with the rebels.[21] Another Hausa aspect of the revolt was the word used both as the common term for the rebels and as their battle-cry: the Hausa 'tawaye', 'rebellion', is found both in books written by Bello in Arabic and in the journals of Clapperton to describe the revolt.[22]

Although this rebellion did not break out before the Shaikh died, the situation was probably known to be precarious.

---

[17] 'Uthmān b. Fodiye, *Naṣīḥat ahl al-zamān*; Muḥammad Bello, *Sard al-kalām* (p. 5), and the letter to Muḥammad Jailani (dated December 1820) in 'Abd al-Qādir b. Gidado, *Majmū'*. Cf. Sa'īd, p. 191, where Bello's troops refuse to divide the booty legally.

[18] A dhimmī classically is one of the people of the Book; i.e. a Jew, a Christian or a Magian. Here it applies to peoples who submitted to the Sokoto Caliph, yet retained their identity and customs. These would include pagans, one Hausa term for whom is Maguzawa (sing: ba-Maguje), derived from 'majūs', 'a magian'. For the use of 'majūs' for the Zamfarawa, cf. Muḥammad Tukur b. Muḥammad, *Qirā al-aḥibbā'* (written in 1809).

[19] Told to me by M. Abbas Yahaya in Sokoto.

[20] *Sard al-kalām*, pp. 4, 11; cf. K.B., p. 10.

[21] *Sard al-kalām*, pp. 5, 10.

[22] e.g. Muḥammad Bello, *al-Qaul al-mauhūb* (Ibadan MS. 120), p. 2; *Sard al-kalām*, p. 11; Sa'īd, p. 189; Clapperton (2nd journey), pp. 150, 154.

'Abd al-Salām had been restive while the Shaikh was alive: as an early follower of the Shaikh, he had been entrusted with seven villages, including Sabuyel (near Gwandu) where he was under the supervision of 'Abdullāh. Dissatisfied with his share, 'Abd al-Salām made contact with dhimmīs, presumably Kebbawa and his own Arewa, with the intention of starting a revolt. However, he was transferred to Sokoto where he could be watched by Bello, and here he was allowed to build a walled town, near by at Kware.[23] Peace was then kept till the Shaikh died, but thereafter the inevitable revolts began.

The Zamfarawa under the leadership of the Banaga had never been reconciled to the Muslims at Sokoto. They had been successful in preventing further settlement in the area of the upper Sokoto and Rima rivers, where Malam Ashafa and his son Muḥammad Sambo, with their followers from the old town of Yandoto, had been trying to establish a town.[24] Further, shortly before the Shaikh died, the Banaga had made a raid in Zamfara.[25] Therefore as soon as recognition had been paid him as Caliph, Bello led an expedition into Zamfara. There, the Burmawa at Bakura had joined the Banaga, and together they surprised Bello's army and defeated it.[26] The reverse made 'Abd al-Salām reopen trade and negotiations with the dhimmīs, and his town of Kware became a centre of the disaffected, who now came in large numbers.[27] Though pressed by Bello to desist from harming the cause of Islam, 'Abd al-Salām called in the Emir of Konni, the Emir of the largest town to the north; Bello, however, managed to depose the Emir and replace him with the Emir's brother who was loyal to Bello.[28] 'Abd al-Salām also opened communications with the Zamfarawa of Sarkin Tleta (Mafara) and the Banaga, but these links were harder for Bello to break. Instead, he offered 'Abd al-Salām a free pass

---

[23] *Sard al-kalām*, pp. 3, 4.

[24] Gusau District notebook. Cf. K. Krieger, *Geschichte von Zamfara* (Berlin, 1959), pp. 84 ff. Muḥammad Sambo was presumably in Sokoto at the time of the Shaikh's death: K.B., p. 9.

[25] R.A., f. 10b.

[26] R.A., f. 11; Sa'īd, p. 190.

[27] *Sard al-kalām*, p. 4.

[28] *Sard al-kalām*, pp. 9, 11.

to anywhere he wished, but 'Abd al-Salām refused to emigrate.[29] 'Abd al-Salām, whose force outnumbered Bello's, continued the fight near Sokoto: Namoda then joined the fighting, which continued till January with 'Alī Jedo, in whose area 'Abd al-Salām's town of Kware lay, as commander.[30] Finally, cut off from his followers and tired of fighting and the public pressure against him, 'Abd al-Salām left Kware for Bakura in Zamfara, but having received an arrow wound in a skirmish he died three days later.[31] His son, Muḥammad Bukhari, who had tried to mediate in the quarrel, was given leave to go down to Jega, close to 'Abd al-Salām's old town of Gimbana and within the sphere of Gwandu.[32] The revolt emphasized the problem of sustaining the loyalty and enthusiasm of the Hausa element, whether Muslims or protected pagans, within the caliphate. With 'Abd al-Salām, the complaint was that he did not receive the large and rich fief he thought he deserved and that the Community had become corrupted by the world. While 'Abd al-Salām's dispute is put in purely Islamic terms, the motives of his Hausa supporters are not mentioned. But the hardship of the jihād and the austerity of the Law, together with the new status of the Fulani clan-leaders on whom Bello had been forced to rely for military support, must have helped to alienate the Hausa peasantry.

Though too late to help 'Abd al-Salām, further revolts broke out in Kebbi and Gobir in January 1818. Bello's

---

[29] *Sard al-kalām*, pp. 11, 12.

[30] Sa'īd, p. 189; *Sard al-kalām*, p. 13. Sa'īd says a dan Jada (presumably a cousin of Namoda, if he is correct) was killed in a skirmish at this time. Abū Bakr dan Jada was killed later at Kiawa.

[31] *Sard al-kalām*, p. 13; Sa'īd, p. 190. Mid-January 1818.

[32] The road taken to Jega was kept open and marked by aguwa bushes as a reminder of the revolt. There are a number of Hausa gibes against 'Abd al-Salām still current: for example, 'an yi rabon kura; ka tafi Bakura, kura ta cinyaka da rana', '(you said) a hyena did the dividing; (well) you went to Bakura (and) a hyena took a bite of you in broad daylight'. 'Abd al-Salām's body was eaten by hyenas at Bakura. The first sentence refers to the 'hyena's share' which 'Abd al-Salām said was taken by the Shaikh's family in the division of territory after the jihād. The saying was told to me by M. Ibrahim Mukoshy in Sokoto.

brother Atiku and his cousin Modibo Muḥammad b. ʿAlī b. Fodiye were sent out against Kebbi, while Bello himself went later that year to Gobir: his cousin Modibo had just been forced to withdraw from the new settlement at Alkalawa.[33] At the same time, a town near Gwandu, Kalembaina, where some of ʿAbd al-Salām's followers had now congregated, threw off allegiance: it held out against ʿAbdullāh for some two years till the combined forces of Bello, Atiku, Muḥammad Bukhari b. al-Shaikh and ʿAbdullāh's son, Muḥammad, succeeded in capturing it.[34]

The capture of Kalembaina for ʿAbdullāh marked the reconciliation between nephew and uncle. ʿAbdullāh had moved to Gwandu permanently eight months after the Shaikh's death. Bodinga had proved too exposed to Sullebawa depredations and he gave the town over to his nephew, Abū Bakr, the son of his elder brother ʿAlī.[35] As leader of the western Emirs and as the senior Vizier, he had not recognized Gidado, who was one of Bello's companions, as the Vizier of the caliphate: after Kalembaina he gave his turban and gown to Gidado as token of his relinquishing office and recognising the new Vizier.[36]

The Gobirawa were still in revolt. Although harassed by Bello's yearly expeditions, they proved elusive, retreating farther from the main valleys, away from Sokoto. In the dry season 1820–1, they had been driven out of the Rima valley; Kadaye had been taken and their leader, Gwomki, killed.[37] But around another Gobir prince, ʿAlī b. Yaʿqūb, there formed a new nucleus of refugees who settled out of reach

---

[33] Tilho, II, 475.

[34] Saʿīd, pp. 193, 194; cf. Saʿd b. ʿAbd al-Raḥmān, *Tartīb al-aṣḥāb*. The leader in Kalembaina, Dan Baiwa, had been a student of ʿAbdullāh, which might partly account for the ideological difference between ʿAbdullāh and Bello over the treatment of rebels as pagans, to which M. Hiskett (T.W., Introduction, pp. 18–20) refers. From a poem by ʿAbdullāh on the capture of Kalembaina, the rebels seem to have been isolated from their allies; some refugees finally settled later near Sokoto.

[35] Saʿd b. ʿAbd al-Raḥmān, *Tartīb al-aṣḥāb*; Bodinga District notebook.

[36] Saʿd b. ʿAbd al-Raḥmān, *Tartīb al-aṣḥāb*. Cf. P. G. Harris, *Sokoto Provincial Gazetteer* (1939), p. 69.

[37] R.A., f. 11.

of Sokoto on the borders of Tuareg country.[38] From there, allied with the Tuareg leader, Ibra, and his Tamesgida, they raided Sokoto.[39] Bello counter-raided. On one occasion, Bello captured a large number of Tuaregs, Tegama according to Clapperton, and had them executed.[40] Bello continued raiding north till eventually the Gobirawa under 'Alī submitted; they were then allowed to settle at Gwongazo, near the old Gobir capital of Alkalawa, but a few years later they again rebelled and moved to Dakorawa, north-west of Konya.[41] Meanwhile, the Zamfara revolt of 1817 continued. Although Bello sent to the area his brother Atiku, 'Umar al-Kammu's son Mudegel, the Galadima Doshero and some of 'Alī Jedo's men, it was not till 1822–3 that the Zamfarawa were decisively beaten.[42]

The pattern of campaigns persisted: raids against Gobir to places like Konya or Dakorawa; against Zamfara to Anka in the Zamfara river valley and Mafara in the upper Sokoto valley; or against Kebbi. In all, Bello conducted forty-seven raids.[43] By the time of his death, opposition to the caliphate had been reduced: in Kebbi, *c.* 1830, the Kebbawa finally made a peace, which lasted till *c.* 1849;[44] in the battle of Gawakuke in Gobir in 1836, a combination of Tuareg, Gobirawa and Katsinawa from Maradi was beaten and the kings of the latter two were killed.[45] In Zamfara, a fort was established at Gandi under a son of Bello, Ibrāhīm, and Atiku

---

[38] R.A., ff. 11, 12: they were at Konya which Clapperton saw being besieged by Bello in 1826 (2nd journey, p. 186). It stood some thirty miles north-east of Alkalawa (near km. 605 of the Madaoua-Maradi road).

[39] K.B., p. 16.

[40] Clapperton (1st journey), p. 107. Cf. Barth, I, 354.

[41] Cf. Tilho, II, 475–6.

[42] Sa'īd, p. 193. Cf. R.A., f. 11b.

[43] K.B. (complete text); 'Abd al-Qādir b. Gidado, *Anīs al-mufīd* (A.M.), p. 28. Twelve of these raids were against Kebbi.

[44] K.B. (complete text); cf. D.M., fols. 50 ff.; Alkalin Gwandu, *History of Gwandu* (trans. McAllister), paras. 50 ff.

[45] K.B., p. 17; the date (1251) is given in a poem by Asmā' bint al-Shaikh. Sa'īd (p. 194) gives the day as Tuesday 11 Dhū'l-ḥijja: i.e. Tuesday 29 March 1836.

was left at Bakura to try to resettle the land after the chronic warfare.[46]

For the continuous campaigning which now seemed necessary, Bello introduced the cotton-padded armour ('lifidi') which was used by the Gobir armies to protect both horses and men against arrows.[47] At the start of the jihād it had been a point of pride that the Muslims fought without the elaborate gear of the Gobir army;[48] but the disasters at Tsuntsua and Alwassa showed how the scholars of the Community could be decimated in battle, and it was on the scholars that the tradition of Islamic learning in the Community depended. The prejudice against armour persisted in that it was usually slaves who wore the 'lifidi'; but freemen were often protected by chain-mail.[49] The infantry Clapperton estimated at nine-tenths of the army, and the army he accompanied at fifty to sixty thousand, giving a possible total of some five thousand cavalry.[50] Barth later calculated that Kano had five to seven thousand cavalry, and that Sokoto could call upon a total of over twenty thousand.[51] Barth never saw an army in action, and his estimates must be second-hand. Nonetheless, the Muslim army was larger than anything any pagan group could muster, and probably larger than the Bornu army.[52] However, it was not a standing force, like the Kanembu spearmen whom al-Kanemi used, and arms practice was never very popular in a society where prowess in fighting was of low prestige.[53]

---

[46] K.B. (complete text); A.M., p. 28; letter of Muḥammad Bello to Abū Bakr Atiku in 'Abd al-Qādir, *Majmū'*.

[47] Muḥammad Bukhari, *Ta'nīs al-ikhwān*. [48] Cf. T.W., pp. 56, 60.

[49] Cf. P. G. Harris, *op. cit.*, p. 272; Clapperton (2nd journey), p. 186. An exception is its use by the Vizier 'Abdullāh Bayero against Argungu early in the 1880's: it seems he had permission from the Amīr al-mu'minīn.

[50] Clapperton (2nd journey,) p. 186.

[51] Barth, IV, 155–6. He assesses Sokoto, Kebbi and Zamfara together at 5,000 horses.

[52] Denham, p. 149, where al-Kanemi has 8–9,000 Kanembu and about 5,000 Shuwa and Bornu men.

[53] *Idem*, pp. 165–6. Archery practice, however, was held frequently in Sokoto.

Muskets were for slaves or servants only. The army of the Amīr al-mu'minīn seems to have had scarcely a single musket, at least in the early jihād.[54] They were found in Kano and Zaria, as well as in Gobir; and, later, Gwandu received them via Nupe, while in Sokoto the Vizier and the Marafa both had followers armed with muskets.[55] Pistols were used by the Arabs living in Sokoto, and the Amīr al-mu'minīn had some given him as presents, but he may never have used them.[56] Still the most effective weapon was the bow, especially when the arrows were tipped with poison, a practice, however, theoretically illegal for Muslims.[57] Equally effective were the barbed spears, sometimes having three or more prongs, for which the Kebbawa were notorious. The musket, by comparison, was unreliable and subject to shortages of flint and powder; but even when out of order, it was a source of security.[58]

Tactics against the Gobirawa, Tuareg or Kebbawa were mainly defensive, to stop the raiding that penetrated the Sokoto hinterland. The threat of an approaching column was usually enough to turn back a raiding party laden with spoils. Occasionally, by error or clever strategy, as in the campaign of 'Alī at Kotorkoshi, a pitched battle took place, but a raiding party, at a disadvantage in numbers and terrain, would try to avoid it. When a band of Tuaregs sacked a town six days north of Sokoto, the main counter-measure taken by Bello had been an edict ordering all the Tuareg of the tribe implicated out of the area, an edict that could be

---

[54] Clapperton (2nd journey), p. 186. Bello wanted, however, to import firearms and rockets (Clapperton, 1st journey, pp. 93, 95, 105); cf. G. F. Lyon (*Travels*, 1821), p. 138.

[55] Cf. Correspondence, IV, 60; P. Staudinger, *Im Herzen der Haussa Länder* (Berlin, 1889), p. 364; cf. Barth, II, 139.

[56] e.g. Clapperton (2nd journey), pp. 188, 196; Barth, IV, 136.

[57] Since the effectiveness of archery lay more in poison than in its penetrating power, arrows in Sokoto were poisoned, despite the Sharī'a. Antidotes for the various local poisons used were known, but men also carried with them general antidotes, a common one being snake venom: cf. Muḥammad Tukur b. Muḥammad, *Qirā al-aḥibbā'*.

[58] Clapperton (2nd journey), p. 195; Staudinger, p. 364.

hard on herds pasturing in the dry season.[59] With Gobirawa, such a measure was of no effect. Instead, punitive expeditions, such as the autumn raid for which all the eastern Emirs were summoned, were aimed at the big towns in enemy hands.[60] Having full-scale armies with them, however, the Caliphs were not afraid of pitched battles. For example, Bello met the combined forces of the Gobirawa, the Katsinawa from Maradi and the Tuareg at Gawakuke in north Gobir, and won decisively.[61] More often than not, the campaign was as inconclusive as the siege of Konya seen by Clapperton.[62] The effect of that campaign was to devastate the surrounding countryside, confine the Gobirawa for a while and demonstrate the strength of Sokoto. Although a long siege which involved an encamped army was impossible due to a shortage of food, and a frontal assault was unlikely to succeed, campaigns, while inconclusive, were not ineffective.

The defence of the caliphate consequently remained a continuous preoccupation despite the frequent expeditions of the Amīr al-mu'minīn. The main threat continued to come from the Gobirawa. After their defeat at Gawakuke in 1836, when their Sultan ʻAlī was killed, they resettled under Mayaki b. Yaʻqūb at Tsibiri, over 50 miles east of Alkalawa on a tributary of the Rima river. From this base, over 125 miles from Sokoto, the Gobirawa launched attacks on Zamfara towns owing allegiance to Sokoto and abetted revolts against the caliphate.[63]

Against the raiding of the Gobirawa, and, to a lesser extent, of the Tuareg and Kebbawa, a policy derived from the history of the Muslim conquest of Persia, Syria and North Africa was adopted. Ribāṭs, walled towns on the frontiers which could serve as bases and rallying-centres against pagan invasions, were established or developed out of existing

---

[59] Clapperton (1st journey), p. 108. The time was late April (1824).

[60] Known as al-ghazw al-kharīfī, or yakin kaka, it was a regular event; letters telling the time and place of meeting were sent out beforehand, and progress reported.

[61] D.M., f. 41.

[62] Clapperton (2nd journey), p. 186.

[63] Barth, IV, 164; Tilho, II, 476.

villages. Although 'Abdullāh had stressed the importance of the ribāṭ in his section on the jihād in *Ḍiyā' al-ḥukkām* (bāb 4), and a pamphlet had been written in 1815 on the necessity of building walled towns (ḥuṣūn), the impetus for establishing ribāṭs seems to have come from Muḥammad Bello. The purpose of the ribāṭ was to close the frontier, and it was to be established where there was danger from unbelievers.[64] It was, therefore, the climax of his Gawakuke campaign in March 1836 to establish ribāṭs on the Gobir frontier at Lajinge, Shinaka and Kware, and later that year after the Zamfara campaign at Bakura and Gandi.[65]

Lajinge was the third attempt Bello made to settle a Gobir town loyal to Sokoto. The first attempt, at Kadaye, across the river from Lajinge, ended when its Sarki, Gwomki, rebelled after the death of the Shaikh.[66] The second attempt was made at Gwongazo, just east of Alkalawa, where Muḥammad b. 'Alī b. Fodiye had been established after the capture of Alkalawa, but had been forced to withdraw in the rebellion that followed the Shaikh's death.[67] The attempt at Gwongazo also ended when its Sarki, 'Alī, rebelled. It was therefore after 'Alī had been killed at Gawakuke that Lajinge was established under a son of Bello by Katembale, a wife of Yunfa captured at Alkalawa. The son, Fodio, was therefore about 26 years old when he was given charge of Lajinge. His duty as the 'āmil or deputy for the area was to close the frontier and protect the roads; to send out raids and night sorties and maintain spies; to establish justice and execute the Law; to avoid insulting, striking, imprisoning or, above all, killing anyone without due process of law; to guard against bribes, illegal taxes and lavish spending; instead, he was to welcome righteous men and listen to their advice, to receive travellers

[64] 'Abdullāh b. Fodiye, *Ḍiyā' al-ḥukkām* (bāb 4). The pamphlet on building towns has neither title nor its author's name: it may have been written by Muḥammad Bello (in N.A.K.: Sokprof 27:6); cf. 'Umar b. Bukhari, *Tanbīh al-ikhwān*.

[65] Two letters of Muḥammad Bello in 'Abd al-Qādir b. Gidado *Majmū'*; K.B. (complete copy); A.M., p. 28; D.M., f. 41.

[66] R.A., f. 11.

[67] Tilho, II, 475 f.

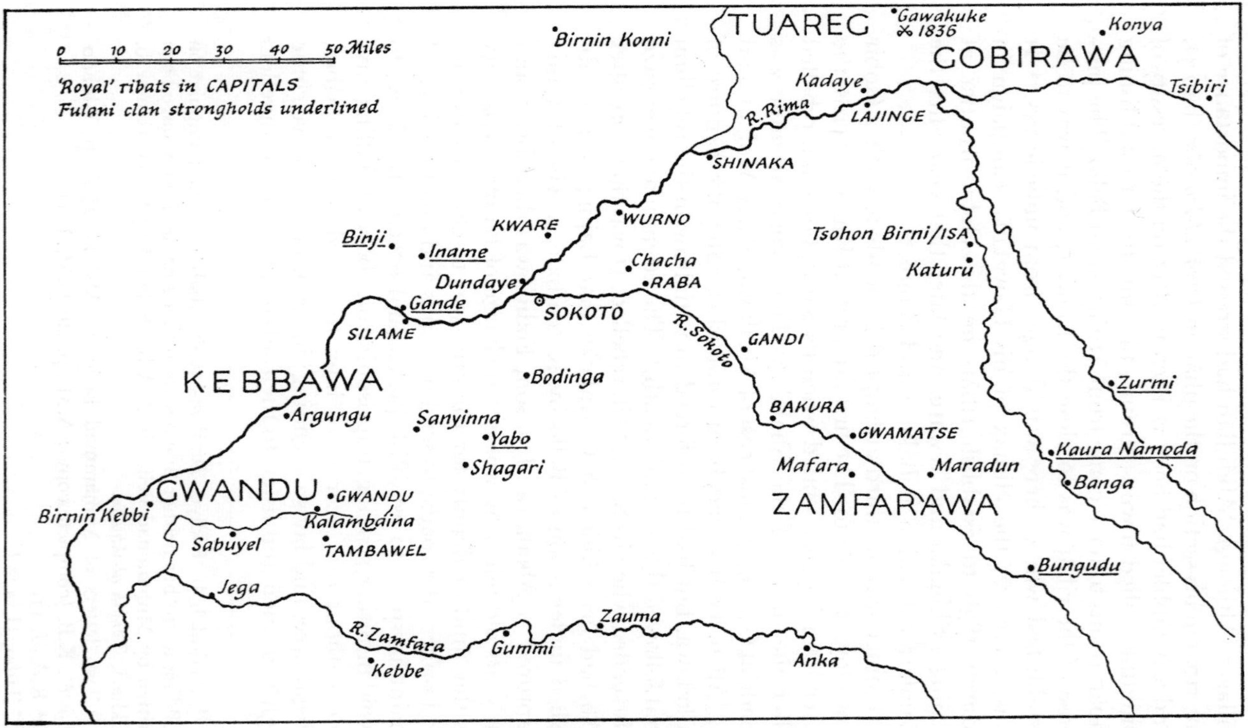

4. Ribāṭs, 1835–1845, in Sokoto

and help the poor. Finally, he had to obey the Caliph, and his people had to obey him, or he would be replaced; his only purpose was to help in maintaining Islam.[68] Fodio, however, did not live up to the standard expected of him, and he was forced by the Gobirawa to evacuate Lajinge.[69]

At Shinaka, Bello established his eldest son, 'Alī, who was about 29 at his appointment. To guide him, Bello wrote a book in which a ribāṭ and the duties of a murābiṭ are defined: for the definition Bello drew on classical authorities and the lessons of the early Muslim conquests described by them.[70] From Shinaka Bello moved farther downriver to Kware, where 'Abd al-Salām had built his walled town. There he left his youngest brother 'Īsa, then less than 20 years old, to rebuild the town and hold it as a ribāṭ against the Tuareg and Gobirawa.[71]

After the autumn raid that year (1836) against Zamfara, Bello established his son Ibrāhīm at Gandi and his brother Atiku in the old Burmi town of Bakura.[72] In a letter to Atiku, Bello told him to keep prepared with spies and all the equipment of war and to beware of the trickery and strife that would surround him as Emir; he was to ensure that the agreements with protected peoples (dhimmīs) were kept, and to restore prosperity to the town, if necessary by distributing land without all the legal formalities.[73] When Atiku left the following year to become Caliph, his sons Aḥmad and, later, Muḥammad took over the ribāṭ.[74]

The establishing of ribāṭs was an extension of Bello's own practice of living in fortified camps, first at Karindaye, then at Magaria and finally at Wurno where he had his own

---

[68] Two letters of Muḥammad Bello in 'Abd al-Qādir b. Gidado, *Majmū'*. Cf. letter of 'Alī (*ibid.*).

[69] Sa'īd, p. 203. Sa'īd confuses Lajinge and Yanshawara here, I believe; I have not found evidence for Fodio being in Yanshawara.

[70] Muḥammad Bello, *al-I'lām bi-mā yajib 'alā 'l-imām.*

[71] Kware District notebook.

[72] K.B. (complete copy); A.M., p. 28; D.M., f. 41.

[73] Letter of Muḥammad Bello in 'Abd al-Qādir b. Gidado, *Majmū'*. Another copy is in the collection of al-haji Junaidu.

[74] Sa'īd, pp. 204, 206. Bakura District notebook.

ribāṭ.[75] There, in sight of the frontier, he insisted he should die and be buried: in this again, he was consciously following a classical precedent.[76]

Of the other major ribāṭs, Silame had been established on the frontier against Kebbi, standing on a ridge where the river Rima runs in a narrow valley between high escarpments. Silame was first entrusted to Muḥammad Mudi (or Mo'i) b. Bello, but he proved disobedient and Atiku transferred the command to Aḥmad Rufa'i b. al-Shaikh, then aged about 25.[77] Aḥmad's mother was related to Waruwa, the important Fulani leader at Gande across the river from Silame: in the later revolt of Kebbi (*c.* 1849), when Silame was sacked, Aḥmad received assistance from his cousins at Gande.[78] Some twelve miles north of Gande, there was also the ribāṭ of Binji, where the sons of 'Alī Jedo were established; 'Alī Jedo himself remained in his old settlement of Iname, to the east of Binji.[79]

On the Gobir frontier, a ribāṭ had been started at Yanshawara, but it had later been evacuated: al-ḥājj Sa'īd mentions Fodio b. Bello, his full brother Mualedi b. Bello and Khalilu b. al-Ḥasan as occupying the ribāṭ, but he may be confusing it with Lajinge.[80] Under Amīr al-mu'minīn 'Alī b. Bello, however, the town of Yanshawara was rebuilt and given to Abū Bakr b. Bello, and later became known as Raba.[81] His cousin, Khalilu b. al-Ḥasan, was established near by at Marnona with the title of Sardauna, while Fodio b. Bello and his brother Mualedi were resettled on the Gobir frontier at the ribāṭ of Tsohon Birni, later Sansanen ('camp') Isa, on the upper reaches of the Rima river.[82] Here Fodio

---

[75] Magaria, Wurno, Karindaye are all on the eastern edge of the Rima valley, Magaria a short distance north-east of Wurno, Karindaye south-west of Wurno. Cf. Clapperton (2nd journey), pp. 192, 199, 200; Barth, IV, 162, 168 f.

[76] K.B. (complete copy). The precedent quoted is that of Abū Ayyūb al-Anṣārī.

[77] Sa'īd, p. 212; cf. Silame District notebook.

[78] Sa'īd, pp. 212, 213.

[79] Cf. Binji District notebook; Sa'īd, p. 199.

[80] Sa'īd, p. 203.

[81] Raba District notebook.

[82] Wurno District notebook; Isa District notebook.

5. Wazirin Sokoto

6. The original room of Asmā', daughter of the Shaikh and wife of the Vizier Gidado

died and the ribāṭ was given to 'Alī b. Bello, a younger brother of the Amīr al-mu'minīn 'Alī b. Bello; Mualedi remained as Dangaladima. Isa thus became the major outpost against the Gobirawa, and a key staging-point on the road to Katsina.[83]

Other ribāṭs were established against Zamfara and Gobir under the control of relatives of the Amīr al-mu'minīn: Katuru, south of Isa, and Gwamatse, east of Bakura, were both in the possession of the family of Atiku. In Gwamatse, at the time of its capture by the Gobirawa, there were said to be over thirty descendants of the Shaikh, but ribāṭs like Gandi or Chancha, which had been given to Khiḍr, a son of the Amīr al-mu'minīn 'Alī, were largely manned by slaves belonging to the major families or to the state.[84]

In the south-east and south there were no major ribāṭs. The towns of Gwandu, under the descendants of 'Abdullāh b. Fodiye, and Tambawel, under the family of Muḥammad Bukhari b. al-Shaikh, were the main strongholds, having subsidiary towns ruled over by members of the family. Similarly, Yabo, the centre of the Kebbi Fulani leader, Moijo, covered the south-eastern approaches to Sokoto which were occupied by the Sullebawa camps, the towns of Bodinga, Sifawa, Shagari, Kasarawa and other settlements founded when the Shaikh was living at Sifawa. Almost every frontier village, however, could qualify as a ribāṭ; but the status of its resident ruler determined the importance of the ribāṭ, partly on account of the following he could command. Some villages, fully walled and strategically placed, were important in the defence of Sokoto. Thus Sanyinna acted as both a staging-point on the route to Gwandu and a listening-post for attacks from Argungu; similarly, Tozo and Gande, near Silame, acted as supporting strongholds against the Kebbawa.[85]

The establishment of ribāṭs was a part of the policy of

---

[83] Barth, IV, 128 ff.; Maradun District notebook.

[84] Sa'īd, pp. 209, 210.

[85] Barth, IV, 193. Sanyinna was held by Fulani from Katsina.

stabilising the frontiers and providing strongholds round which settlement could flourish despite the raids of the Kebbawa, the Tuareg, the Gobirawa and their allies in Zamfara. Likewise Bello encouraged the building within the frontiers of walled towns where mosques and schools could be opened and trade and workshops started: with scholars appointed to these towns as Imams, judges, muḥtasibs (legal inspectors) and teachers, Bello hoped to maintain both the practice of Islam and the military control of the area.[86] Since much of Bello's support had come from cattle-owning Fulani, the Fulani clans were persuaded to join the Community of the Shaikh and accept men to teach their children Islamic practice and behaviour. They were also taught agriculture and encouraged to breed horses, camels and flocks of sheep and goats and to reduce their herds of cattle.[87] By these means, Bello balanced the economy of Sokoto, and the two groups, nomad and peasant, were able to live side by side to mutual advantage; he thus also reduced the military risk involved in the annual exodus for some two months by the cattle Fulani, a practice he could not abolish.

By the time of Bello's death, therefore, the revolts of 1817 and 1818 had been crushed and the frontiers of the caliphate pushed forward and consolidated: frontier towns were placed under the control of members of the family of the Amīr al-mu'minīn; and, within the strongly-held frontier, the hinterland of Sokoto was stabilised by social policies aimed at settling the cattle Fulani in villages. Bello derived the inspiration for these policies from the history and the textbooks of the Arab conquest. He was therefore sure of their success and the rightness of enforcing them. Undoubtedly the sanction given by the Arabic authorities which Bello so often quoted helped to win acceptance for his policies and to generate enthusiasm for the dangerous life in the ribāṭs. Without the cohesion and purpose thus given by Islam, it is doubtful if the Sokoto caliphate would have survived.

---

[86] Muḥammad Bello, *Jawāb shāfi wa-khiṭāb minnā kāfili-Muḥammad al-Jailānī.*

[87] *Ibid.*

(ii) *The Caliphates of Abū Bakr Atiku and 'Alī b. Bello* (*1837–59: 1253–76*)

Muḥammad Bello died after a seven months' illness on 26 October 1837 at the age of 56.[88] He had refused to name any successor, but there was no dispute when Abū Bakr Atiku, a full brother of Muḥammad Bello, was given the appointment in preference to Muḥammad Bukhari, some three years his junior.[89] He was about 54 years old and the most senior of the princes both by age and rank. Although noted for his courage and piety, he was a difficult man, antagonising those who had worked under Bello.[90] He was undistinguished by comparison with his brothers: Bello, a scholar and leader; Sambo, a mystic; 'Abd al-Qādir, a martyr; Bukhari, a poet of distinction.[91] Some of his sisters, too, were famous; 'Ā'isha for her sufism, Asmā' for her learning and poetry.[92] Abū Bakr Atiku claimed one distinction, that the Shaikh had told him 115 secrets. Of these, a hundred died with Atiku: the fifteen that survive are told in a curious manuscript that may, however, prove a forgery.[93]

His rule was not free from trouble: there was a Mahdist movement that alarmed Gwandu, there were the Tuareg crises and the inevitable revolts of Zamfara and Gobir.[94]

---

[88] K.B., p. 24; cf. Sa'īd, p. 198. The day of his death was Thursday; therefore the equivalent of 25 Rajab is 26, not 25 October. Bello was born in October–November 1781 (Dhū'l-qa'da 1195): K.B., p. 4.

[89] K.B., p. 24; Sa'īd, pp. 198–200. In K.B., the claims of kinship in inheritance are stressed; two years earlier Bello had discussed some problems of succession in his *Ifādat al-ikhwān*. Muḥammad Bukhari is said not to have reached Sokoto, and did not contest the election.

[90] Clapperton (1st journey), pp. 102–3; Sa'īd, p. 208.

[91] 'Abd al-Qādir b. al-Muṣṭafā, *Salwat al-aḥzān*; A.M., pp. 28, 31 f.; cf. Sa'īd (p. 195), where 'Abd al-Qādir is said by Bello to have been the principal martyr of the people of Shaikh 'Uthmān. For Bukhari, see his fourteen qaṣā'id in a manuscript in the Shahuci School Library, Kano.

[92] 'Ā'isha: cf. 'Abd al-Qādir b. al-Muṣṭafā, *loc. cit.*: Asmā', *v. infra*.

[93] A copy is in the Shahuci School Library. The secrets are also told in 'Abd al-Qādir b. Muḥammad Bukhari b. Aḥmad, *Tabshīr al-ikhwān*.

[94] See the letters of Abū Bakr Atiku to the people of Gwandu and to M. Adama (enquiring about the state of the road to the Nile). False alarms about the appearance of the Mahdi were endemic in Sokoto

Elected about 1 November 1837, he took out an expedition that dry season up the Sokoto river to Damre and Burmi to quell the Zamfarawa.[95] The following year (1838–9), he went out against the pagan Katsinawa with his cousin Khalilu b. 'Abdullāh from Gwandu. For the next campaign, he sent out Abū'l-Ḥasan, the son of the Commander of the Army 'Alī Jedo, towards Zurmi, and followed this with a combined expedition which the eastern Emirs joined, advancing up from Zurmi towards Tsibiri to fight an alliance of Gobirawa, Katsinawa, Tuaregs and a Bornu contingent (probably from Damagaram). The following year he went, again with Khalilu b. 'Abdullāh, south to the Zamfara river against Gummi and Zauma. Finally, in the autumn of 1842, during the months of Sha'bān and Ramaḍān, he led a combined attack on Tsibiri. All the eastern Emirs were present, except Ya'qūb of Bauchi, who was now old and sent his son Ibrāhīm in his place. In the battle, Atiku was wounded, and, being weak from an earlier illness and from the effects of the fast, died on the road back, at Katuru.[96] It is said that he had prayed to die: his councillors had found it difficult to serve under him and his campaigns had been unsuccessful. He seems to have been a very religious man, and most conscious of the obligations of the jihād: he campaigned annually, going on despite the illness before his last expedition, and he is said to have always had his weapons with him. Clapperton, who met him thirteen years before his accession, reported that he was acknowledged to be extremely brave, though avaricious and cruel.[97]

His yearly campaigns, four of which were directed against Tsibiri or Maradi, reflect the strength of Gobir under their

---

throughout the century, especially in times of trouble: it was the signal to emigrate east. For the Tuareg crises, see three letters of Abū Bakr Atiku in 'Abd al-Qādir b. Gidado, *Majmū'* (filmed also in Antiquities Dept., Jos).

[95] 'Umar b. Bukhari b. al-Shaikh, *Tanbīh al-ikhwān*, from which the details of the following campaigns derive.

[96] 'Umar b. Bukhari, *op. cit.*

[97] Sa'īd, pp. 205 f.; Clapperton (1st journey), p. 102. Al-ḥājj Sa'īd describes him most favourably: age and the caliphate may have mellowed him since Clapperton's visit.

new Sultan, Mayaki. Atiku was trying to prevent the re-establishment of independent Gobirawa on the borders of Sokoto, but proved unable to do so. Instead, Mayaki was taking the offensive, in conjunction with the Maradi Katsinawa and Tuareg, and continued to raid into Sokoto for the next twenty years.

The death of Abū Bakr Atiku on campaign caused a problem.[98] The army needed an Amīr al-mu'minīn since it was still in dangerous territory, but neither the Vizier nor the Amīr al-jaish (Commander of the Army) were present, having sent their sons instead with the expedition.[99] The leading candidates available were the Shaikh's son, Aḥmad Rufaʿi, Bello's son, ʿAlī the elder, and Atiku's son, Aḥmad, the eldest of these being Aḥmad, the youngest Aḥmad Rufaʿi.[100] It seems that Modibo b. ʿAlī (the Shaikh's nephew) and Malam al-Muṣṭafā (a son-in-law of the Shaikh) encouraged some of the expedition to recognise Aḥmad Rufaʿi, who, as the son of the Shaikh, was more 'in line' than the Shaikh's grandsons Aḥmad or ʿAlī. In Sokoto, the Imam Abū Bakr and the Amīr al-jaish ʿAlī Jedo were also in favour of Aḥmad Rufaʿi, while the Vizier was probably in favour of ʿAlī b. Bello. When ʿAlī Jedo came round to supporting ʿAlī (because, according to al-ḥājj Saʿīd, his sons feared the ambitions of the maternal relations of Aḥmad Rufaʿi, the neighbours of ʿAlī Jedo to the south), the Emir of Gwandu Khalilu b. ʿAbdullāh was told by the Vizier that ʿAlī was acceptable in Sokoto.[101] Modibo

---

[98] Late November 1842 (ʿAlī b. Abī Bakr, *Majmūʿ al-khulafā'*; Bukhari b. Aḥmad, *Ta'nīs al-ikhwān*; ʿAbd al-Qādir b. Bukhari, *Tabshīr al-ikhwān*; D.M., f. 46b).

[99] Saʿīd, p. 207; D.M., f. 4b. The accession is described by al-ḥājj Saʿīd, *ibid.*, pp. 207–8. No will was left by Abū Bakr Atiku, but al-ḥājj Saʿīd (p. 205) reports Atiku told his son Aḥmad not to compete for the caliphate.

[100] Muḥammad Bukhari b. al-Shaikh had died in 1840 (A.M., p. 18; Saʿīd, p. 206).

[101] According to ʿUmar b. Bukhari (*Tanbīh al-ikhwān*), Khalilu told the Sokoto electors to choose a Caliph from among the sons of Caliphs, and then he paid homage to the one chosen; cf. al-haji Junaidu, *Tarihin Fulani*, p. 33 (the passage is omitted in D.M.). Al-ḥājj Saʿīd implies Khalilu had hoped for the appointment but was warned off (p. 207).

b. 'Alī and Khalilu were the most senior members of the family, both being nephews of the Shaikh: for this reason Khalilu, who had been Emir of Gwandu for the last seven years, was asked to give his choice second after Modibo b. 'Alī.

'Alī b. Bello had been born of a concubine mother (called Ladi) while Bello was at Sala *c.* 1223 A.H. (*c.* A.D. 1808) and the Shaikh at Gwandu.[102] He presumably fought with his father on the campaigns, but after the battle of Gawakuke (1836) was left in charge of the ribāṭ of Shinaka. Later, he moved down to Wurno, when the Amīr al-mu'minīn was resident in Sokoto, and was given the title his father had held, Amīr al-Sūdān. He seems to have had the support of the younger men, like 'Abd al-Qādir b. Gidado and Abū'l-Ḥasan b. 'Alī Jedo, and before his appointment was clearly a powerful figure.[103] He was himself about 34 years old at his election to the caliphate, though, with the exception of Aḥmad b. Atiku, the eldest of the Shaikh's male descendants. Nonetheless his youth caused him embarrassment: it proved difficult to work with men some twenty years his senior, who had served the Shaikh and Muḥammad Bello since before the jihād. The Vizier in particular, whom 'Alī treated almost as a father, was in an awkward position and soon after 'Alī's accession a crisis over his responsibilities made the Vizier give over his work to his son. Likewise, 'Alī Jedo left the command of the army to his sons, while Aḥmad, the son of Galadima Doshero, deputised for his father.

Khalilu b. 'Abdullāh may also have resented the youth of his superior. A few years after 'Alī's appointment, when the news reached him of a Gobir raid, Khalilu marched into Sokoto territory without asking or seeing 'Alī. When 'Alī summoned him to Wurno, 'Umar b. Bukhari, who was admittedly biased towards Khalilu, reports Khalilu as telling 'all his sons' in Wurno to repent, and then ordering the Amīr al-mu'minīn amongst other things to rebuild Sokoto town and the mosque.[104] Some four years after this (*c.* 1849), Ya'qūb

---

[102] Dogondaji District notebook. [103] Sa'īd, p. 201.

[104] 'Umar b. Bukhari, *Manāqib Shaikhinā Khalīl b. 'Abdullāh.*

Nabame, a son of the previous Sultan of Kebbi, who had been kept under the surveillance of Sokoto since the truce of *c.* 1830, was allowed to settle on the borders of Kebbi: soon after, he organised the Argungu resistance to Sokoto and terrorised the country around Gwandu.[105] 'Alī can hardly have failed to realise that the release of Nabame would result in renewed war; he may have thought the Sokoto-Gwandu forces were sufficient to quell any revolt. Whatever the motive, the renewed raiding by the Kebbawa cannot have improved relations between 'Alī and Khalilu. It was at this time that the traveller Barth passed through Gwandu, to find great insecurity there and the Emir, Khalilu, a recluse.[106] Prior to this, for the first twelve years, he had made or sent numerous expeditions to Yauri, Nupe, Borgu and Yorubaland, showing an activity that rivals that of Bello.[107]

'Alī was equally active as Amīr al-mu'minīn, conducting twenty campaigns in the course of the seventeen years of his caliphate.[108] The Gobirawa under Mayaki were now raiding into Burmi and central Zamfara, with the consequence that southern Zamfara was equivocal, largely depending on internal rivalries within the valley. Responsibility for the area still lay with the Atiku family. Aḥmad b. Atiku, who had been in Bakura till his father died, had moved up to Sokoto, leaving his brother Muḥammad Sambo in Bakura; another brother, 'Umar, was withdrawn from Katuru, where their

---

[105] Barth, IV, 165. Barth calls him Mademe, while D.M. (f. 51) and Sölken (*op. cit.*, p. 154) spell it Nabame. Another result of the Kebbawa revolt was the sack of Silame, the ribāṭ of Aḥmad Rufa'ib. al-Shaikh.

[106] Barth, IV, 197, 201; V, 328–9.

[107] 'Umar b. Muḥammad Bukhari, *Manāqib Shaikhinā Khalīl b. 'Abdullāh* and *Tanbīh al-ikhwān*. These contradict Barth (IV, 197), who thought Khalilu had always been a recluse. The book giving the details of Khalilu's campaigns was probably finished in 1850, thus giving rise to the assumption that he made no campaigns after the book was written. The assumption may, however, be true if Barth's statement is correct for the 1850's: the assumption is made by the Alkalin Gwandu in his *History of Gwandu* (trans. McAllister, 1909), para. 76.

[108] 'Abd al-Qādir b. Gidado, *Manāqib Amīr al-mu'minīn 'Alī*; D.M., f. 52b.

father was buried, and settled at Gwamatse.[109] 'Umar, however, overreached himself and had to be removed by Aḥmad and kept at Sokoto, while Muḥammad Sambo replaced 'Umar.[110] When Muḥammad Sambo sent some of his men to aid the Sarkin Tleta (Mafara), the Gobirawa under Mayaki raided and destroyed Gwamatse.[111] Aḥmad b. Atiku and his brother-in-law, the Ardon Sullebawa, went separately upriver to avenge their brother's defeat: the Ardo was himself defeated and killed near Gora, and Aḥmad was forced to evacuate temporarily the Burmi part of the valley.[112] Once the Gobirawa retired, the situation was retrieved, inevitably, since Burmi lies on the main route to the east. But the murābiṭūn were withdrawn from Bakura, which was now left under a local but loyal ruler, while the ribāṭ at Gwamatse was abandoned. Direct rule by a Sokoto nominee proved a mistake, and the practice of appointing a local ruler, usually adhered to in distinct ethnic areas, was applied here. The 'new' towns, the ribāṭs of Gandi and Raba, remained the strongholds on the upper river, populated largely by slaves or men of mixed ethnic groups.

Bello's closing of the extended frontier could not be maintained. Although 'Alī in his campaign of 1844 had forced the Gobirawa to accept the eastern bank of the upper Rima river as the frontier which they could cross only at their peril, it proved impossible to reduce Mayaki in Tsibiri.[113] He was reinforced, after *c.* 1844, by Ṣiddīq, the ex-Emir of Katsina,

---

[109] Muḥammad Sambo was therefore nicknamed 'Nabakura' and 'Umar 'Nagwamatse'. The Kontagora derivation is improbable (Duff, *Kontagora Gazetteer*, p. 8). Gwamatse is a fairly common place-name: 'Umar's Gwamatse was near Gora, in Zamfara. Cf. Barth, IV, 522–3; Staudinger (map); cf. Hogben and Kirk-Greene, *The Emirates of Northern Nigeria*, p. 500.

[110] More detailed, conflicting accounts are given by Sa'īd, p. 210, and Duff, *Kontagora Gazetteer*, pp. 8–9, *v. infra*, p. 158.

[111] Al-ḥājj Sa'īd says thirty descendants of the Shaikh were either killed or captured on the fall of Gwamatse (p. 210).

[112] The Ardo was probably Gagi b. Nagwanki. The acting Galadima, Abū Bakr b. Galadima Doshero, was also killed in this battle, which took place in mid-1851 (Barth, IV, 157).

[113] Letter from 'Alī in 'Abd al-Qādir b. Gidado, *Majmū'*.

who had been deposed by the Galadima on the instructions of Amīr al-mu'minīn 'Alī.[114] Ṣiddīq, while somewhat of an independent ruler, was also powerful and much respected; together with Mayaki, he led the campaign to Gora which resulted in the deaths of the Ardon Sullebawa and the acting Galadima in 1851.[115] 'Alī was confronted, therefore, with a revolt that included both Kebbi and Zamfara: to the west of Kebbi, Zaberma was also in revolt, while in eastern Zamfara, Kotorkoshi remained unsubdued and in the south Zauma and the other Zamfara river states had rebelled.[116]

It is a measure of the disunity in the pagan areas that there was no co-ordination against Sokoto or Gwandu: only the raids of Mayaki or Ṣiddīq aimed at abetting the revolt. Consequently, when Silame on the Kebbi frontier was sacked, one campaign retrieved the situation.[117] Though Silame was not rebuilt as a ribāṭ till over fifteen years later, and the Kebbi revolt continued, the immediate threat was gone. Similarly in Zamfara, after the withdrawal from the ribāṭs at Bakura and Gwamatse, an expedition in 1853 against Kotorkoshi regained much of the prestige previously lost.[118] The campaign, which Barth disparages, was effective: Kotorkoshi was a major pagan refuge, with, it is said, ninety-nine villages in its cluster of hills, and had been considered impregnable. 'Alī succeeded in taking it after surprising the Gobirawa by a fast march through waterless country. But both 'Alī and Khalilu, the Emir of Gwandu, had difficulty in raising troops for the jihād. 'Alī wrote a general letter to the Community rebuking those who shirked the jihād, and in another letter he praised those who held the ribāṭs and told them to stop the pagans

---

[114] Cf. Barth, IV, 93 f.; Sa'īd, p. 214. Ṣiddīq later seems to have been given hospitality in Sokoto at Gadodi.

[115] Barth, IV, 157. Cf. Edgar (notebook), *Labarin Kano*, pp. 2, 3.

[116] 'Abd al-Qādir b. Gidado, *Manāqib Amīr al-mu'minīn 'Alī*; Sa'īd, p 211; Barth, IV, 164–5.

[117] Sa'īd, pp. 212, 213.

[118] 'Abd al-Qādir b. Gidado, *Manāqib Amīr al-mu'minīn 'Alī*; D.M., fols. 51b, 52; Sa'īd, pp. 213, 214; Barth, IV, 183–4; cf. *ibid.*, p. 164.

from infiltrating by increasing the number of their raids and by joining in the major expeditions.[119]

A longer-term defensive measure was the building of a ribāṭ at Chimola, across the river from Wurno. Here, Aḥmad b. Atiku, having given up his family's responsibilities in Burmi and Zamfara, re-established a sphere of influence for the Atiku branch of the descendants of the Shaikh. Other measures were also being taken: defensive systems with elaborate entrances and cavalry traps were developed to prevent surprise attacks by cavalry:[120] so long as there remained food and water—a problem shared also by the besiegers—the defence could outlast attack. It was the impossibility both of defending the countryside against raids and of destroying the enemy bases that gave the appearance of insecurity which Barth in 1854 thought so remarkable.[121] But Clapperton, visiting Muḥammad Bello in 1824 and 1826, gives a comparable picture;[122] it seems that local insecurity of this kind was chronic.

Similar insecurity was found by Barth on the Bornu marches. There, in an emirate bounded for half its frontier by Bornu, Bukhari, a prince of the ruling house of Hadejia, threw off obedience to the Amīr al-mu'minīn.[123] He had the advantage of a swampy terrain in which he proved invincible; and he had the tacit support of Bornu rulers, who ever since the disastrous raid of 1827 had been trying to regain by more peaceful means the territory lost to the Sokoto emirates. Given these two advantages, Bukhari was able to resist any attempt to bring him to order and, consequently, to keep the surrounding area in great alarm. No other emirate joined him, and he remained independent, but isolated. On his death, the emirate again came under Sokoto leadership.

---

[119] 'Umar b. Bukhari, *Tanbīh al-ikhwān*; letters of 'Alī in 'Abd al-Qādir b. Gidado, *Majmū'*. But compare the letter of 'Alī (*ibid.*) rebuking the Emir of Zamfara (Zurmi) for killing Muslims in a campaign against Muniya.

[120] e.g. Barth, IV, 110, 112, 125, 222.

[121] e.g. Barth, IV, 163, 201; V, 328, 337.

[122] e.g. Clapperton (1st journey), pp. 79, 100, 107 ff., 113; (2nd journey), pp. 195, 226.

[123] *v. infra*, p. 159, for a more detailed account of this revolt.

As with the Kebbi raids in Sokoto, or the Ningi incursions into Kano and Zaria, the revolt of Bukhari did not endanger the hegemony of Sokoto. Bello had left the caliphate at its strongest; the major enemies, Kebbi, Gobir, the Tuareg, were all either subdued or at peace. 'Alī, therefore, was on the defensive, maintaining his father's conquests against a new, unbeaten generation of the enemy. But equally, the new generation of Muslims in the Community had accepted the authority of Sokoto as established; this is shown by the solidarity of the Community under the provocation of Bukhari in Hadejia, Ṣiddīq in Katsina, Mayaki in Gobir or Nabame in Kebbi.

5
The Composition of the Caliphate

(i) *Personnel*

Already when he was the Vizier in charge of the east, Muḥammad Bello had his own household officials. A precise division of responsibilities was probably not made: all are named in the lists as his servants.[1] Apart from the office of Vizier, which seems to have been created from the start, titles such as Magajin gari, Magajin rafi and Galadima did not imply specific jobs: they were names borrowed from Gobir usage.[2] 'Galadima' in Sokoto seems to have grown out of popular usage. The Fulani Doshero b. Mujakka, the first Galadima, had held the title in Alkalawa before the jihād, and the name remained with him in the Muslim Community. Being an important friend of the Shaikh and Muḥammad Bello, he received land and responsibilities which his family inherited with the title.[3]

The first holder of the title Magajin gari, on the other hand, was never in the hierarchy of Alkalawa. The office was of great importance in Gobir, and was probably granted by Muḥammad Bello in imitation. The first Magajin gari is traditionally said to have been Abū Bakr dan Jada (of the Alibawa family), but the earliest occurrence of the title, in

---

[1] Gidado dan Laima, *Majmū' aṣḥāb Amīr al-mu'minīn Muḥammad Bello.* The data that follow are drawn from this book.

[2] For Gobir titles, see the lists in Tilho, II, 480, 520; Perié (*I.F.A.N.*, 1939), p. 191.

[3] The estates were scattered; some, for example, were in Ubandoma and Gwadabawa Districts. See genealogy for his descendants.

Gidado's list of the companions of Bello, is associated with Muḥammad mai alashaf b. Abī Bakr dan Jada who later acted, it is said, as regent for his brother; the title is listed among the five personal servants (kḥuddām ḥaḍratihi) of Bello.[4] Abū Bakr dan Jada died in Zamfara early in Bello's caliphate and was followed by his brother Sulaimān: if Abū Bakr was the first Magajin gari, the title dates from immediately after Bello's accession.[5]

The title of Magajin rafi occurs only late in the century. Barth names the holder of the title in a list of offices, but does not add the title itself.[6] It occurs in the administrative correspondence *c.* 1878, and a reference is made to the Lamido rafi in 1868; the latter, however, probably refers to the Sarkin rafi, a title also found in Sokoto.[7] But it is possible that 'Magaji' and 'Sarki' were interchangeable. Sarkin rafi, but not Magajin rafi, is found in Gobir and Sabon Birni, while Maradi and Kebbi have neither.[8]

Other titles in Sokoto are drawn from Gobir, according to

---

[4] It is possible that Muḥammad mai alashaf was Magajin gari at the time of writing (? *c.* 1838). His brother Nadakura, who followed him as Magajin gari, is listed with him. *v.* Gumbi District notebook.

[5] The brothers Abū Bakr, Sulaimān and Yero (whose son was a Magajin gari) are all listed together as companions of Bello before the hijra. Abū Bakr is again listed as a Vizier and precedes Galadima Doshero. It is possible, but unlikely, that these titles were allowed while the Shaikh lived.

[6] Barth, IV, 155 n. He gives the name Modeggel, which was the nickname of 'Uthmān b. 'Umar who was already dead, according to al-ḥājj Sa'īd (p. 206). His brother, Muḥammad Autanjido, is said to have held the title at this time (Achida District notebook).

[7] Uncatalogued letter, Magajin rafi 'Abd (al-Raḥmān) b. Mudegel to Sultan Bauchi 'Uthmān b. Ibrāhīm. 'Uthmān b. Isḥāq, *al-Kashf wa'l-bayān* (qaṣīda in praise of Aḥmad Rufa'i).

[8] Tilho, II, 520; Perié, *op. cit.*, p. 390; Sölken, *op. cit.* (1959), pp. 144–150. The following list gives other titles used at some time in Sokoto which are also found in the lists of major Gobir and Sabon Birni titles in Tilho (II, 480, 520): Barazaki, Bunu, Dambawa, Dangaladima, Durumbu, Marafa, Sardauna, Sarkin Baura, Sarkin Bazai, Sarkin Tudu, Ubandawaki, Janzami. Other titles in Sokoto are Barade, Sarkin Galma, Shentali, Wombai, Yerima; some of these are probably derived from Gobir. The list is not complete. The modern titles Makama, Tafida, Turaki, were introduced in the twentieth century.

al-haji Junaidu. Few of the Kebbi titles listed by Sölken are found in Sokoto; similarly Perié lists a set of titles for Maradi which are not found either in Gobir or in Sokoto. Fulani titles are few, apart from the use of 'Lamido' for 'Sarki' or 'Amīr', or terms for clan heads, like Ardo or Dikko.[9]

Bello's own household was large and organised. For the stables there are some twenty names and titles, quite possibly of Hausa slaves since their titles are Hausa.[10] Nineteen eunuchs are also listed among Bello's servants. Many are said to have been taken captive at Alkalawa, but numbers dwindled, since castration, properly illegal in Islam, is said not to have been practised. Barth mentions a eunuch official in Gwandu in 1853, and as castration continued outside Sokoto, some must always have been available.[11] Amongst Bello's servants are listed five female slaves. An idea, however, of their status is given by one whom Clapperton met, the Iyargurma Fāṭima, who owned some forty slaves of her own and was a special messenger between the Amīr al-mu'minīn and the Vizier. She had been a messenger for the Sultan of Gobir Yunfa before her capture.[12]

Bello's public appointments included more than nine muezzins, one of whom was a Sharīf. Of the five imams, the most famous was his relative, Abū Bakr 'Malam', mentioned previously.

The eight scribes listed include the Sidi Shaikh whom Clapperton mentions as the 'fighi' (legal adviser) and doctor as well as secretary to the Caliph: he, too, was a foreigner, coming from Tuat, in the Algerian Sahara.[13] The court of

---

[9] One Fulani title in Sokoto is Lumo'o, meaning the man in charge of the market. Lamido Julbe is used for Amīr al-mu'minīn.

[10] The titles are: Maza sirdi, zagi, jan ruwa, dan kanwa, uban turki, wadātawa, barga, maidawa, shamaki (?), buzu dan barga, gurāgiru gudu, gudu, guragiru lumo, zāki, ubandawaki, sakata (?), galadima kan'-barawa.

[11] Barth, IV, 196. Castration was practised, for example, in Damagaram (Abadie, *La Colonie du Niger*, pp. 201 f.). In answer to a letter from the Amīr Yoruba (Ilorin) 'Abd al-Salām 'Abdullāh b. Fodiye gave a fatwa in 1829 that castration was illegal (Muḥammad b. 'Abdullāh, *Risāla*).

[12] Clapperton (2nd journey), p. 249.

[13] Clapperton (1st journey), p. 92; Clapperton (2nd journey), p. 197.

Sokoto attracted several distinguished scholars like the Arab Malam Mūsā who wrote over a period of five years a book on grammar, or the prominent Qādirī Shaikh, Qamar al-Dīn.[14] Such was the welcome given to visiting scholars that under the Shaikh the respect for Arab sharīfs had been abused by impostors.[15] But the tradition of North African scholars in the Muslim states south of the Sahara was long-standing: Sokoto was following in the line of Timbuktu.

The eleven judges appointed by Bello include the son of Jibrīl b. 'Umar, Muḥammadān, who was made Alkalin daji and received the care of a village east of Sokoto;[16] and the sons of Malam 'Ali Bakusani, al-Muṣṭafā and al-Ḥājj, the latter having a son 'Abdullāh who also became a judge. Also listed are two chiefs of police or sheriffs ('Sarkin Yari'), nine other police officials ('amīr al-ḥudūd') and three guards ('ḥaras'). The two sheriffs were brothers, Fulani from Masari in Bungudu district: the family was given the charge of another village east of Sokoto.[17]

Bello drew his advisers from his friends and companions who had been with him before or after the hijra from Degel. They constitute the younger generation—Bello at the hijra was 22 years old—and were mainly taken from among his relations, the sons of his father's students or contemporaries, and the sons of Fulani leaders. Of his relations there were his brothers, Muḥammad Sambo and Muḥammad Bukhari, his first cousins Muḥammad and Khalilu b. 'Abdullāh, Hamma and Modibo b. 'Alī, his cousins Hammada (whose father is not named) and al-Muṣṭafā b. Nakawi. The sons of the

---

[14] The grammar, 197 folios long, is *Ghalīl ṭālib al-naḥw wa'l-taṣrīf wa'l-khaṭṭ al-shāfī*. Mūsā also acted as secretary and adviser and heard complaints. Qamar al-Dīn came in 1836: cf. letters by Bello in 'Abd al-Qādir b. Gidado, *Majmū'*, and Bello's book written after the visit of Qamar al-Dīn, *al-Mawārid al-nabawiyya*.

[15] Clapperton (2nd journey), p. 205.

[16] Wallaka. He (or his descendants) were also responsible for Birnin Goge, Zamo and Wanke (source: al-haji Junaidu).

[17] Mallamawa. One of the guards had the Fulani name of Tando. The later chiefs of police were descendants of the Shaikh's Wālī al-shurṭa, al-Ḥusain. I have not traced the other gaolers or policemen. For the term 'amīr al-ḥudūd', cf. *Kitāb al-farq* (*B.S.O.A.S.*, 1960), p. 563.

Shaikh's friend 'Umar al-Kammu, Aḥmad and 'Uthmān Mudegel, stayed with Bello, as did Yero b. Mudi and Muḥammad b. Gaini, al-Muṣṭafā and Muḥammad (sons of the Malam 'Alī Bakusani mentioned above), and the three sons of the scholar Muḥammad Binduwo filling posts as secretary or judge.[18] In the final group fall the Dagarawa Fulani Mujid and Tamaji, both sons of the Ardo, and the Alibawa Fulani Abū Bakr, Muḥammad Yero and Sulaimān b. Hārūn Jada.

From these were drawn his helpers, or Viziers. The Ibn Jada family held the office of Magajin gari, the family of Mudegel b. 'Umar al-Kammu held that of Magajin rafi, the 'Alī b. Fodiye family that of Ubandoma. The army commanders under Bello follow the same pattern: his cousin Muḥammad b. 'Abdullāh (also a Vizier); Abū Bakr, the son of the Shaikh's Commander of the Army 'Alī Jedo; Mīkā'īl, probably identified as the Sullebawa 'Maiyaki' (commander) who was a friend of Bello; and Maḥmūd, brother of Namoda, the Alibawa leader and cousin of the Ibn Jada family.[19]

Bello drew on two groups for help in the administration of the province that fell to him: his family and those who had helped him in the jihād. The positions held by his family have already been mentioned in the account of the ribāṭs. Apart from these ribāṭs, the territorial administrations were left in the hands of locally-born mujāhidūn: the ribāṭs seem to have been partly chosen so as not to encroach on local vested interests, since these interests would themselves ensure security and make a ribāṭ otiose. The most respected of local interests were those of the key supporters of the Shaikh: 'Alī Jedo and his people in the Konni area, with his base at Iname and later Binji; the Sarkin Kebbi Moijo and his family, leaders of the Kebbi Fulani before the jihād, who were based at Yabo. The third key group, the Sullebawa, were less settled and organised: it was in their sphere that Sokoto and Sifawa were built, and much of their land was given to the Shaikh's friends and scholars who followed him. Thus the

---

[18] Binduwo is the Fulfulde for magatakarda or 'secretary'.

[19] I omit Joda from this list, since he is not yet definitely identified.

family of Garba Ḥājj were based at Kasarawa, Imam Modoma at Danchadi, and Jibrīl b. 'Umar's family at Wallaka. Many refugees from Zamfara were settled here by Bello, and some, like the Sarkin Yari from Bungudu, were given office as well. The Toronkawa land north of Sokoto was also allotted, where it was not already held by one of the Shaikh's friends or kin: for example, Sharīf Baba, who was released from detention by the Sultan of Gobir to act as intermediary with the Shaikh, was given Basansan; Malam al-Muṣṭafā's family received Salame; the Shaikh's servants, Yero and Wodi, received Gidan Kaya and Zaki.[20]

Beyond this circle of friends and refugees, the various Fulani lineages were confirmed in the areas where they were recognised by the villagers as their intermediaries with Sokoto and their supervisors. Thus among the Kebbi Fulani, there were independent clans at Sanyinna (linked to the Galadima);[21] at Birnin Ruwa (related to Bello and Gidado);[22] at Gande (where a daughter married the Shaikh).[23] On the upper Sokoto valley in middle Zamfara, individual scholars who had left this area to join the Shaikh or fight with Bello were given authority, like Dembo in Bungudu or Muḥammad Sambo b. Malam Ashafa at Gusau.[24] In upper Zamfara, the Alibawa predominated among a number of independently recognised towns that owed allegiance to the Amīr

[20] This list is drawn from the notebooks of all the districts near Sokoto town and from my field notes. Sharīf Baba is mentioned in I.M., p. 85.

[21] Sanyinna: Muḥammad Gari Hanaye, whose link with the Galadima was presumably due to their both being Katsinawa Fulani; his house in Sokoto is near that of the Galadima, who acted somewhat as his kofa, or entrée, to the Caliph. He evidently joined the Shaikh to fight at Alwassa. He also had land near Sokoto on the south-west (Sanyinna District notebook; field notes, 1962–3).

[22] Galanko'en Fulani: Bello and Gidado are descended from Jo, a chief of the Galanko'en, through their mothers (Gidado dan Laima, *Risāla fī 'l-nisba*).

[23] 'Ā'isha bint Jobbo, the mother of Aḥmad Rufa'i, *v. infra.*

[24] Their attempts to settle were harassed first by Banaga, and then by successive Zamfara revolts (Gusau District notebook). The area they could physically control was small. Bungudu, according to Barth (IV, 522–3), was in 1853 'said to be the largest place in Zamfara among those which belong to the faction of the Fellani. . . .'

al-mu'minīn direct. Like Katsina and Daura, where various lineages and clans had helped the Shaikh and Bello independently and had received recognition independently, Zamfara formed a kind of province, where the Emir of Zamfara was *primus inter pares.*[25] Several of the Zamfara communities had as intermediary between them and the Amīr al-mu'minīn a member of the Alibawa lineage, the Magajin gari in Sokoto; the Alibawa, from whom were also drawn the Emirs of the two main towns, Zurmi and Kaura Namoda, centralised power, till one ruler for a while ruled both towns at once: but they were never able to force the other towns to relinquish their autonomous status.[26]

In Kano and Zaria, which have fewer clan connections with Sokoto, being more remote and established later and more independently, the fragmentation is less pronounced. Extraterritorial rights seem to date from the time of strong lineage ties when the head of the lineage was responsible for its members. As the lineage ties weaken, whether through intermarriage or a separate settled existence, authority based on geography begins to replace the lineage authority. Its replacement, where it occurs, in Sokoto, Zamfara and Katsina reflects the assimilation of the Fulani into the sedentary society of Hausaland. Likewise, the concept of a *primus inter pares* is more applicable among nomads than among peasants: the centralisation of the provinces coincides with the breakdown of nomadism.

[25] Barth (IV, 120) stresses the later fragmentation of Zamfara. He reads too much into Clapperton's account (Clapperton, 1st journey, pp. 116–17), since the independent towns were then yet to be established. Zurmi, a pre-jihād town, was the Alibawa headquarters; Kiawa, the Zamfarawa capital, captured *c.* 1810, was eclipsed, especially with the founding and growth of Kaura Namoda.

[26] Maḥmūd b. 'Alī, during the caliphate of Amīr al-mu'minīn 'Alī, controlled both Zurmi and Kaura Namoda, but his power was split after his death (to which Barth, *loc. cit.*, presumably refers). Maḥmūd's son, 'Umar, also managed to combine the two towns under his control for the last decades of the century, till it was split again, *c.* 1901. Cf. Zurmi and Kaura Namoda District notebooks. It was not in the interests of the Caliph to lose the allegiance which the various Zamfara towns paid to him direct.

The Caliph, as head of the Muslim community, was never such a *primus inter pares*, but his election in some aspects reflected the Fulani base on which the caliphate depended at first in the jihād. The electors of the Amīr al-mu'minīn were taken from two of the groups given authority in Sokoto: first, the close assistants of Bello, second, the important territorial leaders. The caliphal lineage was excluded from the election, though they, together with the scholars and other officials, doubtless constituted a powerful public opinion. The method of electing the new Caliph, as told to al-ḥājj Sa'īd, shows greater informality, in the manner of the early Muslim caliphate, than later tradition allows.[27] His account suggests the importance attached to seniority, in the deference paid to Modibo b. 'Alī and Khalilu b. 'Abdullāh, who were asked to state their candidates first.[28] Once the candidate's name was given, the openness of the public recognition and respect for seniority ensured that there would be no alternative suggested. Consequently the choice was first made by private agreement: from this there seems to have developed a regular electing council.

The territorial electors were the leaders of the three groups who supported the Shaikh early in the jihād: the Amīr al-jaish from Konni; the Amīr Kebbi and the Ardon Sullebawa. Later, probably after the 1860's, there were two Ardo'en of the Sullebawa, both on the council; a third Sullebawa leader, the Barade, who had been important under the Shaikh, was admitted to the council, according to tradition, in the 1890's.[29] The role of the three groups is stressed only in al-ḥājj Sa'īd and the anonymous pamphlet on the secrets of the Shaikh known to Atiku: both date from the time of the Amīr al-mu'minīn 'Alī.[30] Earlier histories contain little about the activities of the Sullebawa or their leaders in the jihād. However, one of the daughters of the Amīr al-mu'minīn Atiku married the Ardo, who under 'Alī played a part in the Zamfara campaigns. Of the other two territorial leaders, the Amīr

[27] Sa'īd, pp. 199–201, 207–8. [28] *Idem*, p. 208.

[29] Cf. P. G. Harris, *Sokoto Provincial Gazetteer*, p. 94.

[30] Sa'īd, pp. 198, 207; the anonymous pamphlet quoted in 'Abd al-Qādir b. Muḥammad Bukhari, *Tabshīr al-ikhwān*.

al-jaish 'Alī Jedo held an office that required constant contact with the Amīr al-mu'minīn and the court, while the Amīr Kebbi Moijo is sometimes listed among the lieutenants on a par with these of Zamfara and Kano. But Moijo, after giving the Shaikh hospitality at Magabshi, had himself been active in campaigning for the Shaikh, and his son Muḥammad had been associated with Bello.[31]

The other electors were traditionally the Sokoto councillors—the Vizier, Magajin gari, Magajin rafi and Galadima.[32] In the account of al-ḥājj Sa'īd, the Vizier alone of these councillors plays a part in the pre-selection of the Caliph. It is unlikely, then, that a formal electing council had been constituted before the time of the Amīr al-mu'minīn 'Alī. In tradition, the other councillors act as the advisers of the Vizier, separately from the territorial leaders. This was probably their early role, assumed more by virtue of personality than policy. The electors represented the Community as a whole, but no reference was made to the subordinate Emirs for their opinion: seeing that the four Sokoto councillors were the intermediaries for the Emirs at the caliphal court, they can be said to represent the Emirs at the election, but such representation could only be nominal.[33]

Among the qualifications required for the caliphate were closeness of descent from the Shaikh and seniority.[34] For example, after the death of Bello, with 'Abdullāh already dead, Atiku was the next senior. Bukhari, the next eldest and

---

[31] In al-ḥājj Sa'īd's account, Amīr Kebbi Moijo was prevented by 'Alī Jedo from taking part in the deliberations over 'Alī's appointment (p. 207). The role of 'Alī Jedo is possibly exaggerated, since al-ḥājj Sa'īd received some of his information from followers of 'Alī Jedo (p. 199).

[32] The account of al-haji Junaidu. Cf. P. G. Harris, *loc. cit.*

[33] There is an echo of the early Muslim majlis al-shūrā which elected the third Caliph 'Uthmān in A.D. 644. The territorial electors in Sokoto are known, in Hausa, as the sarakunan shawara ('emirs of advice'); the councillors are known as sarakunan karagga ('emirs of the throne'), and the term for a council is majalisa. The term, ahl al-mashūra, is used for a general council by Bello in *Sard al-kalām*, p. 8.

[34] The Emir of Gwandu Khalilu is said to have instituted in 1842 the practice of electing only sons of past Caliphs ('Umar b. Bukhari, *Tanbīh al-ikhwān*).

only alternative to Atiku, died during Atiku's rule, leaving Aḥmad b. Atiku and 'Alī b. Bello as the two most senior: the election has already been described. Of the five succeeding Caliphs, till 1881, it is possible that only one was not the eldest present from the three eligible houses (those of the Shaikh, Bello and Atiku), and he, Aḥmad Rufa'i, was a son of the Shaikh some two years younger than Bello's eldest surviving son at the time.[35] But such a preference for seniority or kinship was not thought to be invariable. Younger brothers, like Atiku in 1817, Bukhari in 1837 or Sa'īd in 1877 could entertain hopes of the caliphate; even 'Umar b. Bukhari hoped for the caliphate in 1859, although his father had not been Caliph himself.[36] The failed candidates could base their claims on merit: Sa'īd was renowned for his scholarship and piety; Bukhari was also a scholar and a writer of excellent poetry in the classical style, while his son was a historian. But there were no wars of succession: 'Umar b. Bukhari had to be disciplined after his bid failed in 1859, but his case was an exception. In a society where learning and piety are more esteemed than warfare, the Caliphs appointed seem to have satisfied public opinion, at least until 1881.

The Caliph relied for the supervision of the Emirs on his councillors, those who had advised the Vizier to elect him. Although the councillors held office longer than the Caliphs they elected and, as sons or nephews of earlier councillors, were educated to their work, the tone of the administration depended on the personality of the Amīr al-mu'minīn: his decision was absolute, and the councillors were only his agents.

The character of the early offices is nebulous. Their spheres of power were not defined: the present Vizier, al-haji Junaidu, suggests the period after 1842 as the time when the work of the vizierate was split up. It would thus coincide with the retirement or death of the first generation: the Vizier Gidado, the Amīr al-jaish 'Alī Jedo and the Galadima

---

[35] 'Umar Nagwamtse b. Atiku, who became established in Kontagora, was probably ineligible.

[36] 'Umar's hopes for the caliphate are the more surprising since he had himself recorded Khalilu's advice on electing sons of Caliphs.

Doshero had retired;[37] Mudegel had just died, while Muḥammad b. Abī Bakr dan Jada, the young Magajin gari, was coming of age.[38] The new Amīr al-mu'minīn, 'Alī, was only 34 years old, and may have wanted to reorganise and control the administration himself. Supervision of the provinces was now regularised, but it is likely that relations between the supervisor and his province had been long-standing. Thus the Abū Bakr dan Jada family, themselves Alibawa from Zamfara, were given responsibility for Zamfara, while the family of the Galadima, Katsinawa Fulani once domiciled in Alkalawa, were given Katsina; Barth refers to Ibn Jodi being Wakilin Daura, but he, like Mudegel also mentioned by Barth, was already dead: it is not certain who Ibn Jodi was, but the only other mention of him as in charge of Daura refers to him as a brother of Ibn Jada; he also, therefore, may be one of the Alibawa Fulani.[39] Under Bello, however, the retirement of the Emir of Daura had been the responsibility of the Vizier.[40] The Ubandoma, an office in the family of 'Alī b. Fodiye, received the supervision of Gusau, and, after 1859, of Kontagora. The new emirate of Raba, the ribāṭ founded in the 1840's for Abū Bakr, the brother of the Amīr al-mu'minīn 'Alī, was responsible for Muri.

Of the royal offices, Amīr al-Sūdān or Sarkin Sudan was the senior title in the family of Muḥammad Bello.[41] He held the family seat at Wurno, when there was no father or brother

---

[37] The Vizier Gidado lived till 1851; the Amīr al-jaish 'Alī Jedo is said to have died either thirty years after the Shaikh, i.e. 1846, or seven years after 'Alī's accession, i.e. 1849; the Galadima Doshero is said to have died in 1847. (Barth, IV, 158; Durbawa District notebook; notes of an interview with the Sarkin Yaki (Binji) in 1963.)

[38] Cf. Gumbi District notebook; Sa'īd, p. 206.

[39] 'Abd al-Qādir b. al-Muṣṭafā: poem on the death of Mudi dan Laima. Barth, IV, 155.

[40] K.B., p.19.

[41] Al-Sūdān means the Blacks as opposed to al-Bīḍān, the Whites, who are the Tuareg. The title was first held by Muḥammad Bello at the suggestion of the Tuareg Sultan of Agades Muḥammad al-Bāqirī who visited Sokoto in 1809. It was given to Bello's eldest son 'Alī, then to 'Alī's eldest son 'Umar. The title was also given to princes of the Atiku family: for example, 'Umar Nagwamatse and his descendants at Kontagora, or Muḥammad Bello b. 'Abd al-Raḥmān (the account of al-haji Junaidu).

as Caliph to reside there. In addition he was responsible for the north-east and the ribāṭ at Shinaka, which was the usual residence when Wurno was occupied. An alternative residence, closer to Wurno, was Kwargaba.[42] Other senior titles like Sarkin Gobir, Sarkin Raba, also had territorial responsibilities and were hereditary within the families of ʿAlī b. Bello and Abū Bakr b. Bello respectively. Junior members of these families might also be given minor territorial responsibility.

The equivalent senior title in the Atiku family was Sarkin Zamfara, with responsibility for Sokoto town, as well as the general supervision of the south-east, dating from the original division by the Shaikh.[43] The house of Atiku, which adjoins the Shaikh's to the south, was the residence of the descendants of Atiku, whether as Amīr al-mu'minīn or Sarkin Zamfara; Bello's house in Sokoto likewise remained in his family. The main ribāṭ of the Atiku family was Bakura, until it was evacuated in 1850.[44] Thereafter, Chimola, built by Aḥmad b. Atiku, became their chief ribāṭ, though other towns were given to various descendants of Atiku: the importance of these descendants depended more on their personalities than their titles.[45]

Though Aḥmad Rufaʿi b. al-Shaikh was Caliph, none of his descendants were elected: the caliphate remained limited to the houses of Bello and Atiku. The sons of Aḥmad Rufaʿi remained at their father's ribāṭ of Silame, with the title of Sarkin Kebbi.[46] Of the other important descendants of the Shaikh only ʿUmar b. Bukhari attempted to get the caliphate:

---

[42] It was built probably before the ribāṭ at Shinaka for ʿAlī b. Bello. Cf. Wurno District notebook.

[43] The first holder is said to have been Aḥmad b. Atiku, but at what time he received it is not clear. The title is not mentioned in either al-ḥājj Saʿīd or Barth in conjunction with Aḥmad. It was later given to Aḥmad's brother al-Ḥasan. The same title was held by the Zamfarawa ruler at Anka, as well as the Alibawa Fulani ruler at Zurmi.

[44] Saʿīd, pp. 204, 206. The Sarkin Zamfara usually stayed near the Amīr al-mu'minīn, instead of living in a major town of his own.

[45] *v. infra*, pp. 125 f.

[46] Not to be confused with the Amīr or Sarkin Kebbi at Yabo, descendants of Moijo, the Kebbi Fulani leader.

the sons of ʿĪsa stayed in Kware with the title of Sarkin Yamma, while the descendants of al-Ḥasan remained in Marnona or Sokoto.[47]

The council of the Amīr al-mu'minīn would consist of such notables as were present. While the closest associates of the Amīr al-mu'minīn, his Vizier, Magajin gari, Magajin rafi and Galadima were the core of his council, much would depend on the individuals and their relationship with the Caliph. Thus Mudegel is said to have gone on Atiku's behalf to accept the homage of the eastern Emirs, a task that the Vizier would be expected to undertake, but since the Vizier had always been closely associated with Bello, relations between him and Atiku seem to have been cool.[48] Other officials or title-holders, such as the Ubandoma, descendants of the Shaikh's elder brother, or the Alkali could attend the council, but would not necessarily follow the Amīr al-mu'minīn round.

The council was usually held in a room facing on to the main courtyard of the palace, at the front of the house. Those of importance greeted the Amīr al-mu'minīn in the morning and he or his councillors attended to any problems which had arisen. These might include the passing of death sentences on cases already heard by the judge, or appeals from the provinces. The latter usually came through the Sokoto official who was recognised as the 'door' for the complainant's area, and who would be left to carry out any decision taken.

(ii) *Revenue*

The administration was supported by revenue from the estates granted to titles or offices and by payments from the

---

[47] The title of Sarkin Yamma was also held by the brother of ʿUmar b. Bukhari, Barau, when he was given Dogondaji after 1859. The title of Sardauna was held by al-Ḥasan's descendants at Marnona. Other less common titles, such as Bunu (e.g. ʿAbd al-Raḥmān b. Atiku), Dambawa (e.g. Khālid b. al-Shaikh), Janzami (e.g. ʿĪsa b. Atiku), Barazaki (held by a son of ʿUmar b. ʿAlī), were found in Sokoto at various times, according to al-haji Junaidu.

[48] Saʿīd, pp. 202, 208.

subordinate Emirs. The estates included land farmed by slaves as well as villages of freemen who gave presents to their patron. In addition to the household, considerable numbers of scholars and poor depended on the great houses for their food and clothing. The food was prepared in the houses, which thus acted almost as communal canteens. The clothing derived largely from the payments from the emirates and was redistributed as presents. In this way, Sokoto could maintain a large scholar community, and keep its position as a religious centre attracting foreigners from northern and western Africa.

Sokoto was exceptional in that no tax other than alms (zakāt) was formally collected from Muslims.[49] A tax on the cattle Fulani, called jangali, used to be levied before the jihād. Since jangali was unpopular and illegal according to the Shaikh, the term was expressly dropped in favour of the legal zakāt.[50] Zakāt in theory should be disbursed locally and immediately for the legally prescribed purposes, and none forwarded. Kharāj (land-tax), a term which became synonymous with tax generally, was not, it seems, paid in Sokoto.[51] All land had been declared waqf—land held for the benefit of the Community, of which only the usufruct can be transferred and, then, theoretically, only for a limited period. As the presence of the Shaikh attracted a great number of immigrants, all of whom would be Muslims, the land round Sifawa and Sokoto was settled by people who were unwilling

[49] The legal taxes and regulations for using them are given, for example, in 'Uthmān b. Fodiye, *Kitāb al-farq*, and 'Abdullāh b. Fodiye, *Ḍiyā' al-ḥukkām*. As books by 'Abdullāh and the Shaikh were the text-books for the Sokoto administration, their authority is quoted for the law. It is clear however that the law was not always fulfilled in detail, and that legal terminology became used as rough descriptions of traditional practice, modified after the jihād.

[50] *Kitāb al-farq* (ed. Hiskett, *B.S.O.A.S.*, 1960), p. 561. Letter of 'Alī b. Bello to Khalilu b. 'Abdullāh in 'Abd al-Qādir b. Gidado, *Majmu'*.

[51] The Hausa term was kurdin kasa ('land tax'). Cf. J. A. Burdon, *Notes on Tribute in Sokoto Province* (7 March 1904), and E. J. Arnett, *Gazetteer of Sokoto Province* (p. 69). As administrators responsible for collecting tax in Sokoto, it is quite possible they were misled; but though revenue reached Sokoto from the surrounding areas, it probably did not come as kurdin kasa. Moreover, no tolls or craft taxes were paid in Sokoto, according to al-haji Junaidu.

to pay any tax like kharāj. Thus when Amīr al-mu'minīn 'Umar tried to introduce a form of head tax, he was prevented on grounds of Islamic Law by public opinion.[52] Kharāj had originally been imposed in Iraq and Syria on non-Muslim farmers, but, owing to the fall in revenue when the farmers became Muslims or their farms were sold to immigrant Muslims, the tax was extended to all those farming conquered land, except in Arabia and Yemen.[53] In the Sokoto caliphate, kharāj was paid, for example, in the emirates of Kano and Zaria; but here little immigration seems to have occurred, since the local farmers either adopted Islam or accepted Muslim protection and paid jizya. In the immediate Sokoto hinterland, it is not clear what population remained in the area during the jihād. While there was an emigration to Argungu on the fall of Birnin Kebbi, and some followed the Gobir princes into exile, the few hunters and peasants near Sokoto, being on the borders, are unlikely to have moved away. It is therefore probable that the majority of the land taken by the Muslims in Sokoto was previously uncultivated. Both uncultivated and abandoned land are legally at the disposal of the Amīr al-mu'minīn.[54]

By declaring the land waqf, the Amīr al-mu'minīn made the selling of farms and houses illegal. In practice, this proved difficult to enforce. The Amīr al-mu'minīn Aḥmad b. Atiku had to give an order to the Sullebawa to refrain from selling farms; but selling became widespread, even for houses, towards the end of the century, especially outside Sokoto. The new farmer in search of land could go into partnership with the owner, in effect paying rent by sharing the produce. Alternatively he could clear land with the permission of the local village head. Some form of rent, by way of a present on feast days, would be given, but any exploitation could be answered by moving away.[55] The village head depended on

[52] P. G. Harris, *Sokoto Provincial Gazetteer*, p. 105. Cf. Burdon, *loc. cit.*

[53] Cf. R. Levy, *The Social Structure of Islam* (Cambridge, 1957), pp. 309 ff.

[54] 'Abdullāh b. Fodiye, *Ḍiyā' al-ḥukkām*; cf. his *Ta'līm al-rāḍī*.

[55] Where there were villages owing allegiance direct to Sokoto, or with other extraterritorial links, these could give asylum. New towns in particular attracted the discontented: for example, Sabon Birni.

the co-operation of his villagers, who could enforce his removal.[56] The district Emir was less amenable to popular pressure; sons and slaves of the Emir were notorious since reports of their behaviour might not reach the Emir. Enforced hospitality and presents became a form of taxation: the Shaikh, in *Kitāb al-farq*, expressly attacked the system of presents, but in the districts, at least, it was too strong a custom.[57]

Presents were the form that much of the revenue which Sokoto received from the emirates took. Kharāj, jizya and terms for other local taxes are usually not mentioned in the letters that accompanied the goods sent: instead the phrase used for the payment was 'the well-known, agreed gift'.[58] Only tax surplus to the needs of the province need be sent to the capital: consequently the revenue sent was somewhat of a voluntary contribution. Non-payment, however, was a sign that relations were broken; the size of the contribution was of little importance, reflecting only the status of the giver, not of the gift itself.[59]

Presents were also given by officials newly appointed. This

---

[56] e.g. Gwaram, in Kano. Correspondence, VII, 4, 5 and 16 (dating from the period 1886–91).

[57] *Kitāb al-farq* (ed. Hiskett, *B.S.O.A.S.*, 1960), p. 561. The term for a present was 'gaisuwa', 'greetings'.

[58] al-Hadiyya al-ma'lūma al-ma'hūda. In Correspondence, VI, 45, the Emir of Zaria 'Uthmān mentions the kharāj owed each harvest. In VII, 114, the Ciroman Kano Mūsā mentions a delay in his payment to Sokoto till the collection of jizya is completed; similarly, in VII, 51, the Emir of Kano Muḥammad Bello reports the jizya and the kurdin karofi (dye-pit tax) have not been collected.

[59] The revenues from important emirates were large, but owing to the semi-voluntary nature of the gifts, details from the accounts of travellers may be misleading. The agreed customary gift referred to above (in Correspondence, VII, 51) consisted of ten million cowries for the Amīr al-mu'minīn, five million for the Vizier and an extra, unspecified five million. The Zaria payment referred to (in VI, 45) was 20 slaves, 70 gowns, of which 20 were fine Nupe gowns. Cf. Barth (IV, 116, 126) on Zaria in March 1853, when he says two million cowries, 500 tobes and 30 horses were sent every second month. Possibly he was misled by the gifts for the two main Muslim festivals which are two months apart, though these had taken place six months before.

practice gave rise to charges of favouritism and of unfair depositions, since on the deposition (or death) of an office-holder, the property of the office was divided into three, one share going to the Amīr al-mu'minīn. The proportion was not rigid. For example, when the Emir of Kano deposed the the Amīr Dutse, his possessions were counted and all the military equipment—horses, swords and guns—were left for the new appointee, while of his eighty slaves forty were taken by the Emir of Kano, who sent twenty of these to Sokoto.[60] The other beneficiaries were normally the new appointee and the previous official or his heirs. At death, in addition to the division just mentioned, there was the further duty of one-tenth on private property which went to the Amīr al-mu'minīn. As zakāt, however, this revenue should be distributed in the home district.

Another source of revenue was the share of booty taken by the Emirs on their expeditions. Expeditions, as part of the jihād, were obligatory, and therefore booty, usually in the form of captives, was sent annually. Legally the share of the Amīr al-mu'minīn was one-fifth but Burdon reports that half the captives taken were forwarded to Sokoto: the latter figure is credible for those emirates whose main revenue was in slaves.[61] In emirates like Kano, surrounded mainly by Muslim areas, where slave-raiding was impracticable, some of the jizya was sent in lieu of slaves. Jizya was paid by non-Muslims who had been granted Muslim protection.[62] In Sokoto, the non-Muslims included not only some Hausa groups, but also some cattle Fulani who were still considered pagan and were thus liable to jizya;[63] in Kano, there were considerable numbers of Maguzawa farming in their own villages. Neighbouring pagan peoples often made peace and agreed to pay the Muslims jizya, in order to retain their pagan beliefs.

---

[60] Correspondence, VII, 34 (dating from the period 1883–6).

[61] Burdon, *loc. cit.* The Hausa term was 'gandu': the term was sometimes used for the whole payment.

[62] Such peoples are known as ahl al-dhimma. Jizya was also known as kurdin kasa.

[63] Letter of 'Alī b. Bello to Khalilu b. 'Abdullāh in 'Abd al-Qādir b. Gidado, *Majmū'*.

Presents were usually sent for the two festivals, the 'Īd al-fiṭr and the 'Īd al-kabīr, and the taxes which were dependent on the harvest were forwarded in the autumn.[64] At such times, subordinate Emirs or allies might come into Sokoto to greet the Amīr al-mu'minīn, or letters be sent with congratulations and a present, in order to show that the bonds of friendship were not broken.[65]

(iii) *A Special Ally: The Tuareg*

The most important group with bonds of friendship with Sokoto were the Tuareg of Adar and southern Ahir. Though they had played a large part in the jihād on both sides, and were within Sokoto's sphere of influence, they were outside its administration.

The Sultan of Agades, Muḥammad al-Bāqirī, was the only ruler in power at the start of the jihād to help the Shaikh.[66] At the time of the battle of Fafara, he ordered the subordinate emirate of Adar to be transferred from Ḥāmid, the leader of the pro-Gobir faction, and be given to Muḥammad b. al-Muṣṭafā who had already campaigned with the Muslims in Gobir and Adar, and whose sons had been with the Shaikh.[67] Muḥammad b. al-Muṣṭafā was later deposed and Ḥāmid reinstated, to be followed on his death by his brother Ibrāhīm who took over the leadership against Sokoto. Despite the antagonism of the Tuareg in Adar, Muḥammad al-Bāqirī visited Gwandu to pay the Shaikh allegiance and to leave his sons there; he died, however, a year later.[68] His brother Muḥammad Kuma succeeded him, and also paid a visit to the Shaikh. He made an alliance with the Muslims, but he

---

[64] A special zakāt is normally paid on the 'Īd al-fiṭr.

[65] e.g. Correspondence, VII, 58; V, 35, 70. Clapperton (2nd journey), p. 228.

[66] R.J., f. 8. Gidado remarks he was the only one, too, to be still on his throne at the end of the jihād. He offered to help in the jihād against Bornu, but died before he could do anything (I.M., pp. 117 f.).

[67] I.M., pp. 117–18, 88. R.J., f. 9.

[68] I.M., p. 117.

seems to have kept the title of Amīr al-mu'minīn, thus putting himself on an equal titular status with the Shaikh.[69]

His power was not extensive. His brother, al-Bāqirī, had not succeeded in keeping Muḥammad b. al-Muṣṭafā on the throne of Adar, and he had little success himself. Though Ibrāhīm was replaced as Emir of Adar by Muḥammad and then Aḥmad b. al-Muṣṭafā, the latter was deposed in his turn and forced to take refuge in Sokoto.[70]

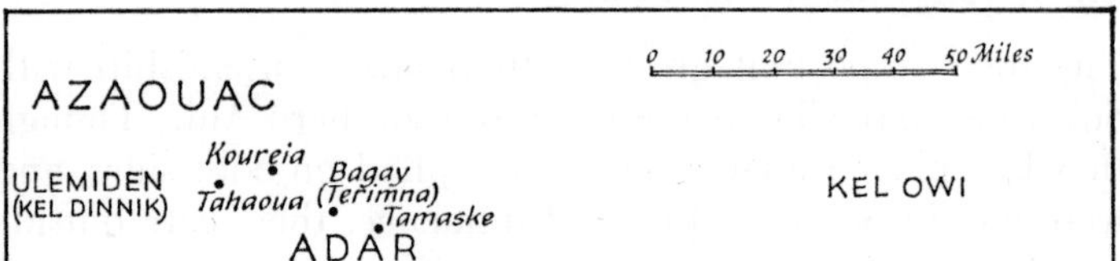

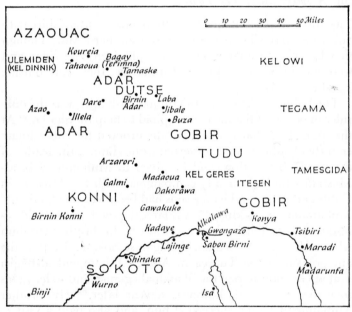

5. Adar and Gobir in the nineteenth century

Outside Agades, the Sultan only had influence if he had allies in one of the major groups like the Kel Geres, Itesen, Ulemiden or Kel Owi. His own appointment was partly in the control of these neighbouring groups, and so liable to

[69] I.M., pp. 174–8.

[70] Tilho, II, 485. Aḥmad was known for his harshness, with the nicknames 'bida', 'mai tsinoni'.

be rescinded suddenly.[71] Likewise, the Emir of Adar had power limited to his towns, and his appointment also was subject to the Tuareg Liswan who formed the Adar aristocracy.[72] The Adar ruling house was split: the sons of al-Muṣṭafā favoured Sokoto and fled there in times of trouble, one branch remaining in Sokoto at Dundaye, the other returning to Adar (the latter's policy was not, however, consistently aligned with Sokoto); the brothers of al-Muṣṭafā and their sons, on the other hand, favoured the Gobirawa, and fled to Tsibiri when in trouble. The Liswan seem to have been similarly split, many taking final refuge in Sokoto.

The history of Adar of this time is dominated by Muḥammad Jailani, the leader of an abortive jihād in Adar.[73] In 1814 a letter had come from a Tuareg scholar who owed allegiance to the Shaikh, asking for advice about a Mahdi who had appeared. Expectation of the Mahdi was widespread, and though this false Mahdi, Hamma, was put to death, the unrest remained.[74] At the same time, the ninth year of the hijra, the jihād of Muḥammad Jailani began.

Muḥammad Jailani was a scholar of the Ineslemen Aitawari, living north-west of Tahoua.[75] The Ineslemen had been granted the right to carry arms after the split of the Kel Dinnik Ulemiden from the Kel Ataram. Then while the Imagerem leaders of the Kel Dinnik were away fighting in the west, Muḥammad Jailani led a force that repelled the

---

[71] Clapperton (2nd journey), p. 228; Barth, I, 422.

[72] Y. Urvoy, *Histoire des populations du Soudan Central* (Paris, 1936), pp. 257–8.

[73] See Urvoy, *op. cit.*, pp. 204–8; F. Nicolas, *Tamesna* (Paris, 1950), pp. 56 ff. Letter of Bello to Jailani (1236 or 1238 A.H.) in 'Abd al-Qādir b. Gidado, *Majmū'*; Muḥammad Bello, *Jawāb shāfi*, and *Jumal min al-mabānī*. Letter of Bello to Ya'qūb in Bivar, *B.S.O.A.S.* (1959), pp. 337–343. R.A., f. 10. Poems (i), (iv) and (vi) of Muḥammad Bukhari b. al-Shaikh in a manuscript in the Shahuci School Library, Kano. *Kashf al-ghumma*, a book (in the Boularaf collection, Timbuktu) by the Kunta scholar 'Umar b. 'Alī, gives an account hostile to Muḥammad Jailani and attributes Mahdist claims to him: this aspect is not mentioned in the other sources so far available.

[74] 'Uthmān b. Fodiye, *Taḥdhīr al-ikhwān* (1229 A.H.), f. 3a.

[75] Nicolas, *loc. cit.*

Tamesgida Imagerem near Tillia, and then turned south into Adar. There he raised a jihād against the pagans. He soon clashed with the Emir of Adar, who, as a Muslim ruler, would not favour another jihād in his territory. The Emir of Adar, though helped by the Kel Geres of Zodi, was beaten in battle east of Tahoua, but subsequently became reconciled to Muḥammad Jailani.

The jihād appealed to all Muslims irrespective of colour or caste. Originally seeking support from the Ineslemen and servile castes against the Imagerem, Muḥammad Jailani broadened the appeal to include Muslims and converts from among the peasant Adarawa.[76] While the restatement of Muslim equality was attractive in the stratified society of the Tuareg, the austerity which Muḥammad Jailani required was excessive: for example, all sounds but that of prayer and religious chanting were prohibited; even the braying of a donkey, so it is said, was thought sacrilegious.

Muḥammad Jailani sought the advice of Muḥammad Bello on the question of maintaining, after the jihād, a Muslim Community among nomads.[77] But he had little success: he alienated too many, since, as well as challenging the position of his own Imagerem, he had fought the Kel Geres and Itesen, the Kel Owi, and the western Ulemiden. Therefore when Ibra, a chief of the Tamesgida Imagerem from Damergu, rallied the dissidents, the allies of Jailani proved insufficient. Ya'qūb b. al-Muṣṭafā was defeated at Daré; then almost all the Ait-awari were killed at Jibale. Ibra took over the town Jailani built at Koureia, and the Imagerem moved back into the Azaouac where once the Ait-awari had been dominant. Jailani fled to Sokoto, and joined Muḥammad Bello in campaigning against Ibra.

Ibra, however, had other enemies in the Ulemiden. Before the rise of Jailani, the Tamesgida and the Ulemiden were contesting northern Adar; with Muḥammad Jailani defeated, the competition was renewed, coming to a head when Ibra

---

[76] Urvoy, p. 206.

[77] Muḥammad Bello, *Jawāb shāfi*; cf. *Jumal min al-mabānī naṣā'iḥ li-Muḥammad al-Jailānī.*

was defeated twice by the Ulemiden under Bodal, who in the second battle had the help of the Liswan of Adar.

In 1836, the conflict was finally resolved by the battle of Gawakuke. Muḥammad Bello, aided by the Kel Geres of Zodi, the Itesen of Wanagoda and the Ait-awari of Muḥammad Jailani, defeated the combination of Ibra, the Sultan of Gobir 'Alī and the Sultan of Katsina (Maradi) Rauda. 'Alī and Rauda were killed, while Ibra died shortly after.[78]

Jailani died near Sokoto in Dundaye district, which had been given over to the Adarawa refugees. They were sufficiently numerous to have a special judge with proceedings in Tamajek. In addition, there was an Adar quarter in Sokoto town, and they were represented at the Caliph's court by the Sarkin Adar, a descendant of Aḥmad b. al-Muṣṭafā.

Not all the refugees from Adar remained in Sokoto. After the Gawakuke campaign, two sons of al-Muṣṭafā, Ya'qūb and Malam, settled in Adar, together with the Liswan; but Illela, in south-western Adar, became the chief town, replacing Birnin Adar.[79] Though the Ineslemen, including descendants of Muḥammad Jailani, were returning north, the Ait-awari were too weak to contest territory: the Kel Dinnik Ulemiden dominated northern Adar, while the Kel Geres of Ṭabl Zodi had received south-eastern Adar and Gobir Tudu from Muḥammad Bello after his victory at Gawakuke.[80]

The jihād of Muḥammad Jailani, while complicated by the appeal to caste and clan antagonisms, was fought, certainly towards the end, on pro- or anti-Sokoto lines. Once Bello had intervened, the war in southern Adar became part of the Sokoto jihād. But there was no attempt to dominate the Tuareg aspect of the jihād or to use local Fulani leaders in Adar: in this the Tuareg jihād differs from the wars which established other communities in the Sokoto caliphate. The

---

[78] K.B., p. 17; D.M., f. 40. Ibra is treated more sympathetically in 'Umar b. 'Alī, *Kashf al-ghumma*.

[79] Barth (IV, 530) heard of four who were said to be Sarkin Adar: Malam was in Illela, while Ya'qūb was in Tahoua and Ḥāmid in Azaw (Asao): the fourth, Sharif, he says, was in Tsambo. Sharif may be a son of Ibrāhīm and a cousin of Ya'qūb and Malam.

[80] Tilho, II, 486; Nicolas, *loc. cit.*; Urvoy, pp. 295–6.

reason lay both in the respect held for the Tuareg scholars and in the physical impossibility of dominating mobile Tuareg clans. Where Tuareg groups were settled, Sokoto negotiated agreements, but always relied on local Tuareg.[81] Apart from Ṭabl Bodal of the Ulemiden and Ṭabl Zodi of the Kel Geres, several Tuareg are listed among the helpers of Muḥammad Bello.[82] The list includes six who were war leaders (Ṭubūl), but it does not necessarily imply they were followed by their clans. For example, the Shaikh Annur listed, whose son, Khiḍr, died fighting for the Muslims, is probably the Kel Owi leader whom Barth met: he had relatives as well as trading connections in Adar and Hausaland, and his relatives are included among the helpers of Bello.[83] But the pact which Bello made with the Kel Owi was only partially kept, depending on local alignments.[84]

The enemies of the Sokoto Muslims also probably reflect local rather than ideological hostilities. For example, of the neighbouring clans based north of Tsibiri in East Gobir, the Tegama and the Teyemawa, the latter accepted the Shaikh's call while the former joined Ibra and raided Sokoto.[85]

The battle of Gawakuke had stabilised Adar and Gobir for the first time. When Bello died, the Amīr al-mu'minīn Abū Bakr Atiku renewed the pacts with the Kel Owi and Ulemiden and acted as mediator for the Itesen and Kel Geres. His authority seems to have been accepted by the Sultan at

[81] An illustration of the seriousness of the Tuareg threat to Sokoto is the number of prayers preserved in which Bello asked for aid against the Tuareg: 'Abd al-Qādir b. Gidado, *al-Iktifā'*. Bello also acted as mediator, as for example in a dispute between the Kel Geres and their neighbours over land: Muḥammad Bello, *Su'lān*.

[82] Gidado dan Laima, *Majmū' aṣḥāb Amīr al-mu'minīn Muḥammad Bello*. Cf. Barth, I, 356, where Wanagoda is the most powerful of the Itesen war leaders. Ṭabl, meaning in Arabic 'drum', is translated as 'Tambari' in Hausa; it is a Tuareg title for a leader in war, but it is found elsewhere in West Africa.

[83] Barth, I, 344. His son-in-law died fighting the Kel Geres (I, 354). 'Abd al-Qādir b. Gidado, *Basṭ al-fawā'id*.

[84] e.g. Barth, IV, 341 f.

[85] The Tamesgida are a sub-group of the Tegama. Barth, I, 529, 536. Urvoy, p. 268. The Teyemawa are a sub-group of the Kel Geres. Cf. J. Perié (*I.F.A.N.*, 1939), p. 381.

Agades and the Emir of Adar, for whose appointment Sokoto approval at least was needed.[86]

These pacts, however, did not prevent raiding or fighting between allies. At the time of Barth's visit to Sokoto, relations with the Kel Owi had improved because the Kel Geres had joined in the raids of the Gobirawa. Likewise, when a usurping leader of the Ulemiden, Bodal Inchilkim, campaigned in Adar and North Sokoto, both the Emirs of Adar, Ya'qūb and Washr, supported him.[87]

Through, rather than despite, this disunity, Sokoto retained among the Tuareg the influence Bello had won by conquest. Sokoto remained a stable and important factor in the diplomacy of alliances. The economics of the salt and other trades prevented the Sultan of Agades in the town from antagonising Sokoto, as much as the needs for dry-season grazing restrained the Kel Geres and Itesen on the marches. A further element was the moral authority which as Caliph and Imam the ruler in Sokoto held: for Sokoto was still the centre for scholarship and pilgrimage, as well as the capital of the largest state in West Africa.

---

[86] Three letters of Abū Bakr Atiku to the Tuareg in 'Abd al-Qādir b. Gidado, *Majmū'* (also, separately, in the Antiquities Dept., Jos). Cf. the role of the Amīr al-mu'minīn 'Alī in the career of the Sultan of Agades 'Abd al-Qādir (Sa'īd, pp. 214, 220; Barth, IV, 185; V, 342); compare also the letter of 'Alī in 'Abd al-Qādir, *Majmū'*.

[87] Nicolas, pp. 60 ff. Urvoy, p. 209.

6

The Period of Security and Settlement (1859–1903: 1276–1320)

(i) *The Caliphate of Aḥmad b. Atiku, 1859–66 (1276–83)*

By the time of the accession of Aḥmad b. Abī Bakr Atiku in 1859 (1276), Sokoto was fully established. The long administration of the Amīr al-mu'minīn 'Alī, who had been a popular, accessible ruler and sufficiently successful in battle, had provided stability.[1] From now the age of the Caliphs at their accessions was to go up, and the length of the reigns grow shorter: the future Caliphs had grown old under 'Alī.

Aḥmad b. Abī Bakr was slightly older than 'Alī.[2] He was the senior member of the house of Abū Bakr Atiku, holding the title of Sarkin Zamfara. He had not always lived in his father's house, at Sokoto, but occupied the ribāṭ of Chimola across the valley from Wurno. As Amīr al-mu'minīn, he used Chimola as Bello had used Wurno.

Though he was the most senior and eligible candidate, his accession was not undisputed.[3] 'Alī's younger brother, 'Alī Karami, left his ribāṭ, Isa, for Sokoto in the hope of becoming Caliph.[4] But a more serious challenge was 'Umar b. Bukhari

[1] For 'Alī's character, cf. 'Abd al-Qādir b. Gidado, *Majmū' al-manāqib*; Sa'īd, pp. 217–18. 'Alī died 21 October 1859 (24 Rabī' I, 1276): 'Alī b. Abī Bakr, *Majmū' al-khulafā'*; Bukhari b. Aḥmad, *Ta'nīs al-ikhwān*, D.M., f. 53b.

[2] Born *c.* 1222 (1807); 'Alī the elder was born *c.* 1223 (1808). His mother may have been an Alibawa Fulani. He is nicknamed 'Zurruku'.

[3] According to Barth (IV, 177), Aḥmad was 'one of the nearest, if not the very nearest, to the succession, but opposed by the greater part of the present courtiers' (April 1853).

[4] 'Alī Karami, according to Barth (IV, 130) in March 1853, was the 'presumed successor'.

b. al-Shaikh, the Emir at Tambawel.[5] His father shared the south with Aḥmad's father Abū Bakr Atiku in the division made by the Shaikh in 1812. His father had been a likely candidate for the caliphate on Bello's death, but he had hurt himself, falling off his horse, and was unable to reach Sokoto: whereupon Abū Bakr Atiku had been elected.[6] When Aḥmad was elected, 'Umar refused to acknowledge him and shut the gates of Tambawel. Aḥmad did not attempt to fight, but removed Dogondaji and Sifawa from the control of Tambawel, giving them to the rival brothers of 'Umar.[7]

Under Aḥmad there continued the expansion and consolidation that was notable in the late 1850's under 'Alī. Towns or ribāṭs such as Moriki, Boko and Birnin Kaya in the old Zamfara were established or re-established; Moriki was founded from Zurmi, while Birnin Kaya was put under Mualedi (a son of Bello by Katembale, the ex-wife of the Sultan of Gobir Yunfa), and Boko under a grandson of Muḥammad Tukur, both being founded from Isa.[8] In the south-east, following 'Alī's campaigns, Chafe was established and a now loyal Kotorkoshi resettled. Raba, upstream from Sokoto, the seat of Abū Bakr b. Bello, was expanded, while to the north-east of Sokoto there was founded Achida. In the river Zamfara valley, new towns were built near Kebbe, while, to the south, the emirate of Kontagora was being created by Aḥmad's brother, 'Umar Nagwamatse. Aḥmad on his accession had given his brother the title of Sarkin Sudan, thus officially recognising his position.

---

[5] Accounts are given in Sifawa and Tambawel District notebooks.

[6] Sa'īd, pp. 199–200.

[7] Barau received Dogondaji, 'Alī Sifawa. Cf. Correspondence, III, 43.

[8] Moriki was ruled by a brother of the Amīr Zamfara (Zurmi), a cousin then being in charge of Kaura Namoda (Moriki District notebook). Mualedi (Mu Alla yidi = 'whom Allah loves') had been with his brother, Fodio, in Lajinge and Tsohon Birni (near Isa). When his brother died, Mualedi acted as Dangaladima to 'Alī Karami, newly appointed Sarkin Gobir at Isa. Failing to become Sarkin Gobir when 'Alī went to Sokoto in 1859, he left Isa and went to Adar and then Tsibiri (Maradun) before founding Kaya. He died *c.* 1874 (Sa'īd, p. 203; Barth, IV, 130; Isa and Moriki District notebooks). Muḥammad Tukur was the famous scholar at the time of the jihād and author of several books and poems.

Two decisions of policy made by Aḥmad were of great importance in the consolidation of Sokoto. The decision to found Sabon Birni involved considerable risk: utilising the chronic divisions within Gobir, he allowed a Gobir prince, Dan Halima, to settle on the piece of fertile but disputed valley where Alkalawa once stood.[9] Standing on the Gobir–Sokoto border, it was to be a buffer between the two. An earlier ribāṭ farther downstream, Lajinge, where Fodio, another son of Bello by Katembale, had been established, proved impossible to retain as a stronghold so long as Mayaki was the Sultan of Gobir. Mayaki was now dead, and when Dan Halima, the cousin of Mayaki's successor Bawa dan Gwomki, asked permission to found Sabon Birni, Aḥmad agreed. Dan Halima linked himself by marriage to Sokoto: he gave his sister to Aḥmad, and their son, Muḥammad Maiturare, was to become the major figure in north-west Sokoto.

Sabon Birni grew quickly, being a refuge for malcontents from both Gobir and Sokoto: it thus became a rival to Tsibiri in Gobir, remaining loyal to Sokoto. The Sultan of Gobir at Tsibiri, Bawa, succeeded, however, in capturing Sabon Birni and the Caliphs Muʿādh and ʿUmar were forced to send expeditions against the town.[10] But it never posed a threat to Sokoto: it was close enough to be cowed into peace, while its only support, Gobir, had its weakness accentuated by internal strife.[11]

The second of Aḥmad's policies was to further the settlement of the Sullebawa, coupled with an attempt to make them keep the Law on certain issues.[12] Aḥmad was in a good position to influence them. His long tenure of office as Sarkin Zamfara under ʿAlī, during which he had responsibility for Sokoto and the south-east, had associated him with the Sullebawa: Barth in 1853 was told that Aḥmad was the head of the Sullebawa.[13] By contrast, Amīr al-mu'minīn ʿAlī at

[9] Tilho, II, 477; Sabon Birni District notebook; P. G. Harris, *Sokoto Provincial Gazetteer*, pp. 167 f.

[10] D.M., f. 58. Tilho, II, 477–8.

[11] Cf. J. Perié, *op. cit.*, on Maradi.

[12] D.M., ff. 53–4.

[13] Barth, IV, 176.

Wurno is said to have had poor relations with them.[14] A further link was the marriage of a sister of Aḥmad to the Ardon Sullebawa Muḥammad Inna; their son later became Ardo also.

Given this position with the Sullebawa, Aḥmad was able to try to persuade them to keep the Law. He ordered them to cease selling farms; not to take rewards for returning missing slaves; to obey the summons of the judges; to obey whoever calls them to a collective duty like jihād; and to respect those in charge of their affairs.[15] The Sullebawa had had a reputation for being rather lawless: with the increasing settlement of the Sullebawa, the problem was evidently acute.

The process of settlement had begun early: some Sullebawa had long been settled near Rikina, and, as Aḥmad's injunction implies, the ownership of land was already an issue.[16] The area in which the Sullebawa settled was their old grazing grounds south-west of Sokoto, in Wamako, Dingyadi and, less predominantly, Kilgori. Already there were villages of immigrants who had stayed here to be near the Shaikh, as well as estates and hamlets which belonged to the Caliph or senior titles like the Sarkin Zamfara or Amīr al-jaish. The settlement of the Sullebawa brought about the regularisation of their leadership on a geographical basis in these areas. Thus the jurisdiction of the Ardo'en of Shuni and Dingyadi and the Barade at Wamako was defined. By the time of the Amīr al-mu'minīn 'Abd al-Raḥmān in the 1890's, all three were in the council for electing the Caliph.[17]

The villages which were built or expanded at this time gave greater depth against the raids of the Kebbawa from Argungu.[18] Wamako, Dingyadi, Kilgori now reinforced the older

---

[14] Barth, IV, 177.

[15] Muḥammad Bukhari, *Ta'nīs al-ikhwān*; D.M., ff. 53b, 54.

[16] R.J., f. 10; Barth, IV, 533–4.

[17] P. G. Harris, *Sokoto Provincial Gazetteer*, p. 194.

[18] The dates for the founding of new villages are difficult to determine. Local evidence, collected in the District notebooks or the Gazetteer, often conflicts with the reports of travellers. In some cases, the dates seem to be those of the building of walls, in others, of moving to a new site. Many sites have names before they have full-scale villages.

centres, like Asari, Gwamatse, Bodinga, Sifawa or Birnin Ruwa. Farther south a line of villages, not always walled, was growing up along the ridges that effectively divide the Burmi-Tureta forests from the higher land. Shuni and Denge became more important, while, later, towns like Wababi, Danchadi and Jabo were strengthened. Tureta itself was developed, perhaps with further Burmawa immigrants from what was now Sullebawa land.

The consolidation of the south-west of Sokoto had been long: the process began with the immigrant villages, like Kasarawa with Jobbawa Fulani or Kalembaina with refugees from Gwandu, and continued throughout the century. The reorganisation of the Sullebawa was an inevitable part of this process: the affluence from owning slaves and the security of the countryside, the increasing population and the need for more arable land, the pressure, which Bello describes, from the Muslim administration to bring the pastoralists within the Law, all made for assimilating the Fulani to town life.[19]

Despite the consolidation of Sokoto, the main anti-Muslim centres remained as bases for raiding expeditions which often went deep into Sokoto territory. Aḥmad continued the jihād, leading punitive expeditions against these bases in Kebbi (to Sowwa), in the new Zamfara (Ruwanbore, Gummi) and in Gobir-Maradi (Tessawa).[20] He campaigned each year, seven times in his seven years as Caliph: these were the expeditions, usually in the autumn, to the frontiers of dār al-Islām, and defensive campaigns against enemy raiding are not included.[21]

(ii) *Four Caliphates, 1866–81 (1283–98)*.

The next four Caliphs are represented in Sokoto as the last descendants of the Shaikh to maintain the traditional values of the Sokoto caliphate. It is a measure of the momentum and strength of the caliphate, attained over the previous forty

---

[19] Muḥammad Bello, *Jawāb shāfi*. Cf. Hopen, *op. cit.*, pp. 14–15.

[20] D.M., f. 54b.

[21] Aḥmad died 2 November 1866 (23 Jumādā II, 1283): D.M., f. 55b.

years, that there was no loss of cohesion or continuity despite the four Caliphs being elderly men and their terms of office comparatively brief.

1866 (*1283*). On the death of Aḥmad the senior candidate was the younger 'Alī b. Bello. Born at the same place, Sala, and about the same time as his brother 'Alī (the Amīr al-mu'-minīn, 1842–59), he was the oldest member of the house of Bello. He had been resident at Isa, the key eastern ribāṭ against Gobir (some twenty-five miles upstream from Sabon Birni), where he had been installed as Sarkin Gobir by his brother, but in 1859 he had left Isa to his son 'Abd al-Raḥ-mān, while he himself went to Sokoto in the hope of being elected Caliph.[22] His nephew 'Umar still held the ribāṭ at Shinaka, it seems with the title of Sarkin Sudan. On his appointment, 'Alī used his father's house at Wurno, leaving Chimola to the sons of Aḥmad. 'Alī, however, died eleven months after his appointment, without having taken out any expedition.[23]

1867 (*1284*). The next Amīr al-mu'minīn, Aḥmad Rufa'i, was distinguished for his piety and learning, and, as a son of the Shaikh, was highly respected.[24] He had been the choice of some for the Caliph in 1842, and presumably had been a candidate at the succeeding elections.[25] Even now, though the closest, he was not the most senior of the descendants of the Shaikh, being about two years younger than Abū Bakr b. Bello.[26] It is possible he was a compromise between the claims of the sons of Bello and those of the sons of Atiku, since till now the caliphate had alternated between the two families. The sons of Bello may have expected the next Caliph also

---

[22] Isa District notebook; Barth, IV, 130.

[23] D.M., f. 55b. He died mid-October 1867 (Jumādā II, 1284). A raid by the Gobirawa and Katsinawa (Maradi) is said to have reached Sokoto at this time (Edgar, notebook, *Labarin Sokoto*, p. 2).

[24] D.M., ff. 55b–7. Cf. 'Uthmān b. Isḥāq, *al-Kashf wa'l-bayān* (1868/1285).

[25] Sa'īd, p. 207.

[26] Born *c.* 1229 (1814), cf. R.J., f. 36, where 'Īsa is the only son younger than Aḥmad Rufa'i.

to be chosen from among them, since the caliphate of the younger ʿAlī had been brief.

Like ʿAlī the younger, Aḥmad Rufaʿi had spent part of his life in a ribāṭ—on an equally dangerous frontier, that of Argungu. He had been driven out of his main town, Silame, by a Kebbawa raid, but had stayed on the frontier at Tozo nearby.[27] His connections with his neighbours across the river had alienated him in the past from the Amīr al-jaish, who feared encroachment on his territory from the south.[28] Already ʿĪsa b. al-Shaikh at Kware, the Adar immigrants in Dundaye and the Sullebawa at Wamako had taken the land between Binji and Sokoto. In the event, Aḥmad Rufaʿi does not seem to have increased his relations' holdings, possibly because the same decline which affected the family of ʿAlī Jedo had also affected the family of Waruwa: the power of the individual leaders was diminishing as the authority of the Amīr al-mu'minīn grew and became established.

Aḥmad Rufaʿi's rule is distinguished for its peace. He himself made in five years only three excursions from Sokoto: once to rebuild his old ribāṭ at Silame for his son Abū Bakr, the Sarkin Kebbi; once to drive some pagans from Kaiama, a village near Kware; and once to attend the funeral of his younger brother, ʿĪsa, at Kware.[29] He put an end to the Kebbawa raids by arranging a truce with the Sultan of Argungu, Toga.[30] On the Gobir frontier, Sabon Birni was still growing under Dan Halima and kept the peace in that area. His five years, in consequence, are uneventful in terms of campaigns and battles. But the peace was probably welcome: the first four Caliphs after the Shaikh had sent out some eighty major expeditions, thirty-three in the last thirty years, while Bello alone had been responsible for forty-seven;

---

[27] Saʿīd, p. 212. He is called ṣāliḥ, rather than murābiṭ, by ʿAbd al-Qādir b. Gidado (*Basṭ al-fawā'id*), who also lists him among the Viziers of ʿAlī (*Majmūʿ al-manāqib*).

[28] Saʿīd, p. 207.

[29] D.M., f. 56.

[30] The terms are given in the *History of Gwandu* by the Alkalin Gwandu (trans., McAllister, 1909), para. 86; they are quoted by Arnett (*Rise of the Sokoto Fulani*, p. 12) and Burdon (*Northern Nigeria*, p. 72). The truce in effect maintained the *status quo*.

and this excludes minor raids. So long as the other Emirs were regular in their presents and their sending of the legal share of the booty and tax, the prosperity of Sokoto did not depend on the spoils of the annual expedition.

If Aḥmad Rufa'i neglected the jihād, he did not neglect the Caliph's duty to urge the Community to do good and avoid evil. Two short works of his survive, couched in the general language of exhortation and political advice.[31] One of these, or a similar sermon, was sent round to the Emirs and they read it out to their Communities.[32] He was evidently rigorous in his application of the Law, and insisted on the cutting off of a thief's hand, the canonical penalty for stealing: despite the fact that this was not an innovation in Sokoto, the presence of such a tradition distinguishes him from the other Caliphs.[33] He also performed the duty of repairing the mosque of the Shaikh in Sokoto while he was occupying a house adjoining the Shaikh's compound.

1873 (*1290*). Whereas Aḥmad Rufa'i was comparatively young at his accession, being aged 53, the next two Caliphs, both sons of Bello, were old: Abū Bakr was 61 and Mu'ādh 62 on their accessions: both died aged 65.[34] Despite his age Abū Bakr b. Bello maintained the Islamic duty of jihād, campaigning three times in his four years against Gobir-Maradi. He had spent most of his life guarding against Gobir raids in the ribāṭ of Raba, which stood on the Sokoto river facing Burmi in the east and Gobir across the Gundumi desert in the north.[35] As Caliph, he strengthened the defences on the river by settling a son of Ibrāhīm b. Bello at Kurya, near

---

[31] *Tanbīh al-umma fī ṭā'at Allāh*; *Tanbīh al-umma 'alā mā 'alaihim min tā'at al-a' imma* (containing, *inter alia*, a call to individuals to make the jihād and to Emirs to stop confiscating private farms).

[32] Correspondence, IV, 16.

[33] P. G. Harris, *Sokoto Provincial Gazetteer*, p. 103.

[34] Abū Bakr was born *c.* 1227 (1812), Mu'ādh *c.* 1231 (1816). Aḥmad died in mid-March 1873 (Muḥarram 1290), aged 61: D.M., f. 57.

[35] 'Abd al-Qādir b. Gidado calls him 'mujāhid' and 'murābiṭ' and a 'nā'ib' of Amīr al-mu'minīn 'Alī as the 'Amīr Raba' (*Basṭ al-fawā'id*; *Majmū' al-manāqib*).

Ibrāhīm's old town of Gandi.[36] On the Kebbi frontier, the peace made by Aḥmad Rufa'i was broken during Abū Bakr's rule, but no expedition against Argungu is mentioned.[37]

Abū Bakr was noted for his piety and austerity: for example, he is famous for making ropes to sell in the market and so providing himself with his own livelihood.[38] No writings of his have yet been found.

1877 (1294). On his death both Mu'ādh and Sa'īd, sons of Bello by the same mother, 'Ā'isha bint 'Umar al-Kammu, were eligible for the caliphate but the appointment was made according to seniority.[39] Sa'īd, the junior brother, was a scholar of some distinction, writing much poetry and some prose in Arabic, Fulfulde and Hausa.[40] He had also taken a part in the administration: he had acted as a 'sort of mayor' in Sokoto, according to Barth, when the Sarkin Zamfara Aḥmad was away;[41] and he represented Aḥmad Rufa'i, when Amīr al-mu'minīn, at the appointment of al-Muṣṭafā as Emir of Gwandu.[42] He had been resident in the ribāṭ at Gandi, which had proved awkward to administer, partly due, it seems, to the large and powerful section of caliphal slaves there. Sa'īd's brother, Ibrāhīm, had had difficulty there in the 1840's, while Sa'īd's son, Ḥayāt, ran into trouble and was forced out, it is said, by popular action.[43] Ḥayāt went to the east, to Adamawa and the Bornu marches, and became the representative for the Sudanese Mahdi in the west, telling the

---

[36] Abū Bakr b. Ibrāhīm (Gandi District notebook).

[37] Alkalin Gwandu, *History of Gwandu* (trans., McAllister, 1909), para. 89; Burdon, *op. cit.*, p. 72. Cf. the *History of Missau* by the present Emir of Missau, Aḥmad b. al-Ḥājj, written *c.* 1928, on some campaigns of Abū Bakr.

[38] The account of M. Yahaya Abd al-Qadiri. Cf. D.M., f. 57. There is a reference to a plot against Abū Bakr by the Sarkin Zamfara al-Ḥasan in (Anon), *Faiḍ al-qadīr*; but I have not been able to substantiate it.

[39] Abū Bakr b. Bello died mid-March 1877 (Rabī' I, 1294) ('Abd al-Qādir b. Bukhari, *Tabshīr al-ikhwān*; D.M., f. 57b).

[40] e.g. *Irshād al-'ābid ilā ḥaḍrat al-ma'būd*; *Markab al-'awām*.

[41] Barth, IV, 179.

[42] P. G. Harris, *Sokoto Provincial Gazetteer*, p. 201; Arnett, p. 41.

[43] Gandi District notebook: cf. P. G. Harris, *op. cit.*, pp. 138 f.

Mahdi that his father had foretold his coming. Sa'īd, however, declined to join his son, and died in the 1880's.

Mu'ādh, before his election as Caliph, had always lived in Sokoto:[44] he was therefore the first Caliph not to have commanded a ribāṭ on the frontier. Though he began the building of the walls of Denge for his son 'Alī and may have had earlier connections with the village, there is no evidence that he had any following comparable to that of the Sarkin Sudan 'Umar b. 'Alī who succeeded him in the caliphate.[45] Mu'ādh, on his election, faced a hostile Sabon Birni which Bawa, Sultan of Gobir, had succeeded in capturing from Dan Halima. Mu'ādh therefore concentrated on retaking the town, but although he had some success against Bawa (celebrated in a poem by Mariam bint al-Shaikh), he did not recapture the town.[46] The next Amīr al-mu'minīn 'Umar b. 'Alī continued the campaign against Sabon Birni, but, soon after, Bawa died and the town was no longer a threat.[47]

(iii) *The Caliphate of 'Umar b. 'Alī, 1881–91 (1298–1308)*

1881 (1298). Mu'ādh died in late September 1881, leaving Sa'īd and Yūsuf from the sons of Bello as the senior eligible candidates to succeed him.[48] From the house of Atiku there was the Janzami, 'Īsa b. Abī Bakr Atiku, whose brother, al-Ḥasan, the Sarkin Zamfara, had died during the rule of Mu'ādh; also seeking election were Abū Bakr b. Aḥmad Rufa'i and 'Umar b. Bukhari b. al-Shaikh.[49] None of these, however, were elected; instead, a great-grandson of the Shaikh was chosen. 'Umar b. 'Alī b. Bello had held the title of Sarkin Sudan since 1842 and had lived at the ribāṭ of Shinaka before moving to Wurno when the Amīr

[44] According to al-haji Junaidu.

[45] Denge District notebook; P. G. Harris, *op. cit.*, p. 133.

[46] D.M., f. 58; cf. Aḥmad b. al-Ḥājj, *op. cit.*, on the campaigns of Mu'ādh.

[47] Tilho, II, 477.

[48] 3 Dhū'l-qa'da 1298 (D.M., f. 58).

[49] 'Alī b. Abī Bakr, *Majmū' al-khulafā'*. Mischlich (*M.S.O.S.*, 1908), p. 66.

al-mu'minīn was no longer resident there. He was aged 57 at the time of his election.[50]

In his nine years as Caliph, three expeditions are mentioned. The first was to follow up Mu'ādh's campaign against Sabon Birni; the second was against Madarunfa, *c.* 1886, and the third against Argungu, *c.* 1889.[51] Although 'Umar continued to go to Kaura Namoda each year, the virtual ceasing of the autumn campaigns rendered the annual mustering of the Muslim forces otiose:[52] consequently the eastern Emirs more frequently excused themselves the journey and sent larger presents instead. This loosening of ties, which had begun before 'Umar, was compensated by Sokoto's greater interference in the domestic politics of the emirates, as, for example, in Zaria where the continual imbalance and rivalry of the tri-dynastic system had begun to require an outside stabiliser.[53] In Kano, too, the new Emir, Muḥammad Bello b. Ibrāhīm, proved most amenable to Sokoto wishes.[54]

The annual expedition, by bringing together the combined forces, had been a reminder to all, Muslim and non-Muslim, that a strong force could be mobilised readily. Once the practice lapsed, it was less easy to get the forces to come together, even for a major expedition. While the Emirs themselves were not particularly lax in the jihād, there had always been a reluctance on the part of the peasants to go to war; after eight years of peace under Aḥmad Rufa'i and with the stability of Sokoto secured, lack of enthusiasm for the jihād was probably widespread. The walls of Sokoto were left to decay and the gates stood unhinged.[55]

Uninterrupted by the Kebbawa, trade was flourishing in the south-west;[56] in Gobir, the Sultan Ibrāhīm b. 'Alī was

---

[50] Born *c.* 1239 (1824). His mother was a daughter of Abū Bakr dan Jada, Bello's close adviser. For some details of the election, *v. infra.*

[51] D.M., f. 58b. Cf. Tilho, II, 478.

[52] Cf. Muḥammad Bukhari b. Aḥmad, *Ta'nīs al-ikhwān.*

[53] Cf. M. G. Smith, *op. cit.*, pp. 178 ff.

[54] (Anon), *Faiḍ al-qadīr.* Cf. Correspondence, VII, 13, 45, 51, 56, 59, 85; and one uncatalogued.

[55] Thomson, *Good Words*, p. 326; in May 1885.

[56] Thomson, *op. cit.*, pp. 324–5.

reconciled to Sokoto, though the peace was broken both during his sultanate and following his deposition in 1886. Ibrāhīm's successor, however, re-established good relations with both 'Umar and 'Abd al-Raḥmān.[57]

A corollary of the lessening campaigning was the increase in revenue that was sought by the Amīr al-mu'minīn, since 'Umar did not share the austerity of a Caliph like Aḥmad Rufa'i. However unsuccessful the expedition in terms of capturing major towns—and success was rare—there was usually some booty by way of captives and livestock, or a payment made in return for the expedition's withdrawal. Though presents were often received instead of booty, the expectations of the Amīr al-mu'minīn 'Umar for revenue are said to have continued to increase. There is a story that he attempted to impose a tax on Sokoto for the first time: the story, even if untrue—and it is denied by the present Vizier, al-haji Junaidu—suggests there was some financial irregularity under 'Umar.[58]

The period 1881–1903 was nonetheless one of expansion and settlement. Towns or reorganised villages dating from this period are numerous, most notably in the north of Sokoto.[59] The outstanding figure of this area was the Marafa, Muḥammad Maiturare, the son of the Amīr al-mu'minīn Aḥmad by the sister of the Gobir ruler of Sabon Birni, Dan Halima. Muḥammad Maiturare himself married a Tuareg chief's daughter. Given Gwadabawa, a town west of his father's ribāṭ of Chimola, he assumed the leadership of the northern quarter.[60] The heirs of 'Alī Jedo, the family of the Amīr al-jaish, were eclipsed: no outstanding figure had emerged, and the importance of their military contribution to Sokoto had decreased. Since the Kebbawa from Argungu were still

---

57 Tilho, II, 477–8.

58 Burdon, *Notes on Tribute in Sokoto Province* (7 March 1904).

59 Gwadabawa District notebook; P. G. Harris, *Sokoto Provincial Gazetteer*, pp. 145, 181.

60 His elder brother, Muḥammad Attahiru, was living in Chimola, while other brothers were Abū Bakr and 'Abdullāh who during this period held the title of Sarkin Zamfara with charge of Danchadi. Cf. F. Edgar, *Litafi na Tatsuniyoyi na Hausa* (Belfast, 1911–13), III, 413–15.

actively raiding in this direction and the Amīr al-jaish was too weak to protect his followers, the Marafa moved in, controlling towns on the Kebbi river and leaving the Amīr al-jaish confined to the hinterland of Binji. Arming with guns a contingent of Azbinawa immigrants who were thus loyal to himself, the Marafa proved to be the most effective force in the area. Despite this force—and he was not above threatening his fellow princes—he could not wholly overawe them. He did not, for example, manage to take control of Shinaka, the ribāṭ under the Sarkin Sudan.[61] With his uncle, 'Abd al-Raḥmān, as Amīr al-mu'minīn, he may have been allowed a freer hand than he had had under 'Umar b. 'Alī b. Bello. He had increased his strength by building up the land north and west of Chimola. He developed Gwadabawa into a major centre; he walled some of the older villages like Abdallo, and encouraged immigrants from Adar, Gobir and elsewhere to settle in the new villages he organised, and farm. He could ensure the stability of the area, in contrast to the comparative turbulence beyond the Sokoto borders.

Elsewhere, expansion continued. In the east, in Zamfara, a new ribāṭ was being planned by the Sarkin Kaya, after the boundary with Isa was delineated;[62] in Burmi, a ribāṭ was built at Modochi by the local ruler of Bakura.[63] In the south-east, the town of Danchadi was walled, while a new ribāṭ was proposed south of Dogondaji.[64] The Vizier Muḥammad Bukhari built towns and a ribāṭ in the same area after an expedition to Bunja.[65] The impression Thomson received while he travelled through these parts was one of a densely populated land under annual cultivation.[66] Though villages continued to be built or expanded close to Sokoto, as for example were Durbawa and Mallamawa upriver from Sokoto, the main areas of settlement had now to be in the north or in the less secure region of Zamfara.

---

[61] Goronyo District notebook.

[62] Correspondence, V, 43.

[63] Correspondence, I, 48. It may have been built during the Mafara revolt: *v. infra.*

[64] Correspondence, III, 40.

[65] Correspondence, III, 36; I, 12.

[66] Thomson, *op. cit.*, p. 324.

(iv) *The Caliphates of 'Abd al-Raḥmān b. Atiku, and Muḥammad Attahiru b. Aḥmad, 1891–1903 (1308–20)*

1891 (1308). When Amīr al-mu'minīn 'Umar died at night while on campaign at Kaura Namoda, there was an emergency; it was imperative that the army should not be leaderless so long as the enemy were near. At a late session presided over by the Vizier, 'Abd al-Raḥmān b. Abī Bakr Atiku was chosen, some three hours after 'Umar's death.[67]

He was an old man, 62 at his appointment.[68] Fourteen years old when his father died, he was overshadowed by his elder brothers, Aḥmad, 'Umar Nagwamatse, Muḥammad Nabakura, al-Ḥasan, 'Īsa, or even his nephew Muḥammad Maiturare b. Aḥmad. 'Abd al-Raḥmān's career before his election as Amīr al-mu'minīn, therefore, is obscure. He had held the title of Bunu when Abū Bakr b. Bello had sent him to southern Zaria to bring back Bayero b. Abī Bakr b. Bello to Sokoto;[69] but since his later reputation generally was not good, material about him is scarce. He seems to have taken offence easily and to have been harsh and uncompromising. His nickname 'unbaked pot' was not complimentary.[70] The oral tradition, in which the nickname is always used, concentrates on his propensity for executing people for little or no reason.[71] As soon as he was elected, he was annoyed at the Sarkin Mafara for only sending his Galadima for homage and so precipitated a crisis which left middle Zamfara devastated.[72]

---

[67] 25 March 1891 (14 Sha'bān 1308). D.M., fols. 59, 59b. It seems that the Sarkin Raba Muḥammad whom Staudinger (p. 374) was told was the future Caliph, was not present: he died soon after 1891. Also absent was 'Uthmān b. 'Alī, the Sarkin Gobir (Isa).

[68] Born *c.* 1244 (1828–9). al-Ḥasan, the Sarkin Zamfara before his death under Amīr al-mu'minīn Mu'ādh (1877–81), was his full brother.

[69] *Labarin yakin Bayero,* in the notebook of F. Edgar. As Bunu, he had charge of the village Dambiso, north of Wurno.

[70] In Hausa, 'Danyen kasko'. Cf. the proverb:

Danyen kasko ba shi kai ruwa ban daki
An unbaked pot does not carry water to the back of the house.

(*Hausa and Fulani Proverbs*, ed. Whitting, Lagos, 1940, p. 120.)

[71] e.g. Edgar, *Litafi na Tatsuniyoyi na Hausa* (Belfast, 1911–13), I, 212–213; II, 341–2; II, 360–1; II, 366–7; cf. II, 335.

[72] *v. infra*, pp. 131 ff.

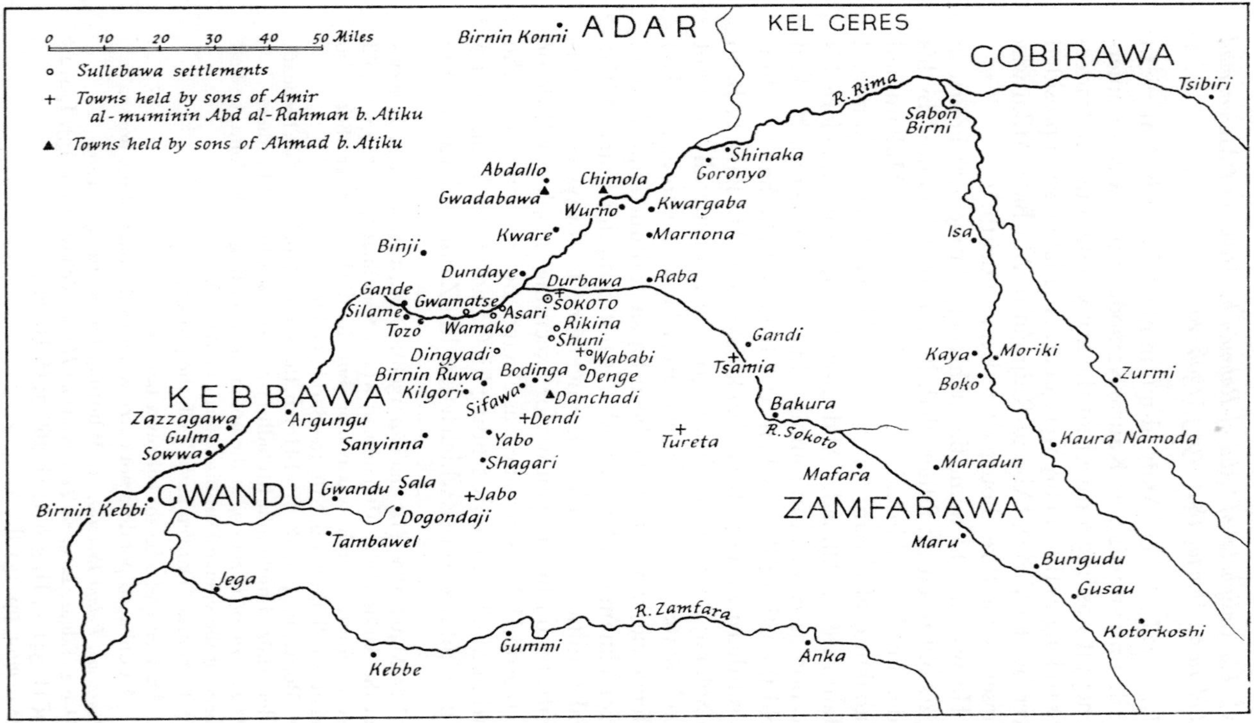

6. The Sokoto Area *c.* 1890–1900

Two years later, when the Emir of Kano died, the stubbornness of 'Abd al-Raḥmān over the succession gave rise to another crisis which more than any other lowered Sokoto's prestige in the caliphate.[73]

Scepticism about 'Abd al-Raḥmān's intentions and motives is common in the oral tradition: he seems to have been singularly unpopular, especially after the catastrophes of the first four years of his rule. There is a resemblance to his father's position in Sokoto: and even more than in his father's case, the sources are not in his favour.[74] His sons did not increase his popularity by being overbearing. 'Abd al-Raḥmān appropriated or built towns for them, along the edge of middle Zamfara; for example at Jabo, Dendi, Wababi, Tsamia, Durbawa, Tureta.[75] But these towns are also part of the general expansion mentioned previously.

In addition to founding towns, he took out expeditions for which he summoned all the eastern Emirs. Five campaigns are mentioned in the ten years of his rule, but none were markedly successful.[76] The expedition against Argungu *c.* 1892 was a disaster. Though all the eastern Emirs were present, only Tukur, the Galadima of Kano and leader of the Kano contingent, was interested in fighting the Kebbawa. The others are said to have expected that no share of the booty would be given them. In the event, the besieging army was routed and the Sokoto drums were lost.[77]

But the very occurrence of such expeditions was confining the Kebbawa to four walled towns packed with refugees:[78]

---

[73] *v. infra*, pp. 134 ff.

[74] Edgar (*op. cit.*) is the main written source, together with the accounts copied down by the early British administration. The Arabic accounts written by the Viziers of Sokoto are only critical by implication or omission.

[75] Jabo—Muḥammad Maigari; Dendi—Sarkin Mafara Mahe; Wababi—Muḥammad Sambo; Tsamia—Marafa Abū Bakr; Durbawa—Yerima; Tureta—Bunu 'Alī. Another son, Muḥammad Bello, had the title of Sarkin Sudan. According to al-haji Junaidu, Mahe, Sambo, Abū Bakr and Bello married daughters of the Vizier Bukhari.

[76] D.M., f. 63b.

[77] Cf. Edgar, II, 337–40.

[78] Sowwa, Zazzagawa, Gulma and Argungu (P. L. Monteil, *De Saint-Louis à Tripoli par le lac Tchad*, Paris, 1894, p. 227).

that the towns were unassailable meant they could hold out unless there was treachery, but their future was hopeless. Gobir-Maradi were in a better position, but so decisively divided within themselves that they were now never a threat, only a nuisance.[79] No revolt which they might incite by their raiding could be sustained after the raid was over: a revolt, therefore, dependent on the Gobirawa, was not likely to be a threat to Sokoto.

The Tuareg were likewise within the orbit of the caliphate: intermarried with, for example, the Marafa, or preoccupied with internal rivalries, they accepted the hegemony of Sokoto. With the continuous southward attraction of pasture and the north-west expansion under the Marafa, the Tuareg came more directly into contact with the Sokoto administration, which for the most part acted only as arbiter.

The established strength of Sokoto is shown by two crises, those of Mafara and Kano, which compare in importance with the crises in Bakura and Hadejia nearly fifty years before under 'Alī. The politics of middle Zamfara, where Mafara is situated, were based on internal, indigenous competition over which Sokoto arbitrated. The early Caliphs suffered setbacks when they tried to take part in this strife by controlling Bakura directly or maintaining a ribāṭ at Gwamatse. After the crisis of 1851, this control was withdrawn, but loyal rulers were kept in charge and frequently supervised since the main road to the east ran upriver past them.

Mafara was on a tributary off this route; to the south lay the pagan strongholds which Bello had once reduced, Morai, Kanoma or Ruwanbore, the object of recent raids. Farther south were the Zamfara valley territories of Anka, Zauma, Gummi and Kebbe. Continuous rivalry and occasional fighting were maintained along the valley, with Sokoto favouring one side or the other: all except Kebbe were, like Mafara, once part of the Zamfara kingdom and now housed its refugees.[80]

Political life within these Zamfara and Burmi communities

---

[79] J. Perié (*I.F.A.N.*, 1939), pp. 383 ff.
[80] Cf. Anka, Gummi, Kebbe District notebooks.

was unstable: *coups d'état* provided rapid political change, and Sokoto, where necessary, recognised the ruler *post-facto*. Border disputes were frequent: the area of a state and its strength are correlative. As there were numerous refugees exiled from neighbouring states, the opportunities for subversion were many.

The vague character of the 'protectorate' that Sokoto held over the area is shown by the continued pagan practices, such as throwing dust on the head as a token of submission.[81] But though control was limited, the Amīr al-mu'minīn expected homage and presents from the local rulers. The autumn expedition of the Amīr al-mu'minīn, which frequently went across towards Kaura Namoda where the eastern Emirs met, ensured this. Doubtless much food was contributed locally. Similarly, passing officials received hospitality. In addition, those pagan communities which had submitted were taxed for jizya. Any deviation in payment might be interpreted as the preliminary to rebellion.

Thus when the Sarkin Mafara excused himself on grounds of sickness from travelling the ten miles from Mafara to Gora to pay homage to the new Amīr al-mu'minīn 'Abd al-Raḥmān, and sent his Galadima instead, he was understood to be showing disrespect to the Caliph.[82] When the Sarkin Mafara then refused to accept the decision of the Amīr al-mu'minīn which allotted a disputed town to his neighbour, the Sarkin Burmi (the nominee of Sokoto at Bakura), 'Abd al-Raḥmān declared Mafara in revolt and the Sarki deposed. Anka joined its relative, Mafara, in the revolt; Donko,

---

[81] To throw dust on the head is an old practice. J. S. Trimingham (*History of Islam in West Africa*, p. 53, n. 3) refers to it in Gana, Mali, Songhai and Jolof. Cf. Thomson, *op. cit.*, p. 328, where his bearers throw dust on their heads before the Amīr al-mu'minīn in Wurno. The Shaikh in *Kitāb al-farq* (ed. Hiskett, *B.S.O.A.S.*, 1960, p. 563) says it was a pagan practice in Hausaland and quotes Ibn al-'Arabī for it being 'a sign of excess' ('alāmat al-ighrāq).

[82] The chief source is Muḥammad Bukhari b. Aḥmad, *Rauḍ al-rayāḥīn*. The Sarkin Mafara here is the Zamfara ruler of Mafara; the Sarkin Mafara (Gummi) is the Zamfara ruler of Gummi. The time of year was late dry season (1891), when disease would be prevalent.

therefore, stayed by Sokoto.[83] The Sokoto forces were mobilised, and letters were sent to the eastern Emirs to boycott Mafara trade.

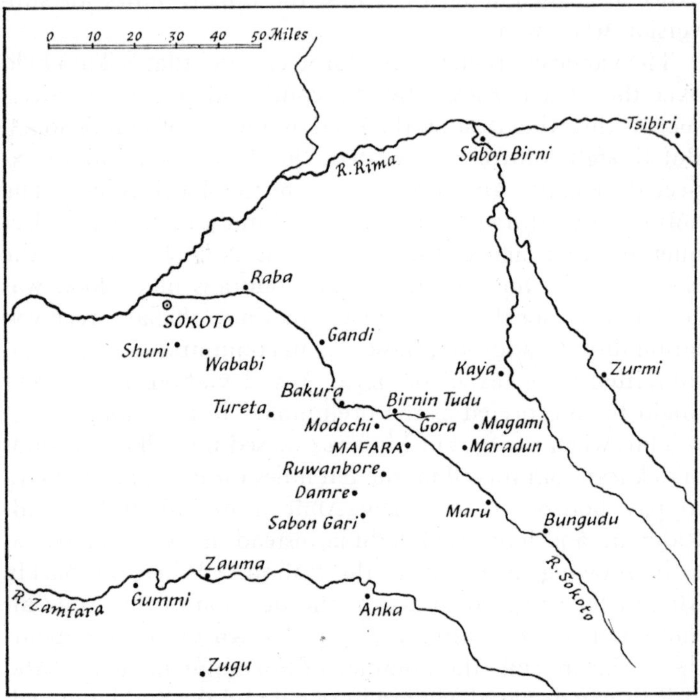

7. To illustrate the Mafara Revolt, 1891

The forces at Sokoto's immediate disposal were considerable. The Emir of Zamfara at Zurmi was to hold the east against Gobir; the Amīr Rafi at Kaya was to move to Magami and blockade Maradun from the north; the Sarkin Burmi (Bakura) moved upriver to the ribāṭ at Modochi to block Mafara from the west. The Ardon Sullebawa also started raiding from the west, out of Shuni; the Sarkin Donko was

[83] The Sarkin Donko was in Sokoto at this time. Cf. Krieger, *op. cit.*, pp. 111 ff. Correspondence, V, 72, probably refers to this revolt.

sent to join the Sarkin Mafara (Gummi) Laje in attacking Zauma and Anka;[84] the Marafa was sent against Damre, while the Magajin gari, being in charge of Zamfara, was sent south-east of Mafara to raise cavalry from Maru. The Amīr al-mu'minīn sent out a force to Wababi, which then went on to Mafara and captured Ruwanbore; Sabon Gari and Damre were taken from the south, while in the north Maradun was captured. Meanwhile, the Sultan of Gobir had come down through north-east Sokoto and joined Mafara, but after destroying Tureta, they separated, the Gobirawa returning home, while the Sarkin Mafara (Mafara) sent an army, unsuccessfully, against the Sarkin Burmi (Bakura). In the course of the war there was a surprise attack on the Mafara market, followed by a massacre. The people of Mafara could no longer continue the war, and, deposing their Sarki, asked the Sarkin Burmi to mediate. The terms seem stiff; all captives to be released and a thousand slaves given up; all conquered land to be surrendered to the Amīr al-mu'minīn, and Birnin Tudu, Sabon Gari, Ruwanbore and Damre to be ceded to the Sarkin Burmi, Maradun to be given to Amīr Rafi al-Ḥājj, while Zauma was to be divided between the Sarkin Donko (at Zugu) and the Sarkin Mafara (at Gummi); all (escaped) slaves taken by them were to be returned; and certain practices, like pouring dust on the head, were to end.

This effective end to the revolt demonstrated the striking power of Sokoto and how little the Caliph would tolerate even the beginnings of disobedience. Mafara, once isolated—and this was easily done owing to the internal rivalries of Zamfara—was no match: the Gobirawa could march down with impunity, but, beyond the particular raid, were of little help. In 1846, when Gobir was raiding through to Zamfara regularly and the land was sparsely populated, middle Zamfara could not be held. But now Kaya and other Zamfara Fulani

---

[84] The Sarkin Donko had been forced out of Zugu by the previous Sarkin Zamfara (Anka) (P. G. Harris, *op. cit.*, p. 117; Bukwium District notebook). Krieger (p. 121) identifies Laje as the Sarkin Mafara at Garangi: Garangi and Gummi are neighbouring towns. Cf. Gummi District notebook and Correspondence, IV, 71.

settlements were well established in the north, the Sullebawa were settled in the west, Bakura was loyal to Sokoto, and in the east were the other Muslim centres like Maru or Bungudu.

While Sokoto was strong enough to deal with its own revolts, it relied on the other emirates for support for external decisions. This being so, the authority of the Caliph rested largely on the justice of those decisions: he was incapable of enforcing a decision if the other Emirs felt it was unjust. The same attitudes and policies for Sokoto province did not hold for the subordinate emirates. In Zaria, Sokoto had been able to impose its will, since the tripartite division left Zaria weak.[85] In Kano, however, the tactics that succeeded in Mafara or Zaria were inapplicable, and 'Abd al-Raḥmān failed to see the limitations of his power. Since his decision to appoint Tukur as Emir was of doubtful justice as well as being unrealistic, he found little sympathy among the Emirs by whom alone his decision could have been enforced.

The origins of the crisis go back to the lengthy rule of the Emir of Kano 'Abdullāh b. Ibrāhīm and the consequent strength of his sons who had held high office under him.[86] There were at least five sons of distinction.[87] When their uncle, Muḥammad Bello b. Ibrāhīm, had been appointed, there could be little opposition. But Muḥammad Bello hoped to secure the succession for his son, Tukur; he appointed him Galadima and sent unusually large presents to Sokoto, while Tukur showed his friendship with the Amīr al-mu'minīn 'Abd

---

[85] Sokoto had once to call upon the Emir of Kano 'Abdullāh to help in enforcing the return of 'Abdullāh as Emir of Zaria *c.* 1873 (Edgar, notebook, *Labarin Kano*, p. 2).

[86] See Muḥammad Bukhari b. Aḥmad, *Kitāb fī-mā jarā bainī wa-bain Amīr Hadijia wa-Yūsuf*. Edgar, *Litafi*, I, 187–91; III, 410–13. Correspondence, VII, 2, 3, 8, 9, 12, 19, 32, 39, 53, 60, 82, 87, 97, 103, 104; III, 9; V, 36. (Anon), *Faiḍ al-qadīr*; *Wajīz mulakhkhaṣ*. Cf. Muḥammad b. Ṣāliḥ, *Taqyīd al-akhbār*. Kano Chronicle (in H. R. Palmer, *Sudanese Memoirs*, III, 130–2). W. Wallace, *Geographical Journal* (1896), pp. 211 ff. C. H. Robinson, *Hausaland*, pp. 82–3, 211, 217. al-haji Abubakar Dokaji, *Kano Ta Dabo Cigari* (Zaria, 1958), pp. 61–7.

[87] al-haji Abubakar Dokaji (*op. cit.*, p. 58) lists twenty-eight sons of 'Abdullāh.

al-Raḥmān by his help on the abortive expedition against Argungu. When, therefore, Bello died, 'Abd al-Raḥmān ordered the Vizier to appoint Tukur as Emir of Kano. Though the Vizier advised against it, the Amīr al-mu'minīn paid no heed, and the Vizier was obliged to appoint Tukur surreptitiously and present a *fait accompli.*[88] Once the appointment was learnt, the sons of 'Abdullāh b. Ibrāhīm left the town, with Yūsuf as claimant to the Kano emirate. Yūsuf's following was large and included not only his brothers and their followers, but also officials like the Madawaki and the state and personal slaves who had followed his father. The crisis split the ruling families in almost every major town of the emirate. With a few important exceptions the incumbent ruler followed the legally appointed Tukur, while an uncle, brother or nephew followed Yūsuf and 'Alī. Yūsuf is also said to have made contact with the anti-Sokoto states, such as Damagaram, Gumel and Ningi, as well as attracting the lawless element in Kano itself.

An attempt was made to isolate Yūsuf. Letters were sent to the Emirs ordering them to boycott Yūsuf, but without asking for aid. The Vizier went personally to Hadejia, but failed to get the Emir's active co-operation since Yūsuf was there at the same time and loyalties were divided in Hadejia. A small force, however, from Hadejia which was with Tukur was defeated by Yūsuf. The other emirates, while not helping Yūsuf, made no move to help either Tukur or the Vizier. It is said that in Kontagora the Emir, Ibrāhīm b. 'Umar, refused to fight Yūsuf, as a fellow-Muslim. Meanwhile, the devastation was great: Yūsuf's army foraged outside Kano city; inside Kano city, Tukur executed captives as pagans, and there was a severe shortage of food.[89]

When Yūsuf died in his camp, 'Alī, a son of 'Abdullāh by a daughter of the Amīr al-mu'minīn 'Alī (1842–59), took over the leadership and some two months later managed to

---

[88] Bello died in late November 1893 and Tukur was probably turbanned the following month (D. M. Last, *op. cit.*, *J.H.S.N.*, 1966).

[89] The execution was ordered by the Amīr al-mu'minīn: (Anon), *Faiḍ al-qadīr*, f. 12; cf. Wallace, *op. cit.*, p. 212.

win control of Kano city.[90] Once Tukur was out of Kano, his cause was known to be lost, and no help could be expected from the Emirs: the Amīr al-mu'minīn is said to have wanted to summon the eastern armies for an expedition, but it proved impossible. The Emir of Katsina, who was embarrassed by Tukur taking refuge in his emirate, sent out a force against 'Alī, but it was routed; the Emir then returned to Katsina, which was threatened from Maradi. The Emir of Zamfara came, and started raiding Kano, while the Emir of the South (Adamawa), returning home from Sokoto, avoided meeting either Tukur or 'Alī. The Vizier remained in touch with everyone, trying to arrange action. The affair was ended by Tukur being cornered by 'Alī's forces, and killed by 'Abbās, a brother of 'Alī.[91] 'Alī was then recognized as Emir by the Amīr al-mu'minīn; a reconciliation was attempted, and some of Tukur's supporters returned.[92] In consequence of this dispute with Sokoto, 'Alī is said to have reduced the annual presents to the Amīr al-mu'minīn, but conditions in Kano after the civil war, as well as the past generosity of the Emir of Kano Muḥammad Bello, must have made the previous level of giving too difficult to maintain.[93]

In contrast to the Mafara affair, this crisis shows the impotence of the Caliph, should he try to enforce a personal preference. Against Hadejia in the years after 1846, the Amīr al-mu'minīn had support from the neighbouring emirates, and an army could be sent out under the Vizier or his lieutenant. In Kano, there was no attempt to use force to intervene. Only the death of both Tukur and Yūsuf, which allowed the solution of accepting 'Alī, saved face for the Amīr al-mu'minīn.

---

[90] Entry into Kano *c.* September 1894 (Rabī' I, 1312); Yūsuf died probably in June 1894 (Dhū'l-ḥijja 1311); cf. al-haji Junaidu, *Tarihin Fulani*, pp. 66 f.

[91] Tukur died in March 1895 (Ramaḍān 1312); cf. Robinson, *op. cit.*, p. 217.

[92] Tukur's brother, the Sarkin Shano Ibrāhīm, however, continued to oppose 'Alī from neighbouring emirates, such as Katsina. He also sought help from the Sultan of Damagaram; but the latter was badly defeated by 'Alī (*Faiḍ al-qadīr*, fols. 22–5).

[93] J. A. Burdon, *Notes on Tribute in Sokoto Province* (7 March 1904).

The evident powerlessness of Sokoto to assert its will must have harmed the prestige of the caliphate. Whereas Bukhari in Hadejia in the 1850's was inaccessible on the Bornu marches and relied on the Shaikh of Bornu for protection, Kano, the most populous of the emirates, was central and vulnerable to the Maradi and Damagăram forces that took advantage of the disunity. At the same time the Ningi pagans too were a threat, being liable to use this opportunity to raid into both Zaria and Kano. The situation looked more precarious than it in fact was: as soon as the crisis resolved itself—after nearly two years—the situation returned to normal. There was little advantage to be gained by 'Alī if he had seceded from the caliphate: he would have jeopardised his case—that he had been wrongfully treated by the Amīr al-mu'minīn—and lost much of his support from the neighbouring emirates whose own legitimacy he would have been denying if he had refused to acknowledge the caliphate. Further, the prosperity of Kano and its Emir depended on a secure government which secession would destroy, and which the two years of civil war had already seriously damaged. Lastly, to men brought up in the strongly Islamic atmosphere of the caliphate, the threat of excommunication, of being declared an apostate, would not be a matter to be lightly disregarded. As in Hadejia, the dispute was fundamentally over succession, not over the legitimacy of the Sokoto caliphate. Collectively, the caliphate, in moral authority if not in armed force, was too strong to be broken.

Many of the crises in or between emirates were solved locally, with the minimum of interference from Sokoto: appeal, however, was usually made to the Caliph. An example is the Ako crisis in Gombe *c.* 1899–1900.[94] Here, the Amīr Bornu (Missau), exercising his extraterritorial rights on the Bornu marches, was in a strong position to aid the Galadima of Ako to defy his Emir, the Amīr al-jaish (Gombe). Without the support or approval of the neighbouring Emirs,

[94] Gombe Correspondence: 13, 19, 28, 30, 34, 35, 61, 67, 72, 73, 80, 81, 89, 101, 127, 130, 137, 139, 140, 142, 150, 154–7, 160, 163, 167–8, 170–4, 177, 180, 200, 202, 206, 207, 209, 212, 220, 224.

the Amīr al-jaish, who seems to have been unjust in his treatment of Ako, was powerless. Sokoto could only arbitrate: the Vizier told the Amīr Bornu (Missau) to withdraw, and the Amīr al-jaish was ordered to pardon the Galadima, who himself sent to seek pardon. When this failed, the senior Emir of the area, the Emir of Bauchi, was told to mediate and bring the Galadima and his Emir together. The Emir of Bauchi was not wholly impartial: the Galadima was with him in Bauchi, and a settlement, somewhat unfavourable to the Amīr al-jaish 'Umar, was negotiated. Death, however, eliminated some of the hostility: 'Umar's Galadima, who had suffered at the hands of Ako's ally, the Amīr Bornu, died, followed not long afterwards by the Amīr Bornu himself.

Minor rebellions did not warrant an expedition from Sokoto. Though Mahdism challenged the religious leadership of Sokoto, the caliphate was too well established: the forces of the local Emirs were left to contain, if not destroy, the rebels. Thus Jibrīl Gaini withstood the ostracism of Sokoto and the armies of his neighbours for some fifteen years.[95] Based on the walled town of Burmi, which, with Bima hill, was soon associated with supernatural legends, he attracted many through his religious activities, using the appeal of Mahdism: but he was unable to expand very far territorially. Similarly Ḥayāt b. Sa'īd, though he might draw adherents to himself as the lieutenant of the Sudanese Mahdi for the west, could not succeed so long as the surrounding Emirs, as well as the Caliph, scorned his call to them to join the Mahdi.[96] This is the more remarkable since Hausaland had long been excited by expectations of the coming of the Mahdi, and the overthrow of Bornu by Rābiḥ, and the penetration of the Christians elsewhere, suggested that the coming was soon.[97]

[95] e.g. Correspondence, II, 28, 30, 32, 34, 35; IV, 48, 40, 43, 28; two uncatalogued.

[96] e.g. Correspondence, IV, 24, 26; three uncatalogued letters. Cf. letter from Mariam bint al-Shaikh to the Emir of Kano (Muḥammad Bello), quoted in al-haji Junaidu, *Is'āf al-zā'irīn*.

[97] For Mahdism in nineteenth-century Hausaland, see S. Biobaku, M. A. al-Hajj, 'The Sudanese Mahdiyya and the Niger-Chad region' in *Islam in Tropical Africa* (edited I. M. Lewis, I.A.I. and Oxford, 1966, pp. 425 ff.).

The coming of the British, on the other hand, looms larger after the event than before it: it was not the preoccupation of Sokoto. Although refugees from the French capture of Segu were received in Sokoto and given land, their constant jeremiads were of little effect.[98] The Amīr al-mu'minīn 'Abd al-Raḥmān followed a policy of closing the frontiers and markets to traders from hostile territories: it was the policy used against Bornu and Faḍlullāh, against Argungu and the Christians.[99] But with the seizure of Bida and Ilorin by the Christians, followed by the consolidation of the Royal Niger Company, and, after 1900, of Lugard's Government in the southern dependencies of the caliphate, the attitude of Sokoto stiffened:[100] Christians were asked to leave and their agents treated with only the minimum courtesy.[101] Till then, they had been given the hospitality afforded foreign traders and travellers who had been frequenting Sokoto in large numbers since the days of the Shaikh, while the Royal Niger Company paid the annual traditional gift.[102] More ominous

---

[98] Burdon (*Northern Nigeria*, p. 74) gives their number at about 10,000, which is surely an exaggeration. They were allowed to settle at Karantudu; their leader, Aḥmad, is said to be buried at Maikulki, south of Binji. They also became unpopular through their constant begging. Cf. an anonymous MS. on Aḥmad b. al-ḥājj 'Umar from the *Fonds Vieillard* (I.F.A.N., Dakar; Ibadan photo-copy, No. 176); and Gombe Correspondence, Nos. 20–7 (where Aḥmad's seal is still being used by the refugees then in the Bornu marches).

[99] Cf. Clapperton (2nd journey), p. 237; Robinson, *op. cit.*, p. 120. Backwell (letter) No. 28; Gombe Correspondence, Nos. 91, 92, 94, 100, 178, 193; both contain requests by Rābiḥ and Faḍlullāh for opening trade, which in the latter's case was granted. Cf. Royal Niger Co., *Arabic Letter Book*, pp. 25–6. Cf. Journal of Cazemajou in *B.C.A.F.* (vol. X, 1900), pp. 281, 243. Correspondence, III, 34 (blockade of Argungu), but cf. III, 17. Also cf. Bello, *Sard al-kalām*, p. 5.

[100] Cf. *Arabic Letter Book*, p. 12. A year after the taking of Bida and Ilorin (January–February 1897), a French expedition under Cazemajou was refused entry into Sokoto. He had, however, already made a treaty with Argungu. Three years before, in 1895, Dr. Grüner had been refused a treaty by the Emir of Gwandu (cf. forthcoming article in *J.H.S.N.* by Professor W. Markov and P. Sebald).

[101] Cf. Royal Niger Company, *Arabic Letter Book*, pp. 111–12, 165.

[102] Cf. Backwell, letter No. 30.

had been the French expedition under Voulet and Chanoine which passed through northern Sokoto, burning and sacking as they went.[103] Salame, near Wurno, was burnt, and the ribāṭ at Shinaka destroyed. But these French were birds of passage, and Salame was rebuilt, while Goronyo replaced Shinaka. The Christians, it was said, were like a stream that would soon dry up after the storm.[104]

Above all, there was the sure belief that what is the will of Allah must come to pass. The best defence, therefore, was prayer. Apart from prayer and the making of protective charms against bullet wounds, few other preparations for defence were made in Sokoto. The Amīr al-mu'minīn 'Abd al-Raḥmān had died the October before the British threatened, and his successor, Muḥammad Attahiru b. Aḥmad, was not popular in Sokoto: the sons of 'Alī b. Bello disapproved of his election, while the sons of 'Abd al-Raḥmān feared expropriation.[105] With the Caliph new and Sokoto somewhat divided and unsettled, opinions conflicted: not all were prepared to emigrate.[106] Nonetheless the contingents were called in from the local towns in the Sokoto hinterland, and a large army assembled. But there was no co-ordination with the Kano force which had come to Sokoto with the Emir of Kano to greet the Amīr al-mu'minīn and was on its way back when it met a small force of British-led troops. The Emir of Kano here deserted his army and fled north to Gobir, planning to go to Mecca.[107]

Bauchi and Zaria were under British control; the French were north of Katsina, while Bornu was in confusion after the

---

[103] May 1899. Gombe Correspondence, Nos. 1, 131. D.M., ff. 74b, 75. Birnin Konni was also sacked.

[104] Cf. notes to a poem, collected by F. Edgar, in National Archives, Kaduna (Kadcap 2:6) on the capture of Sokoto.

[105] The election of Muḥammad Attahiru was on 13 October 1902 (Rajab 1320), three days after 'Abd al-Raḥmān's death, and the battle at Sokoto took place on 15 March 1903 (Dhū'l-ḥijja 1320): *v. infra*, p. 175; D.M., ff. 84b, 85.

[106] D.M., f. 85b.

[107] Passes were prepared for the Emir of Kano addressed to the Sultan of Gobir to let him travel through. Correspondence, VII, 124–9. Cf. Backwell (letter), No. 125; (Anon), *Faiḍ al-qadīr*.

defeat of Rābiḥ and Faḍlullāh.[108] Given these conditions, the scarcity of water and food late in the dry season and the delays involved in summoning the Emirs and their forces, a large mustering of the eastern Emirs in the manner of the autumn expedition was impracticable. Moreover, the small numbers of the invaders would scarcely warrant it. Nonetheless, there had been talk of emigrating to the east, as pilgrims probably rather than as Mahdists, since there is no mention of the Amīr al-mu'minīn recognising the Sudanese Khalīfa till later, at the battle of Burmi.[109] Thus when the battle at Sokoto was lost, the Amīr al-mu'minīn started slowly making his way east, followed by some scholars and gentry.[110] Most of the office-holders, however, remained behind to maintain the dār al-Islām under a new Amīr al-mu'minīn.[111] News of Christian control of other Islamic states—Algeria, Tunisia, Egypt and the Sudan—must have made emigration or the pilgrimage to Mecca appear hopeless: it seemed better to accept, together with British control, Lugard's promise not to interfere with the practice of Islam, than to abandon the jamā'a of the Shaikh.

---

[108] French in Ahir, Zinder and Baghirmi: cf. Correspondence (uncatalogued), Aḥmad b. Tanima, Sultan of Damagaram to Amīr Kano 'Alī b. 'Abdullāh (two letters).

[109] e.g. Backwell (letters), Nos. 125, 128; cf. *Faiḍ al-qadīr*, ff. 25, 26. According to Muhammad al-Hajj, Sa'īd b. Ḥayāt claims that Attahiru accepted Mahdism at Burmi.

[110] Burdon, Second Monthly Report (30 April 1903).

[111] *v. infra*, pp. 176f.

Part III:

The Vizierate in Sokoto, 1804–1903

7
The Viziers

(i) *Introduction*

Of the offices in the administration of Sokoto, the vizierate is the best documented after that of the Amīr al-mu'minīn. There are the writings of Viziers on the careers of the three Caliphs—the Shaikh, Bello and 'Alī; there are their polemical and explanatory writings on the religious affiliations of Bello; there are an index of names, a little poetry and a moral fable. In addition, there are over six hundred letters addressed to the Vizier or Amīr al-mu'minīn and covering for the most part the last twenty years of the century. Finally, the present Vizier is acknowledged as the most learned historian in Sokoto.

For the other lineages of major officials, little has yet been recovered; some material on the Magajin gari family is said to have been burnt. None of the other officials seem to have written anything, at least that has survived: scholarship was not part of their traditional work, as it was for the Vizier. Consequently their characters and achievements are somewhat shadowy; their importance, then, may be underrated. This is probably the case for 'Uthmān Mudegel b. 'Umar al-Kammu, whose name recurs for offices more important than those the Vizier first held.

Nonetheless, the vizierate was the leading office under the caliphate. Its character was sanctioned and defined by classical antecedents as none of the other major offices, such as the Magajin rafi, were sanctioned. Its primacy was established by these antecedents. Thus while the character of the individuals determined the measure of the influence of the other offices, the vizierate, like the caliphate, was too powerful to suffer through a particular holder of the office. The other offices appear still more insubstantial because of the shadowiness of the holders' characters. The Viziers, on the other hand, seem to adopt the stereotyped substance typical of the office: at least, in the histories, only the qualities appropriate to a Vizier are mentioned. While probably not untrue—since the image of an office imposes its own character—the portrait must be partial: but how partial it is, is not clear. The history of the vizierate, therefore, is a history more of the office than of the men who held it.

The classical vizierate is based on the text: 'Appoint for me from my folk a wazīr [helper], Aaron, my brother; by him confirm my strength and join him with me in my affair.'[1] Vizier was not an official title before the Abbasid caliphate: wazīr is one who bears a burden, and thus came to mean a helper.[2] But when the Abbasid bureaucracy was developed and specific offices and titles were defined, the classical theory of the vizierate, expressed for example in al-Māwardī, *al-Aḥkām al-Sulṭāniyya*, was based on Abbasid practice.[3] The administration of most succeeding states had a Vizier, but the number of Viziers, their importance and their sphere of influence varied. Among the Seljuks, the Vizier was low in the hierarchy; in Spain, they were so numerous that the senior Vizier was called Chamberlain; the Hafsids gave the office military duties, the Almohads only secretarial work, while the Fatimids changed it from a civilian to a military appointment.[4] The Ottomans also modelled their vizierate on the Abbasid system, but so extended the office that the senior Vizier was given the title Grand Vizier, al-Wazīr al-A'ẓam.[5]

The Sokoto vizierate is based on the Abbasid theory and

---

[1] Quran, 20: 28–32. Translation of F. H. El-Masri.

[2] D. Sourdel, *Le Vizirat Abbaside* (Paris, 1959–60), vol. I, pp. 50 ff.

[3] Mawerdi, *Les Statuts Gouvernementaux* (trans. Fagnan), pp. 43 ff.

[4] Ibn Khaldūn, *The Muqaddimah* (trans. Rosenthal), II, pp. 3 ff.

[5] H. A. R. Gibb and H. Bowen, *Islamic Society and the West*, pt. I, pp. 107 ff. The English 'vizier' is derived from the Turkish form. The Hausa form is 'waziri'.

did not specifically copy any more recent Muslim state. The two books written early in the jihād—the Shaikh's *Bayān wujūb al-hijra* (November 1806) and 'Abdullāh's *Ḍiyā' al-ḥukkām* (*c.* 1807–8), while not actually mentioning al-Māwardī, follow the arguments made familiar by him. *Bayān wujūb al-hijra* is general:

'The first pillar [of a kingdom] is an upright wazīr over the wilāya who wakens [the king] if he sleeps and gives him sight if he cannot see and reminds him if he is heedless. The greatest catastrophe which could befall the wilāya and its subjects is to be deprived of good wazīrs and helpers. One of the requirements of a wazīr is that he should be truly benevolent and kind-hearted towards the people.'[6]

Later, it continues: 'As for the office of wazīr, it is in conformity with the Sharī'a; it centres on a man, trustworthy both in his religion and intelligence, who is to be consulted by the Caliph in all matters of his concern. God has said through the tongue of Moses, "Appoint for me from my folk a wazīr, Aaron, my brother; by him confirm my strength", and a tradition of the Prophet says, "My wazīrs from the folk of heaven are Gabriel and Michael, and my wazīrs from among the folk of the earth are Abū Bakr and 'Umar".'[7]

'Abdullāh, in *Ḍiyā' al-ḥukkām*, is more concerned than the Shaikh with the offices in the government. He distinguishes between the vizierates having delegated, executive or consultative authority, but only the delegated authority is described in detail.[8] The distinction between executive and delegated authority, such as is found in al-Māwardī, derives from the varied careers of the Abbasid Viziers, and was not applicable in the new communities. No mention is also made of the well-known division of government into the 'sword' and the 'pen', which is described by Ibn Khaldūn and al-Qalqashandī: deriving from late Abbasid practice, it was particularly developed in Egypt, but it too was as little relevant to Sokoto conditions as it was to the classical period.[9]

---

[6] Chapter 9. Translation by F. H. El-Masri. [7] Chapter 10.

[8] Bāb 2, faṣl 1. The third group, the consultative viziers, are simply helpers.

[9] Ibn Khaldūn, *loc. cit.* al-Qalqashandī, *Ṣubḥ al-a'shā*, book III.

The needs of the newly established Community in Sokoto were more akin to those of the early Muslim Community than the organised bureaucracies of North Africa. Therefore the pattern adopted was that of the early Community as translated into Abbasid practice and idealised by Abbasid theorists.[10]

The first Vizier in Sokoto, as suggested above, was in the Quranic sense: 'Appoint for me from my folk a wazīr [helper], Aaron, my brother.' 'Abdullāh, the Shaikh's brother, was acknowledged the senior Vizier, Wazīruhu al-akbar wa-ruknuhu al-abhar.[11] Except when he left for Kano in 1807–8 (1222) or went on campaigns, 'Abdullāh kept close to the Shaikh. He lived next to him at Degel; he was the first to acknowledge the Shaikh Amīr al-mu'minīn.[12] His work was not defined: he was one of the 'helpers' of the Shaikh and his title showed he was the most senior of them. But he valued the title, even after the Shaikh died, when he was unwilling at first to recognise any new Vizier. One of the other Viziers of the Shaikh was 'Umar al-Kammu, the first student of the Shaikh and his close friend; he had been given the care of the booty after the capture of Matankari, but he never appears as leading military expeditions or taking part in other battles, in which work 'Abdullāh distinguished himself. Muḥammad Bello was another 'helper', wazīr, but like 'Umar al-Kammu only listed as such, without ever bearing any title.[13] The absence of 'Abdullāh in Kano for the dry season 1807–8 underlines the titular nature of the vizierate at this period. He did not forfeit the title then, since his role in Sokoto required no replacement. It was Bello who had gone to give the oaths to the eastern Emirs on the Shaikh's behalf, or who was to build the walls of Gwandu for the Shaikh. On his return from Kano, 'Abdullāh seems to have resumed his

[10] Cf. Hiskett, 'An Islamic tradition of reform in the Western Sudan', *B.S.O.A.S.*, 1962, p. 592.

[11] I.M., p. 188.

[12] Gidado dan Laima, *Majmū' khiṣāl al-Shaikh*. I.M., p. 70.

[13] The fourth of the Shaikh's Viziers, his cousin Sa'd, does not seem to have been sufficiently distinguished to merit frequent mention. It is possible he is the Sa'd who carried the flag at Tsuntsua and was killed there (I.M., p. 87).

place in the Sokoto command, and four years later became responsible for the western emirates.

Though it could be argued that 'Abdullāh and Bello exercised considerable 'delegated authority' as Viziers, leading expeditions or supervising emirates, the vizierate only moved markedly from the early Quranic to the Abbasid ideal when Muḥammad Bello succeeded to the caliphate and appointed his messenger as his Vizier. No longer is the Vizier a helper from the family, but the first minister in a government. This is expressed in eligibility for the caliphate: 'Abdullāh expected or hoped to become Caliph, whereas to elect Gidado was inconceivable. The change was part of the establishment of organised government which Bello undertook. Bello, who, of the three, had specialised in writing books on politics and who had expressed the need for evolving or adapting theory to suit local contemporary conditions, transformed the simple administration that had sufficed the Shaikh.

(ii) *The Vizier Gidado 1817–42*

The first Vizier under Muḥammad Bello, and founder of the line, was 'Uthmān, known as Gidado, b. Abī Bakr, known as Sambo Laima, b. 'Umar, known as Gabinda, b. Aḥmad. Gidado was his Fulani name, meaning 'beloved'; his father's nickname, Sambo Laima, distinguished him from his brother Abū Bakr 'Garba Laima', but the exact implication of Laima here is not known.[14] Laima is a common place-name (meaning 'dampness' in Hausa), and occurs, for example, in north-east Konni and west Kebbi: with both areas his family was connected.

The background of the family was mixed. His father's ancestors were Torobe (Toronkawa) from Konni, but no more specific relationship with the Shaikh is recorded.[15] The

[14] Gidado dan Laima, *Risāla fī l'-nisba*. The genealogical details that follow also derive from this book.

[15] Gidado's line is traced from Belari ('Black'), the 'son' of Mūsā Jokollo, while the Shaikh is from 'Alī, also a 'son' of Mūsā Jokollo (source: al-haji Junaidu; D.M., f. 8).

family was accustomed to going to Kebbi, if not staying there, and Gidado's paternal grandfather, 'Umar, had married into a Kebbi Fulani family, who had immigrated from Bornu in the days of the Kanta. This family may have been of some standing: the head of it was Malam Muḥammad Yerima whose name implies he was a scholar and includes a title that originated in Bornu.

Gidado's mother was of equally diverse origins: her father was from the Galanko'en Fulani and so linked to the mother of Muḥammad Bello through an ancestor, the chief Jo; her mother was from a leading family of Sullebawa.

The grandparents of Gidado, then, were Torodo, Kebbi-Bornu Fulani, Galankejo and ba-Sullebe. Such Fulani cosmopolitanism is a corrective to the image presented by the introverted Torodo genealogy of the Shaikh; there is no evidence, however, to show which pattern predominated in eighteenth-century Fulani society. The connections which this diversity of background represents may have served Gidado in good stead, first as a messenger and then as Vizier: but it cannot be assumed that such a background was a necessary qualification for these offices.

Gidado was born about 1776 (*c.* 1190 A.H.)—five years before Muḥammad Bello. He joined the Shaikh, and then persuaded his father and uncle to come up from Kambaza in Kebbi and join also. His father, given the title of a Shaikh, composed some praises of the Shaikh;[16] both father and uncle died at Degel, but the house there is not recorded by Gidado.[17]

Gidado himself remained close to the Shaikh and his family, and, probably shortly after the jihād, married a daughter of the Shaikh, Asmā'. Her mother, Maimūna, was the senior wife, and first cousin, of the Shaikh, but Asmā' was probably not the first wife of Gidado; she was about eighteen years his junior.[18] From the early accounts which mention

---

[16] R.J., f. 12b. 'Abd al-Qādir b. Gidado, *Basṭ al-fawā'id,* section 1.

[17] Source: al-haji Junaidu.

[18] He also married a daughter of the Zaria leader M. Mūsā, Ṣāliḥa (or Ḥalīma: M. G. Smith, *op. cit.*), whose children remained in Zaria. I do not know the date of this marriage, but it was probably after the marriage to Asmā'.

her, it seems her truthfulness drew her close to the Shaikh; she was clever, picking up Tamajek from a concubine at Degel, and, in later years, was noted for her learning.[19] She composed poems in Arabic and Fulfulde and wrote three books in Arabic.[20] The last survivor of the hijra from Degel, she was greatly respected as an authority and arbiter. She died twelve years after Gidado, having borne him five sons. Two of them became Viziers, the third the Dangaladima of the Vizier.[21] Her twin brother, al-Ḥasan, died early, aged 23, leaving a son who received the title of Sardauna and the charge of Marnona.[22] Her full sister, Ḥafṣa, married a servant of the Shaikh, Dembo, and later married Mudegel, but died before 1837.

Of Gidado's brothers, little is heard. Only Muḥammad Mudi is known as helping Gidado: Clapperton draws a sympathetic picture of him, while an elegy on his death was written by ʻAbd al-Qādir b. al-Muṣṭafā.[23] He had lived on the frontier at Goronyo and died there a martyr, fighting the pagans.

Gidado mainly appears, prior to his official position of Vizier, as a messenger or special envoy. Before the jihād, for example, he accompanied Muḥammad Bello to Kadaye to fetch books.[24] Though Gidado was a good Arabist, at least by the style of his later books, and spoke it fluently according to Clapperton, he was never listed as a scribe of either the Shaikh or Bello.[25] Most of his time was spent with Bello, who used to send him with messages to the Shaikh.[26] But his most crucial tasks were in Bornu. He was sent to collect the Caliph's share of the booty from Birnin Gazargamu in 1808: in the course of the rather perilous journey, he met all the Fulani

---

[19] R.J., f. 36. [20] See bibliography.

[21] One died of smallpox in April 1824 (Clapperton, 1st journey, p. 108).

[22] A.M., p. 13. The son was Khalilu: cf. Sa'īd, p. 203.

[23] e.g. Clapperton (1st journey), pp. 101 f., 105. The elegy consists of twenty-three lines rhyming in ā' (copy in Niz.). Mudi's descendants are now in Danmaliki.

[24] K.B., p. 8. It is possible it was the Shaikh, not Muḥammad Bello who went to Kadaye. Gidado carried books for Bello: Sa'īd, f. 112a.

[25] Clapperton (1st journey), p. 81. [26] e.g. K.B., p. 19.

leaders.[27] This knowledge of conditions in Bornu was probably a good reason for sending him a few years later to negotiate the truce with al-Kanemi at Siko, and carry the letters between the Shaikh and al-Kanemi.[28]

Both in *Rauḍ al-jinān* and in the lists of Bello's companions, he refers to himself as one of the messengers. He also, in these lists, bears the title of Amīr al-maṣāliḥ.[29] This title, later found usually in conjunction with a rhyming second half, wālī al-naṣā'iḥ, may be of classical origin, but I have been unable to trace it.[30] 'Abdullāh b. Fodiye is said to have invented it, although it never occurs in connection with him or in his books.[31] 'Maṣāliḥ' usually refers to good works, or, in a governmental sense, public works and welfare.[32] Wālī al-naṣā'iḥ, 'lord of advice', is appropriate for any counsellor. In *Infāq al-maisūr*, a certain learned Muḥammad is called wālī al-naṣā'iḥ, but no significance is there attached to it.[33] It is likely that the phrase was used primarily as a rhyme, having a suitable meaning. The full title, however, was largely confined to written Arabic documents; the title in common use was waziri.

The position of Gidado before Bello's caliphate was personal rather than public. Without strong clan ties or geographical links, he was never the leader of a particular group. Gidado did not usually lead armies, nor did he receive territorial responsibilities; he was less of a public figure than, for example, Mudegel, whose father had held a high place in the Community's affairs.[34]

---

[27] R.J., ff. 4, 4b. Gidado was not the only messenger: his cousin Muḥammad Sambo was sent to Katagum (K.B., p. 12). The sword, 'Bi-salām', captured from the Mai Bornu, was given to Gidado and became the sword of office. Cf. R.J., f. 8b.

[28] I.M., pp. 144; 162, 167; 120.

[29] R.J., f. 12; *Majmū' aṣḥāb . . . Muḥammad Bello.*

[30] M. Sourdel, in a personal communication, says he has not met the title in works of the classical period.

[31] Al-haji Junaidu attributes the coining of the title to 'Abdullāh.

[32] It is sometimes translated into Hausa as Sarkin gyara: gyara means 'repair'.

[33] I.M., p. 23.

[34] In the *Majmū' aṣḥāb Bello* (al-haji Junaidu's copy), he is listed as a wazīr of Muḥammad Bello.

On Bello's election as Amīr al-mu'minīn, Gidado became the Vizier of the caliphate. The title was already held by the Shaikh's Vizier, 'Abdullāh b. Fodiye, who was unwilling, it seems, to surrender it. Only after the capture of Kalembaina, when Bello and 'Abdullāh were reconciled, in Gidado's second year as Vizier, did 'Abdullāh formally recognise the new Vizier, giving Gidado his robes in token.[35] Nonetheless, the title was not in frequent use: Clapperton, who stayed eight months in Sokoto under the care and hospitality of Gidado, mentions that Gidado was the Vizier, but refers to him usually as 'the Gadado'.[36] It is possible that out of deference to 'Abdullāh Gidado did not call himself Vizier.

The work of Gidado did not change on his appointment except that in so far as the status of Bello and Sokoto had increased, so his responsibility was greater. While retaining the title of Amīr al-maṣāliḥ, he still lists himself among the messengers of Bello, although there are others now he names as messengers along with him. The 'Viziers' he lists are the other officials, relatives of Bello and Fulani leaders.[37]

As the Vizier, Gidado had considerable freedom of judgement. On his own initiative he retired the Emir of Daura, Isḥāq, and appointed his son, Zubair b. Isḥāq. This was later approved by Bello.[38] When al-Kanemi was invading the Bornu marches and eastern Kano, Gidado was sent out to take command of the joint army.[39] At this time he was responsible for all the Emirs under the caliphate, as Bello's minister. Although the Emirs would normally come to greet the Amīr al-mu'minīn once a year and join the autumn expedition, much travelling was involved. During some of Bello's campaigns Gidado was evidently away, but the Vizier's place was generally at the Caliph's side, both in war and in council. At the siege of Kalembaina, he took the ultimatum to the rebels and escorted their messenger back.[40] At the attack on Konya, which Clapperton witnessed, the Vizier

---

[35] Sa'd b. 'Abd al-Raḥmān, *Tartīb al-aṣḥāb*.

[36] Clapperton (1st journey), pp. 76, 81. He thought 'Gidado' meant 'Vizier'.

[37] *Majmū' aṣḥāb Bello*.

[38] K.B., p. 19.

[39] Clapperton (2nd journey), p. 243.

[40] K.B., p. 15.

was camped and stationed near to the Amīr al-mu'minīn.[41] Again, when Ibra was raiding near Sokoto, Gidado was left at the camp to warn Bello, who had gone into Sokoto to preach on the Thursday evening.[42] Or when a new town site was to be marked out, Bello and Gidado went together, with only a few others.[43]

The early Caliphs appear to have done much, if not all, of their correspondence themselves. Though Gidado, like Malam al-Muṣṭafā, wrote to Shaikh Aḥmad of Masina, the letters have not survived. The letter to Masina was one of several written from Sokoto: not only Bello himself, but also 'Abdullāh b. Fodiye, Khalilu b. 'Abdullāh, Muḥammad Bukhari b. al-Shaikh and, after Bello's death, Abū Bakr Atiku had all written.[44] The letter of Gidado, then, was supplementary.

Little of the routine correspondence has survived from the early period: with one exception such that has survived is written by Bello, since his writings would be of greater value to preserve.[45] Consequently, it is not clear how far Gidado acted as an official secretary in the manner of the later Viziers. There is nothing in the accounts of Clapperton to suggest it. The letters that Bello wrote himself range from politics and medicine to current news: he gave political advice to the Tuareg Muḥammad Jailani;[46] he gave medical advice to the Emir of Zaria who was suffering from an undefined pain which Bello diagnosed as kidney trouble;[47] he sent Ya'qūb, Emir of Bauchi, the latest news of his movements and plans.[48] He also wrote to Malam Adama forwarding the Sharīf Qamar al-Dīn *en route* to Egypt.[49] These letters are in a personal style and deal with matters (with the exception of

[41] Clapperton (2nd journey), pp. 188, 190; 181, 185; cf. 1st journey, p. 106.

[42] K.B., p. 15.

[43] Clapperton (2nd journey), pp. 223 f.

[44] Abū Bakr Atiku to Aḥmad b. Muḥammad (*Fonds Brevié*, Dakar).

[45] Gidado to M. Adama (calling on him to renew his allegiance): the original (which I have not seen) is said to be in Garoua.

[46] 'Abd al-Qādir b. Gidado, *Majmū'* (letter 1).

[47] *Ibid.* (letter 7).

[48] A. D. H. Bivar (*B.S.O.A.S.*, 1959), pp. 337 ff.

[49] 'Abd al-Qādir b. Gidado, *op. cit.* (letter 8).

medicine) that later were usually left to the Viziers. Some are claimed to be in Bello's own handwriting, but there is not enough comparative material to be precise on this:[50] as there were several scribes and one man listed as 'secretary' in the caliphal household, one of them might have been employed, in the manner of the later secretaries.[51]

Less can be said of the letters of Abū Bakr Atiku.[52] All six were sent in his name, three to the Tuareg, one to Shaikh Aḥmad of Masina, one to M. Adama and one in general on Mahdism; though they deal with official matters, there is nothing in them to suggest they are the work of the Vizier or a secretary. Similarly, those of 'Alī are all in his name, though two-thirds of those preserved by the Vizier 'Abd al-Q̱ādir are generally addressed to the Community, and are therefore less personal in style and could be 'set pieces' by the Vizier or one of his staff.[53]

Under an active and young Caliph like Bello, the Vizier had less responsibility than his successors were to enjoy, and the area of that responsibility was less defined by consequence: Bello was the executive, and Gidado his assistant. Such a system depended on friendship to work well. When Bello died, relations between the new Amīr al-mu'minīn Abū Bakr Atiku and Gidado were not good. Gidado virtually retired from public work, though he retained the title of Vizier. His brother, Muḥammad Mudi, who had been his senior assistant, died in the course of Abū Bakr's caliphate; 'Abd al-Q̱ādir b. Gidado therefore acted for the Vizier.[54]

---

[50] Bivar, *op. cit.*

[51] The term used for 'secretary' is magatakarda (Hausa) or binduwo (Fulfulde). For the Sokoto Chancery, *v. infra.*

[52] Four in 'Abd al-Q̱ādir b. Gidado, *op. cit.*: copies are also found in Jos and in Ibadan (microfilm). The Masina letter, *v. supra.* The letter to M. Adama is in Garoua.

[53] The letters of 'Alī are (*a*) on microfilm in Ibadan; (*b*) in 'Abd al-Q̱ādir b. Gidado, *op. cit.* In letter 18 in 'Abd al-Q̱ādir b. Gidado, *Majmū'*, a passage is quoted as deriving from the Shaikh; the same passage without ascription occurs in Gidado dan Laima, *Majmū' khiṣāl al-Shaikh*, and 'Abd al-Q̱ādir b. Gidado, A.M., p. 10.

[54] It is possible that Tabi b. Mudi had acted as the Vizier's assistant for a while.

'Abd al-Qādir had had experience of campaigns from an early age: he was on twenty-five of Bello's forty-seven raids; on four with his uncle Abū Bakr Atiku before 1837 and on one to Nupe with his uncle 'Abd al-Qādir b. al-Shaikh and cousin Muḥammad b. 'Abdullāh.[55] These expeditions were the training ground for many of the young men, the sons of princes or councillors, as the lists of the mujāhidūn show.[56]

Other councillors also had retired: the Galadima Doshero sent his son Aḥmad to campaign with the Gwandu forces, while even the Commander of the Army (Amīr al-jaish) 'Alī Jedo used his sons as his deputies. His senior son, Abū Bakr, acting as Amīr al-jaish, had been killed on one expedition at which 'Abd al-Qādir b. Gidado was present under the command of Abū Bakr Atiku.[57] Abū 'l-Ḥasan b. 'Alī Jedo then campaigned alongside 'Abd al-Qādir b. Gidado as the representative of his father. But neither of them could act independently of their fathers in the matter of electing the new Amīr al-mu'minīn on the death of Abū Bakr Atiku. Although, since they were the acting officials, they doubtless influenced their fathers, both Gidado and 'Alī Jedo played their part in choosing the new Amīr al-mu'minīn.[58]

When 'Alī was elected to the caliphate after Abū Bakr Atiku, Gidado was over thirty years his senior: at 66, Gidado could scarcely fulfil the work of a Vizier, quite apart from the embarrassing disparity in age. After his years of service under Bello, the relationship between Gidado and 'Alī was more that of a father to his son than a minister to his Caliph. Since 'Alī wanted to reorganise and regularise the administration, which involved curtailing the responsibilities of the Vizier, it was necessary for Gidado to remain in retirement.[59] Though Gidado wanted to resume work, he was dissuaded by his wife, Asmā', and 'Alī. When Gidado objected to the reorganisation, his retirement was made final.[60] He kept, however, the

---

[55] A.M., p. 31.

[56] 'Abd al-Qādir b. Gidado, *Basṭ al-fawā'id*, Sections 2 and 3.

[57] A.M., p. 31. 'Umar b. Muḥammad Bukhari, *Tanbīh al-ikhwān*.

[58] Sa'īd, pp. 208 f.

[59] *v. supra*, p. 99.

[60] On the authority of al-haji Junaidu and M. Abd al-Qadiri Yahaya. Cf. Sa'īd, p. 208.

emeritus title of Vizier. What title ʿAbd al-Qādir took is not clear; he was not, it seems, given the title of Dangaladima, yet in the books he wrote he does not always style himself Vizier. Al-ḥājj Saʿīd refers to him as Vizier before the death of Gidado.[61] It is therefore possible that he was turbanned Vizier, while his father kept the honorary title.

The retirement of Gidado reflects the basis on which the early vizierate was built: friendship between Caliph and minister, which had grown up from the days of Degel over forty years before. A similar bond developed between ʿAbd al-Qādir and ʿAlī. As suggested previously, so long as titles and offices were ill-defined, personality played a great part in the fluid administration of the early caliphate: the example of Mudegel being sent instead of the Vizier by Atiku to the eastern Emirs has already been given.[62] The relationship between Vizier and Amīr al-mu'minīn was more personal than official, with the result that when the personal relationship proved impossible, the official relationship had to cease.

(iii) *The Vizier ʿAbd al-Qādir b. Gidado 1842–59*

ʿAbd al-Qādir b. Gidado was described by Barth as ʿAlī's 'greatest friend and principal minister' and as one 'who, although not very energetic, and still less war-like, is a man of cheerful disposition and good principles . . .'[63] Barth described ʿAlī in similar terms.[64] Although Barth's standards of energy were high and his criticism of ʿAlī and ʿAbd al-Qādir unjust on that score, Barth's general description of both ʿAbd al-Qādir and ʿAlī is borne out by their kindness towards him. ʿAbd al-Qādir also stresses in his biography of ʿAlī his open friendliness and accessibility.[65] ʿAbd al-Qādir was evidently of a similar nature, although Barth, being introduced by the

---

[61] Saʿīd, p. 211. Gidado died in February 1851 (Barth, IV, 178).
[62] *v. supra*, p. 102. Cf. Saʿīd, p. 202.
[63] Barth, VI, pp. 184, 178.
[64] *Ibid.*, p. 154.
[65] ʿAbd al-Qādir b. Gidado, *Manāqib ʿAlī*. Cf. Saʿīd, p. 217.

Galadima, did not see as much of the Vizier as had Clapperton.[66]

Under 'Alī, the territorial responsibilities of the Vizier had been limited. The emirates were divided between the major councillors and, in a few cases, princes. The Vizier received Kano, Zaria, Hadejia, Katagum, Missau, and Adamawa: to these can be added Gombe, and a general supervision of local Sokoto emirates like Tambawel.[67] Two events illustrate the effectiveness and limitations of the administration under 'Alī and 'Abd al-Qādir.

When 'Umar b. Abī Bakr Atiku, 'Umaru Nagwamatse', having already been recalled from Katuru, proved unsuitable as a ruler for the second time, the Vizier, or, in the account of al-ḥājj Sa'īd, the Sarkin Zamfara Aḥmad b. Abī Bakr Atiku ('Umar's elder brother) went to Gwamatse with an army and ordered 'Umar out.[68] 'Umar's reputation was that of a successful, independent and somewhat high-living prince, but against the authority of the Caliph he attempted nothing: he went to see the Amīr al-mu'minīn, as instructed. The Sultan of Gobir, Mayaki, at this period was raiding into the area of Zamfara, yet there was no attempt by 'Umar to desert to the Gobirawa or to use the insecurity in order to be independent himself. Sokoto had both the authority and the army to prevent independence and extravagance on the part of a prince within its own hinterland. The example of 'Umar

---

[66] Barth stayed only about a month each time: April 1853 and September 1854. Clapperton spent eight months there in all.

[67] Cf. Barth, IV, p. 155. See map, p. 200.

[68] The two main, and divergent, sources are (i) *Ta'rīkh Kontagora*, the account by 'Umar's grandson, 'Uthmān b. Ibrāhīm, written in a'jamī Hausa, *c.* 1918, and condensed in Duff, *Kontagora Gazetteer* (the *Ta'rīkh* was found in the Kontagora Divisional Office by Mr. E. J. Lannert); (ii) Sa'īd, pp. 210 f. Cf. Edgar, *Litafi*, I, 236; Burdon, *Northern Nigeria*, p. 71. Though the main accounts diverge, the point at issue, that the deposition was effective and peaceful, is not disputed. The Kontagora account says the Vizier was on his way with an army to depose Bukhari in Hadejia. This is chronologically awkward: the disaster at Gora following 'Umar's deposition was in 1851 (Barth, IV, 157; the Abū Bakr referred to by Barth died at Gora); Bukhari was probably deposed in 1846 (Sa'īd, p. 211; Barth, II, 175 ff.).

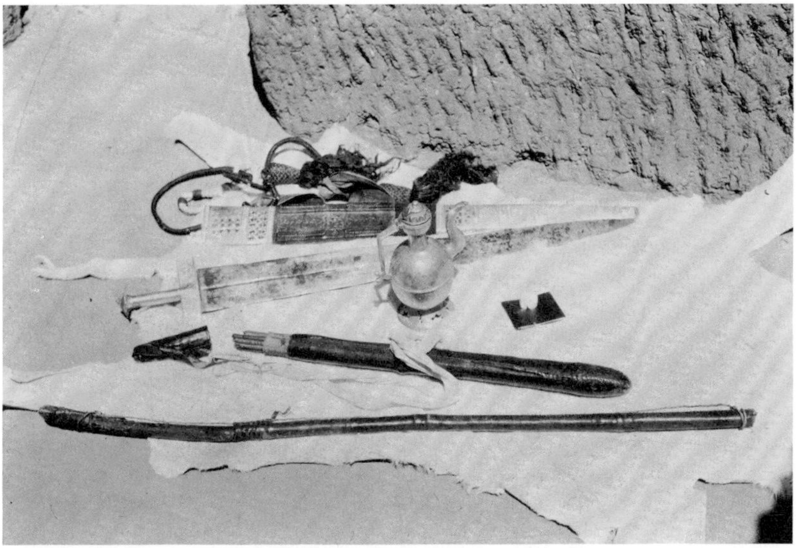

7. Symbols of the Vizier's office

8. Pens and pen-and-ink case of the Alkalin Waziri

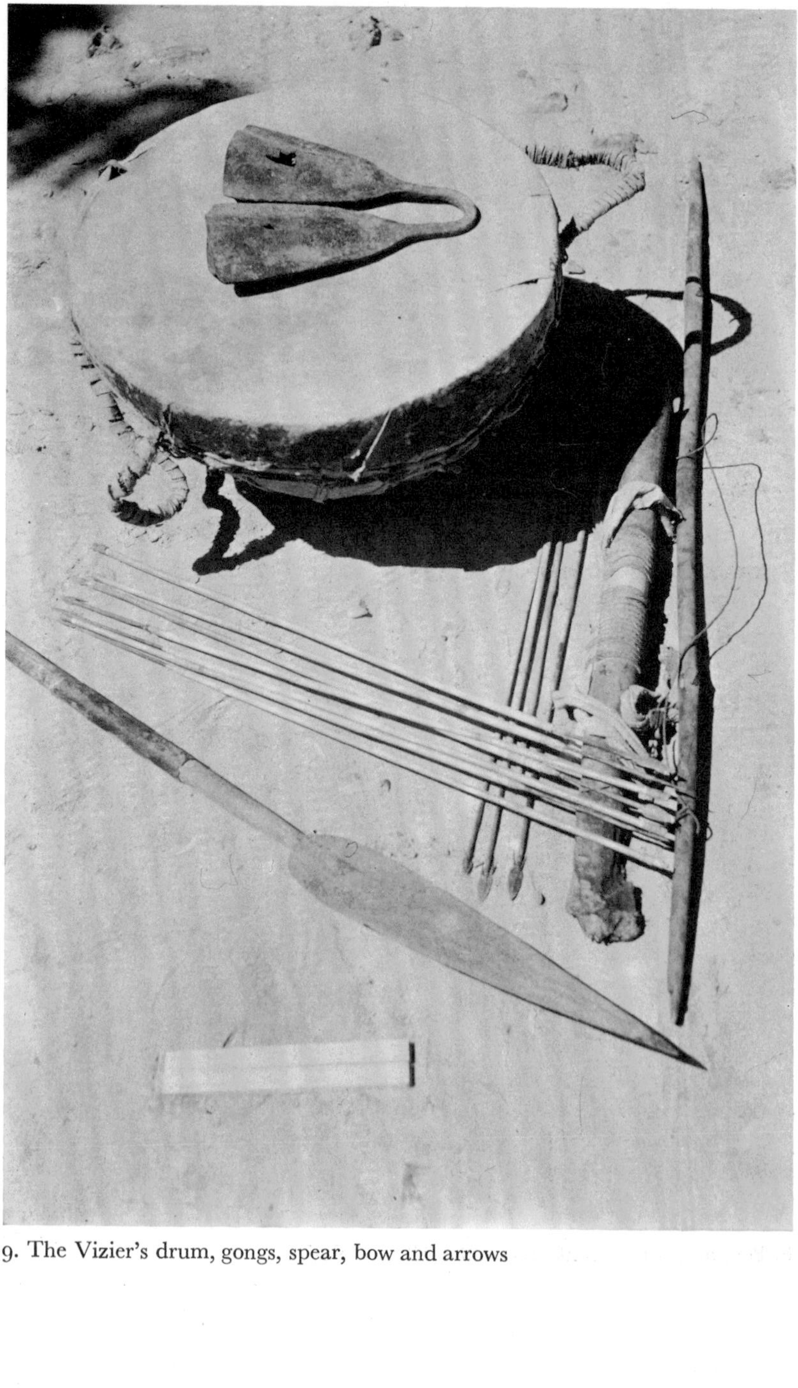

9. The Vizier's drum, gongs, spear, bow and arrows

Nagwamatse may have prompted other frustrated younger brothers to seek their fortunes outside Sokoto: 'Umar himself soon left secretly for Nupe and later founded an emirate at Kontagora where he accepted the suzerainty of his brother, then Amīr al-mu'minīn at Sokoto.[69]

Whereas no prince within Sokoto proved beyond the jurisdiction of the Amīr al-mu'minīn, an Emir of a subordinate province at this time was able to throw off the authority of Sokoto, despite the counter-measures of the Vizier. About the time of the deposition of 'Umar, when the Emir of Hadejia, Bukhari, having obtained power by force, had become the cause of much complaint, 'Abd al-Qādir was sent out to take charge of the situation.[70] He went to Katagum and summoned Bukhari; Bukhari threatened him with his troops, was declared a rebel and was replaced as Emir by his brother Aḥmad. The ensuing battle was indecisive, but Bukhari removed to a town under the protection of Bornu. Later the Vizier's brother and Dangaladima, Aḥmad, led an army jointly with Sambo Lai from Jamaari but could make no impression. Then about 1853, a bigger army, with contingents from Zaria and Kano as well as from Zamfara and Sokoto, led by the Vizier himself, was again turned back. Meanwhile, Bukhari had killed his brother Aḥmad and taken Hadejia town. The key to the success which Bukhari maintained for some fifteen years, devastating the lands of his

---

[69] 'Umar was accompanied or joined by others from Sokoto and Gwandu. His Ubandoma, 'Alī, was a son of the Sarkin Tudu Alami, who had fought at Alkalawa, and Mariam, a daughter of 'Abdullāh b. Fodiye ('Uthmān b. Ibrāhīm, *op. cit.*; Gidado, *Majmū' aṣḥāb Bello*). Compare the careers of other young princes: e.g. Ḥayāt b. Sa'īd in Adamawa, or Bayero b. Abī Bakr b. Bello in Doma (M. G. Smith, *op. cit.*, p. 171; F. Edgar, notebook).

[70] Two contemporary sources for the Vizier's role are (i) 'Abd al-Qādir b. Gidado, *Manāqib 'Alī* and (ii) Sa'īd, pp. 211, 212. Sa'īd, as elsewhere, is harsh on the Vizier. Another contemporary source is Barth (II, 175–7). If Sa'īd's date is correct for the deposition of Bukhari —i.e. early 1846, coinciding with the death of the Emir of Kano Ibrāhīm —, then it is necessary to assume that Bukhari spent the five years between his initial deposition and his counter-attack in building up his forces in western Bornu.

neighbours in Katagum and Kano, was the help he received from Bornu.[71] In addition to having a friendly frontier behind him, he had for his base the difficult marshy country of the Komadugu Yobe.

The revolt, though effective in itself, demonstrates the overall strength of the Sokoto hegemony. Despite the favourable circumstances, the revolt spread no further; and on the death of Bukhari, when his son succeeded, a brother of Bukhari seized control and the emirate was reintegrated into the caliphate.

Events in Zaria during the vizierate of 'Abd al-Qādir, as told by M. G. Smith, show further this strength of Sokoto and the physical weakness of the Vizier's position.[72] First, Hammada, Emir of Zaria in 1847, refused to be turbanned by the Vizier or his deputy; his successor, however, Muḥammad Sani, allowed himself to be turbanned. The next Emir, Sidi, in 1854 refused the Vizier entrance to Zaria, making it clear that he rejected Sokoto intervention in the affairs of Zaria. But when the Vizier returned to Sokoto, Sidi was summoned and deposed: he did not return to Zaria before his death.

While the Vizier was unable to impose his will on the Emir directly or immediately, when it came to a showdown with the power the Vizier represented, the Emir did not resist. Though, as M. G. Smith argues, Sidi's going to Sokoto may have been the only course feasible, the deposition nonetheless demonstrated the authority of Sokoto, which otherwise might be thought to have suffered from the continued success of Bukhari in Hadejia.[73]

In crises such as those in Zaria and Hadejia, there was a certain inevitability in the succession. The local electors suggested or sanctioned the candidates, who in effect chose themselves through descent and seniority of title if not of age. But the ultimate responsibility for recommending the appoint-

---

[71] Cf. Sa'īd, p. 216, where 'Abd al-Raḥmān, the rival to Shaikh 'Umar in Bornu, tried to win Sokoto support by opposing Bukhari in 1853–4.

[72] M. G. Smith, *op. cit.*, pp. 155 f., 163 f. (with the chronology emended: cf. D. M. Last, 'A solution to the problems of dynastic chronology in nineteenth-century Zaria and Kano', *J.H.S.N.*, 1966).

[73] M. G. Smith, *op. cit.*, p. 164.

ment, say, of Bukhari, was the Vizier's. Here he was open to charges of corruption. Considering the hostility of al-ḥājj Sa'īd to the Vizier, it is impossible to accept the wholesale charge of bribery in his account.[74] With presents as part of the normal courtesies of life, a charge of bribery is easily made, especially against an official whose duty is to recommend new appointments.

Such presents by the new Emirs became regularised under Amīr al-mu'minīn 'Alī, according to M. G. Smith; similarly, the Vizier began regularizing his presents as a form of tax.[75] It was also customary for the Caliph to receive a proportion, sometimes a half, of the official property of a deposed Emir, in the same manner as the Emir received that of an official subordinate to him. Some of the property thus allotted to the Caliph was given to the Vizier. Though the wealth of the Emir of Kano Dabo or the Emir of Zaria Muḥammad Sani, for example, was said to have been considerable, it was not taken as an excuse for frequent depositions. Outside Zaria, few Emirs were deposed; in Zaria, the deposition of Sidi was due to his misrule.[76]

The appointments made by Sokoto in this period proved, in general, successful. In the course of 'Alī's caliphate, 1842–1859, the remaining jihād leaders died: for example, Ibrāhīm Dabo of Kano, Ya'qūb of Bauchi, Adama of Adamawa.[77] Thus a generation who had grown up under the Sokoto hegemony took over. The stability in rule which 'Alī and his Vizier 'Abd al-Qādir provided, and which was paralleled by the twenty-five years of the Emir of Gwandu Khalilu (1835–1860), consolidated the authority of Sokoto over its more recently appointed Emirs. This was of particular importance since the personal ties of the jihād which linked Muḥammad Bello or 'Abdullāh to their fellow mujāhidūn had passed away. Some of the ties were renewed by marriage: for example, the Vizier 'Abd al-Qādir married the daughter of the new Emir of Kano he had appointed in 1846. Such links,

---

[74] Sa'īd, pp. 211, 122. *v. supra*, p. xli.
[75] M. G. Smith, *op. cit.*, pp. 154 ff.
[76] Cf. Sa'īd, p. 219. [77] *v.* Sa'īd, p. 220.

while they could not replace the Islamic bonds of the caliphate, in a group so conscious of its genealogy and relationship to the Shaikh undoubtedly increased the solidarity of the Community in a way the Shaikh himself had recommended.

(iv) *The Vizier Ibrāhīm Khalilu b. 'Abd al-Qādir 1859–c. 1874*

After seventeen years of partnership, 'Abd al-Qādir, like his father Gidado, was identified with the Amīr al-mu'minīn he served. Consequently when 'Alī was getting old, there was some canvassing for the vizierate under the next Amīr al-mu'minīn. That this was practicable shows the extent to which the vizierate was not yet an hereditary office, but a post for a close and suitably learned friend and adviser of the Amīr al-mu'minīn.

While Aḥmad b. Abī Bakr Atiku was living in his ribāṭ at Chimola, he had 'Abd al-Qādir b. al-Muṣṭafā for a neighbour at Salame, some two hours' ride north up the Rima valley: the court at this time was at Wurno, across the valley from Chimola.[78] A friendship seems to have grown up between them: 'Abd al-Qādir b. al-Muṣṭafā won a promise from Aḥmad that should Aḥmad become Amīr al-mu'minīn, he would appoint him his Vizier. 'Abd al-Qādir was qualified by the Sokoto standards. Barth had been told by a Tuat scholar in Katsina that 'Abd al-Qādir was the 'most learned of the present generation of the inhabitants of Sokoto'.[79] He had written a geography of the Sudan, a history of Gobir and the annals of the jihād, a sufic work and a mystical biography of Muḥammad Sambo, and a book of answers to various questions.[80] In addition he was a prolific poet, writing, in particular, several elegies. A further qualification was his descent from the Shaikh. His mother, herself a noted Sufi,

[78] The following is based on the account given me verbally by M. Abd al-Qadiri Yahaya in 1963.

[79] Barth, IV, p. 101.

[80] See bibliography. He also set an 'exam' consisting of tricky legal and historical questions; an answer in verse was given by the Zaria scholar 'Umar b. Aḥmad.

was Khadīja bint al-Shaikh, while his father was a scholar and a scribe at Degel.[81] 'Abd al-Qādir was thus of the same generation as Aḥmad b. Abī Bakr Atiku, 'Alī b. Bello, and 'Abd al-Qādir b. Gidado. He did not have the connections or experience that the Gidado house had built up over the years of managing relations with the eastern Emirs; as most of the assistants of the Vizier were his relations, the expertise would remain within the family. Nonetheless, Aḥmad evidently felt 'Abd al-Qādir was sufficiently qualified to be his Vizier.

The Vizier 'Abd al-Qādir, however, was told of this promise. When the Amīr al-mu'minīn 'Alī died, the Vizier refused to nominate Aḥmad to succeed as Amīr al-mu'minīn unless he swore to make Ibrāhīm Khalilu b. 'Abd al-Qādir, his son, the next Vizier. Aḥmad agreed, and became the next Amīr al-mu'minīn.

The situation that made Gidado retire under Aḥmad's father, Abū Bakr Atiku, had no chance to develop. The Vizier 'Abd al-Qādir b. Gidado, upset, so it is said, at the death of 'Alī, died forty days later.[82] The Amīr al-mu'minīn Aḥmad kept to his oath and appointed Ibrāhīm Khalilu Vizier. The appointment was made hastily, before either 'Abd al-Qādir b. al-Muṣṭafā or the brothers of 'Abd al-Qādir b. Gidado could object effectively. The latter were on their way to Aḥmad to contest the office, when they heard the news of the appointment of their nephew, Khalilu. Of the eligible sons of Gidado by Asmā', there were 'Uthmān ('Shehu'), 'Abdullāh ('Bayero') and Muḥammad Laima. Aḥmad b. Gidado, also a son of Asmā', who had been the Dangaladima for 'Abd al-Qādir and the senior son after 'Abd al-Qādir, had died in 1853 when accompanying the Amīr al-mu'minīn at Katsina. Another son of Gidado, but not by Asmā', Muḥammad Bukhari, had been the Sarkin Fada, but, though married to a daughter of Amīr al-mu'minīn 'Alī, he was not eligible: he had been removed from office, at the request of 'Alī, for extravagant living. Aḥmad, a son of the Vizier 'Abd al-Qādir,

---

[81] 'Abd al-Qādir b. al-Muṣṭafā, *Salwat al-aḥzān*; R.A., f. 12b.

[82] The account of M. Abd al-Qadiri Yahaya. The date of 'Abd al-Qādir's death was, therefore, *c.* 1 December 1859.

and Khalilu's younger brother, had been appointed in his place.[83]

On hearing the news of Khalilu's appointment, Muḥammad Laima, the youngest brother, was so annoyed he turned back, refusing to acknowledge Khalilu as Vizier. Shehu, the eldest of the three, appears to have joined Muḥammad Laima: he did not proceed to Wurno. Only 'Abdullāh went on, to mourn his brother and greet his nephew. His mother, Asmā', consoled him, promising him a long life if he was patient; she succeeded in getting him appointed the Dangaladima to Khalilu, thus virtually assuring him of the vizierate some time. Aḥmad b. 'Abd al-Qādir thus remained Sarkin Fada, while both Shehu b. Gidado and 'Abd al-Qādir b. al-Muṣṭafā died shortly after.[84]

The appointment of Khalilu has its rationale. Though young—he must have been in his mid-thirties, and so young enough to be the son of the Amīr al-mu'minīn he served—he is said to have been older than the sons of Gidado who also sought the post.[85] Of more importance, he also had been the Dangaladima to his father for the previous six years, and had therefore not only seniority but also experience. His only disqualification was that he was not as closely descended from Gidado and the Shaikh as were his uncles, a factor that counted in Sokoto.

He was, however, well connected. His mother, Mariam, was a daughter of the Commander of the Army 'Alī Jedo, and thus both his grandmothers were daughters of the Shaikh; he married, among others, the daughter of the Emir of Kano 'Abdullāh whom his father had appointed.[86] Later the Emir

---

[83] This and the following are based on accounts given by al-haji Junaidu.

[84] 'Abd al-Qādir died in 1280 (1863–4). An ode on his death was written by Asmā' (died 1280).

[85] Chronologically, this is somewhat difficult, since it implies that Asmā', born *c.* 1794, had her first child ('Abd al-Qādir) *c.* 1809; a second (who died in 1824) *c.* 1815 (?); a third (Aḥmad) *c.* 1820; and the remaining three sons born between 1826–34, since her eldest, 'Abd al-Qādir, would have his first son, Ibrāhīm Khalilu, *c.* 1826.

[86] Cf. Edgar, *op. cit.*, II, 342.

of Zaria Abū Bakr b. Mūsā, himself a brother of a wife of Gidado, made Khalilu's first cousins, Muḥammad and al-Ḥasan b. 'Abdullāh b. Gidado, the Wali and Makama Karami respectively. The next Emir appointed another cousin, Fate, to be Fagaci.[87]

Documentation for the activities of Khalilu in Sokoto is scant. His reputation is that of a scholar, working long into the night: but only two poems of his survive, both classically elegant. He was noted, as a great malam, for superiority over charms: a story tells how a concubine paid no heed to his warning about a bird, and died. He died young himself, in his mid-forties, and there is a story that he was victim of the hostility of the Caliph's secretary.[88]

One event illustrates the position of the Vizier *vis-à-vis* the Caliph in this period. In Zaria, the Emir 'Abdullāh was deposed by Amīr al-mu'minīn Aḥmad Rufa'i in 1870, since 'Abdullāh had persisted in attacking Keffi against the orders of the Amīr al-mu'minīn.[89] Evidently, the deposition was made without the proper form or trial. When the death of the succeeding Emir of Zaria Abū Bakr followed soon after the death of the Amīr al-mu'minīn Aḥmad Rufa'i, 'Abdullāh was reinstated as Emir. Khalilu was still the Vizier, and he had to write formally to the Emir of Kano 'Abdullāh that the 'Amīr al-mu'minīn had favoured the Emir of Zaria 'Abdullāh with the return of his sultanate'.[90] It reveals the dependence of the Vizier's position that he was unable to have a consistent policy of his own: the Vizier was, ultimately, only the agent of the Amīr al-mu'minīn .This subordination may have

---

[87] M. G. Smith, *op. cit.*, pp. 173, 176. The Emir of Zaria Sidi, deposed under 'Alī, was also a brother of this wife of Gidado.

[88] Bi Sa'd, whom Khalilu had had sacked. The story was told me by M. Abd al-Qadiri Yahaya, but according to al-haji Junaidu only other men called Ibrāhīm Khalilu were affected. There are stories about Khalilu also in Edgar, *op. cit.*, II, 334, 342–6. One of Khalilu's teachers was the famous muḥtasib, Muḥammad Julde.

[89] M. G. Smith, *op. cit.*, pp. 170 f. (chronology emended).

[90] Uncatalogued letter in the collection of al-haji Junaidu. On this occasion, Sokoto depended on the Kano army to enforce its will in Zaria (F. Edgar, notebook, *Labarin Kano*, p. 2).

been increased by the fact that Khalilu was still young, over ten years younger than the Caliphs he served.

Khalilu died not long after the accession of the Amīr al-mu'minīn Abū Bakr.[91] He had been Vizier for over fourteen years, and in that time he had served four Caliphs: there cannot have existed quite the close partnership that had been built up by Gidado or 'Abd al-Qādir, but there is no evidence, beyond that already cited, to suggest that any definite change had taken place in the relationship between Vizier and Caliph.

(v) *The Vizier 'Abdullāh Bayero c. 1874–86*

Khalilu's uncle, 'Abdullāh Bayero b. Gidado, who had been acting as his Dangaladima, was appointed Vizier in his place. 'Abdullāh was still young: like Khalilu, he was in his forties, and therefore considerably younger than the Amīr al-mu'minīn, Abū Bakr, who had been 61 at his accession. The Sarkin Fada, Aḥmad b. 'Abd al-Qādir, Khalilu's younger brother, was passed over for the vizierate. He had been appointed Sarkin Fada presumably after 1853 when his elder brother became Dangaladima. When Asmā' persuaded Khalilu and the Amīr al-mu'minīn Aḥmad to make her son 'Abdullāh Dangaladima, it meant he superseded Aḥmad b. 'Abd al-Qādir. 'Abdullāh and Aḥmad were contemporaries, but being a son of Gidado and Asmā' counted in 'Abdullāh's favour.

In addition to the vizierate, 'Abdullāh took over Khalilu's widow, the daughter of the Emir of Kano 'Abdullāh, and had children by her: they did not, however, hold any major posts in the Vizier's household. 'Abdullāh also married a daughter of Mu'ādh b. Bello, perhaps on Mu'ādh's election to the caliphate which took place during the vizierate of 'Abdullāh.[92]

His reputation is of being 'of the old school', a true son of Asmā' bint al-Shaikh and stricter than some of his younger

[91] About 1874, before the death of the Emir of Gwandu al-Muṣṭafā, *c.* 1875 (?) (Correspondence, I, 9).

[92] Genealogical details given by al-haji Junaidu.

contemporaries. In this, he appears to have shared the standards of the first two Caliphs he worked for, Abū Bakr and Mu'ādh b. Bello. But his relations with Amīr al-mu'minīn 'Umar b. 'Alī b. Bello were strained.

He had been forced into agreeing to the nomination of 'Umar for the caliphate. On the death of Amīr al-mu'minīn Mu'ādh, the three eligible candidates were Sa'īd b. Bello, Yūsuf b. Bello and 'Umar b. 'Alī b. Bello. The Vizier wanted Sa'īd as Amīr al-mu'minīn, who as well as being both very learned and pious was a grandson of the Shaikh; the other electors preferred 'Umar b. 'Alī, whose mother was a daughter of the first Magajin gari and who was known for his more liberal habits. Confronted with a deadlock, the other electors suggested Yūsuf b. Bello. The nomination of Yūsuf, a grandson of the Shaikh but less learned than Sa'īd, presented the Vizier with an awkward choice: he had married the ex-wife of Yūsuf, while his nephew, the Dangaladima Muḥammad Bukhari, had married Yūsuf's daughter. Since to elect Yūsuf was dangerous, 'Abdullāh agreed to 'Umar b. 'Alī as Caliph.[93] It is possible he opposed 'Umar because he foresaw that 'Umar would pay less heed to the council than had the previous Caliphs; but in his strictness, he was out of step with his colleagues.

It is a reflection on the elective nature of the caliphal succession that the Vizier, though having a veto, could not force his choice on the council: the Vizier, especially if isolated in the council, was scarcely more than *primus inter pares*. To the stranger, 'Abdullāh's position seemed stronger than this. Joseph Thomson, visiting Wurno in May 1885, said, '... the present Wazir has occupied that position during the reign of several Sultans and is now Crown lawyer, general adviser and depository of all the Acts of the various Sultans under whom he has served. Nothing is done except by his advice, and he is thus really more powerful than the Sultan himself.'[94] This

[93] This is based on the account given me by al-haji Junaidu.

[94] *Good Words* (vol. 27, 1886), p. 327. Thomson lost his diaries and based this account on some letters he had written, adding to them from memory. Consequently, these remarks may reflect as much his general notion of a Vizier as the contemporary scene in Wurno.

is in contradiction to tradition which credits the Vizier with more moral authority than physical power: certainly having served as Dangaladima or Vizier under six Caliphs over the previous twenty-six years, he was the most experienced councillor 'Umar had. But tradition asserts that 'Umar was less receptive to advice than the previous Caliphs.[95]

An example of the way the Vizier 'Abdullāh influenced fractious princes is the poem he wrote to the Emir of Tambawel, 'Umar b. Muḥammad Bukhari b. al-Shaikh. Relations between Sokoto and 'Umar b. Muḥammad Bukhari had not been good since the refusal of 'Umar to recognise Aḥmad b. Atiku as Amīr al-mu'minīn in 1859 and his subsequent loss of territory to his brothers.[96] In the rather forced poem the Vizier 'Abdullāh wrote to reconcile 'Umar, he appealed almost solely to the bonds of kinship and solidarity between 'Umar and the Amīr al-mu'minīn and Sokoto generally. The Amīr al-mu'minīn, Abū Bakr b. Bello, was a first cousin of 'Umar, and a daughter of Abū Bakr was married to 'Umar's eldest son. In addition, a sister of 'Umar's had married the brother of the Vizier 'Abdullāh, and the son by that marriage was the Vizier's Dangaladima, Muḥammad Bukhari.[97]

The network of kinship seems to have kept the Community together. For example, sisters of 'Umar were also married into the ruling houses of Gwandu, Bodinga and Jega; a brother, admittedly a rival of 'Umar, was married to a daughter of the Emir of Gwandu 'Alī b. 'Abdullāh. Although Tambawel was under Sokoto, relations between Tambawel and Gwandu were close: 'Umar's father, Muḥammad Bukhari b. al-Shaikh, had been brought up in Gwandu, and princes from

---

[95] According to al-haji Junaidu. Cf. P. G. Harris, *op. cit.*, p. 105.

[96] 'Umar was still without Kebbe, which had been transferred to Sokoto since early in the caliphate of 'Alī; it was returned to Tambawel under 'Abd al-Raḥmān. (*History of Gwandu* by Alkalin Gwandu Aḥmad, translated by R. McAllister (1909) and quoted in Arnett, *The Rise of the Sokoto Fulani* (p. 39). Cf. Correspondence, V, 35; and the note in Backwell, *The Occupation of Hausaland*, p. 41.)

[97] These and the following genealogical details were given me by al-haji Junaidu and by the present Emir of Tambawel.

Tambawel campaigned on Gwandu expeditions. The Gwandu Emirs could therefore be a restraining influence on Tambawel, especially when Sokoto–Gwandu relations were cordial. The Vizier 'Abdullāh was a close friend of the Emir of Gwandu al-Muṣṭafā b. Muḥammad and on his death wrote a classical elegy and takhmīs.[98]

Such ties, while they did not prevent disputes—there are several examples of rivalry between brothers—did make the Vizier's diplomacy easier. But diplomacy was subject to the changes of Caliph. Although, as Dangaladima, 'Abdullāh would have had no direct responsibility for either deposing the Emir of Zaria 'Abdullāh in 1870 or reinstating him in 1873, the final deposition of 'Abdullāh fell to him when Mu'ādh b. Bello succeeded his brother, Abū Bakr, as Caliph. According to M. G. Smith, the new Amīr al-mu'minīn maintained the first deposition was legal and justified: although the Vizier might advise the Caliph on this, M. G. Smith implies the deposition was the decision of the Caliph himself.[99]

There is nothing in the surviving correspondence to suggest that the Vizier had any motives for replacing 'Abdullāh with Muḥammad Sambo as Emir of Zaria.[100] One early letter to the Vizier from Muḥammad Sambo sends the usual compliments and a small present of two shirts, and adds: 'I take refuge and put myself under your wing and your tail.'[101] Another letter, just before his appointment, carries compliments and a present of four black tobes. Once appointed Emir, Muḥammad Sambo filled certain key offices as the Amīr al-mu'minīn suggested to him: but even a minor appointment like the Makama Karami was discussed and approved by the Vizier.[102]

---

[98] In the collection of al-haji Junaidu.

[99] M. G. Smith, *op. cit.*, pp. 177 ff. (with the chronology emended).

[100] It is, of course, not very likely that any incriminating letter, if it existed, would survive. The presents mentioned in the letters are too small to be significant.

[101] Correspondence, VI, 6.

[102] M. G. Smith, *op. cit.*, p. 179. Correspondence, V, 39 ('Abd al-Karīm b. Muḥammad Sambo is called by M. G. Smith (p. 180) by his nickname 'Tsoho').

In Kano, where the Emir, 'Abdullāh, had been ruling since 1855, the Vizier had less power. Although relations were not disturbed, the Emir showed little subservience: he could send his son, the Wombai 'Uthmān, to pay homage for him to the Amīr al-mu'minīn 'Umar.[103] He had already been married to 'Umar's sister, Sauda, while his own daughter had been married to the Viziers Khalilu and 'Abdullāh. On the death of the Emir 'Abdullāh, the succession was problematical: 'Abdullāh had kept control of his princes by frequent dismissals.[104] His son Yūsuf had once been Galadima, and then been dismissed, evidently with a warning curse from his father: though he was the eldest son and the most eligible to succeed, the warning was enough to make the Vizier use it as a pretext to oppose his election.[105] The Amīr al-mu'minīn 'Umar, however, was in favour of Yūsuf's appointment. The Vizier preferred Dan Lawal, a brother of the late Emir, but he was unacceptable to the Amīr al-mu'minīn who, at the time Dan Lawal had refused the Amīr al-mu'minīn a saddle-cloth, had said he would never be Emir. When deadlock was reached, Mariam, a daughter of the Shaikh then in her sixties and much respected, suggested the appointment of Muḥammad Bello, a full brother of the Emir 'Abdullāh and who had been Dan Turaki. Muḥammad Bello was appointed. He seems to have been a pious and generous man: he gave large sums to the Amīr al-mu'minīn, the Vizier and the Dangaladima; of the last he was particularly fond, but there is no

---

[103] Correspondence, VII, 70. The Emir, though old and infirm, was fit enough to start the journey the following year: he died on the way, however. Homage in person was considered important.

[104] Cf. Kano Chronicle (trans. Palmer, *Sudanese Memoirs*, III), pp. 130–1.

[105] Muḥammad b. Ṣāliḥ, *Taqyīd al-akhbār* (1284/1868), f. 24b; Correspondence, VI, 121 (datable to 1873); (Anon), *Faiḍ al-qadīr*, f. 3; Mischlich (*M.S.O.S.*, 1908), pp. 65 f. *Labarin Kano* (Edgar, notebook, pp. 1–4) makes the election take place at Kaura Namoda; the Vizier opposed Yūsuf on the grounds that he would be too powerful and unruly to control from Sokoto. The version here was given by al-haji Junaidu. The appointment took place probably in September 1882 (Dhū'l-qa'da 1299) (D. M. Last, *op. cit.*, *J.H.S.N.*, 1966).

evidence that the friendship originated before his appointment.[106]

Some three years after the appointment of Muḥammad Bello as Emir of Kano, the Vizier 'Abdullāh died; Staudinger heard the news in the course of his journey back to Loko, that is, about March 1886.[107]

(vi) *The Vizier Muḥammad Bukhari 1886–1903*

The Dangaladima Muḥammad Bukhari b. Aḥmad b. Gidado was appointed to succeed 'Abdullāh as Vizier. 'Abdullāh had no sons of suitable age to contest the appointment: both sons by the daughter of the Emir of Kano, Muḥammad Babba and Muḥammad Bello, were too young; of the sons of Khalilu, the eldest, Adili, was now about 18, and Yahaya 14. There were no sons of Gidado by Asmā' still alive, and the Wali 'Uthmān b. 'Abd al-Qādir was the only eligible son of 'Abd al-Qādir b. Gidado surviving; Aḥmad b. 'Abd al-Qādir, who had served as Sarkin Fada under his father, brother and uncle, died during the vizierate of 'Abdullāh, as did his brother 'Abbās. The post of Wali seems to have been given to 'Uthmān while Aḥmad was Sarkin Fada and Muḥammad Bukhari Dangaladima: though eligible for the vizierate, he was junior to Muḥammad Bukhari. The Sarkin Fada after Aḥmad was the younger brother of Muḥammad Bukhari, 'Abd al-Qādir b. Aḥmad b. Gidado. Another brother, Adilijo, son of Khadīja, the daughter of Muḥammad Bello, does not seem to have ever held office.[108]

---

[106] Cf. Correspondence, VII, 97, 82. Cf. VII, 120, 59. Dan Lawal, who was sick at the time of the election, died immediately afterwards. In al-haji Abubakar, *Kano ta Dabo Cigari* (1958), p. 58, a son of 'Abdullāh, Ayuba, is given as Dan Lawan.

[107] Staudinger, *op. cit.*, p. 373 The Dangaladima Bukhari whom MacDonald (Report on his visit to the Niger and Oil rivers, 1890, p. 13) met in 1889 was Bukhari b. Abī Bakr b. Bello, the Raba representative to Muri, and not the Dangaladiman Waziri.

[108] Details for this and the early life of the Vizier Bukhari are based on information given by al-haji Junaidu, who is a son of Bukhari. For the death of the Sarkin Fada, cf. letter on microfilm (5A S2) at Jos.

Though his father had not been Vizier, Muḥammad Bukhari was well connected. His mother was the daughter of Muḥammad Bukhari b. al-Shaikh; consequently when his father died when he was about 12, he stayed with his mother in Tambawel. There he married his cousin, a daughter of Barau b. Muḥammad Bukhari b. al-Shaikh, while his brother Ambo married another cousin, a daughter of 'Umar b. Muḥammad Bukhari b. al-Shaikh. He studied in Tambawel, making use of the large library of the Emir of Tambawel 'Umar and being taught by Malam Ḥamīd.[109]

Following the practice of the vizieral family, Muḥammad Bukhari married into the house of the Caliph. He was given a daughter of the Amīr al-mu'minīn Abū Bakr b. Bello, but he had no children by her; he also married a daughter of Yūsuf b. Bello. Despite the rivalry of Yūsuf for the caliphate, in which Muḥammad Bukhari probably supported Yūsuf, his relations with Amīr al-mu'minīn 'Umar are said to have been good. Similarly, his relations with the Emir of Kano Muḥammad Bello—for whom, as Dangaladima, he was responsible to the Vizier—were very cordial: Muḥammad Bello was delighted when 'Umar made Muḥammad Bukhari the Vizier, and sent the Amīr al-mu'minīn fourteen horses to mark the occasion.[110]

On his appointment, however, he had to solve the crisis in Zaria. Attacks from Ningi and Maradi had increased: a Ningi expedition had devastated areas around Zaria city itself, and the Emir had to be ordered to rebuild the walls.[111] Muḥammad Bukhari had no direct experience of Zaria, for which he had to rely on his brother the Sarkin Fada, and no letters have survived addressed to Muḥammad Bukhari as Dangaladima. But as soon as Bukhari became Vizier, the Galadima in Zaria, Sulaimān, fostered good relations with the Vizier; one letter from the Galadima is addressed in abject terms to Majidadi and refers to an agreement between

[109] His teachers in Sokoto included the Muḥtasib, Malam na Khalifa, and M. Akali.

[110] Correspondence, VII, 52.

[111] Correspondence, VI, 30. Two uncatalogued letters.

them.[112] The Galadima had been dangerously placed since his collusion with the Ningi, but he retained his office despite the attempts of the Emir, Sambo, to isolate him.[113] Sambo himself was deposed not long after the start of Bukhari's vizierate, but the part Bukhari played in the deposition is not documented: the Vizier 'Abdullāh and the Sarkin Fada had already once successfully dissuaded the Amīr al-mu'minīn from deposing Sambo.[114]

The death of the Amīr al-mu'minīn 'Umar caused a minor crisis which illustrates the competence of the Vizier. The occasion was an expedition to Zamfara and Gobir in March; although the eastern Emirs are said to have been called, it was not the autumn expedition and it is unlikely that all forces were mustered. Late one night, while camped at Kaura Namoda, the Amīr al-mu'minīn 'Umar died. The enemy Gobirawa were in the vicinity, thus making it imperative for the Muslims to have a leader.[115] The Vizier was present, but there was not time to summon any of the electors or await candidates who were absent. After a three-hour session in the middle of the night, 'Abd al-Raḥmān b. Abī Bakr Atiku b. al-Shaikh was chosen and the homage paid to the new Caliph in the Vizier's house. No one is said to have questioned the election or its legality.

Although the Vizier may have been decisive in the election of 'Abd al-Raḥmān, he remained the instrument of the new Amīr al-mu'minīn. In the crisis in Kano described above, the Vizier's advice was neglected, and the Caliph's orders had to be carried out whatever the consequences.[116] Although he had a free hand over the means of carrying out the orders,

---

112 Correspondence, VI, 7; 4; 53. Majidadi was Bukhari's servant.

113 M. G. Smith, *op. cit.*, p. 183.

114 Staudinger, *op. cit.*, pp. 323 f.

115 al-haji Junaidu, *Ḍabṭ al-multaqaṭāt*, f. 59b. Burdon's note on the translation of the Vizier Bukhari's *Ta'nīs al-ikhwān*, which he discussed with the author, gives shortage of food as the reason for haste; since it was March, this is very likely.

116 *v. supra*, p. 134. The main source of the Vizier's movements is his own account: *Kitāb fī-mā jarā bainī wa-bain Amīr Hadijia wa-Yūsuf*. A hostile account is (Anon), *Faiḍ al-qadīr* (*v. supra*, p. xliv).

the orders were final: the Vizier was not to return to Sokoto till they had been fulfilled. During the crisis the Vizier was respected by both contestants and could move about without being molested. Though accused of duplicity by the partisans of Tukur, he must have realised the hopelessness of Tukur's position against the sons of 'Abdullāh: the Vizier's policy, confronted with the obstinacy of the Amīr al-mu'minīn, was to wait till the contestants decided the issue themselves and presented a *fait accompli* to the Amīr al-mu'minīn. The Vizier, having appointed Tukur officially, had fulfilled his orders in part, but that was as far as his power ran. None of the other Emirs on whom the Vizier would normally rely for military assistance were eager to fight Yūsuf or 'Alī, whose cause, if not their action, seemed just. The Vizier therefore went down towards Zaria and then stayed in Kano, keeping out of Sokoto till the Caliph withdrew his threat of dismissal.[117] The threat was evidently real enough, though neither the dismissal of a Vizier nor the forced retirement of a Caliph had ever occurred in Sokoto. But when Tukur was finally killed and 'Alī was recognised as Emir by the Amīr al-mu'minīn, relations between the Vizier and his Caliph were restored: the Vizier returned to Sokoto, although he still had to arrange for the care of Tukur's supporters.

The experience in Kano affected events in Zaria some two years later, in 1897, when the hand of the Vizier was forced into choosing Muḥammad Kwassau as Emir over both the Amīr al-mu'minīn's nominee, the Iya 'Uthmān, and the nominee of the Galadima.[118] Muḥammad Kwassau commanded a force of gunmen loyal to himself: like Yūsuf in Kano, he could defy the Vizier militarily, while, in addition, he had the sympathy of the opponents of the Habe Galadima Sulaimān. The Vizier, it seems, appointed Kwassau without

[117] 'Abd al-Raḥmān ordered him back to Sokoto in the middle of the crisis, but later told him again not to return home till Tukur was reinstalled in Kano (Bukhari, *op. cit.*). His coming to Sokoto was the occasion he escorted Wallace to the Amīr al-mu'minīn, in May 1894 (Wallace, *op. cit.*, pp. 211 ff.).

[118] Edgar, *Litafi*, I, pp. 198–202. M. G. Smith, *op. cit.*, pp. 193–4.

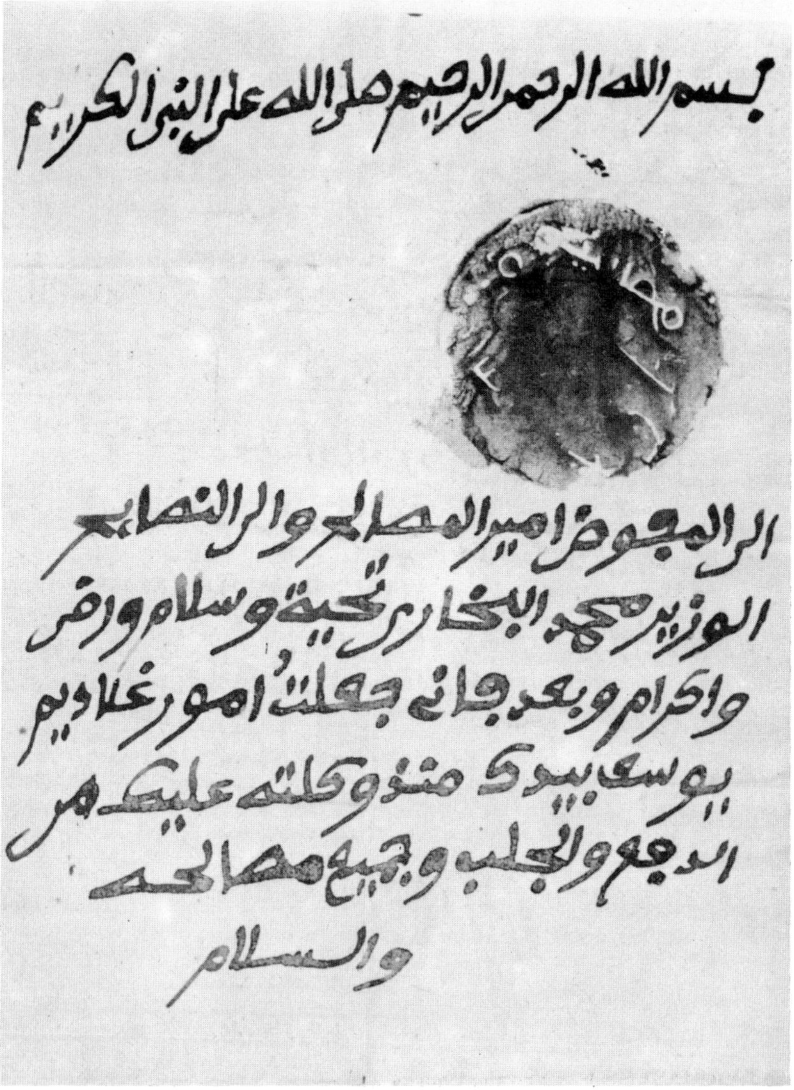
بسم الله الرحمن الرحيم صلى الله على النبي الكريم

الى المحبوب امير المصالح والى النصايح
الوزير محمد البخاري تحية وسلام ورضى
واكرام وبعد فاني جعلت امور غلاديم
يوسف بيوك منذ وكلته عليك من
الدفع والجلب وجميع مصالحه
والسلام

10. Letter from the Amīr al-mu'minīn to his Vizier
(*for translation see p. 197*)

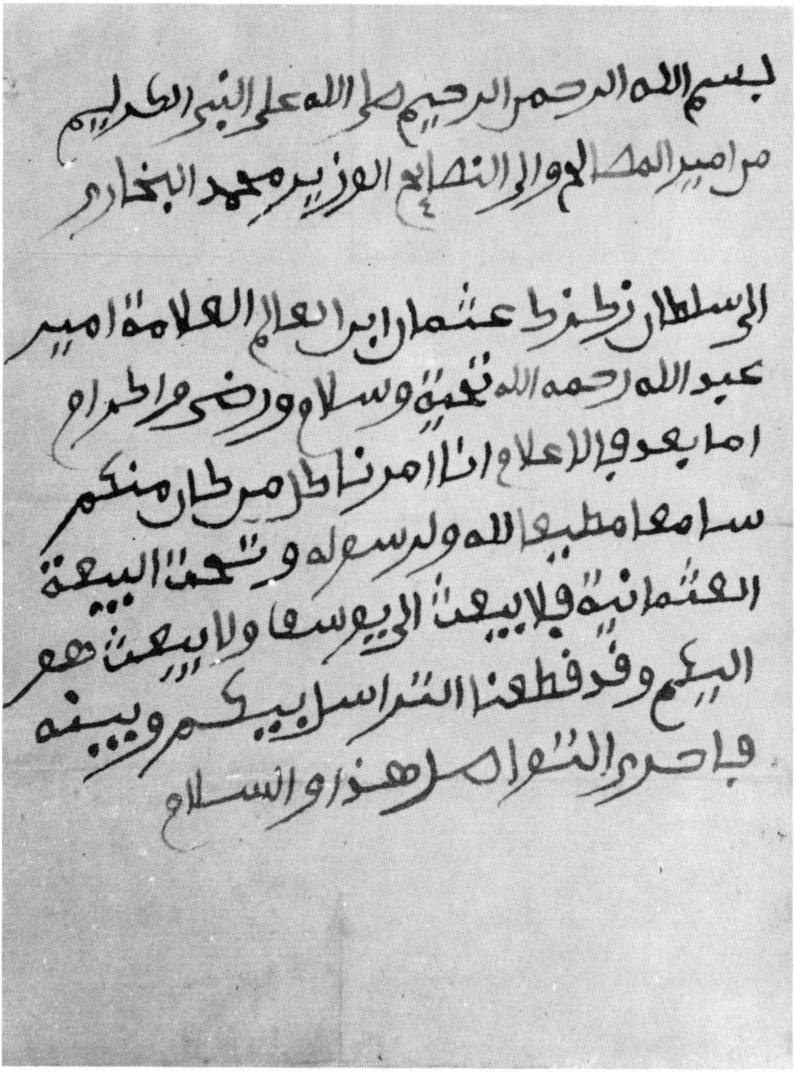
بسم الله الرحمن الرحيم صلى الله على النبي الكريم
من امير المصالح والي النصائح الوزير محمد البخاري
الى السلطان زكزك عثمان ابن العالم العلامة امير
عبد الله رحمه الله تحية وسلام ورضى واكرام
اما بعد فالاعلام انا امرنا كل من كان منكم
سامعا مطيعا لله ولرسوله وتحت البيعة
العثمانية فلا يبعث الى يوسف ولا يبعث هو
اليكم وقد قطعنا التراسل بينكم وبينه
فاحذر التواصل هذا والسلام

11. Letter from the Vizier to the Emir of Zaria
(*for translation see p. 198*)

first referring to Sokoto. The Amīr al-mu'minīn who was not, it seems, strongly committed to his candidate nor prepared, after Kano, to face another crisis, accepted the Vizier's decision.

Despite the strain of the Kano crisis, which evidently affected his eyes, the Vizier remained active, accompanying the Amīr al-mu'minīn or travelling round the emirates: in March 1902, for example, he visited Zaria, collecting, it seems, the fifth of the booty due to the Caliph.[119]

Though no other major crises occurred, relations are said never to have been very good between the Amīr al-mu'minīn and the Vizier.[120] Like other Viziers, however, he had marriage links with the Caliph. Four daughters of his each married a son of 'Abd al-Raḥmān. But since there were complaints about the high-handedness of these sons, the link may rather have embarrassed the Vizier.

The death of 'Abd al-Raḥmān left the caliphate open to a son either of Aḥmad b. Atiku or 'Alī b. Bello. Though the son of 'Alī was the popular choice, Muḥammad Attahiru b. Aḥmad was chosen through pressure from the Marafa, Muḥammad Attahiru's brother, with his contingent of Azbinawa gunmen.[121] Muḥammad Attahiru b. 'Alī stepped down and avoided conflict. The extent to which the Vizier's hand was forced is not clear. Though over 60 years old and nearly blind, he was a strong personality and able to take charge, as later events proved, in a succession crisis. After thirty years as Vizier or Dangaladima, he was the dominant figure in the Sokoto administration. For example, on the coming of the British, the course he took was crucial: while the Amīr al-mu'minīn went off to the east, intending to go to Mecca, the majority of the administration waited, and followed the Vizier's lead.[122]

---

[119] Letter of Abadie to Lugard, 5/4/1902, in Kaduna Archives (Kadcap 11:17). Cf. Gombe Correspondence, 28.

[120] Cf. Edgar, *op. cit.*, III, pp. 413–14.

[121] Edgar, *op. cit.*, III, pp. 400 f.

[122] Muḥammad Bukhari b. Aḥmad, *Risāla*. Cf. the monthly reports by Residents J. A. Burdon and H. R. P. Hillary, beginning 31/3/1903 (that is, a fortnight after the battle of Sokoto).

After the British had won the battle on 15 March 1903 outside the south-western suburbs of Sokoto town, the Vizier, like the others, left by the north towards Wurno, the second capital. He had lost contact with the Caliph, and spent the night at Marnona. There, many people had gathered round him to ask his advice: guessing that the main road to the east, up the Sokoto river, was closed, they knew that the shortage of water elsewhere made emigration *en masse* impossible. It was March, late in the dry season, and no preparations had been made. The Vizier, therefore, ordered each man to make his own way; he himself went the few miles on to Dinawa where his wife's family was in charge. The Amīr al-mu'minīn evidently discouraged others from joining him. For example, the Emir of Raba Ibrāhīm b. Amīr al-mu'minīn Abī Bakr b. Bello, who had gone straight to Raba after the battle, tried to join the Amīr al-mu'minīn that evening, but could not: his Dangaladima Hamza and Sarkin Fada 'Alī, however, did, but were told to return. The Emir of Raba thereupon wrote to the Vizier, whom he, with some anxiety, knew to be staying behind: 'all who do not find the Amīr al-mu'minīn', he said, 'must seek you'. With the Emir of Raba were one of the senior councillors, the Magajin rafi Macha, and the Amīr Burmi Maigari b. 'Abd al-Raḥmān.[123]

Thus when the Vizier moved back into Sokoto after receiving assurances that the practice of Islam would be guaranteed, others gradually followed.[124] The Galadima and the brother of the Amīr al-mu'minīn, the Marafa, returned shortly after, followed by the Amīr al-jaish and the other royal electors. The Magajin gari, who had been badly wounded in the battle, returned to Sokoto during April.[125] Only the Ubandoma and the Alkali, of the senior officials, were still with the Amīr al-mu'minīn.[126] In the extraordinary

[123] Letter from the Amīr Raba to the Vizier Muḥammad Bukhari in the collection of the late Sardauna of Sokoto.

[124] Muḥammad Bukhari, *Risāla*.

[125] J. A. Burdon, monthly report, No. 2 (30/4/1903); H. R. P. Hillary, monthly report, No. 16 (July 1904).

[126] C. L. Temple, in his Report on the death of the Amīr al-mu'minīn Attahiru (8 August 1903: NAK. SNP., 10) gave a list of the Sokoto men

circumstances, with the British present and wanting either to see the Amīr al-mu'minīn Attahiru b. Aḥmad or to have a new Caliph appointed immediately, the Vizier called on the Galadima, the Marafa and the Sarkin Galma to help him choose the new Caliph. Attahiru b. Aḥmad, although still quite close to Sokoto, did not return; in his place, Attahiru b. 'Alī, the popular candidate of the year before, was elected Amīr al-mu'minīn. The election was later approved by the Amīr al-jaish and the other proper electors on their return to Sokoto.[127] With the co-operation of the Vizier and the Marafa, the new Amīr al-mu'minīn was able to continue the Sokoto administration; but he depended heavily on the Vizier, who knew more of the internal politics of the caliphate and was thus left with most of the work.

Though the Vizier had decided to maintain the administration of the caliphate despite the presence of the British, some of his family joined the ex-Amīr al-mu'minīn in emigrating to the east. Two sons of Muḥammad Bukhari left Sokoto, one as late as April: one died at Burmi, the other reached the Sudan, along with a son of the Vizier Khalilu.

Muḥammad Bukhari kept the title of Vizier till his death on 6 October 1910; but the vizierate had entirely changed under the British reorganisation. The history of that change is outside the limits of this study.

---

reported killed at Burmi: Attahiru, Ubandoma, Alkali, Dan Maji, Dan Magaji, Dan Waziri, Sarkin Kwani, Madaki.

[127] H. R. P. Hillary, *loc. cit.*; M. Perham, *Lugard* (London, 1960), II, 128 ff. Lugard installed Attahiru b. 'Alī on 22 March 1903. The Sarkin Galma was a descendant of the sister of the Shaikh.

8
The Work of the Viziers

(i) *Their Work in Sokoto*

In the administration of the Sokoto caliphate, the Vizier was second only to the Caliph. His sphere, as the Caliph's deputy, in theory covered everything; in practice, certain geographical areas and commands were delegated to others who were responsible directly to the Caliph. The Shaikh had several Viziers and commanders, but under Bello the Viziers were differentiated by titles, to leave a single Vizier who retained his overall seniority.

The vizierate in Sokoto does not fit either of the classical divisions between delegated and executive authority—as discussed by al-Māwardī or Ibn Khaldūn.[1] The Vizier's authority, and the consequent relationship between Caliph and Vizier, depended on personalities and experience: while the Vizier had freedom of decision in many appointments and problems, the final word was with the Caliph. But as the Caliph relied on the Vizier's advice, this final word need only be a formality.

The Vizier was, above all, the senior councillor.[2] In the

---

[1] al-Māwardī, *op. cit.*, pp. 53 f.; Ibn Khaldūn, *op. cit.*, II, pp. 10–11. In some letters, the Vizier is called al-mufawwaḍ, implying that he had delegated authority (tafwīḍ); but the term is not always used.

[2] For much of the details of the nineteenth-century vizierate I am indebted to al-haji Junaidu, Wazirin Sokoto. Unless explicitly stated otherwise, the data given in what follows is true for the period 1880–1900. The documentation does not cover in any detail the vizierate of the earlier period.

early morning, after sending one of his men to the palace to find if his arrival would be convenient, he went to greet the Amīr al-mu'minīn. Most houses have a reception room off the main courtyard: in the Shaikh's house in Sabon Birni (Sokoto), the meeting-room seems to have been a separate building; in Bello's house Clapperton describes a formal chamber reached through a series of rooms.[3] At Degel, the meetings were held at the door of the house.[4]

Before the council met, the Amīr al-mu'minīn received the greetings of others, who came out of courtesy or to make a request. Similarly, at the Vizier's house, before the Vizier left for the palace, his followers were present to greet him. The council of the Amīr al-mu'minīn seems not to have been strictly defined: the key officials were there—after the Vizier, the Magajin gari, the Magajin rafi, the Galadima, the Ubandoma, the chief Qāḍī (judge). Other officials like the Amīr al-jaish, or important princes, if in town, might be there. If there was a serious crisis, a kind of outer council, which would include the electing councillors, notable scholars and others, could be summoned by the Vizier. If there were decisions to be made public, such as to keep the cattle in town and off the crops, or to get ready for an expedition, a drum was beaten at the palace gate and the Vizier proceeded to the market with his gongs and trumpets. If he was away, his Dangaladima acted for him. But this seems not to be invariable, or else to be a late development: Clapperton describes a town-crier announcing an expedition.[5]

The Vizier's authority *vis-à-vis* the other councillors was shown at the election of a new Caliph. He summoned the council—the Magajin gari, Magajin rafi, Galadima—and the representatives of the three major Fulani groups, the Amīr al-jaish (Konni), the Amīr Kebbi (Kebbi) and the

---

[3] al-haji Junaidu, *Bughyat al-rāghibīn*, p. 19 (printed by the Gaskiya Corp., Zaria). Clapperton (1st journey), p. 82; (2nd journey), p. 208.

[4] K.B., p. 7.

[5] Clapperton (1st journey), p. 97. He says the crier shouts 'This is the will of the Sultan' at the end of each sentence, and people reply, 'Whatever the Sultan does, is good; we will do it.'

Ardo'en of the Sullebawa.[6] The Vizier had the final word, and unless he agreed, no one was elected: in al-ḥājj Sa'īd's accounts of the early elections, the Vizier acted as chairman, presiding over the council.[7] The candidates came in from their ribāṭs or towns to press their claims and their qualities: for this reason, the election of a new Caliph was not normally finished until four to seven days after the death of the previous Caliph. The bay'a was then made, in a mosque or, on two occasions, in the house of the Vizier.[8]

For other appointments, the Vizier advised the Amīr al-mu'minīn, and the appointment was made in the Amīr al-mu'minīn's name. Nonetheless, two sets of letters were written, one from the Amīr al-mu'minin and one from the Vizier: they were in identical or nearly identical terms, written by the same scribe. Each set consisted of a letter of condolence for the late Emir and a letter of appointment, congratulations and good advice for the new Emir. The letters were taken by the Vizier, or, if he could not travel, either by one of his lieutenants responsible for the emirate, or, sometimes, in the case of Gwandu, by one of the royal princes.[9] The new Emir came later to greet the Caliph.

If the issue was clear and the Vizier was on the spot, he could appoint a new Emir on his own initiative. For this purpose he carried round on tour papers ready stamped with the caliphal seal to fill in the appropriate appointments or depositions. For example, Gidado deposed the old Emir of Daura, Isḥāq, and installed the Emir's son without reference to Muḥammad Bello.[10] In difficult appointments, such as

---

[6] Cf. Barth, IV, p. 528, where he mentions only one Ardo (or Sarki) of the Sullebawa on the electing council. I suggested above that the other Ardo was appointed after the settling of the Sullebawa in the 1860's.

[7] Sa'īd, pp. 207 f.

[8] The bay'a to 'Abd al-Raḥmān in 1891 and to Attahiru in 1902 took place in the house of the Vizier Bukhari, the first in Kaura Namoda, the second in Wurno (Muḥammad Bukhari, *Ta'nīs al-ikhwān*).

[9] For a late description (1903), see Burdon, monthly report No. 3, paras. 19–22.

[10] K.B., p. 19. In the *History of Missau* written by the present Emir, Aḥmad b. al-Ḥājj, in *c.* 1928, it is said that Muḥammad Bello reversed Gidado's deposition of Muḥammad Manga.

Kano in 1893, he had to wait for explicit instructions. In practice, the Vizier's responsibility was limited by the small choice of candidates, and the local nominee was usually accepted. The local electoral council represented the local community and was not easily by-passed. In Zaria, much manœuvring was done by both Sokoto and the Zaria electors to maintain at least a semblance of local autonomy in the election of a new Emir.

Minor provincial appointments were similar: if they were controversial, they were referred to the Amīr al-mu'minīn or the Vizier. Thus at Gwaram in Kano, the dispute warranted Sokoto intervention, and it was then made clear that appointments had to be popular.[11] Depositions were also within the jurisdiction of the Vizier: when the Amīr Dutse was deposed, the Vizier received his share of the property.[12] On one occasion when the Emir of Zaria was threatened with dismissal, the Vizier and his deputy, the Sarkin Fada, intervened and dissuaded the Amīr al-mu'minīn.[13] If deposed, an Emir was brought to Sokoto; he might, like the Emir of Bauchi, be put in chains and suffer much abuse.[14] He was then lodged on the estate of his Sokoto supervisor, like the Emir of Zaria Sambo on the Vizier's estate at Bado.[15] Depositions, however, were uncommon.

The Vizier also advised the Amīr al-mu'minīn on the choice of officials. The appointment of judges within Sokoto is said to have come under the Vizier, though some local autonomy must have occurred in practice. The Vizier was generally responsible for legal education, but this was not formalised in the nineteenth century. The Law was an integral part of Muslim learning, but those who wished to be trained as judges acted as clerks in the courts, assisting the judge.[16] The Vizier did not directly handle cases—though

[11] Correspondence, VII, 4, 5, 16 (from the period 1886–91).

[12] Correspondence, VI, 34 (from the period 1882–6, in Kano).

[13] Staudinger, *op. cit.*, pp. 323 f. (*c.* 1885).

[14] Staudinger, *ibid.*

[15] Cf. Staudinger, *op. cit.*, p. 342. He died and was buried there. The Emir of Zaria 'Abdullāh was also detained at Bado.

[16] Cf. J. A. Burdon, monthly report No. 2.

under the British administration he did on occasion. Appeals were made to the chief judge in Sokoto town or to the Amīr al-mu'minīn if necessary. Capital cases were reviewed by the Amīr al-mu'minīn, but he relied on advisers, leaving the judge to do the investigation.[17] On difficult cases, other learned men were called in to advise. The Vizier, who was always distinguished for his learning, might be consulted.

The Vizier also promoted Quranic education. His house supported scholars and teachers to instruct their circles of students in the Quran and the Islamic sciences. The Vizier's family was itself the largest group of scholars and judges in Sokoto, with ability and learning above average. The Vizier had the further responsibility of helping the Imams and Quran readers.

Any stranger, orphan or destitute who appealed to the Amīr al-mu'minīn was sent to the Vizier. Gidado, it is said, used to go round seeing if there was anyone who was hungry or without clothes or whose house needed repair, and see to it that all was put right. The care of the two mosques in the town was also given to the Vizier:[18] repairs, however, were usually done by communal effort, each house supplying something as alms—water, labour, straw. Gidado was building a third mosque at his own expense when Clapperton was in Sokoto, but by Barth's day it had fallen down, due, presumably, to Amīr al-mu'minīn 'Alī's preference for Wurno and the moving of the court there.[19]

In Sokoto town, the Vizier's quarter, Gidadawa, occupied the north-east of the old town.[20] The quarter was under the

---

[17] Bello is said to have reversed the decisions of the judges frequently (Sa'īd, p. 197). According to M. Yahaya Abd al-Qadiri, formal review of capital cases began under 'Alī al-kabīr, following an incident in which the Arab scholar, Mūsā, intervened to stop a miscarriage of justice. Later, the Amīr al-mu'minīn was informed, in writing if necessary, of important cases. (Cf. Correspondence, V, 31, 34.) The office of Alkalin Garka was introduced early in the twentieth century for political reasons; it is said to have had no nineteenth-century precedent in Sokoto.

[18] The Friday mosques of the Shaikh (in Sabon Birni) and of Bello (in Sokoto proper). There were, of course, several prayer places.

[19] Clapperton (1st journey), p. 103; Barth, IV, p. 179.

[20] See map on next page.

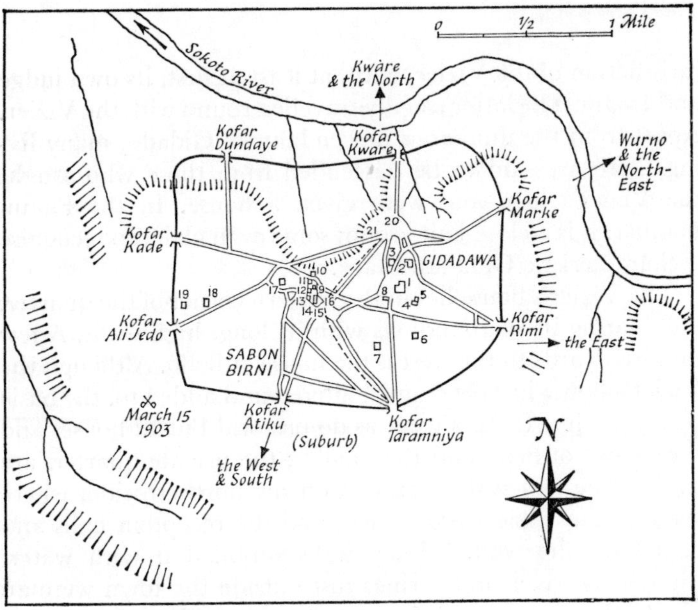

8. Sokoto Town in the nineteenth century

1. House of Muḥammad Bello b. al-Shaikh
2. House of the Vizier
3. House of Magajin gari
4. House of Galadima
5. House of Ubandoma
6. House of Magajin rafi
7. House of the Gaoler (Yari)
8. The Mosque of Muḥammad Bello
9. House of the Shaikh
10. House of al-Ḥasan b. al-Shaikh
11. House of 'Īsa b. al-Shaikh
12. House of 'Abd al-Qādir b. al-Shaikh
13. House of Aḥmad Rufa'i b. al-Shaikh
14. House of Muḥammad Sambo b. al-Shaikh
15. House of Muḥammad Bukhari b. al-Shaikh
16. House of Abū Bakr Atiku b. al-Shaikh
17. Mosque of the Shaikh
18. Mosque of the Vizier Gidado (disappeared by 1853)
19. House of the Amīr al-jaish (Sarkin Yaki)
20. Market
21. Dajin Maleri (execution ground)

The walls were rebuilt *c.* 1818 to include Sabon Birni: they were about 24 ft. high. There were originally more than eight gates.

jurisdiction of the Vizier, with, at least at first, its own judge and Imam. The latter usually travelled round with the Vizier. Apart from the numerous descendants of Gidado, many living there are said to be descended from those who sought the Vizier's help and were given a house. In the Fulani manner, it is a close-knit group: some even claim to recognise a characteristic Gidadawa face.

The Vizier's house lies in the western corner of the quarter, dominating its surroundings with its long, high walls. A few hundred yards to the west is the house of Bello. Although the Vizier's house has been much altered and added to, the basic plan remains. It faces west, as do pastoral Fulani houses and the houses of Bello and the Shaikh; the private quarters are against the east wall, a garden on the northern side, where some of the Viziers are buried, and the reception halls and courts on the west.[21] Deep wells supplied it with water, though the river and springs just outside the town were an alternative source.

As successive Caliphs preferred to live either in Sokoto or in Wurno, and sometimes moved between the two, the Vizier maintained two establishments. It was in these moves to and fro that the vizieral archives were damaged or lost. His house at Wurno was large—it contained its own mosque—and stood on a slight rise south-west of Bello's house. Only the Vizier 'Abd al-Qādir is buried there, and the house no longer stands.

Outside Sokoto town, several villages came under his jurisdiction. These were distinct from his own farms, though such villages may well contain some estates of his.[22] The land was transferable: Dendi, for example, was given by Gidado

---

[21] Compare Clapperton's description of the house of Muḥammad Bello (2nd journey, pp. 208–9). The Viziers buried there are Ibrāhīm Khalilu, 'Abdullāh and Muḥammad Bukhari. Gidado and Asmā' are both buried in the house of the Shaikh. Aḥmad b. Gidado is buried in Katsina in the house of the Emir.

[22] e.g. Bado, Gandi. He also had lands, for example in Adamawa, according to al-haji Junaidu. Gidado is credited with introducing from Kano the 'kutara', or the pole of a shadūf, for irrigating the farms around Sokoto. (P. G. Harris, *op. cit.*, p. 320, confirmed by al-haji Junaidu.)

to the Amīr Kebbi (Yabo), while Yartsokwa was established by Khalilu and handed over to his Magaji.[23] He also had both slaves and followers settled in villages outside his control. His following, then, was scattered over a large area, with no single stronghold except in his own quarter in Sokoto town. This was true of the other councillors and officials in Sokoto, including the Caliph.

Having these estates, neither the Amīr al-mu'minīn nor the Vizier had any need of support from the treasury. Bello had insisted on being self-supporting, and the ideal remained.[24] The Amīr al-mu'minīn, therefore, had his own treasury under one of his servants. Presents from both his followers and the provincial Emirs and officials supplemented the income of the Vizier and the Amīr al-mu'minīn considerably. The presents received were redistributed to their followers in need, providing food, clothing, horses.

The public treasury was under the Vizier, and the Ajia in charge was appointed by him. The building that housed it stood a little to the west of the Vizier's house. The first treasurer mentioned had been 'Umar al-Kammu, chosen on the spot to take care of and divide the booty after the battle of Matankari.[25] However, in Sifawa, one of the Shaikh's servants, Wodi, was responsible. On Bello's accession, he probably added the treasury to the Vizier's responsibilities, and the Vizier in turn appointed his own Ajia. Al-ḥājj Sa'īd suggests that Amīr al-mu'minīn 'Alī al-kabīr wanted to take the treasury out of the Vizier's control, and that this alienated the Vizier.[26] The story may be another example of al-ḥājj Sa'īd's bias, but since there was a redistribution of responsibilities at this time, it is possible that the treasury was at first included. However, the treasury is said by al-haji Junaidu to have remained under the Vizier throughout. Payments into the treasury took the form of kharāj tax from the subordinate emirates, jizya from protected peoples, and the fifth

---

[23] Yabo District notebook; Gandi District notebook. The Sarkin rafi in the Vizier's household was given Arba, in Wurno District (*v.* Wurno District notebook).

[24] Sa'īd, p. 197; cf. 'Abd al-Qādir b. Gidado, *Manāqib 'Alī.*

[25] I.M., p. 73.

[26] Sa'īd, p. 208.

of the booty; the zakāt was usually disbursed locally and immediately in the Community. The goods or money (cowries) received were used for public works and for rewarding those who joined the campaigns.

Though in overall charge of the treasury, the Vizier was not involved in tax-collecting or assessing. Such of the tax as went to Sokoto was forwarded by the Emir through his or the Vizier's servants—whoever was available. In the case of Hadejia, the tax was sent from the Emir via Kano, as a matter of convenience. Barth met the Galadima in Katsina when he was with his brothers collecting what was owed; Katsina, however, was the only responsibility of the Galadima.[27] The Vizier, by contrast, with seven major emirates to supervise, required a large household.

(ii) *Their Household*

The household, like the village, was a microcosm of the state, repeating the names if not the functions of state offices, and copied from the common fund of Gobir titles. The selection of titles seems arbitrary: there is little uniformity of usage between household and household, village and village, state and state. In the vizieral household, the most senior official was the Dangaladima. He was the Vizier's messenger to Kano, and, as such, the intermediary between the Emir of Kano and the Vizier. The Dangaladima deputised for the Vizier, handling correspondence if the Vizier was away. As he was usually a close relation of the Vizier and next in line for the vizierate, he was the object of attention for aspiring Emirs.[28] His influence was, therefore, considerable in Kano, and by virtue of this and his marriage ties in Sokoto, he could become a potential rival of the Vizier himself.

The first Dangaladima, or at least the first of Gidado's lieutenants, was his brother, Muḥammad Mudi.[29] The

---

[27] Barth, IV, pp. 98, 155.

[28] Cf. Correspondence, VII, 12, 82, 97, 8, 53, 103.

[29] The sword of office is said to have been given to the Dangaladima by Bello; but it does not necessarily imply the title was current at the time.

Dangaladima's special responsibility for Kano may not have been formulated at this time. Clapperton, who met Muḥammad Mudi often, makes no mention of his activities except that he commanded the escort that took Clapperton across to Zamfara.[30] On the death of Muḥammad Mudi during the caliphate of Abū Bakr Atiku, Gidado's son 'Abd al-Qādir acted for the Vizier and continued to do so under 'Alī, though he seems not to have taken the title.[31] The younger brother of 'Abd al-Qādir, Aḥmad, became his Dangaladima and led, for example, the expedition against Bukhari in Hadejia on his brother's behalf. In 1853, however, aged 33, he died while with the Amīr al-mu'minīn at Katsina, and Khalilu, the Vizier's son, became Dangaladima. When Khalilu succeeded to the vizierate, he accepted his uncle 'Abdullāh as his Dangaladima on the insistence of Asmā': she promised 'Abdullāh the vizierate. 'Abdullāh, when Vizier in his turn, made his nephew Muḥammad Bukhari Dangaladima; the latter on becoming Vizier took his brother Ambo as Dangaladima, and he in turn was followed by Bukhari's son Machido.[32] Apart from Muḥammad Mudi and Ambo, the Dangaladimas were young at the time of their appointment, in their late 20's or early 30's, in contrast to the Viziers, who were usually at least ten to twenty years older. The apprenticeship as Dangaladima was consequently long, enabling a continuity of administration to be established.

Although in theory others among the Vizier's subordinates could become Vizier, none did. The eligible titles were the Sarkin Fada and the Wali: both were held by descendants of the Shaikh, through Gidado's wife Asmā'.

The Sarkin Fada was the second in seniority, the messenger to Zaria. His position, though important as intermediary in Zaria politics, never approached that of the Dangaladima: for example, he led no major campaign. The Sarkin Fada was usually a son or a younger brother, who largely escaped

[30] Clapperton (1st journey), p. 110. But other messengers with geographical responsibilities were also operative at this period: *v. infra*.

[31] It is possible that Tabi b. Mudi acted as Dangaladima for a while at this time.

[32] The list of Dangaladimas was given me by al-haji Junaidu.

fame and lived long. The first was a son of Gidado, Muḥammad Bukhari; the second, a son of 'Abd al-Qādir, Aḥmad, while the third was Bukhari's younger brother 'Abd al-Qādir.[33]

The third eligible title was Wali, but only one is now known to have been appointed, 'Abd al-Qādir's son 'Uthmān, who held the title during the vizierate of Bukhari. He was the messenger to Gombe, which was given first to Asmā', and then to her descendants, to administer.

Other relatives, though not descended from Gidado and Asmā', acted as messengers for the other emirates. The title of Magaji was first held by Gidado's nephew, Sambo dan Garba dan Laima, and remained in that family: they were responsible for Katagum.[34] The Galadima travelled to Missau, the Sarkin Rafi to Hadejia, the Wombai to Adamawa; all were distant relations of the Vizier.[35] These posts tended to be hereditary or at least kept within the descendants of the first title-holder. There was, therefore, no promotion from one post to another. Officials were removed from office, but only rarely.[36]

Though these officials as representatives of the Vizier had some latitude of action, and on occasions formed an advisory council for the Vizier, much of the administration was done through letters, leaving the Vizier's officials as simple mes-

---

[33] Source: al-haji Junaidu. The Sarkin Fada Muḥammad Bukhari married a daughter of the Amīr al-mu'minīn 'Alī.

[34] The sons of Sambo, Muḥammad Bukhari and 'Abdullāh, both held the job of Magaji (Backwell, *op. cit.*, letters 6, 7). The earliest reference to Sambo travelling to Katagum is in K.B., p. 12; but in 1824 Muḥammad Dumbojee (i.e. Buji), 'one of the gadado's officers', escorted Clapperton to Katagum (Clapperton, 1st journey, pp. 113, 132). Sambo was noted for his knowing the Quran by heart; a poem on his death was written by Ibn Isḥāq.

[35] The first Galadima was Sambo (Aḥmad b. al-Ḥājj, *op. cit.*, para. 27 ff.). The Wombai was assisted by the Ubandawaki, who was normally resident in Gandi or Tsamia. (Contrast Monteil, *op. cit.*, p. 254.)

[36] For example, the Sarkin Fada Muḥammad Bukhari was dismissed for luxurious living at the request of Amīr al-mu'minīn 'Alī. Galadima Shehu b. Sambo was deposed by order of the Amīr al-mu'minīn Aḥmad b. Atiku, but no reason is given. (Source: al-haji Junaidu.)

sengers.[37] But there were in addition a number of other messengers, such as Nawurno who regularly went to Kano, escorting goods, horses or people as well as carrying letters.[38] They tended to specialise in a particular route, having regular halting-places, and escorts were provided by the local village heads over the dangerous stretch between Zamfara and Katsina. The volume of traffic was considerable, judging from the correspondence, and urgency, coupled with delays, required a large staff. Thus servants of the Amīr al-mu'minīn like Dagamalle were also used as need or convenience dictated.

The Vizier himself was for much of the year on tour round the emirates under his supervision: thus his nickname Shekaran tafi, 'year-long traveller'. He was usually accompanied by a retinue to which would be added the escort of the local Emir.[39] He moved slowly, averaging fifteen to twenty miles a day, and sometimes at night.[40] While the Vizier was on tour, his household would keep in touch with him, forwarding letters, supplies and news of messengers or the attitude of the Amīr al-mu'minīn.[41] The Vizier also informed the Amīr al-mu'minīn of his acts and movements, while the Amīr al-mu'minīn sometimes sent him instructions, though this was, it seems, uncommon, the Vizier having usually a free hand: the delays would make diplomacy otherwise impossible.[42] Officials like the Galadima or Magajin rafi also kept the Vizier informed of their plans and movements.[43]

Of the other officials directly appointed by the Vizier, the

---

[37] After the Kano crisis of 1893–5, it is said that the Magaji, Bukhari, threatened to resign over the Vizier's proposal to return Tukur's followers to Kano after Tukur's death. (Bukhari b. Aḥmad, *Kitāb fīmā jarā bainī wa-bain Amīr Hadijia wa-Yūsuf*; (Anon), *Faiḍ al-qadīr*.)

[38] e.g. Nawurno: cf. Correspondence, VII, 44, 68, 82, 97; Dagamalle: VII, 33; VI, 69; V, 59; Sarkin Baka: VII, 46, 59, 68, 83; VI, 1. Messengers till recently escorted horses along the same routes.

[39] e.g. Backwell, *op. cit.*, letter 27; Correspondence, VII, 72.

[40] Backwell, *op. cit.*, letters 30, 31.

[41] Correspondence, I, 18; V, 25, 59.

[42] Correspondence, V, 1; one uncatalogued; Backwell, *op. cit.*, letters 30, 31.

[43] Correspondence, V, 79, 50; I, 51.

Ajia, in charge of the public treasury, was a distant relation of the Vizier. The appointments of Alkali (al-qāḍī) and Imam for the quarter, however, were not hereditary, but based on merit; considering the scholastic ability of many among the descendants of Gidado, the appointment, however, might still be made from within the family.[44]

The titled and untitled followers and servants of the Vizier were numerous. There were the campaign officials like the Sarkin Yaki and the Barde, as well as the usual complement of stable-men. In his personal entourage, the Majidadi acted as his private servant and constant companion, and the Shentali as his confidential messenger to the Amīr al-mu'minīn: the Shentali kept the caliphal seal which was used on the correspondence.[45]

(iii) *The Chancery*

The Chancery, or secretariat which produced the correspondence for the Vizier and the Amīr al-mu'minīn, was part of the Vizier's household. The writing was done in the courtyard of the house by some scribes sitting on a mat beside the inkpot, while others stamped the completed letters with the seal of the Amīr al-mu'minīn, under the supervision of the chief scribe.[46] The letters were taken for checking to the Vizier who read them through. The Vizier kept extensive files of letters in leather bags, but not, it seems, copies of letters sent. Two copies were frequently made and sent, one in the Caliph's name, the other in that of the Vizier: the texts were virtually identical. Since the caliphal correspon-

---

[44] The names and dates of the first appointments to these offices are not known. The Alkali towards the end of the century became little more than a scribe, and during the vizierate of Bukhari was a scholar from Shira.

[45] Staudinger, *op. cit.*, pp. 318, 320. The office of Majidadi dates at least from the vizierate of Khalilu; the holders could be either free men or slaves. The office of Shentali was held by the brother of the Imam of the Bello mosque in the 1850's and both offices have remained in that family. Originally, the Shentali, as the name implies, was the custodian of the Vizier's water jug (for ritual ablution).

[46] Staudinger, *op. cit.*, p. 365.

dence was handled by the Vizier, his files contained letters addressed to the Caliph, but not those dealing with emirates outside his jurisdiction. Letters from the Caliph to these emirates were nonetheless written in the Chancery.

The Chancery remained in Sokoto or Wurno. When the Vizier was away, the letters continued to be written by the same hands, sometimes in the name of the Dangaladima, Sarkin Fada or Wali.[47] The number of scribes seems to have been small. Over thirty years, four hands are recognisable: for example, in the latter part of Bukhari's vizierate, the highly individualistic hand of the scribe Muḥammad predominates.[48] In the other emirates too, such as Kano, the scribe continued despite the change of Emir.[49] Styles of writing, therefore, change little. It is probably the practice of Sokoto that is followed: not only is the handwriting surprisingly uniform, but so are the terms and the style of composition used. Comparatively few letters emanating from Sokoto have survived: to be kept in the Vizier's files, for the most part they would have to be letters or versions never sent. So far only a small number of letters have been collected from the emirates, with the exception of Gombe and Bauchi, and even these collections are limited.[50] The Gombe letters are those that have survived from the period *c.* 1898–1901: they total 227, of which twenty-five are from Sokoto, four of these being second copies; the Sokoto archives contain no letters from Gombe for this period. Considering how much will have been lost or destroyed, the volume of correspondence is great.

It is possible to distinguish the general characteristics of the Sokoto Chancery for the last two decades of the nineteenth century.[51] All the letters without exception are written in

---

[47] e.g. Correspondence, I, 18; Gombe Correspondence, 28.

[48] Cf. Correspondence, I, 29; V, 25. This Muḥammad held the title of Alkalin Waziri.

[49] Thus the writer of letters VII, 27, 46, 61, 63, etc., under Emir of Kano 'Abdullāh (died 1882) wrote letters VII, 18, 83, 88, 90, etc., under Emir of Kano Muḥammad Bello (1882–93).

[50] But only in Gombe and Sokoto has any serious attempt been made to collect letters. The total number of letters so far collected is over a thousand.

[51] Cf. A. D. H. Bivar (*B.S.O.A.S.*, 1959), pp. 325 ff.

Arabic. The use of Hausa in Arabic script for administrative correspondence was introduced by the British, who were ignorant of Arabic. Arabic was the lingua franca of the learned; being not merely a literary but also a spoken language (admittedly in the classical form) throughout Muslim West Africa, it was often the only means of communication between the communities of Tuareg, Kanuri, Hausa, Fulani, Nupe or Yoruba. Further, the religious and scholastic character of the Sokoto caliphate ensured that Arabic was the language of state.

The seal used on the letters of the Amīr al-mu'minīn was a cone made of brass, with the inscription cut into the face: when it is dipped in black ink, the stamp appears black with white writing.[52] On some seals, a ring is inscribed round the edge. The diameter of the seal varies slightly with each Amīr al-mu'minīn, from $1\frac{9}{16}$ in. to $2\frac{7}{16}$ in. Except in the early years of a caliphate, or when a new one is made, the seal is illegible, and is sometimes stamped upside down. The seals of Muḥammad Bello and 'Alī b. Bello are clear, but from the blurred patterns of later seals, it is possible to see that the wording did not always remain the same. The following seal, *mutatis mutandis*, was used by Muḥammad Bello and his sons, 'Alī the elder and younger, Abū Bakr and Mu'ādh.

Amīr
al-mu'minīn 'Alī
bin Muḥammad Bello naṣarahu
Allāh rabbī wa-huwa
ḥasbī[53]

The seal is placed between the bismillah and the name of the

[52] Cf. Staudinger, *op. cit.*, p. 365.

[53] 'Commander of the Faithful 'Alī b. Muḥammad Bello, help him Allāh, my Lord, and He is sufficient for me.' Bello on his seal called himself Muḥammad Bello b. 'Uthmān b. Fūdī. (Cf. letters in NAK; cf. Bivar, *B.S.O.A.S.*, 1959, pp. 338–9. But it is possible Bello needed two seals during his caliphate.)

addressee. The name of the Caliph does not appear except on the seal: sometimes the phrase 'from us' is used before 'to the Amīr . . .' On the Vizier's letters the seal is not used, and beneath the bismillah, usually after a small gap, the text begins with the Vizier's titles and name. No date is given in the text. This is true for the other emirates, none of which, except Katsina, use a seal. The Emir of Katsina writes his name as well as having the seal, which is placed usually at the foot of the text.

The style of the letters is distinctive, and differs, for example, from that of North Africans settled in Kano or from that of Bornu; nor is it the style of the correspondence manual such as the one which was written in 1877 and was in circulation in the Sokoto caliphate.[54] Of the very early correspondence, little survives except in a reproduced form which omits the opening. What does survive suggests that a formal style was not established early.[55] The later style was a short bismillah at the head of the page; then, with a gap left, the sender's title and name, the addressee's title and name with a phrase or two of pious epithets, then the rhymed greetings 'taḥiyya wa-salām wa-riḍā wa-ikrām' followed by 'wa-ba'd' or 'ammā ba'd'.[56] Occasionally, there is an enquiry after the health of the addressee, followed by 'the purpose of this is to . . .' or 'to inform [you] that . . .' The purpose of the letter is expressed succinctly and seldom exceeds a page; writing on the reverse is rare.[57] Pious phrases like 'May Allah

[54] 'Umar b. Abī Bakr b. 'Uthmān, *Kitāb al-sarḥa al-warīqa fī 'ilm al-wathīqa* (*G.A.L.*, S.I., 483). The author, a Kebbi man born in Kano, was resident in Salaga (in modern Ghana). A copy is in NAK (Sokprof 4:15). Cf. Bornu letters, on microfilm (uncatalogued) at Ibadan; letters 77, 78 in Backwell, *op. cit.*; letter 5 in B. G. Martin (*J.H.S.N.*, 1962).

[55] A. D. H. Bivar, *B.S.O.A.S.*, 1959, p. 337. It does not seem, as Bivar (pp. 327–8) suggests, that a distinctive 'alāma was used by each Amīr al-mu'minīn; nor was there much need of one, since the origin of the letter would be well known.

[56] 'Greetings and peace and contentment and honour; and after [this] . . .'

[57] The average page is more or less 6¼ in. by 9 in., the double page 9 in. by 12½ in.; this is also the standard size of page for manuscript books. The pages are cut out of larger sheets. The writing averages two lines per inch.

prolong your life' (an equivalent of the common Hausa, 'Ranka ya dade', or Fulfulde 'Allah sabbinane') recur towards the end. The letter is closed by 'hadhā wa 'l-salām'.[58]

The most striking facet of these letters is their brevity: the subject-matter is given without discussion; the greetings and pieties are formal but generally unobtrusive; even the congratulations and regular greetings or thanks are kept down to a few sentences. By comparison, the diplomatic letters of North Africa are verbose.[59] Equally, in this succinctness literary elegance is lost. Some writers do use the stylish phrase and the high-flown titles: they were familiar to the poets of Sokoto, but the scribes whose style determined the formulas generally avoided them.[60]

With the small turn-over in scribes, consistency in style was maintained in most emirates. The handwriting is clear and distinctive: documents from Bornu and the lands west of Sokoto are written in a somewhat different hand.[61] Being a product of scholars, the handwriting is in sharp contrast to that of areas where scholars are rare. There is a tendency for the earlier writing to be smaller; possibly this was due to the scarcity of paper, which, being largely of Italian manufacture, was imported over the Sahara from Tripoli.[62]

Another aspect of the coherence of practice in the caliphate is the manner of folding letters: one predominates.[63] First,

---

[58] Literally 'furthermore, peace'.

[59] e.g. Bivar (*B.S.O.A.S.*, 1959), pp. 345–6; cf. Martin (*J.H.S.N.*, 1962), letter IV in contrast to the baldness of letters I, II, III.

[60] Letters from the Emir of Tambawel, for example, are more high-flown than average (Correspondence, III, 10 ff.).

[61] For the differences, see A. D. H. Bivar (*B.S.O.A.S.*, 1959), pp. 328 ff., 336 ff. I have not studied the handwriting west of Sokoto, but a cursory survey of material from Segu in the Bibliothèque Nationale, Paris, revealed no non-Sokoto material in the 'Sokoto' style.

[62] Professor H. F. C. Smith, who studied the watermarks, found that they were of little use for chronology, since paper imported in bulk might be used over a long period.

[63] The letter of Muḥammad Bello, published by Bivar in *B.S.O.A.S.*, 1959, facing p. 336, was not folded in this pattern: it may have been folded by later owners. The final fold is usually shown by indigo dye-stains.

fold lengthwise down the middle; then divide into fifths, folding the top two fifths over on to the next two, and refolding those two fifths into half; finally the bottom fifth is folded over the remaining fifth. The address 'to the hand of Amīr—' is written diagonally in the top left-hand corner on the back of the penultimate fifth. No sealing-wax was used to close it: presumably if the messenger was unscrupulous, the contents could be widely known. Yet in the Kano succession crisis, the Vizier could keep secret the Amīr al-mu'minīn's letter appointing the unpopular candidate. In that same crisis, however, the caliphal messenger showed a letter for the Vizier to the Emir of Kano, who then told the Vizier.[64]

The answers to these letters often returned with the messenger, who also brought a present from the Emir back with him; some of the answers were a simple acknowledgement of the letter received, though acknowledgement seems not to have been invariably made. According to Staudinger, the letters brought were given by the Shentali to the Vizier who passed them to the Amīr al-mu'minīn. After glancing at the letters, he returned them to the Vizier who read them out, if there was no other malam present.[65]

Of the in-coming letters preserved in the Vizier's house, about a quarter of those from Kano and Zaria are addressed to the Amīr al-mu'minīn, the rest to the Vizier; the proportion of letters addressed to the Amīr al-mu'minīn from the other emirates under the Vizier's control is smaller. Some of the incoming letters were duplicated, a copy of the letter being sent to the Vizier as well as the Amīr al-mu'minīn. In general, the duplicates may not have been kept, and thus any statistics are invalid. It does seem that the Emirs of Kano and Zaria felt more free to address the Amīr al-mu'minīn direct than the less powerful Emirs. Some fourteen letters from the Emirs of Katsina and Bauchi are kept in the vizieral archives: only one is addressed to the Vizier, but another two are forwarded by an Emir under the Vizier.[66] Since Katsina and

---

[64] Correspondence, VII, 33.

[65] Staudinger, *op. cit.*, p. 320.

[66] Correspondence, II, 33, 35 and one uncatalogued; one letter is addressed to the Vizier Bukhari by the Galadima of Katsina (V, 14).

Bauchi were the charges of the Galadima and Magajin rafi, it is probable that the letters went to them and the Vizier only on occasions kept the original or the Amīr al-mu'minīn's copy. Since problems of general importance were discussed in the council, the Vizier took part in making any decision. In the Jibrīl Gaini affair, when co-ordination was required between Bauchi and the other emirates which were under the Vizier, the Vizier has retained at least some of the correspondence.[67]

The style of the letters, as has been said, followed the Sokoto model of simplicity bordering on curtness. The titles given to the Amīr al-mu'minīn were seldom flowery or eulogistic: rarely is the Amīr al-mu'minīn even called 'Khalīfa'.[68] 'Sulṭān' is not used for him except in conjunction with other honorific titles, but the Emirs of Kano, Zaria and Bauchi are so called, especially by the minor Emirs.[69] With the Emirs of Gwandu, all mention of Gwandu is omitted, 'the Emir' being sufficient.[70] Similarly, the Vizier is usually addressed with his traditional title of Amīr al-maṣāliḥ wālī al-naṣā'iḥ, with only a few compliments added.[71]

An in-coming letter was often accompanied by some gowns or cloths, occasionally a slave or a horse or a parcel of kola-nuts.[72] A note of what was being sent was usually written

[67] Correspondence, II, 34, 35; one uncatalogued.

[68] The Emirs of Gwandu, Tambawel and Kaya (Maradun), or their scribes, were unusual in addressing the Amīr al-mu'minīn as Khalīfa.

[69] For example, both Gombe and Bauchi (e.g. Correspondence, II, 33) refer to the Emir of Kano as Sulṭān, as on occasions does Sokoto (e.g. VI, 81; VII, 127). The Emir of Bauchi both styles himself, and is addressed as 'Sulṭān'.

[70] That is, in letters addressed to Sokoto. Muḥammad b. 'Abdullāh, in one of the earliest extant Gwandu letters (to the Amir Yoruba 'Abd al-Salām in 1829), uses the title Amīr al-gharb, Emir of the West. Foreign correspondence required different forms: for example, in the letter on the back of the treaty collected by Dr. Grüner, the Emir of Gwandu 'Umar calls himself: Amīr aqālīm al-gharb al-falatiyya wa'l-sūdāniyya (*v.* forthcoming article by W. Markov and P. Sebald in *J.H.S.N.*).

[71] Al-mufawwaḍ, the deputy, is sometimes written; e.g. Correspondence, VII, 15, from the 'Sulṭān Kano' Muḥammad Bello to 'Amīr al-maṣāliḥ wālī al-naṣā'iḥ al-wazīr al-a'ẓam al-mufawwaḍ'.

[72] Kola-nuts particularly from Gwandu (e.g. Correspondence, I, 8, 69).

after the letter, at right angles to the text, saying 'by the hand of [bearer] . . .' or 'our present to you is . . .'. These presents were not tribute, but a courtesy: they were not compulsory, and do not always reflect the contents of the letter, although begging letters were usually accompanied by a present, which was seldom large.[73] Sometimes the gifts were to be shared between the Amīr al-mu'minīn and the Vizier.[74]

Letter 1 (the Arabic text faces p. 174)

Translation:

'In the name of Allāh the Compassionate the Merciful; may Allāh bless the Generous Prophet.

'To the deputy, the Emir of affairs, the Wālī of advice, the Vizier Muḥammad al-Bukhārī, greetings and peace, joy and honour. Next, I have put the matter of the Galadima Yūsuf into your hands since I have entrusted you with control over him and all his affairs.

'Peace.'

Origin: uncatalogued letter from the collection of alhaji Junaidu, Wazirin Sokoto.

Date: within the period 1886–91.

Seal: probably that of the Caliph 'Umar b. 'Alī.

Handwriting: that of the scribe Muḥammad (Alkalin Waziri); several letters in this handwriting are found.

Size: approximately 6½ in. by 9 in.

Note: Yūsuf b. 'Abdullāh was the ex-Galadima of Kano and hoped to become Emir of Kano on the death of his uncle Muḥammad Bello. Bello's son, Tukur, had been appointed Galadima and was also a candidate for the throne of Kano.

---

[73] e.g. Correspondence, VI, 90, 95; but cf. VI, 10.

[74] Correspondence, VI, 27.

Letter 2 (the Arabic text faces p. 175)

Translation:

'In the name of Allāh the Compassionate the Merciful; may Allāh bless the Generous Prophet.

'From the Emir of affairs, the Wālī of advice, the Vizier Muḥammad al-Bukhārī.

'To the Sultan of Zakzak 'Uthmān, son of the most learned Emir 'Abdullāh—Allāh be merciful on him—greetings and peace, joy and honour. Next, the news is that we have ordered all who are with you who hear and obey Allāh and his Messenger and pay allegiance to [the caliphate of the Shaikh] 'Uthmān not to send to Yūsuf, nor is he to send to you. We have broken off communications between you and him; therefore see that this is maintained. Peace.'

Origin: Letter VI, 100, from the collection of al-haji Junaidu, Wazirin Sokoto.

Date: *c.* 1893–4.

Handwriting: not known; it does not occur frequently in the surviving correspondence.

Size: approximately 6½ in by 9 in.

Note: When Tukur b. Muḥammad Bello was appointed Emir of Kano after his father, Yūsuf b. 'Abdullāh left Kano with a large following. His withdrawal from Kano implied rebellion, and measures such as those mentioned in the letter were taken in order to isolate him.

(iv) *Their Work Outside Sokoto*

The work of the Vizier is partly reflected in these letters. As they seldom form a series, and the Vizier's replies are missing, a comprehensive and exact analysis of the whole correspondence is impossible.[75]

---

[75] It should be remembered that almost all this correspondence dates from the period 1881–1903.

A large proportion of the letters are complimentary: greetings on appointment, on celebrating 'Īd al-fiṭr or 'Īd al-aḍḥā, on returning home, enquiries after health, reminders of friendship. Such letters accompanied payments like the kharāj sent each autumn, or came from officials in Zaria seeking promotion.[76] News of appointments was circulated and congratulations came in from all concerned. The Emir of Kano, for example, congratulated the Amīr al-mu'minīn on appointing Bukhari Vizier and sent along fourteen horses.[77]

Personal requests or problems were comparatively rare. The Vizier of Dogondaji asked for a dictionary; the Emir of Dogondaji wanted a builder; branches for house-building were sought from Raba; the wife of the Emir of Hadejia had learnt the Quran by heart, and arrangements were to be made to send her to Sokoto; a lion-skin was requested from the Sultan of Damagaram who had to forward the request to Kukawa since he had none.[78] The Emir of Kano, controlling the main trading centre, was used as a banker and payments were often made through him.[79] Riyals were sent to be exchanged there; silver anklets and musk were procured there, and the Vizier ordered his paper from his Kano counterpart.[80]

The most common complaint in the letters involved slaves who had either run away or claimed they were free men. Decisions were usually taken by the local Emir, and the matter reported again to Sokoto. In other inter-emirate problems, such as inheritance or blood-money, the case might be reported to the Vizier, who would then urge the Emirs to co-operate.

---

[76] Correspondence, VI, 45, e.g. VI, 14, 15, 16, 52. Cf. Kano, VII, 20, 22. Large sums were transferred to Sokoto—ten million cowries being normal—as the 'agreed gift' (VII, 14, 41, 56, 85). Cowries were packed in 20,000-cowrie bundles: one man could carry a bundle, though with difficulty (cf. M. F. Smith, *Baba of Kano,* London, 1954, p. 81).

[77] Correspondence, VII, 52.

[78] Correspondence, III, 41–5, 46; V, 29; IV, 17, 23, 47. Uncatalogued.

[79] Correspondence, VII, 65, 45, 40, 70, 84. Cf. Monteil, *op. cit.*, p. 252.

[80] Correspondence, VII, 107, 11, 95. The Amīr al-mu'minīn 'Umar received some paper from Katsina (VI, 14), as did Mu'ādh (V, 2).

Complaints against Emirs and District Heads were forwarded to Sokoto, and in one case, at least, the complaint was upheld and the District Head removed.[81] Local appointments and depositions were often reported to Sokoto; in depositions part of the deposed official's property was sent to Sokoto.[82] Sokoto had the right to 'bind and loose' in the

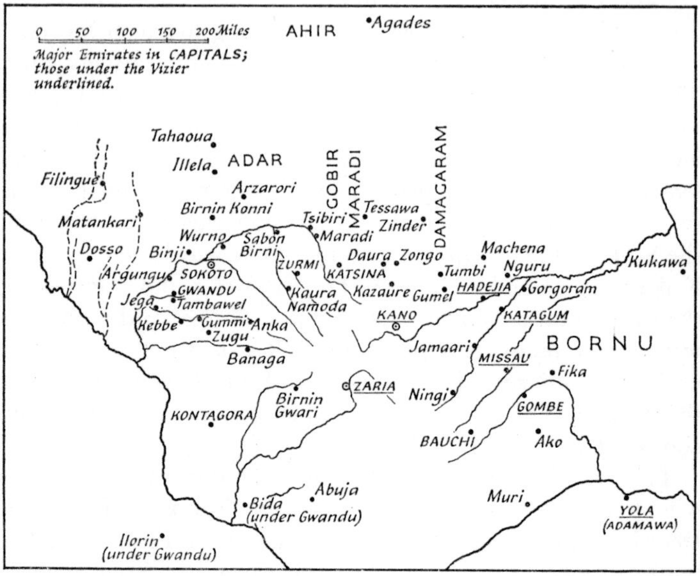

9. The Sokoto Caliphate *c.* 1890

emirates, giving orders to depose or reinstate officials.[83] But the electors of Adamawa, on the other hand, told Sokoto of their choice for the Emir of the South, expecting approval.[84] In a complaint against the Emir of Zaria, the people appealed

[81] Correspondence, VII, 4, 5, 16. At Gwaram; during the period 1886–91.

[82] e.g. Correspondence, VII, 34 (from the period 1882–6).

[83] Correspondence, VII, 57; VI, 81, 83. The phrase 'bind and loose' (al-'aqd wa'l-ḥall) is classical.

[84] Uncatalogued; *c.* 1872, on the death of Muḥammad Lawal and the appointment of 'Umar as Emir.

direct to the Emir of Kano to intervene on their behalf. He forwarded the appeal to Sokoto.[85]

The majority of complaints were probably made direct to the Vizier on his frequent tours, which would explain the letters reporting the settlement of cases. Nonetheless, petitioners did come in person to Sokoto, sometimes with the permission of the Emir, or were able to use relatives in Sokoto as intermediaries: thus when ʻAlī al-kabīr b. Amīr Kano ʻAbdullāh complained of oppression by one of the slaves of the Emir of Kano Muḥammad Bello, he wrote to his mother's brother, and the letter was passed to the Vizier.[86]

In most inter-emirate problems, the Vizier was only an adviser, using the Emirs to resolve the crises and encouraging their mutual dependence and co-operation: thus the Emir of Kano was asked to vouch for the Emir of Zaria Muḥammad Sambo.[87] Much of the correspondence will never have been forwarded to Sokoto. Territorial disputes, however, usually required mediation, and boundaries were adjusted. In the Bornu marches, for example, there was conflict between Katagum and Missau over certain towns in Katagum which had previously owed allegiance to Missau. Earlier, the Amīr Bornu (Missau) Muḥammad Ṣāliḥ had appealed to the Amīr al-mu'minīn to have his rights given him in Bauchi. But when the Caliph ʻUmar had deprived the next Amīr Bornu (Missau) Muḥammad Manga of all his extraterritorial rights for refusing to go to Sokoto, and only Amīr Bornu (Katagum) carried the order out, fighting occurred: the Amīr Bornu (Missau) attacked one of his lost towns, Isawa, and continued till the Amīr Bornu (Katagum) gave up his claims. The Vizier was kept informed, but there was little he could do beyond meeting the Amīr Bornu (Missau) outside Kano.[88] The dispute with Katagum extended over

---

[85] Correspondence, VII, 102 (from the period 1877–81).

[86] Correspondence, VII, 104. Cf. VII, 88.

[87] Correspondence, VI, 81 (probably written early in ʻUmar's caliphate, i.e. 1881–*c.* 1885).

[88] Correspondence, IV, 14, 15; V, 59. Cf. II, 4, 7, 11; IV, 34, 22, 30, 37, 38; one uncatalogued. J. M. Fremantle, *J.A.S.*, X, 40 (1911), pp. 417–19. The letters do not allow precise dating.

the Bornu frontier, when Katagum attacked a town owing allegiance to the Emir of Fika, who had a treaty with Missau. Once again, the matter was referred to the Vizier, as had been the letter of the Emir of Fika announcing his succession and renewing his treaty with Missau.[89]

The Vizier was informed of any developments in relations with Bornu. Although the policy was one of peaceful co-existence, it did not prevent expeditions across the border against dissident towns.[90] Relations with the Shaikh of Bornu were, however, sedulously preserved; despite frontier incidents caused by subordinates, communications were kept open and trade encouraged.[91] The Emir of Kano in one instance showed great care not to disturb friendly relations when a dispute arose in Kano over two Bornu men sold as slaves in Hadejia.[92] Nonetheless, a close watch was kept on the movements of the Shaikh of Bornu whenever he was approaching the border.[93] Damagaram, though a province under Bornu with which peace had been made, had invaded northern Kano and had to be watched: any troop movements were reported.[94] Similarly, the Emir of Katsina warned Sokoto of impending invasions from Maradi and the Amīr Gobir (Sabon Birni) and Amīr Raba of raids from Tsibiri.[95]

When Rābiḥ and Faḍlullāh were conquering Bornu, the Emirs on the border kept the Vizier informed of their progress and the rumours about their intentions.[96] The Emir of Gumel warned the Emir of Kano, who forwarded the letter

---

[89] Correspondence, IV, 6; two uncatalogued letters. (Early in 1886 (?).)

[90] Cf. letter in A. D. H. Bivar (*B.S.O.A.S.*, 1959), pp. 332–3.

[91] Correspondence, VII, 65; two uncatalogued letters. The Emir of Hadejia informed the Vizier of the death of Ibrāhīm, the Shaikh of Bornu, and the succession of Hāshim (II, 41).

[92] Uncatalogued letter (from the period 1886–92).

[93] Correspondence, IV, 6; one uncatalogued letter (from the period *c.* 1886–90).

[94] Correspondence, VII, 36, 64; II, 2 (? from the period 1884–91).

[95] Correspondence, IV, 70; V, 76, 77; one uncatalogued letter (from the period *c.* 1882–91).

[96] Backwell, *op. cit.*, letters 93, 94, 97 (from the period 1895–1900).

on to Sokoto.[97] Likewise when the British were moving into the regions of Bauchi and the Benue, reports reached Sokoto.[98] The Egyptian messengers sent up to Kukawa by the Royal Niger Company to negotiate with Rābiḥ caused the Vizier to write to the Royal Niger Company and demand to know who they were.[99]

The Vizier was also told of the activities of the Ningi and other pagans, of both their defeats and their victories in Zaria and Kano. When Hārūn of the Ningi sought a truce, his letter to the Emir of Kano was forwarded to Sokoto, where the decision was taken: the Emir of Kano refused to make any move till he had heard from Sokoto.[100] But when the Sultan of Damagaram wrote asking for a truce, the Emir of Kano first wrote a curt reply before informing Sokoto.[101] Again, till Sokoto had given permission, trade could not be opened with Faḍlullāh: the Emir of Bauchi sent Faḍlullāh's messengers back the same day.[102] Since Sokoto had been hostile to Faḍlullāh and had not made a truce with him, the caution is understandable.[103]

Likewise, when the Royal Niger Company was trading on the Niger and Benue, correspondence continued between Ādam Jekada for the Company and the Vizier, and an annual agreed present was sent up to Sokoto. Thus Wallace thought it advisable to explain to the Vizier exactly why nothing was sent the year that Akassa was sacked.[104]

While on occasion an Emir might ask permission to raid,

---

[97] Backwell, *op. cit.*, letter 95.

[98] e.g. Backwell, *op. cit.*, letters 114–18.

[99] Uncatalogued letter, *c.* 1894 (A. H. M. Kirk-Greene, *Adamawa, Pas and Present*, p. 48; J. E. Flint, *Sir George Goldie*, p. 296).

[100] Correspondence, VII, 61, 62 (from the period 1859–73).

[101] Correspondence, VII, 64 (from the period 1881–91).

[102] Gombe Correspondence, 178. Cf. Backwell, *op. cit.*, letter 98. The letters of Faḍlullāh are dated January and February 1901 (Gombe Correspondence, 94, 100, 193).

[103] Gombe Correspondence, 53. Similarly, Kano referred to Sokoto a request for trade from the French-appointed Emir of Kukawa, *c.* 1900 (Royal Niger Company, *Arabic Letter Book*, pp. 95–6).

[104] Three uncatalogued letters. Akassa was sacked in December 1894. (Flint, *op. cit.*, pp. 201 ff.)

local campaigns were usually left to the Emir's initiative. Thus, although the subversive letters and proclamations of Ḥayāt b. Sa'īd were sent back to Sokoto by the Emirs of Bauchi, Missau and Katagum, the Vizier only encouraged co-ordination and co-operation between the local Emirs.[105] News of campaigns might be relayed by a neighbouring Emir, but if the expedition was successful, the Caliph received his share of the booty, along with a share for the Vizier and other officials in Sokoto.[106]

The Vizier's relations with emirates not in his portfolio, such as Bauchi or Katsina, extended only to matters in which the Amīr al-mu'minīn or an Emir under the Vizier was also involved. No dealings were had directly with the Emirs under Gwandu; when the British were in Nupe, information reached Sokoto via Gwandu, and the Emir of Gwandu on the Caliph's behalf told the Emir of Nupe to keep the agreement with the British.[107] The surviving correspondence also shows considerable co-operation between Gwandu and Sokoto, in dealing with the chronic problem of escaped slaves and the blockade of Argungu or in quelling a small revolt in Yabo: in the last incident, the Amīr al-mu'minīn called on Gwandu to give him armed assistance, which was done.[108] The Vizier personally was on good terms with the Emir of Gwandu, exchanging information and plans.[109]

Within the Sokoto hinterland the Vizier exercised only a nominal supervision. The princes required no intermediary to the Amīr al-mu'minīn, and being at most three days' journey away were not given to correspondence. The Emirs

[105] e.g. Correspondence, IV, 24; four uncatalogued letters; II, 17, 34 (all date probably from the period 1881–91).

[106] Correspondence, VII, 15, where 100 slaves were sent to the Amīr al-mu'minīn, 50 to the Vizier, 10 to the Dangaladima, 10 to the 'Emirs' of the Caliph, 10 to his sons and brothers, 10 to the women in his house, plus 10 in case of accident, one for the 'kofa' (intermediary) and 5 of the remaining 9 for the house of the Shaikh (from the period 1886–93).

[107] Backwell, *op. cit.*, letter 111.

[108] Backwell, *op. cit.*, letters 1, 2, 4.

[109] Correspondence, IV, 60; I, 8; e.g. V, 3, 4, 9, 12, 7, 13. All but V, 9 are from the Emir of Gwandu Malik (died *c.* 1888). V, 9 is from the Emir of Gwandu 'Umar (died *c.* 1897–8).

at Tambawel and Dogondaji shared the local interests of Gwandu such as escaped slaves and the Kebbawa. Problems outside the emirate, however, they had to refer to the Vizier, such as conflicts between Gummi and Kebbe, confiscations of traders' goods by the Emir of Zamfara, or border disputes.[110] In the succession crisis at Tambawel, appeal was made to the Vizier in person, but later the Ubandoma was sent down to read out the letters of appointment from the Amīr al-mu'minīn and the Vizier.[111]

The other states round the Sokoto borders which had treaties with Sokoto submitted their complaints or requests to the Amīr al-mu'minīn or the Vizier. Thus the Sultans of Gobir, Maradi and Agades, Tuareg chiefs and more especially the rulers of Anka, Gummi, Kebbe, Mafara and Burmi were in occasional correspondence with Sokoto.[112] The last five, being subject to Sokoto, though keeping their own identity, had to refer their complaints to the Amīr al-mu'minīn or the Vizier, lest their action be construed as rebellion.[113]

The Vizier himself did not normally lead or accompany expeditions in the subordinate emirates, since apart from the use of Katsina by the Caliph 'Alī once as a base from which to attack Maradi, the Amīr al-mu'minīn did not leave the Sokoto area: his campaigns were directed only against the enemies surrounding Sokoto itself. For these campaigns, the Vizier sent out summonses to all the eastern Emirs as well as the princes, such as Amīr Tambawel, to converge at a certain place and time.[114] Gwandu was informed, but not requested

---

[110] Correspondence, III, 11, 21, 43, 47; cf. 54.

[111] Backwell, *op. cit.*, letter 65 (*c.* 1902–3).

[112] *Gobir*, e.g. I, 58, 41; Backwell, *op. cit.*, letter 14. *Maradi*, I, 24, 25; V, 55; I, 22; IV, 72. *Agades*, I, 47. *Kel Geres*, IV, 52, 69, 73; cf. VII, 45. *Ulemiden*, I, 59.

[113] e.g. *Anka*, V, 71; I, 40; V, 73, 74. *Kebbe*, V, 44, 49. *Burmi*, Backwell, *op. cit.*, letters 69, 71.

[114] e.g. Correspondence, III, 22, 25. Clapperton (1st journey, p. 75) met near Zurmi two messengers from Sokoto summoning 'all Felatahs' to go to Sokoto for an expedition: they did not know where the expedition was going.

to come. The expedition was normally annual, after the harvest in the autumn, and attendance was expected even from emirates as distant as Adamawa.[115] Emirs sometimes sent letters telling the Vizier of their progress to the main meeting-place or to a preliminary rendezvous where the eastern Emirs would join to go to the Amīr al-mu'minīn.[116] Once assembled, the contingents camped in surrounding villages, the Vizier remaining with the Amīr al-mu'minīn. On the march the Vizier continued to keep by the Amīr al-mu'minīn, preceded by the Barade, Amīr al-jaish and Magajin gari and followed by the Magajin rafi and Galadima. The Vizier was accompanied by a large retinue. Clapperton in September 1826 saw the Vizier arrive 'with a numerous train of attendants on horseback and on foot. The horsemen armed with spears, swords and shields; the foot with swords, bows and arrows. The women were behind; some riding on horseback a-straddle, some on camels, others less fortunate, were walking and carrying the gourds and kitchen utensils . . . he had four long trumpets and a pipe, like the pipe of a bagpipe and two drums before him.'[117] To this there could be added, by 1886, some one hundred gunmen.[118]

On two occasions the Vizier was called upon to take charge of expeditions. Once when al-Kanemi invaded the eastern emirates in 1826, Gidado was sent by Bello to command the combined forces which had mustered under Ya'qūb, Amīr Bauchi. However, al-Kanemi was defeated before Gidado arrived.[119] The second time, 'Abd al-Qādir was sent by 'Alī to lead the attack on the rebel Bukhari in Hadejia, after his Dangaladima, Aḥmad, had gone the previous year.[120]

But the qualities valued in Sokoto were not military. Although Bello and 'Abdullāh in their poems glorify their battles, and although the ideal of the murābiṭ, the defender of Islam on the frontier who would be rewarded in Paradise if he

[115] It was known as al-ghazw al-kharīfī, 'the autumn expedition'.

[116] e.g. Correspondence, VII, 17, 66, 92, 117 (*c.* November–December 1889).

[117] Clapperton (2nd journey), p. 177.

[118] Staudinger, *op. cit.*, p. 364.

[119] Clapperton (2nd journey), p. 243.

[120] *v. supra*, p. 159.

died fighting for the Faith, was extolled in the early jihād, scholarship was still at a premium. Ideally those who thought only of fighting were not complete members of the Community. The characters of the Shaikh and Bello were the models; and in the early histories, such as those written by the Viziers, the virtues stressed are learning and piety.[121]

(v) *Their Writings*

The literary climate in which the Viziers wrote their collections of miracles (karāmāt), although dominated by theological works of exegesis, encouraged differing genres. In the quantity of legal, political and doctrinal material which was necessarily produced in the early decades of the jihād to disseminate Islamic ideas to a wide but newly-awakened class of scholar-reformers, the originality in the selection of authorities often passes unnoticed. Despite the constant use of quotations, independence of thought remained: Bello advocated interpreting Islamic political science in terms suited to local conditions, while the Shaikh expressed his opinion on such controversial topics as the legal restriction of women.[122] There was enough divergence of character and opinion to cause prolonged disputes: the Shaikh disagreed with his teacher Jibrīl b. 'Umar on what constitutes a Muslim, and with 'Abdullāh, for example, on the relative meaning of sulṭān, malik and amīr.[123]

A wide range of books was imported and copied: although most Sokoto texts have little or no indication of the date of copying, the extent of the quotations or allusions indicates the sources that were available in the Community before and after the jihād.[124] Their libraries also contained

[121] e.g. Gidado dan Laima, *Majmū' khiṣāl al-Shaikh*; R.J., f. 11; K.B., pp. 6, 20 ff. 'Abd al-Qādir b. Gidado, *al-Iktifā'*, *Manāqib 'Alī*.

[122] Muḥammad Bello b. 'Uthmān, *Kitāb al-taḥrīr fī qawā'id al-tabṣīr li'l-siyāsāt*. 'Uthmān b. Fodiye, *Irshād al-ikhwān ilā aḥkām khurūj al-niswān* (attributed), *Nūr al-albāb*.

[123] 'Uthmān b. Fodiye, *Shifā' al-ghalīl*. 'Abdullāh b. Fodiye, *Ḍiyā' al-sulṭān*; 'Uthmān b. Fodiye, *Najm al-ikhwān*.

[124] Cf. Hiskett (*B.S.O.A.S.*, 1957), pp. 550 ff.

locally written works of authors such as Aḥmad Baba of Timbuktu or Ibn Māsanih of Katsina.[125] Some scholars who were of repute in orthodox subjects had also specialised in numerology and astrology, and against these the Shaikh protested.[126]

It was at dissident scholars and critics that much of the historical literature of Sokoto was at first aimed.[127] When al-Kanemi asked the Shaikh to explain the attack on Bornu, it became necessary to produce an official account of the causes and course of the jihād. This was written at the Shaikh's request by ʻAbdullāh and was used by the Shaikh both in his reply to al-Kanemi and in his book *Tanbīh al-ikhwān* in 1811 (1226 A.H.).[128] Bello, who in his answers to al-Kanemi had also discussed the history of the movement, in 1812 (1227 A.H.) added a detailed account of the campaigns to his general discussion of pre-nineteenth-century bilād al-Sūdān, to make *Infāq al-maisūr*. ʻAbdullāh a year later collected his poems to illustrate the history of the Shaikh (1228 A.H: *Tazyīn al-waraqāt*). The next year another book, in which the distribution of Muslims in the western Sudan was discussed, was written by the Shaikh (1228 A.H: *Ta'līm al-ikhwān*): the subject was of great importance in justifying both the jihād and the quelling of dissidents, which had already been argued in the *Ḍiyā' al-sulṭān* (1227) of ʻAbdullāh and *Sirāj al-ikhwān* (1226) and *Najm al-ikhwān* (1227) of the Shaikh.

Interest in Sokoto was not confined to the history of the jihād. ʻAbd al-Qādir b. al-Muṣṭafā, *c.* 1824, wrote a history of the western Sudan, in which he draws, presumably, on Gobir chronicles before giving a brief annalistic account of

---

[125] Even a book by Aḥmad Baba on smoking tobacco (*al-Lam' fī'l-ishāra li-ḥukm tibgh*, A.D. 1607) was copied *c.* 1800 by a relation of the Shaikh (in Nizamiyya School Library). Aḥmad Baba, unlike the Shaikh, did not condemn the use of tobacco.

[126] Astronomy for calendrical purposes was acceptable to the Shaikh: cf. two of his poems in Fulfulde, and Muḥammad Bello, *Tanbīh al-fuhūm*, *al-Kitāb al-kāfī fī ʻilm al-jafr wa'l-khawāfī*.

[127] Few books are dated. What follows only takes into account the books that are dated, and is therefore no more than an outline.

[128] I.M., p. 167.

events between 1804 and 1823.[129] Details of the Shaikh's life were also being written down: his genealogy, his wives and children, the Shaikhs who taught him and their relationships to him, the places he stayed in after his hijra. Both 'Abdullāh and Bello wrote on their own Shaikhs and their families as well as those of the Shaikh.[130] The Shaikh himself recorded his sufic chains of authority in the Qādiriyya, and in this he is followed by Bello: similarly both Bello and the Shaikh wrote on their experiences in their fortieth year.[131] 'Abd al-Qādir b. al-Muṣṭafā shared the interest in mysticism, and like Bello, wrote on the various forms of foretelling the future.[132] In other books Bello discusses the legal uses of charms and other non-physical remedies, the diseases of the eye or the cures for kidney trouble.[133] When Clapperton visited Sokoto, he was nonplussed by the range of Bello's interests and knowledge of history and doctrine.[134]

The Vizier Gidado was part of this court, reading the *Jawāhir al-ma'ānī* on Aḥmad al-Tijānī to Bello or writing the *Ba'ḍ tanbīhāt* at Bello's dictation.[135] When Bello died, and

---

[129] *Rauḍāt al-afkār* (*v. supra*, pp. xxxiii f.). His work on the geography of the Sudan, *Qaṭā'if al-jinān*, I have only seen in an incomplete copy.

[130] 'Abdullāh b. Fodiye, *'Īdā' al-nusūkh*. Muḥammad Bello b. 'Uthmān, *Ishāra wa-i'lām fī ba'ḍ umūr ṣilat al-arḥām*; *Nasab*. An anonymous list of the Shaikh's halting-places is dated 1237.

[131] 'Uthmān b. Fodiye, *al-Salāsil al-qādiriyya*; *Wird*; *al-Salāsil al-dhahabiyya*; Muḥammad Bello b. 'Uthmān, *Miftāḥ al-sadād*; *al-Durar al-zāhiriyya*; *Kitāb al-nisrīn* (1235).

[132] 'Abd al-Qādir b. al-Muṣṭafā, *Salwat al-aḥzān*; *Kashf al-ghiṭā'*. Muḥammad Bello, *al-Kitāb al-kāfī fī 'ilm al-jafr wa 'l-khawāfī*.

[133] *'Ujālat al-rākib fī 'l-ṭibb al-ṣā'ib*; *Ṭibb al-hayyīn*; *Ṭibb al-Nabī*; *al-Mawārid al-nabawiyya*; letter in 'Abd al-Qādir b. Gidado, *Majmū'*; cf. Muḥammad Tukur's *Qirā al-aḥibbā'* on the remedial use of Islamic formulae, which was written specially for Bello. It is likely that his interest in medicine, astronomy and divination was partly due to a desire to replace the non-Islamic magic current in Hausaland with practices sanctioned by Islam.

[134] Clapperton (1st journey), pp. 82, 85, 96, 109; (2nd journey), p. 198. Bello, for example, introduced a novel sugar-refining process on one of his farms.

[135] 'Alī b. al-'Arbī, *Jawāhir al-ma'ānī wa-bulūgh al-amānī fī faiḍ Sīdī Abī'l-'Abbās al-Tijānī* (*G.A.L.*, S. II, 876); Gidado dan Laima, *Kashf*

the unliterary Atiku was elected, the court lost much of its creative activity. It was in this atmosphere, a year after Bello's death, that Gidado finished his *al-Kashf wa'l-bayān* in which he recounts some of the wonders Bello performed during his life, as well as giving lists of his books and campaigns.[136] Fourteen weeks later he finished a work on the virtues of the Shaikh, adding a plan of his house and neighbours at Degel and an account of his death.[137] A third book, completed nearly two years afterwards, gives Gidado's own genealogy and children.[138] To this same period, I suggest, belong the undated *Rauḍ al-jinān* and the *Majmū'* of Bello's companions and helpers.[139]

The dating of *Rauḍ al-jinān* to the period following the writing of *al-Kashf wa'l-bayān* has no direct proof. However, *al-Kashf wa'l-bayān* reads as if it was the first of its genre: it opens with a preface giving the reasons for writing on the karāmāt; it contains the date of the Shaikh's birth, omitted in *Rauḍ al-jinān*, along with the birth-date and character sketch of Bello; karāmāt are contained in *al-Kashf wa'l-bayān* which would more properly belong to *Rauḍ al-jinān*, if the latter had been written first. Similarly, much of the material in *Majmū' khiṣāl al-Shaikh* would be more suited to a first work on the Shaikh, but this book lacks a proper title and is only four folios long. *Rauḍ al-jinān* has a short introduction saying there are going to be mentioned the wonders, virtues

---

al-ḥijāb wa-raf' al-niqāb; (*Ba'ḍ tanbīhāt al-imām Muḥammad Bello*), dated 2 Rabī' I, 1239/6 November 1823. Cf. 'Abd al-Qādir b. Muḥammad Bukhari, *Tabshīr al-ikhwān*, f. 11.

136 Dated 6 Rajab 1254/25 September 1838.

137 Dated Thursday 16 Shawwāl 1254/3 January 1839. There is no formal title beyond '*Majmū' . . . ba'ḍ khiṣāl . . . 'Uthmān*'.

138 Dated Wednesday 1 Jumādā I, 1256/(Wednesday) 1 July 1840. There is no formal title beyond *Risāla . . . fī 'l-nisba.*

139 *Majmū' . . . aṣḥāb Amīr al-mu'minīn Muḥammad Bello* is attributed to Gidado dan Laima, and he is the most likely author. Another work attributed to Gidado is a book called *Riyāḍ al-ṣāliḥīn*, mentioned to M. Hiskett (T.W., p. 20, n. 2). I have not seen it, nor is it known to the present Vizier, al-haji Junaidu; similar material is given by Sa'd b. 'Abd al-Raḥmān in *Tartīb al-aṣḥāb wa-tajmī' al-arbāb min aṣḥāb al-Shaikh 'Abdullāh.*

and characteristics of the Shaikh from the beginning to the end of his life, then starts abruptly with the first of the karāmāt. With its lists included at the end, it is a more complete book than *al-Kashf wa'l-bayān*, which required a further *Majmū'*; *Rauḍ al-jinān* contains none of the material to overlap either *al-Kashf wa'l-bayān* or the *Majmū' al-khiṣāl*.

Since Gidado was almost in retirement during this period under Amīr al-mu'minīn Atiku, it is likely he devoted his time to collecting and codifying the oral material at hand. In this his wife Asmā' bint al-Shaikh clearly helped; some of her own work in Arabic and Fulfulde deals with the family of the Shaikh, while a few karāmāt are derived from her experience.[140] A corpus of Traditions about the lives of the Shaikh and Bello has grown up, having multiplied considerably since the *Karāmāt* of Gidado. Although the stories, antedating the works of Gidado, were current during the lifetimes of the Shaikh or Bello, both 'Abdullāh and Bello ignore any miraculous element in their histories. 'Abdullāh does not refer to any karāmāt;[141] Bello, however, acknowledges the ability of the Shaikh to have supernatural powers and to have, for example, jinns as messengers after the capture of Alkalawa, but in his account of the battle of Tabkin Kwotto, around which traditions have since multiplied, there is no trace of such intervention.[142] In *Rauḍ al-jinān*, on the last day of the battle of Alwassa, a causal relationship is implied between the Shaikh's words and the Muslim victory: 'when [the pagans of Gobir and the Tuaregs] . . . approached the village of the Shaikh, he said, "You will see, if Allāh wills, how Allāh will confound them", and when they came to the Shaikh's village, they fled and scattered . . .'[143] Bello, in his account in the *Infāq al-maisūr*, while noticing the Shaikh's words of encouragement and the prayers, does not juxtapose

[140] Asmā' wrote a poem in Fulfulde on the family of the Shaikh. Another poem by her, also in Fulfulde, is on the history of the jihād and is dated 1256 (1840). She appears in karāmāt on folios 3 and 3b. On folio 2, the mother of Asmā' is referred to as 'our mother'.

[141] F. H. El-Masri pointed this out to me.

[142] I.M., pp. 41, 116.

[143] R.J., f. 10b.

them causally: the emphasis in the *Infāq al-maisūr* is on the work of Allāh.[144]

Although the Shaikh was evidently conversant with jinns, he seldom refers to them in his books. In the example quoted above, when Bello says the news of the fall of Alkalawa was brought to the Shaikh, some said by jinns, others said by revelation, no mention of any such miracle is made by the Shaikh at the end of his book *Tanbīh al-fāhim*: he says, 'I finished it at midday on Saturday, the day of the bringing of the news of the conquest of Alkalawa. . . .' In *Taḥdhīr al-ikhwān* (1229 A.H.) he says jinns have been appearing to him intermittently since his boyhood and still do so, but only when they choose. He denies he has any control over them, in the ways people suggest, such as flying, walking over water, crossing the earth or going to Mecca and Medina: only complete saints can do that.[145]

Gidado drew on such popular material for his book. The stories used fall into two groups, the miracles (karāmāt) and the incidents which illustrate the character of the Shaikh. The miracles are of four general kinds. The first is where the Shaikh is conversant with jinns and saints; the second, where he shows his mastery of worldly things—a mastery that saints and jinns possess—such as travelling immediately, stopping rain clouds or animals (a miracle that Bello performed more often than the Shaikh), or causing real things or unreal people to appear; the third, where this power is used in answer to a prayer by one of his followers, to rescue or guide them in a place completely remote from the Shaikh; the fourth kind shows him not only knowing what is happening elsewhere but also what will happen.[146] The other group of

---

[144] I.M., p. 100.

[145] pp. 13, 15 (Ibadan, No. 116). In a somewhat strange poem in Fulfulde he records conversations among jinns, and mentions in passing his ability sometimes to take their form. It seems that in the excitement of the Community in his earlier years he felt a readiness to show off his supernatural powers which he did not feel later; the legends current about him in his lifetime may have disturbed him.

[146] The proportion, approximately, is (i) 10; (ii) 7; (iii) 7; (iv) 5. Only one involves distant prophecy (folio 4).

stories demonstrates (i) the austerity of his life and his unconcern for property, (ii) his feats of memory and learning, and (iii) his authority and control of the situation, these last being almost indistinguishable from historical narrative. Together they illustrate the learning, piety and lofty idealism which Gidado mentions as the three parts of the Shaikh's 'house'.[147]

In *al-Kashf wa'l-bayān*, where the karāmāt of Bello are given, the superhuman element is underplayed. Jinns have no specific part: but Bello does know the special name of Allāh that gives him supernatural power, and in another instance his command changes the course of battle; on a third occasion he transfers the corpse of 'Umar al-Kammu to Sokoto.[148] Otherwise, most of the spectacular karāmāt show either his control over weather and beasts for himself and his followers, or foreknowledge and foretelling. The miracles were mostly done for himself: only two (one concerning rain, the other concerning a lion) were in answer to a prayer.[149]

Curiously, some of Bello's karāmāt are done at the expense of the Shaikh. Not only is Bello at times elevated above the Shaikh explicitly, but also it is Bello who is compared to Joseph, the Shaikh to Joseph's parents.[150] This aspect can be better understood if *al-Kashf wa'l-bayān* was written before *Rauḍ al-jinān*.

The difference between the two books is reflected in the frequent use of the first person in *al-Kashf wa'l-bayān*. Gidado was often present, with Bello or being sent by Bello, at the times the karāmāt occurred.[151] Having been Bello's companion since the early days of the Community, and writing less than eleven months after his death, he was in a better position to obtain the material for *al-Kashf wa'l-bayān* than for *Rauḍ al-jinān*.

The two books became the standard sources for later historians of the lives of the Shaikh and Bello. 'Abd al-Qādir b. Gidado uses the chapter in *al-Kashf wa'l-bayān* on the virtues of Bello to supply the title and the corresponding chapter,

---

[147] R.J., f. 11.
[148] pp. 10–11, 15, 19.
[149] pp. 12, 13.
[150] e.g., pp. 7, 8, 9–10.
[151] e.g. p. 8, 13, 15–16, 19. Cf. R.J., fols. 4b, 5.

with alterations of order, for his *al-Iktifā' li-ahl al-ta'assī*; the virtues of the Shaikh reappear in 'Abd al-Qādir's *Anīs al-mufīd*, while one paragraph found without ascription in both Gidado's *Majmū' al-khiṣāl* and *Anīs al-mufīd* is quoted again in a letter of Amīr al-mu'minīn 'Alī as the words of the Shaikh.[152]

Anīs al-mufīd, being a history of the Shaikh, 'Abdullāh and Muḥammad Bello and detailing their families, books and karāmāt, naturally draws heavily on material already written, such as Gidado's works or the poems of the three subjects of the book. But 'Abd al-Qādir b. Gidado does add material of his own where he was a contemporary. Similarly he depends on his father's works for his index of locally famous men, *Basṭ al-fawā'id*, a list of some 450 names divided into three chapters roughly corresponding to the Shaikh and his contemporaries, the Shaikh's sons and their contemporaries, and the third generation, of the 1840's. Since notes on the names are largely lacking, the book is more a roll of honour than a biographical dictionary.

The Vizier 'Abd al-Qādir, like his father, acted as biographer of the Amīr al-mu'minīn he served; but 'Abd al-Qādir's *Manāqib* was written during the lifetime of 'Alī.[153] By comparison with *al-Kashf wa'l-bayān* or *Rauḍ al-jinān*, it is simple: a preface on the virtues of 'Alī, a chapter in verse on his Viziers, another on his lieutenants and a third on his campaigns; there are no karāmāt, and the virtues discussed are specific and humane, as, for example, his accessibility and friendliness which remained unchanged even after his appointment.

Somewhat earlier than the period in which 'Abd al-Qādir was writing the *Manāqib 'Alī*, an equivalent book had been written by 'Umar b. Muḥammad Bukhari b. al-Shaikh on the virtues of the Emir of Gwandu Khalilu and his campaigns to the south and west.[154] Another book by 'Umar b. Muḥam-

---

[152] K.B., p. 20. *al-Iktifā' li-ahl al-ta'assī* is dated 1265 (1848–9).

[153] *Majmū' dhikr manāqib Amīr al-mu'minīn 'Alī.* The last campaign mentioned was in 1853 (cf. Barth, IV, 183 f.).

[154] *Nubdha li-izhār ba'ḍ manāqib Shaikhinā Khalīl b. 'Abdullāh.* The last campaign mentioned was in *c.* 1849.

mad Bukhari, a general history of Sokoto till the present, treats the lives of the Shaikh, Bello and Atiku, but adds at the end the praises of the Emir of Gwandu Khalilu.[155] These books are not simply Gwandu histories: they omit any history of ʻAbdullāh, more of which is given in ʻAbd al-Qādir's *Anīs al-mufīd*. Since both of ʻUmar's books and the two histories of ʻAbd al-Qādir are undated, definite proof of priority is lacking. ʻUmar's two books end with events in the mid-1840's, while ʻAbd al-Qādir's *Manāqib* extends into the 1850's; *Anīs al-mufīd* is less datable, but was written after 1851, when his father died.[156] No clear borrowing seems to have occurred.

The difference in the relationship between ʻAlī and his Vizier and Bello and Gidado is also reflected in the fact that whereas Gidado copied out some of Bello's tanbīhāt for him, ʻAbd al-Qādir collected the letters of Amīr al-mu'minīn ʻAlī, some of which were possibly the composition of ʻAbd al-Qādir himself.[157] As so far we have nothing else written by ʻAlī, proof again is lacking. The collection is dated March 1849, and it is quite possible that the Vizier Gidado may have written or dictated some of them; it must have been he who preserved the letters from Bello and Atiku in the collection.

As the leading authorities on the biography of Bello, both Viziers, ʻAbd al-Qādir and Gidado, were engaged in defending Bello against the claims that he was a Tijānī. Both were somewhat *parti pris*. Gidado was a Qādirī and had been instructed in it by Bello, although both of them had taken it from al-sharīf al-ḥājj ʻAbdullāh al-Makkī and Ḥamīd b. al-Hindī.[158] ʻAbd al-Qādir was also instructed and both Gidado and ʻAbd al-Qādir were leaders in the Qādiriyya at Sokoto.[159] ʻAbd al-Qādir's son, Ibrāhīm Khalilu, also followed

---

[155] *Tanbīh al-ikhwān fī amr al-sūdān*. The last campaign mentioned was in *c*. 1845.

[156] A.M., p. 8, where reference is made to Gidado as if he was dead.

[157] *Majmūʻ baʻḍ rasā'il*. It contains thirteen letters of Muḥammad Bello and four of Abū Bakr Atiku, some of which have been found elsewhere separately; and twelve letters of ʻAlī b. Bello.

[158] Gidado dan Laima, *Kashf al-ḥijāb*.

[159] The ʻchains' of ʻAbd al-Qādir in the Qādiriyya derive from Muḥammad Bello: ʻAbd al-Qādir, *al-Lawāmiʻ al-nūrāniyya*.

his father in the Qādiriyya. The Qādiriyya was the 'established' ṭarīqa: the Sokoto Community, like that of Kano, was called, and addressed as, Kadirawa; there were arguments that since the Shaikh was Qādirī, every jamā'a that followed him was, or should have been, Qādirī.[160] But unlike the Tijāniyya, the Qādiriyya as found in Sokoto tends to be individualistic and does not practise group recitations. Thus there is less community of feeling demonstrated among Qādirīs.

The issue of whether Bello was a Tijānī or not is still important because Tijānīs continue their claims.[161] It was the writings of the Viziers which were largely responsible for refuting those claims.[162] Gidado's argument was straightforward:[163] I was with Bello, before and during the last two years at Wurno, and had there been any change, I would have known it. Bello was an accredited Qādirī; so was I, having learnt it from Bello. He visited the tomb of his father [prohibited by Tijānīs]. I read him Tijānī books, but he said nothing of following the Tijāniyya. Why should we follow it?

---

[160] e.g. Gloss on final folio of *Kashf al-ḥijāb*; an anonymous manuscript in the Kaduna archives (Sokprof 22:39) claims that all the land from Adamawa to Gonja was Qādirī.

[161] The Tijānī claim is based on the inferences to be drawn from the *Rimāḥ* (*G.A.L.*, S. II, 896) of al-ḥājj 'Umar b. Sa'īd, where it is implied that Bello was a follower of Aḥmad al-Tijānī (1345 edition: part I, pp. 207–11). Another contemporary Tijānī source, Muḥammad Raji b. 'Alī, reports that Sa'd (b. Muḥammad Aminu) was told by Bello that since there is now the Tijāniyya, Sa'd should join that ṭarīqa. (*Risāla*: copies in Ahmadu Bello University, no. 86b, and BN 5716, p. 65b ff.). A third Tijānī source contemporary with Bello, al-ḥājj Sa'īd, without stating explicitly that Bello was a Tijānī, does imply that he recognised the sufic worth of al-ḥājj 'Umar and the Tijāniyya. This respect is openly expressed in Bello's *Raf' al-ishtibāh* (1836) in which, as Omar al-Nager has kindly pointed out to me, Bello is quoting extensively and admiringly from *Jawāhir al-ma'ānī*. That Bello was unwilling to deny the claims of Aḥmad al-Tijānī is clear, but evidence for his actual conversion away from the Qādiriyya is unconvincing.

[162] Gidado dan Laima, *Kashf al-ḥijāb*. 'Abd al-Qādir b. Gidado, *al-Mawāhib al-rabbāniyya* (dated 23 December 1855); *al-Lawāmi' al-nūrāniyya* (no date); *al-Iktifā' li-ahl al-ta'assī* (dated 1265/1848–9).

[163] *Kashf al-ḥijāb*.

'Abd al-Qādir al-Jailānī is excellent, and we made a bond with him. Only the young or later generations could follow al-Tijānī, those who never knew the Shaikh or those good for nothing. Good men would not leave the Qādiriyya: how much less likely, then, that Muḥammad Bello would.

The Vizier 'Abd al-Qādir continued the argument, but largely on literary grounds: he used the books, poems and prayers of Bello and the Shaikh which expound the Qādirī doxology, and by doing so showed that Bello was a Qādirī; an argument *ex silentio*, it omits the possibility of a late conversion, since most of the dated Qādirī books in Sokoto are early.[164] The literary argument used Bello's *Miftāḥ al-sadād* and *al-Durar al-ẓāhiriyya*, the Shaikh's *al-Salāsil al-qādiriyya*, *Tabshīr al-umma al-aḥmadiyya*, and *Irshād al-sālik*: apart from giving the Qādirī chains of the Shaikh, Bello and 'Abd al-Qādir himself, the bulk of the book is an exposition of the Qādiriyya.

Another book by 'Abd al-Qādir adds, though not explicitly, to the *ex silentio* argument.[165] After giving briefly the description, genealogy and qualities of Muḥammad Bello, it contains in some seventy-six folios Bello's poetry and his prayers for times of victory, joy or distress. The various Shaikhs are invoked, 'Abd al-Qādir al-Jailānī, Ibrāhīm al-Dasūqī, Abū Bakr al-'Atīq and Aḥmad al-Badawī, as well as locally famous scholars like 'Uthmān b. Fodiye, Jibrīl b. 'Umar and al-Murtaḍā—but Bello never invokes Aḥmad al-Tijānī.

In what was probably his last book, *al-Mawāhib al-rabbāniyya*, 'Abd al-Qādir explicitly attacks the Tijānīs. He says that the Qādiriyya is the best of ways and that the Shaikh was always teaching it in his Arabic books and non-Arabic poems, as did also 'Abdullāh and Bello; anyone who says Bello was a Tijānī is seduced by self-aggrandisement and Satanic maliciousness. The argument divides into two: first, on literary evidence, Bello was a Qādirī, and 'Abd al-Qādir quotes the Shaikh's *al-Salāsil al-qādiriyya*, Bello's *Infāq al-*

---

164 'Abd al-Qādir b. Gidado, *al-Lawāmi' al-nūrāniyya*.

165 'Abd al-Qādir b. Gidado, *al-Iktifā 'li-ahl al-ta'assī* (1265/1848–9).

maisūr and *al-Durar al-ẓāhiriyya* in support. Second, that while no aspersions are thrown on the Tijāniyya or Aḥmad al-Tijānī, he had heard nothing about the Tijāniyya from Bello, nor did he see how Bello could be one: for Bello took the Qādiriyya from his father, remaining in it till his father died; on becoming Caliph, Bello confirmed his link with the Qādiriyya, reading and commenting on the Qādirī books; he once spent three days in the Shaikh's house and used to visit the house at other times; he instructed his children and other relatives in the shorter wird of the Qādiriyya and commended it to them; at the end of his life, he continued reading Qādirī books, and visited the tomb of his father nine months before he died.

The visiting of tombs is important, since the Tijānīs did not allow it. A letter of al-ḥājj 'Umar suggests that visiting or praying at the Shaikh's tomb was an issue at Sokoto in April 1836:[166] ten months later Bello made the visit to his father's tomb mentioned above.[167] The reason for Bello not visiting the tomb during the eight months before he died is that he was ill for his last seven months and wanted to die at Wurno in sight of the frontier.[168]

Reasons for the polemics over Muḥammad Bello being a Tijānī probably lie in the spread of the Tijāniyya in the late 1840's and 1850's in Gwandu, Kano and Zaria.[169] The years

---

[166] Bibliothèque Nationale 5693, f. 7b. Dated 14 Dhū'l-ḥijja 1251. Al-ḥājj 'Umar finished his *Suyūf al-sa'īd*, on the Tijāniyya, in March 1837.

[167] Gidado dan Laima, *Kashf al-ḥijāb*. Here, it is said the visit, lasting three days, took place at the end of Shawwāl (1252; February 1837): Bello died 25 Rajab 1253 (October 1837). 'Abd al-Qādir b. Gidado in *al-Mawāhib* says Bello's visit was eight months before his death, which suggests that 'Abd al-Qādir was not borrowing directly from Gidado's work. Another visitor to the Shaikh's tomb at this time (1836) was the noted Qādirī scholar Qamar al-Dīn. Bello saw a vision of 'Abd al-Qādir al-Jailānī, who told him to welcome Qamar al-Dīn, from whom he would derive much benefit ('Abd al-Qādir b. Gidado, *Majmū'*; Muḥammad Bello, *al-Mawārid al-nabawiyya*). It is possible that Qamar al-Dīn had come to counter al-ḥājj 'Umar's influence on Bello.

[168] Bello's illness: Sa'īd, p. 198. Death in Wurno; K.B., p. 24.

[169] In Gwandu there were Tijānī scholars like Muḥammad Raji b. 'Alī, who was the Emir Khalilu's deputy before he started in the 1850's on the pilgrimage with a large following of students from Gwandu and

immediately following 'Umar's departure from Sokoto in 1838 seem to have been free from controversy, but the calm was broken in 1845 when 'Umar finished his major text on the Tijāniyya, *Rimāḥ ḥizb al-raḥīm 'alā nuḥūr ḥizb al-rajīm*, and it started to circulate in Sokoto. The book contains references which tend to lower Bello's standing *vis-à-vis* 'Umar and in general reflect poorly on Sokoto: Aḥmad al-Tijānī is quoted as referring in a vision to Hausaland as 'that land in ruins'.[170] It was presumably against such comments, and the claims of local Tijānīs, that the Viziers wrote their books.

Such polemical books are rare in Sokoto. Although polemical letters and poems were written, the books are usually informative. This partly explains the academic turn of these anti-Tijānī works: the argument is brief compared with the exposition of the Qādirī way or the narrating of historical data.

The form of explanatory pamphlet in defence of his actions or the Caliph's was taken up later by the Vizier Muḥammad Bukhari. In 1892, he wrote *Rauḍ al-rayāḥīn*, in which he describes the course of action taken by Sokoto over the Mafara revolt; in 1895 he wrote an account of his part in the Kano crisis; in 1903, he explained his conduct after the British came.[171] In the latter two crises he was personally under strong fire; but his role in the Mafara crisis is not clear. The Mafara and Kano pamphlets contain a straightforward narrative of events or the Vizier's movements; the 1903

Kano (they stopped, however, in Adamawa); and Sa'd b. Muḥammad Aminu, whose son Aḥmad became the Alkalin Gwandu. In Zaria there was, among others, 'Umar b. Aḥmad, a young son of the Vizier of Zaria and member of the ruling Bornawa dynasty, who was inducted into the Tijāniyya in 1850 by a visiting Tijānī, Isḥāq al-Fūtī. For the ten years before *c.* 1845 Muḥammad Raji says he refrained from active teaching of the Tijāniyya (*Risāla*). It is possible that the reason for al-ḥājj Sa'īd leaving Sokoto in *c.* 1855 was because as a Tijānī he felt he had already outstayed his welcome.

170 *Rimāḥ*, I, 211 (1345 edition).

171 Kano crisis: *Kitāb fī-mā jarā bainī wa-bain Amīr Hadijia wa-Yūsuf.* The 1903 crisis: *Risālat al-wazīr ilā ahl al-'ilm wa'l-tadabbur*. It is possible that the books on the Mafara and Kano crises were written after 1903 for the new British administrators.

pamphlet opens with such a narrative and then quotes a letter of advice which he had sought from M. Aḥmad b. Sa'd. No personal arguments are advanced: the tone is factual and without colour.[172] The Vizier did not defend his policy; his position was above question. He did, however, relate what happened.

When the British came, the Vizier was asked for a history of Sokoto. This, his last work, was dictated to his son, 'Abd al-Qādir Machido, in September 1905: called *Ta'nīs al-ikhwān bi-dhikr al-khulafā' al-'uẓamā' fī 'l-sūdān*, it was a model for 'Abd al-Qādir Machido's own *Tabshīr al-ikhwān bi-akhbār al-khulafā' fī 'l-sūdān* (1912–13). Some of the 'king-list' material may have been derived from a history of Sokoto by the Imam 'Alī, completed *c.* 1873–7, which was brought up to date (1903) by the Vizier's Alkali, Muḥammad.[173] The king-list material records the length of reigns, the dates of the bay'a of each Caliph and his death, his virtues, and any event that would distinguish him from any other Caliph, such as the first use of iron-faced gates. This form is traditional: it is found in the *Kano Chronicle*, and 'Abd al-Qādir b. al-Muṣṭafā drew on a similar chronicle for Gobir for his *Rauḍāt al-afkār*.[174]

Though the Vizier Bukhari and his son were thus maintaining the Vizier's role as historian and pamphleteer, Muḥammad Bukhari also tried a genre new to Sokoto. His *Ḥikmat al-abrār* was written for Muḥammad Lawal, the son of the Emir of Zaria 'Uthmān, and reads like an exercise in elegance and vocabulary: it is a conversation between an ibex and a camel on the subject of Man.[175]

---

[172] Only in the 1903 *Risāla* does he mention any criticism or anxiety he felt about his actions. Aḥmad b. Sa'd was the Alkalin Gwandu at the time, and, though a Tijānī, had been a close friend of the Vizier's family for several years.

[173] *v. supra*, p. xliii.

[174] *Kano Chronicle* (trans. Palmer) in *Sudanese Memoirs*, v. III; Arabic text in NAK (Sokprof 1:25). *Rauḍāt al-afkār*, ff. 5b–8. The *Kano Chronicle* gives a list of the forty-seven Sultans of Kano, with the events in their reigns, up to 1883.

[175] The long, florid invocation is probably by the scribe, and not by Muḥammad Bukhari. I am indebted to F. H. El-Masri for his help on this manuscript.

Comparatively little literature has survived from the Sokoto of this later period, a fact which makes the *Ḥikmat al-abrār* still more unusual. Muḥammad Bukhari was also a poet, writing long didactic and historical poems, which are still sung or recited, and composing an elegy on reaching the age of 55. The Viziers were otherwise not distinguished for their poetry: Gidado wrote little or no poetry that has survived, while 'Abd al-Qādir's poetry is mostly in Fulfulde.[176] By contrast, the Shaikh, 'Abdullāh and the children of the Shaikh, Muḥammad Bukhari, Bello, Asmā', 'Īsa or scholars like 'Abd al-Qādir b. al-Muṣṭafā were prolific poets. Fulfulde and Arabic were the most common media, but some poems were written in Hausa, and later more translations were made into it.[177] Many subjects were covered: instructional and religious poems, war narratives, arguments and challenges in verse, satire and conventional love poetry, odes on the deaths of relatives or in praise of the Amīr al-mu'minīn. This tradition was kept up through the century: Asmā' and 'Abd al-Qādir b. al-Muṣṭafā continued to write till their deaths in *c.* 1864.[178] The Vizier Khalilu has left two poems, written elegantly in the classical manner and borrowing the conventional imagery. The Vizier 'Abdullāh Bayero wrote three poems that have survived; one, an ode on the death of the Emir of Gwandu al-Muṣṭafā, is completely classical, and to it he added a takhmīs; another is a somewhat awkward poem appealing to 'Umar b. Muḥammad Bukhari not to break the ties of kinship.[179] 'Īsa b. al-Shaikh and Sa'īd b. Bello were writing at this time, but both were overshadowed, in volume, by 'Uthmān b. Isḥāq who wrote, in addition to poems on Sokoto and Gwandu, encomia on most of the

---

[176] Examples of his Arabic poetry are in his *Manāqib 'Alī.*

[177] Although the Shaikh wrote mostly in Fulfulde, some poems were in Hausa: cf. R.J., f. 6, 6b; T.W., p. 51. 'Īsa b. al-Shaikh translated a poem of Asmā' into Hausa as well as several by the Shaikh. Other translations were made by Sa'īd b. Bello and Asmā' herself.

[178] e.g. 'Abd al-Qādir b. al-Muṣṭafā, *Mauṣūfat al-sūdān* (1280 A.H./A.D. 1863–4). Asmā' wrote an elegy on his death.

[179] I am indebted to Muhammad al-Hajj for his help on these poems of the Viziers.

figures of the 1870's, the Amīr al-mu'minīn, the Emirs of Tambawel, Kontagora, Kano, Zaria, Nupe and Ilorin.[180] The other small poems that survive in the Sokoto collections, such as the poem on a grammarian Qudāma by the Muḥtasib Muḥammad, indicate how common was the art of poetry. The Viziers of the twentieth century continue this tradition, as they do that of the historian, celebrating or satirising events, recording their moods or Sokoto history: the present Vizier is distinguished for both his histories and his poetry. To write poetry in Arabic was the attainment of a cultured man, and the famous poems of the founders of the Sokoto caliphate became part of Sokoto culture: the poems of the Shaikh, Bello and others were learnt by rote by children; today they are broadcast over the radio.[181] Few, however, of the praise-songs and genealogical poems have survived, presumably because, being in Hausa and composed for only oral recitation, they were seldom committed to writing; for the poetic tradition described is that of the scholar, not of the professional praise-singer.

(vi) *Their Position*

The vizieral house, alone of the major dynasties, maintained the tradition of scholarship throughout the nineteenth century. Relatives of the Vizier were frequently to be found as scholars and judges, and by their importance added to the influence of the Gidado family. But the Vizier was also linked to the major royal families by marriage.

The Shaikh had tried to break the clannish pattern of families and replace it with a pattern incorporating the Community of Muslims. His daughters were therefore married to the various leading scholars who were helping him. Thus Gidado married the Shaikh's daughter, Asmā'. Of her sons, 'Abd al-Qādir married a daughter of the Emir of Kano and

---

[180] All these poems are in the collection of al-haji Junaidu.

[181] In strongly Fulani areas the religious poetry of the Shaikh and others in Fulfulde is still widely sung, in the houses by women, and outside by blind men.

the daughter of the Amīr al-jaish (who had himself married a daughter of the Shaikh); ʻAbdullāh married both a daughter of Muʻādh b. Bello and his own nephew's widow, the daughter of the Emir of Kano; Aḥmad married a daughter of Muḥammad Bello as well as a daughter of Bukhari b. al-Shaikh; another son of Gidado married, at least for a while, Mariam, the Shaikh's youngest daughter. Apart from Asmā', Gidado married Ṣāliḥa, a daughter of Malam Mūsā, the leader of the Zaria community, where the children of the marriage were brought up and held office. ʻAbd al-Qādir's son, Ibrāhīm Khalilu, married a daughter of the Emir of Kano ʻAbdullāh, while the Vizier Bukhari married two granddaughters of Bello and gave four of his daughters to four sons of the Amīr al-mu'minīn ʻAbd al-Raḥmān.

It was usual for the Vizier to have as one of his wives a daughter of the Amīr al-mu'minīn he served, or vice versa: this, in addition to the common Fulani practice of marrying first cousins, made for a closely knit aristocracy. The links, however, included the subordinate Emirs: for example, the Emir of Kano Sulaimān married a daughter of Bello, the Emir of Kano ʻAbdullāh a daughter of ʻAlī b. Bello, the Emir of Bornu (Missau) Ṣāliḥ married daughters of Abū Bakr and Muʻādh b. Bello.

Asmā' bint al-Shaikh, the wife of Gidado, was an important figure in her own right: her sons, ʻAbd al-Qādir, Aḥmad, or ʻAbdullāh, were known as 'Dan Nana' (son of Nana—Nana being a nickname) more frequently than 'Dan Gidado'. She was one of the most learned of the Shaikh's children, a poet in Fulfulde and Arabic, and an author of three books in Arabic. She is considered a 'Wali', a saint; as the last survivor of the original emigrants from Degel, and as a confidante of her father, her authority was greatly respected.

Such ties to distinguished families were a factor, together with their scholarship and ability, in maintaining the Viziers' position *vis-à-vis* the royal families. A third factor, largely dependent on the success of the Viziers, was the numerical strength of their followers. As officials without a geographical basis of support, they commanded followers by virtue of their office, whereas the princes in charge of ribāṭs commanded the peasantry in their area. Further, since they were based at court, there was a limit to the number of followers who could be supported there. However, the Vizier evidently had a considerable following. Clapperton in 1826 speaks of 'a numerous train of attendants on horseback and on foot'; Staudinger in 1886 says the Vizier had considerable 'house-power' ('eine ziemliche Hausmacht'), having a hundred gun-men in his following.[182] The estates and villages under him were several, but their inhabitants, being scattered and often distant from Sokoto, would join the Vizier only for a major expedition.

The Vizier's position in the 1880's and 1890's struck foreign visitors as all-powerful: Thomson thought him 'really more powerful than the Sultan himself', since 'nothing is done except by his advice'; Staudinger reported that he was the most powerful of the ministers, almost more so than the Sultan, since all government business went through him; Wallace found that 'the grand Vizier practically rules the whole Fulah Empire' and holds 'all the real power, the Sultans being completely hedged in by formalities'.[183] Though these impressions are exaggerated, the Vizier did appear to have the whole civil service under his control.

These impressions were not due to any magnificence or pomp surrounding the Vizier. While there was considerable ceremonial attached to the vizierate, with its symbols of office, a sword, bow and arrows, a ring and water jug, and with the trumpets, drums and gongs that accompanied him on the move, the Vizier dispensed with most of the trappings of high office. Wallace, when he first saw the Vizier Muḥammad Bukhari in Kano in 1894, found him 'seated on a mat placed on the mud floor of the small house he occupied in Kano, quietly studying, through a pair of large horn-rimmed spectacles, an Arabic manuscript. It struck me as a curious contrast to see him sitting in the darkened house, without kingly garments or the least sign of state, while within a few

---

182 Clapperton (2nd journey), p. 177. Staudinger, *op. cit.*, p. 365.

183 Thomson, *op. cit.*, p. 327. Staudinger, *op. cit.*, p. 365. Wallace, *op. cit.*, pp. 212, 217.

hundred yards the emir of the province of Kano was seated in embroidered robes on a gaudy throne, and was surrounded by a courtly retinue dressed in all the tawdry imitation of Eastern courts.'[184] Similarly, Staudinger had remarked on the poor lodgings which the Vizier's official, the Sarkin Fada, had in Zaria.[185]

The qualities of austerity and scholarship, descent from the Shaikh and high office together command immense respect in Sokoto. In addition, the first three Viziers were leaders in the Qādirī order. In the public mind, therefore, the Viziers had considerable 'baraka', which was balanced by the unpretentiousness of its holders. The Vizier Khalilu, however, who was popularly known for his supernatural powers, was the object of sometimes derisive stories about his private life.[186] Another story, about the Vizier Muḥammad Bukhari, stresses his impotence *vis-à-vis* the Amīr al-mu'minīn 'Abd al-Raḥmān.[187]

The Amīr al-mu'minīn, as the Caliph and direct descendant of the Shaikh, had all the authority that Islam and Sokoto tradition gave to his position. His authority was absolute, but its misuse diminished the personal prestige of the Caliph: thus while he was above being the butt of a joke, the Caliph could be still the subject of derogatory stories, which expressed, in the case of the Amīr al-mu'minīn 'Abd al-Raḥmān, the resentment of people against his arbitrary abuse of power. The extent of this caliphal power was never tested: no revolt or mass resignation by officials ever took place, while any incipient revolt by a prince was forestalled by persuasion or diplomacy. Similarly, the extent of the vizieral power was untested. Though deposition was threatened by Amīr al-mu'minīn 'Abd al-Raḥmān, the Amīr al-mu'minīn was so unpopular with officials and princes that it would have precipitated a crisis in which 'Abd al-Raḥmān

---

[184] Wallace, *op. cit.*, p. 212. Wallace saw him in 1894 during the Kano crisis, when the Vizier was in a difficult political position.

[185] Staudinger, *op. cit.*, p. 201.

[186] Edgar, II, 342–6, 334.

[187] Edgar, III, 413 f.

might have found himself impeached. Resignation, not revolt, was the protest open: the position of the Vizier was that of the senior civil servant, connected with the royal house but ineligible to succeed, and having the authority given by long and effective administration.

Some Concluding Remarks

This study on the history of Sokoto depends heavily on the Arabic sources. Not only were the most detailed accounts of the jihād written by Bello and 'Abdullāh, but also the origins and the philosophy of the jihād are to be derived from the writings of the Sokoto leaders. Similarly, the fullest histories of the first fifty years of the nineteenth century are those written in Arabic by the Viziers Gidado and 'Abd al-Qādir and their contemporaries, 'Umar b. Bukhari, 'Abd al-Qādir b. al-Muṣṭafā and al-ḥājj Sa'īd. For the later period, it is the Arabic sources again, the pamphlets of the Vizier Bukhari and his files of correspondence, that provide the data for the Sokoto administration and its crises during the last two decades of the nineteenth century. For these sources, the journals of travellers provide the eyewitness illustrations and, on occasions, serve as points of chronological reference. The various kinds of oral tradition, on the other hand, deriving from less authoritative sources than the Arabic material, both supply additional data on the minor figures and towns of the Sokoto caliphate and preserve a popular view of the major figures.

Without recourse to the Arabic sources, no adequate study of Sokoto, I believe, is possible. Most modern historians have overlooked the importance of the Arabic sources in relation to the oral tradition, owing to the poverty of published texts or translations. Further, since the translations that are generally known are sometimes misleading, scholarship based on them is somewhat vitiated. Equally it is not sufficient to rely on the few famous books that have been published: first, to circumvent corrupt texts some collation is necessary, and few published texts are adequately collated; second, much detail is to be gleaned from such minor works as letters, pamphlets and poetry. Much material of this minor kind remains to be recovered and analysed: there has yet to be made for any of the emirates under Sokoto a study which utilizes these Arabic sources. For this reason the summary given above of the development of the Sokoto community is somewhat introverted, being limited to the Sokoto hinterland. But not until there are detailed studies of all the areas under the Sokoto caliphate will it be possible to give more than an outline of Sokoto in the nineteenth century.

Nonetheless, within the limits of the sources available, certain patterns can be seen in the account already given of the way in which the Community of the Shaikh confronted the demands of almost continual war, while still maintaining the ideal of the Islamic state. The aim of the Shaikh had been to restore purity to the Islam practised in the neighbouring Hausa kingdoms. Although he had started by preaching, it became clear that the rulers of Gobir were not prepared to reform, and that Muslims had to be ready to defend themselves and conquer. The nature of the Community was scholastic. Though the majority of the scholars were Fulani, many of whom were related to the Shaikh, the Community also included non-Fulani scholars and enjoyed popular support among the non-Fulani population, who doubtless welcomed the Shaikh's demands for Islamic legality.

When war was declared, however, the Community, hitherto primarily scholastic, required military support: this tended to come from the Fulani whose clan-leaders were associated with the Community. When the demands of war and of food involved attacking non-Fulani villages, the Community lost much of its support among the peasants. Movements in the jihād were dictated by the need for food and the position of strong Fulani leaders who could afford the Community both food and protection: for wherever the migrant Community stayed, it made enemies of the peasants who had previously been its allies.

With the war, the nature of the Community changed.

Although the leaders, the family of the Shaikh, were still dominant, clan-leaders such as 'Alī Jedo in Sokoto and Namoda in Zamfara superseded in importance the scholars such as the non-Fulani 'Abd al-Salām. Territorially, the Fulani received the larger share of the land, while the scholars tended to stay by the Shaikh and 'Abdullāh, and the younger men of the Community with Bello. The Shaikh, in conformity with the ideals expressed in his books on Islamic Law and practice, created an elementary administration. Though books were written for their guidance, the men who became territorial leaders seldom had the training suitable for creating an ideal Islamic state. Dissatisfaction with the territorial administration was expressed by the leaders of the Community, most forcibly by 'Abdullāh. At the death of the Shaikh, a revolt within Sokoto centred round the non-Fulani scholar 'Abd al-Salām, while on the borders the Hausa peoples renewed their hostility to the caliphate. The revolt of 'Abd al-Salām, aimed in particular at the monopoly of leadership within Sokoto by the family of the Shaikh but receiving general support from Hausa under the caliphate, accentuated the need for an organised administration through which Bello could both combat the enemies of the Sokoto caliphate and contain his Fulani supporters, thereby ensuring the continuity of the Shaikh's Community.

The policies of Sokoto towards its immediate neighbours fall into two phases. The first phase, 1817 to *c.* 1853, was one of conquest in Adar, Gobir, Zamfara and Kebbi. By 1836, after more than forty-seven campaigns Bello had forced the Kebbawa and Zamfarawa into peace, and had driven the Gobirawa and Tuareg out of the area immediately north of the Rima valley. To close the frontiers, Bello stationed his sons, relatives or companions in ribāṭs in potentially hostile territory, while nearer to Sokoto were settled immigrant Muslims, often Fulani from outlying areas. Non-Muslim groups who submitted to Sokoto were recognised as protected peoples.

This policy was maintained for some ten years after Bello's death in 1837: it was terminated by a revolt that spread through Kebbi, Burmi and Zamfara and was abetted by the successful leader of the Gobirawa, Mayaki. It proved impossible for Sokoto to put down the revolt completely; instead the ribāṭs that had been sacked were abandoned.[1]

In the second phase, from *c.* 1853 to 1903, the policy was largely defensive. The major ribāṭs were retained, but the new posts in Gobir and upper Zamfara were put under either locally born or locally established leaders, while in Burmi and the upper Sokoto river valley the local rulers were recognised. A treaty, *c.* 1866, was made with Kebbi; Gobir, with Mayaki dead, was less menacing, with the result that the Sokoto expeditions tended to be punitive, to exact payment and submission. The phase was one of consolidation and increased settlement, which was sufficiently effective that when a Zamfara revolt occurred in 1891, loyal forces could be mobilised from all sides and the rebels quickly contained.

The military success of Sokoto was inevitable so long as the cohesion of the caliphate was maintained and its enemies lacked co-ordination. As Sokoto fought on interior lines, Kebbi, Zamfara or Gobir could be attacked separately. But they also lacked the unity which Islamic ideals gave to the Sokoto caliphate.

The ideals of the jihād seemed to be in jeopardy when the influence of the Fulani clan-leaders exceeded that of the scholars. By containing the power of the clans and strengthening the centre, Bello could reassert the Islamic character of the jihād. His policy of establishing the ribāṭs did this. The men placed in command followed Bello alone and were without the existing loyalties which made the clan-leaders powerful. As the ribāṭs grew, they counterbalanced the support the caliphate received from the Fulani clans. To ensure Islamic government Bello addressed to some of the ribāṭ commanders short pamphlets on how to conduct their ribāṭs, while many of those sent to the ribāṭs had been brought up in the scholastic atmosphere of the Shaikh's camps.[2]

---

[1] Except Silame, rebuilt some twenty years later.

[2] Muḥammad Bello, *al-I'lām bi-mā yajib 'alā 'l-imām*. Muḥammad Bello, Letters 11, 12 and 13 in 'Abd al-Qādir b. Gidado, *Majmū'*; cf. Letter 1, and Muḥammad Bello, *Jawāb shāfi wa-khiṭāb minnā kāfi* (both to Muḥammad Jailani).

At the centre, in Sokoto or in his camps, Bello gathered round him a circle of scholars and the sons of the generation that had been with the Shaikh. In addition, he had his own household. From the Sokoto group, Bello drew the officials and subordinate administrators who were to balance, first the clan-leaders, and then the ribāṭ-holding princes.[3] These officials, although Fulani, were neither descendants of the Shaikh nor members of any of the three major clans.

The third group to counterbalance the three clans were the immigrant Fulani who settled near Sokoto. Their leaders were often past followers or students of the Shaikh; their loyalties were to the Caliph and they thus constituted a large part of his following. Similar communities were attached to the major officials, though to a lesser degree.

The settlement of such primarily scholastic families was made possible through the large numbers of captives taken on campaigns or sent to Sokoto from subordinate Emirs as the Caliph's share of the booty. Land was available, since the area around Sokoto was thinly populated before the jihād; being on the borders of Kebbi, Zamfara and Gobir, there was little conflict with established peasant interests. The Sullebawa, whose grazing grounds the area had been, were also gradually persuaded to settle in walled villages there.

Two advantages derived from this settlement. The existence of slaves to do the manual work enabled the tradition of Islamic learning to spread among those Fulani who as cattle-owners had had little opportunity for it previously; secondly, Islamic Law could be enforced. Settlement in towns was a policy actively pursued by Bello; to support it, he quoted the experience of the Prophet who had found it was imperative to get the Beduin to settle in order that they might practise Islam.[4] But for these communities settled

[3] The private army of gunmen used by the Marafa in the last decade of the century was new to Sokoto politics. Developments in this direction were stopped by the coming of the British. Cf. Yero in Zaria (M. G. Smith, *op. cit.*, pp. 190 ff.).

[4] Muḥammad Bello, *Jawāb shāfi wa-khiṭāb minnā kāfi*; cf. an anonymous, untitled manuscript (2 fols.) on the building of walled towns (ḥuṣūn), dated 1230 A.H. (A.D. 1815) (NAK, Sokprof 22:6).

round Sokoto and elsewhere, it was necessary to find scholars able to act as judges and maintain the Law. Thus the Shaikh, ʿAbdullāh and Bello wrote their books of Law and politics for the guidance of both the Emirs and the judges who were being newly appointed. These books later became the standard texts also for the new caliphates in Masina and Segu.

Respect for the Law and Islam was the source of authority for the Sokoto caliphate. So long as the Caliph upheld the Sharīʿa, he was unimpeachable, and those who denied his authority were unbelievers. Although men might grow less enthusiastic for the jihād, they did not cease to recognise the Islamic tradition on which it was based. The universal nature of the Law, having an existence and validity separate from the Sokoto caliphate, gave Sokoto the power it did not have militarily. The Emirs outside Sokoto, such as those of Gwandu, Kano or Adamawa, respected this Law, and obeyed Sokoto as established under it. Thus the armies of the subordinate Emirs could be relied upon to fight the wars of Sokoto against anyone who could justly be called a rebel. Clearly, it was in the interests of the subordinate Emirs to maintain the *status quo*: it gave to their position the same universal legality which the caliphate possessed.

In each emirate there developed an administrative aristocracy which included Emirs, their officials and scholars. In Sokoto this aristocracy was closely intermarried; disunity was prevented by appeal to these family links and by the distribution of offices and wealth. In this way both the tradition of scholarship was maintained and the competition for office limited. Ties were also extended to include subordinate Emirs, so that the various administrations of the caliphate were linked by marriage. Thus while there could be intense competition for the office of Emir, as in the Kano crisis of 1893–5, the dispute did not disrupt the caliphate: the eventual Emir of Kano was a great-grandson of Muḥammad Bello and the author of learned books of advice in Arabic.[5]

These emirates provided a further counterbalance to the

[5] ʿAlī b. ʿAbdullāh, *Kalima manqūla fī aqwāl ʿulamāʾinā al-sāda*. Cf. his *Irshād al-ikhwān ilā ṭarīq al-khair waʾl-iḥsān* (NAK, Bauprof 16:1).

power of any single group in Sokoto. Each year they were expected to join the autumn expedition against Gobir-Maradi or Kebbi. Their presence emphasised the breadth of the caliphate, as well as its solidarity. This solidarity rested on consent and, as has been said, respect for legality. The Emirs, by having their own revenue and armed forces, were important to Sokoto for their presents and the military support they provided; but they were largely free to determine the amount they would give to Sokoto.

It was from the supervision of the emirates that the officials of the Caliph obtained their importance. The Caliph depended on them for their advice in handling the emirates and their diplomacy with which they obtained his wishes. Though the officials were in the last resort only the agents of the Caliph, their popularity with the Emirs they supervised and the following they built up in the course of their work gave them a certain independence *vis-à-vis* the Caliph.

The most important of the officials, the Vizier, was second only to the Caliph he served. So long as power remained at the centre, the Vizier, as an agent of the centre, shared in that power. It was the Vizier, for example, and not the Konni Fulani leader having the title of Commander of the Army, who led the army in 1826 and *c.* 1853. The vizierate, however, never rivalled the Caliph's position. The Vizier remained the chief supporter, adviser and friend of the Caliph, and in that position was able to reassert the Islamic tradition in Sokoto.

The Viziers, by being from the most learned family in Sokoto, learned not only in the legal and political aspects but also in the mystical side of Islam, acted as a stabilising, conservative element in the course of several caliphates. Their books stressed the saintliness and orthodoxy of the early Caliphs and helped to maintain the values established by the Shaikh and Muḥammad Bello. Similarly, the houses in which the Caliphs were buried were preserved and became places of pilgrimage and retreat.

The tenor of Sokoto was also classically Islamic in aspects other than the observance of Islam and the Sharī'a Law. Primary education involved learning the Quran and, in addition, some knowledge of Arabic. Languages other than Arabic were commonly written in the Arabic script, and literature, in both prose and verse, echoed the classical styles; books quoted classical authorities in support of arguments or as historical parallels, while medical textbooks referred back to Arabic sources.[6] The administrative correspondence, being written all in Arabic, used Arabic technical terminology and forms of titles. But not all such correspondence was confined to the administration: there was evidently enough demand to make 'Umar al-Salagawi compose his manual, in Arabic, on how to write various forms of letters.[7] Although the majority of the titles were not Arabic, a few, such as Waziri, Sa'i, Limam, Alkali, retained their Arabic form in common speech. The method of investiture of officials also followed the classical model in that a turban and cloak were ceremonially put on the new official.

The use of a turban, once the mark of the Shaikh's Community at Degel, remained customary. Similarly, in the use of veils, women, at least in the families of high position, followed Islamic practice. Although purdah was observed, it did not prevent women from being educated: many of the daughters and wives of the Shaikh and his students were also his students and attained great learning; nor was this confined to Sokoto.[8] Slave women, however, were not veiled, but slaves in general were encouraged to become Muslim and their children were given Muslim education.

Clearly, the reforms did not cover all the Community; music and gambling, for example, continued despite dis-

---

[6] Books are occasionally dated from the hijra of the Shaikh as well as from the hijra of the Prophet e.g. T.W., p. 83.

[7] 'Umar b. Abī Bakr, *al-Sarḥa al-warīqa fī 'ilm al-wathīqa*, dated 1294 A.H. (A.D. 1877) (NAK, Sokprof 4:15).

[8] R.J., ff. 2, 12b. Correspondence, IV, 17; Clapperton (2nd journey), p. 214. Cf. 'Uthmān b. Fodiye, *Nūr al-albāb* (*Revue Africaine*, 1898), pp. 62 ff., and *Irshād al-ikhwān* (attributed to the Shaikh). It is a tradition still continued in important Fulani households for the early Islamic and Arabic education of all the children to be done by women. The conservative piety of these elderly women of the household plays a major part in maintaining the strict observance of Islam.

approval.[9] But so long as the Sharī'a was upheld, and the practice of the Caliphs and the court was Islamic, the framework was maintained for a society in which a man could not only be a good Muslim but could also call others to the Faith. It was for this that the Shaikh had fought the jihād; and for the pattern of this society he had looked to the classical Islamic texts in order to reproduce as far as possible an Islamic state. Although, despite the abhorrence of innovations, some modifications proved necessary, they were justified on the lawful grounds of *ijtihād*.[10] Similarly, when it proved impossible to stop the British conquest, co-operation with Christians was justified because Islamic society was to be maintained. Throughout the century, then, the ideals, and to a large extent the practice, of Sokoto did not change. This was achieved because the Caliph and his court upheld the traditions of the Shaikh, and the caliphate itself remained strong.

---

[9] Al-ḥājj Sa'īd, p. 201. Clapperton (2nd journey), p. 201. The Shaikh in his poetry had specifically condemned the use of such musical instruments as molo, goge, and kalangu; similarly he disapproved of dancing, possession ceremonies and prostitution, but, like music, these proved too popular to stamp out completely.

[10] Muḥammad Bello, *Kitāb al-taḥrīr fī qawā'id al-tabṣīr li'l-siyāsāt.*

Bibliography

(i) *Arabic*

Note: The Arabic bibliography is in two parts: first, books which were written within the Sokoto caliphate and are specifically relevant to Sokoto; second, general books. In the list of Sokoto authors, the Shaikh, ʻAbdullāh and Muḥammad Bello are listed separately. I have not read all the works which I list under their names, nor is the list complete: works are mentioned only if copies are obtainable in the libraries mentioned. These libraries have been described in the note on the sources above. The symbols used are:

K. —in the catalogue published by W. E. N. Kensdale and preserved in Ibadan.

SDL. —Sokoto Divisional Library.

TCL. —Sokoto Town Council Library.

Niz. —Nizamiyya School, Sokoto.

Ko. —Shahuci Judicial School, Kano.

NAK.—National Archives, Kaduna.

Jos —Department of Antiquities, Jos

BN. —Bibliothèque Nationale, Paris.

I.F. —Institut de France, Paris.

Pr.1. —the private collection of al-haji Junaidu, Wazirin Sokoto.[1]

Pr.2. —the private collection of M. Yahaya, Alkalin Lardin Sokoto.[1]

ABU.—Ahmadu Bello University, Zaria.[2]

CAD.—Centre of Arabic Documentation, University of Ibadan.[2]

[1] Texts are only mentioned as being in this collection if they are otherwise unobtainable or rare. In most cases photographs have been made of these texts for the collections in Ibadan and Zaria.

[2] All texts in this collection are on *microfilm*, and therefore only comparatively rare texts are listed here. A simple catalogue for ABU has been published in the Northern History Research Scheme *Interim Report* (1966), while a descriptive catalogue for CAD is being published in the Centre's *Research Bulletin.*

'UTHMĀN B. FŪDĪ

al-Ajwiba al-muḥarrara 'an al-as'ila al-muqarrara fī wathīqat Shīṣmāṣ		SDL; TCL; Ko; Jos; NAK; printed, Kano.
Akhlāq al-Muṣṭafā		ABU.
Amr al-sā'a	1218	SDL; NAK.
al-Amr bi'l-ma'rūf wa'l-nahy 'an al-munkar		SDL.
al-Amr bi-muwālāt al-mu'minīn 1227 (or 1226, wrongly?)		K; SDL; Niz; NAK; printed, Zaria.
Anwā' māl Allāh	1224	Jos; NAK; I.F.
'Aqīdat al-'awāmm		Pr.1.
Asānīd al-ḍa'īf al-mutashaffi' bi'l-mushaffa' Aḥmad al-Sharīf		K; NAK.
Asānīd al-faqīr al-mu'tarif bi'l-'ajz wa'l-taqṣīr	1213	Niz.
Bayān al-bida' al-shaiṭāniyya		K; SDL; TCL; NAK; BN.
Bayān wujūb al-hijra 'alā 'l-'ibād	1221	K; TCL; Niz; NAK.
Bayān wujūb al-hijra wa-taḥrīm muwālāt al-kafara		Niz; NAK.
Hidāyat al-ṭālibīn		Niz (incomplete).
Hidāyat al-ṭullāb		published, Gaskiya Corp., Zaria; K.
Ḥaqīqat al-īmān		SDL; Niz.
Ḥiṣn al-afhām	1225	published, Cairo, 1959; K; SDL; Niz; Ko; BN.
Ḥukm juhhāl bilād Ḥausa		K; SDL; NAK.
I'dād al-dā'ī ilā dīn Allāh		TCL; NAK.
Ifḥām al-munkirīn 'alayya fī-mā āmuru al-nās bihi		SDL; Ko; NAK.
Iḥyā' al-sunna		published, Cairo, 1962; K; SDL; Niz; NAK; Jos; BN.
Irshād ahl al-tafrīṭ wa'l-ifrāṭ		K; TCL.
Irshād al-ikhwān ilā aḥkām khurūj al-niswān (attributed)		SDL; NAK.
Irshād al-sālik al-rabbānī ilā aḥwāl al-shaikh 'Abd al-Qādir al-Jailānī		CAD.

Irshād al-'ubbād ilā ahamm masā'il al-jihād		NAK.
Irshād al-umma		ABU.
Ittibā' al-sunna wa-tark al-bid'a		K.
Kashf mā 'alaihi al-'amal		K; NAK; CAD.
al-Khabar al-hādī ilā umūr al-imām al-mahdī		CAD.
(Khamsa kalimāt)		SDL.
Kifāyat al-muhtadīn		SDL; CAD.
Kitāb al-ādāb		Ko; NAK.
Kitāb al-farq bain 'ilm uṣūl al-dīn wa-bain 'ilm al-kalām		K; SDL; NAK; Jos.
Kitāb al-farq bain wilāyāt ahl al-Islām wa-bain wilāyāt ahl al-kufr		published, *BSOAS*, 1960; Ko; NAK; Jos.
Kitāb al-maḥdhūrāt min 'alāmāt khurūj al-mahdī		NAK.
Kitāb muddat al-dunyā		NAK.
Kitāb al-tafriqa bain al-wu''āẓ al-maḥmūdīn wa-bain al-wu''aẓ al-madhmūmīn		NAK.
(al-Masā'il min shaikhinā 'Uthmān ibn Fūdī)		TCL; NAK.
Masā'il muhimma	1217	K; SDL; Niz; Ko; NAK; BN.
Mawāḍi' auhām al-ṭalaba		K.
Mi'rāj al-'awāmm ilā samā' 'ilm al-kalām		TCL.
Mir'āt al-ṭullāb		K; SDL; TCL; NAK; Jos.
Miṣbāḥ li-ahl hadhā 'l-zamān min ahl bilād al-Sūdān	1223	I.F.
Miṣbāḥ al-muhtadīn		K; Niz.
al-Nabā' al-hādī ilā aḥwāl al-imām al-mahdī		Pr. I.
Najm al-ikhwān	1227	K; SDL; Niz; Jos.
Naṣā'iḥ al-umma al-muḥammad-iyya		K.
Naṣīḥat ahl al-zamān	1226	K; SDL; TCL; Niz.
Nūr al-albāb		published, *Revue Africaine*, 1897–8; printed, Kano (?); K; SDL; TCL; Niz; NAK; Jos.

Qaṭ‘ al-khiṣām		K; NAK.
Qawā‘id al-ṣalāt		K; NAK; Jos.
Qawā‘id ṭalab al-wuṣūl ilā Allāh		Ko.
Rujū‘ al-shaikh al-Sanūsī ‘an al-tashdīd ‘alā ’l-taqlīd fī ‘aqā’id al-tauḥīd		Niz.
al-Salāsil al-dhahabiyya		K; SDL; NAK.
al-Salāsil al-qādiriyya	1225	K; SDL; TCL; NAK.
Sauq al-ṣādiqīn (*or* ṣiddīqīn)		K; SDL; NAK.
Sauq al-umma		K; SDL; Niz; NAK; Jos.
Shams al-ikhwān yastaḍī’ūna bihā fī uṣūl al-adyān	1228	Jos; BN; Pr.I.
Shifā’ al-ghalīl fī-mā ashkala fī kalām shaikh shuyūkhinā Jibrīl		Ko; NAK; Jos.
Shifā’ al-nufūs		SDL; NAK.
Sirāj al-ikhwān	1226	K; SDL; NAK; Jos; BN.
Tabshīr al-umma al-aḥmadiyya bi-bayān ba‘ḍ manāqib al-qādiriyya	1209	TCL; Ko; NAK.
Tabṣirat al-mubtadi’ fī umūr al-dīn		I.F.
Taḥdhīr ahl al-īmān		CAD.
Taḥdhīr al-ikhwān	1229	K; SDL; Niz; NAK.
Taḥqīq al-‘iṣma li-jamī‘ ṭabaqāt hādhihi ’l-umma		TCL; Niz.
Ta‘līm al-ikhwān	1228	TCL; Niz.
Talkhīṣ asrār kalām al-Maḥāsibī (*or* Minhāj al-‘ābidīn)		K; NAK.
Tamyīz ahl al-sunna		SDL; Niz; NAK.
Tamyīz al-muslimīn		K; SDL; Niz.
Tanbīh al-fāhim ‘alā ḥukm ta’rīkh muddat al-dunyā wa-khalq al-‘ālam	1223	NAK.
Tanbīh al-ghāfilīn		K; SDL; TCL; NAK.
Tanbīh al-ikhwān ‘alā aḥwāl arḍ al-Sūdān	1226	SDL; Niz; NAK; Jos.
Tanbīh al-ikhwān ‘alā jawāz ittikhādh al-majlis li-ajl ta‘līm al-niswān ‘ilm furūḍ al-a‘yān min dīn Allāh al-Raḥmān		ABU.

Tanbīh al-ṭalaba 'alā anna Allāh ma'rūf bi 'l-fiṭra	1217	NAK.
Tanbīh al-umma 'alā qurb hujūm ashrāṭ al-sā'a		SDL; Niz; Ko; NAK.
Tarwīḥ al-umma bi-bayān taisīr al-milla		SDL; TCL; Niz; NAK.
Tauqīf al-muslimīn 'alā ḥukm mad-hāhib al-mujtahidīn	1228	SDL; TCL.
Tuḥfat al-ḥabīb		K; SDL; NAK.
Ṭarīq al-janna		K; SDL; Niz; Ko; NAK.
'Ulūm al-mu'āmala		SDL; TCL; Niz; NAK.
'Umdat al-bayān fī'l-'ulūm allatī wajabat 'alā 'l-a'yān		SDL; TCL; Ko; NAK; Jos.
'Umdat al-muta'abbidīn		K; Niz; NAK.
'Umdat al-'ubbād		published, Gaskiya Corp., Zaria; K; SDL; TCL; Niz; Ko; NAK; Jos.
'Umdat al-'ulamā'		K; SDL; Ko; NAK.
Uṣūl al-'adl	1224	K; SDL; TCL; Niz; NAK; Jos.
al-Uṣūl allatī naqaltu 'an Abī 'Abbās Aḥmad b. Muḥammad b. 'Īsa al-Zarrūq al-Fāsī		NAK.
Uṣūl al-dīn		printed, Zaria; K; SDL; NAK; Jos.
Uṣūl al-wilāya wa-shurūṭuhā		printed, Zaria; K; NAK.
Wathīqat al-ikhwān li-tabyīn dalī-lāt wujūb ittibā' al-kitāb wa'l-sunna		published, Gaskiya Corp., Zaria; NAK.
Wathīqa (ilā jamī') ahl al-Sūdān		published, *J.A.H.*, 1961; I.F.; CAD.
Wird		published, Gaskiya Corp., Zaria; K; SDL; NAK.

'ABDULLĀH B. FŪDĪ

Ādāb al-'ādāt 'alā sunnat al-Rasūl		SDL; TCL; Niz; NAK.
Ādāb al-mu'āshara li-ṭalab al-najāt		SDL.
'Alāmāt al-muttabi'īn		K; SDL; Ko; NAK; Jos.
Alfiyyat al-ūṣūl		published, Cairo, 1961.

Aṣl al-Fullātīn		NAK.
al-Baḥr al-muḥīṭ	1237	K; Jos.
Bayān al-arkān wa'l-shurūṭ li'l-ṭarīqa al-ṣūfiyya		TCL; CAD.
Bayān al-nasab wa-aṣl al-dār (rā' iyya)		Pr. I.
Dawā' al-waswās	1242	K; SDL; NAK.
Dir' al-kai'a fī hijā' 'ilm al-hai'a	1242	Niz; NAK.
Durar ḥikam al-Rasūl		SDL.
Ḍau' al-muṣallī	1213	published, Abeokuta, 1953; and at Sokoto; SDL; NAK; Jos.
Ḍiyā' ahl al-iḥtisāb 'alā ṭarīqat al-sunna wa'l-ṣawāb		ABU; BN.
Ḍiyā' ahl al-rashād fī aḥkām al-hijra wa'l-jihād wa'l-sunna fī siyāsat al-'ibād		CAD.
Ḍiyā' al-anām		K; NAK.
Ḍiyā' al-ḥukkām	(ca. 1221)	K; SDL; NAK; Jos; BN.
Ḍiyā' al-mujāhidīn	1226	K; NAK; I.F.
Ḍiyā' al-muqtadīn li'l-khulafā' al-rāshidīn (attributed)		I.F.
Ḍiyā' al-qawā'id wa-nathr al-fawā'id li-ahl al-maqāṣid	1243	ABU; CAD.
Ḍiyā' al-sanad	1228	SDL; NAK.
Ḍiyā' al-siyāsa (*or* siyāsāt)	1235	K; SDL; TCL; Niz; NAK; BN.
Ḍiyā' al-sulṭān	1227	NAK; I.F.; Ibadan.
Ḍiyā' al-ta'wīl	1230–1	published, Cairo, 1961; K; SDL; NAK.
Ḍiyā' ūlī al-amr wa'l-mujāhidīn	1225	Niz; NAK; BN.
Ḍiyā' 'ulūm al-dīn (attributed)	1228	SDL; NAK.
Ḍiyā' al-umarā' fī-mā lahum wa-'alaihim min al-ashyā'		NAK.
Ḍiyā' al-umma	1226	K; NAK.
Ḍiyā' al-wilāyāt	1230	SDL; Niz; NAK; I.F.

al-Farā'iḍ al-jalīla wasā'iṭ al-qawā 'id al-jamīla	1211	SDL; NAK; Jos.
Fatḥ al-baṣīr fī 'ilm al-tabṣīr	1210	Pr.2.
Fatḥ al-laṭīf al-wāfī li-'ilm al-'urūḍ wa'l-qawāfī		NAK; Pr.1; CAD.
al-Ḥiṣn al-raṣīn	1216	K; NAK, Jos.
'Īdā' al-nusūkh	1227	published, *BSOAS*, 1957; SDL; NAK.
Jūdat al-sa'āda	1224	TCL; NAK.
Kashf al-ghumma fī bayān marātib al-umma (attributed)		NAK.
Kashf al-lu'm lanā wa-li-man tabi 'anāfī amr al-sharīf 'Abdullāh Hannun Giwa (forged?)		NAK.
Khulāṣat al-uṣūl (li'l-kaukab al-sāti')	1227	Jos; ABU.
Kifāyat al-'awāmm fī'l-buyū'	1224	Niz; Pr.2.
Kifāyat ḍu'afā' al-Sūdān fī bayān tafsīr al-Qur'ān	1238	K; Ko; NAK; Jos.
Kifāyat al-ṭullāb fī'l-nikāḥ	1232	K; SDL; NAK.
Kitāb la'ālī al-mawā'iẓ wa'l-ḥikam al-manthūra wa'l-manẓūma	1242	Niz; NAK.
Kitāb al-nasab		SDL; Niz; NAK.
Kitāb al-targhīb wa'l-tarhīb		CAD.
Lam' al-barq li-dhī tashābuh min al-farq	1237	Ko.
Lubāb al-mudkhal fī ādāb ahl al-dīn		K; SDL; TCL; NAK; KO; Jos.
al-Lu'lu' al-maṣūn	1231	K; SDL; NAK.
al-Masā'il		K.
Maṣāliḥ al-insān al-muta'alliqa bi'l-adyān		Niz; NAK.
Maṭiyyat al-zād ilā 'l-ma'ād	1233	K; SDL; TCL; Ko; NAK.
al-Miftāḥ li'l-tafsīr	1209	K; SDL; Ko; NAK.
Miftāḥ al-taḥaqquq li-ghālib mā yuḥtāju ilaihi fī'l-manṭiq		NAK.
Minan al-Mannān	1201	SDL; TCL; NAK; Jos.
al-Nafaḥāt al-bashriyya sharḥ al-qaṣā'id al-'ashriyya	1243	Pr.2.

Nail al-ma'mūl min jawāmi' kalim al-Rasūl		ABU; CAD.
Nail al-marām min shiyam al-kirām	1242	Pr. 1; CAD.
al-Naṣā'iḥ fī ahamm al-maṣāliḥ	1242	K; SDL; NAK; Jos.
Naẓm (al-'aqīda) al-wusṭā	1207	K; Jos.
al-Niyyāt fī'l-a'māl al-dunyawiyya wa'l-dīniyya		K; SDL; TCL.
Qawā'id al-ṣalāḥ ma'a fawā'id al-falāḥ		NAK.
Rauḍ al-'āshiq		Niz; NAK; Jos.
Sabīl al-najāt		K; SDL; Niz; NAK.
Sabīl al-ṣalāḥ li'l-falāḥ		NAK; ABU; CAD.
Sabīl al-salāma fī'l-imāma	1232	ABU (c.f. I.F.).
Sabīl al-sunna al-muwaṣṣila ilā 'l-janna		NAK.
Shifā' al-nās min dā' al-ghafla wa'l-waswās	1241	NAK.
Shukr al-iḥsān 'alā minan al-Mannān	1244	SDL; Niz; Ko; NAK; BN.
Sirāj jāmi' al-Bukhārī	1212	K; SDL; Niz; Ko; NAK.
Sulālat al-miftāḥ	1210	K; SDL; NAK.
Tahdhīb al-insān min khiṣāl al-shaiṭān	1244	Niz.
Takhmīs al-'ashriyyāt	1235	Niz; Ko; NAK; Jos.
Ta'līm al-anām	1240	SDL; NAK; CAD.
Ta'līm al-rāḍī asbāb al-ikhtiṣāṣ bi-mawāt al-arāḍī		Ko; NAK, I.F.
Taqrīb ḍarūrī al-dīn		K; SDL; TCL; Niz; NAK; Jos.
Taqrīb fī 'ilm ahl al-dhauq	1221	SDL.
Tazyīn al-waraqāt	1228	published, Hiskett, 1963; K; NAK; Jos.
al-Tibyān li-ḥuqūq al-ikhwān	1243	Niz; NAK.
al-Ṭarīq al-jādda mā iḥtawat 'alaihi min al-hādda (?)		SDL; TCL; Niz.
Ṭarīq al-ṣāliḥīn		Niz.

MUḤAMMAD BELLO B. 'UTHMĀN B. FŪDĪ

(Asbāb al-naṣr li'l-mujāhidīn)		I.F.
al-'Awāmil fī'l-naḥw (attributed)		Niz.
al-Badr al-lāmi' fī wird al-jāmi'	1246	Ko; BN.
al-Budūr al-musfira fī'l-khiṣāl allatī yudraku bihā al-maghfira		ABU.
al-Burd al-yamanī fī akhbār Uwais al-Qaranī		SDL.
al-Dhikrā		Ko.
(Dhikr (*or* Ifrād) man yuṣallī Allāh 'alaihi wa-malā'ikatihi)		ABU; CAD.
al-Durar al-ẓāhiriyya fī'l-salāsil al-qādiriyya		Niz.
Ḍiyā' al-'uqūl fī bayān ghilaẓ taḥrīm al-ghulūl	1235	Jos.
Fatḥ al-bāb fī dhikr ba'ḍ khaṣa'iṣ al-shaikh 'Abd al-Qādir		TCL; Niz; NAK.
Fatḥ al-ighlāq fī ma'nā ḥadīth bu 'ithtu li-utammim li'l-nās makārim al-akhlāq	1235	Pr.2.
Fawā'id mujmala (Birr al-wālidain)		K; Niz; NAK; Jos.
al-Ghaith al-shu'būb fī tauṣiyat al-amīr Ya'qūb		K; NAK.
al-Ghaith al-wabl fī sīrat al-imām al-'adl	1236	SDL; Ko; NAK.
Ghāyat al-su'l fī tafsīr al-Rasūl		NAK.
Ḥilyat al-baṣā'ir 'an al-aḥkām al-lāzima	1236	SDL; TCL; NAK.
Ifādat al-ikhwān	1251	NAK.
al-I'lām bi-mā yajib 'alā 'l-imām min ḥifẓ baiḍat al-Islām		ABU.
Infāq al-maisūr	1227	published, Whitting, 1951 (London); Abubakar Gummi, 1964 (Cairo); SDL; Niz; NAK; Jos.
al-Inṣāf fī dhikr mā fī masā'il al-khilāfa	1232	K.
al-Ishā'a fī ḥukm al-khārijīn 'an al-ṭā'a		TCL; NAK.

Ishāra wa-i'lām fī ba'ḍ umūr ṣilat al-arḥām		Pr. 1.
Jalā' al-ṣamam fī maraḍ al-aqwāl wa'l-af'āl wa'l-himam		TCL; Niz; NAK.
Jalā' al-ṣudūr	1229	K; SDL; TCL; Niz; Ko; NAK; Jos; BN.
Jam' al-nuqūl fī aḥkām al-ghulūl		ABU.
Jawāb li'l-sayyid Aḥmad b. Ḥamma Lobbo		ABU.
Jawāb shāfi wa-khiṭāb minnā kāfi ilā Muḥammad al-Jailānī		Niz.
Jumal min al-mabānī naṣā'iḥ li-Muḥammad al-Jailānī		Ko.
Jumla munabbiha fī-hā al-ishāra al-muwaqqiẓa		Ko.
Kaff al-ikhwān 'an ittibā' khaṭawāt al-shaiṭān	1226	TCL.
Kashf al-ghiṭā' wa'l-sitr fī muwālāt al-kuffār	1235	Niz; ABU.
Kashf al-khafī min akhbār al-imām al-mahdī		Ko.
al-Kawākib al-durriyya fī dhikr ba'ḍ muṣṭalaḥāt al-ṣūfiyya		NAK; Pr. 2
Kifāyat al-muhtadīn fī aḥkām al-mukhallafīn min al-mujāhidīn		Ko.
(Kitāb fī aqwām al-muhājirīn wa'l-mujāhidīn) (attributed)		Niz.
al-Kitāb al-kāfi fī 'ilm al-jafr wa'l-khawāfī		ABU.
Kitāb al-nasab		I.F.
Kitāb al-nisrīn fī-mā qīla fī-man balagha min al-sinn arba'īn	1235	NAK; Jos.
Kitāb al-nisrīn (dhail)	1235	Pr. 2.
Kitāb al-taḥrīr fī qawā'id al-tabṣīr		published, Gaskiya Corp., Zaria; TCL.
Madārij al-salāma		I.F.
al-Maḥṣūl fī dhikr jumla min masā'il al-ghulūl		Jos.
Manẓūm al-durr	1236	Niz.

Marthiyyat ʿammihi ʿAbdullāh		K; NAK.
Masā'il ʿan sha'n najm ṭalaʿa fī Ṣafar	1241	Ko.
Masā'il muhimma wa-fawā'id ʿaẓīma		Pr.2.
al-Mawārid al-nabawiyya fī'l-masā'il al-ṭibbiyya	(1252)	Niz.
Miftāḥ al-baṣā'ir (forged?)		ABU.
Miftāḥ al-sadād fī aqsām hadhihi 'l-bilād		SDL; TCL; Niz.
Miftāḥ al-sadād fī dhikr al-auliyā' al-khawāṣṣ al-afrād		CAD.
Nail al-raghā'ib fī silsilat al-quṭb al-Thaʿālibī	1235	Jos.
al-Naṣīḥa bi-taqrīb mā yajib ʿalā ʿāmmat al-umma		K; SDL; Niz.
al-Naṣīḥa al-waḍi'a		Ko.
Nūr al-fajr fī'l-ayyām al-maʿlūmāt		SDL; TCL; Ko; Jos.
Nuṣḥ kāfi wa-li'l-amrāḍ shāfi		K; SDL; TCL; Niz; NAK.
Qadḥ al-zinād fī amr hadhā 'l-jihād (attributed)		NAK.
al-Qaul al-mabdhūl	1238	NAK.
al-Qaul al-manthūr fī bayān adwiya ʿillat al-bāsūr		SDL; Niz; Ko.
al-Qaul al-manʿūt		K; SDL; TCL; NAK.
al-Qaul al-marham		K.
al-Qaul al-mauhūb		K.
al-Qaul al-mukhtaṣar fī amr al-imām al-mahdī al-muntaẓar	(1235. 1204, wrongly?)	SDL; NAK.
al-Qaul al-sanā' fī wujūh al-taliyīn (?) wa'l-tamashshī bi'l-sanā'		SDL; Niz; NAK; Jos.
Qawāʿid al-ṣalāḥ	1249	K.
Rafʿ al-ishtibāh fī'l-taʿalluq bi-Allāh wa-bi-ahl Allāh		TCL; Niz; Ko; Jos.
Rafʿ al-shubha	1216	K; SDL; TCL; Niz; NAK; Jos.
al-Raghba		NAK; I.F.
al-Ribāṭ wa'l-ḥirāsa		K.

Risāla ilā jamā'at al-muslimīn	Niz; Ko; NAK; I.F.
Risāla ilā Muḥammad al-Mukhtār	Ko.
Risāla li'l-amrāḍ shāfiyya fī-hā naṣīḥa fī'l-aghrāḍ kāfiyya	Niz; NAK.
Sard al-kalām	K; SDL; TCL; NAK.
Shams al-ẓahīra fī minhāj ahl al-'ilm wa'l-baṣīra	Ko; NAK.
Sharḥ al-qaṣīda al-ṭā'iyya al-badamāṣiyya	K; NAK.
Sharḥ al-ṣadr fī taḥrīr jawāb jināyat al-raqīq 'alā 'l-ḥurr	CAD.
Shifā' al-asqām fī ma'rifat madārik al-aḥkām	Pr.1.
(Su'ālān)	Pr.2.
Taḥqīq al-murībīn wa'l-mushakkikīn (attributed)	NAK; Jos.
Takhmīs Bānat Su'ād	Ko; NAK.
Takhmīs al-Burda	Pr.1.
Ta'līq 'alā abyātinā al-manẓūma fī'l-fitan al-muttaṣila bi-khurūj al-mahdī	Ko.
Ta'līq 'alā qaṣīdatinā fī mauḍū' al-Qur'ān	Ko.
Talkhīṣ al-maqāṣid al-mujarrada fī 'l-adwiya al-farīda	NAK
Tanbīh (ahl) al-fuhūm 'alā wujūb ijtināb ahl al-sha'dhaba wa'l-nujūm 1236	K; SDL; TCL; Niz; Ko; NAK; Jos.
al-Tanbīhāt al-wāḍiḥāt fī-mā jā'a fī'l-bāqiyāt al-ṣāliḥāt	BN.
Tanbīh al-ikhwān 'alā adwiyat al-dīdān	Niz.
Tanbīh al-ikhwān 'alā aḥkām al-amān	TCL.
Tanbīh al-jamā'a 'alā aḥkām al-shafā'a	TCL.
Tanbīh al-rāqid 'alā mā ya'tawir al-ḥājj min al-mafāsid	SDL; Niz; NAK.

Tanbīh al-ṣāḥib ʻalā aḥkām al-makāsib	1235	K; SDL; Niz; NAK; Jos.
al-Tawaṣṣul bi-khair al-rusul		Ko.
al-Turjumān ʻan kaifiyyat waʻẓ al-shaikh ʻUthmān	1217	SDL; TCL; Niz; Ko; NAK.
Ṭibb al-hayyīn		SDL; NAK; BN.
Ṭibb al-Nabī		SDL; Pr. 1.
ʻUjālat al-rākib fī'l-ṭibb al-ṣā'ib	(1245)	NAK; CAD; BN.
Uṣūl al-siyāsa		Niz; Ko; NAK.
Wathīqa ilā jamāʻat al-muslimīn		SDL; Ko.

ʻABDULLĀH B. MUḤAMMAD AL-KANĀWĪ

(35 dā'ira)	1229	NAK; CAD.

ʻABD AL-QĀDIR B. GIDĀDO

Anīs al-mufīd		K; NAK.
Basṭ al-fawā'id wa-taqrīb al-maqāṣid		Pr. 1.
al-Iktifā' li-ahl al-ta'assī	1265	Niz; CAD.
al-Lawāmiʻ al-nūrāniyya		Pr. 2.
Majmūʻ manāqib amīr al-mu'minīn ʻAlī		Pr. 1; CAD.
(Majmūʻ al-rasā'il)	1265	ABU; CAD.
al-Mawāhib al-rabbāniyya	1272	CAD.

ʻABD AL-QĀDIR B. MUḤAMMAD AL-BUKHĀRĪ

Tabshīr al-ikhwān bi-akhbār al-khulafā' fī'l-Sūdān	1331	Niz; NAK.

ʻABD AL-QĀDIR B. AL-MUṢṬAFĀ

Baʻḍ tanbīhāt li'l-shaikh ʻUthmān wa-ʻAbdullāh		ABU.
Kashf al-ghiṭā' wa'l-raib fī dhikr anwāʻ mafātīḥ al-ghaib		Pr. 2.
Majmūʻ kalimāt al-shaikh ʻUthmān		Niz.
al-Masā'il		SDL.
Mauṣūfat al-Sūdān	1282	K; SDL; TCL; Niz; NAK.

Qaṭā'if al-jinān fī dhikr aḥwāl arḍ al-Sūdān — Pr. 1 (incomplete).
Rauḍāt al-afkār (akhbār al-bilād al-Ḥausiyya) — K; Niz; NAK.
Salwat al-aḥzān fī dhikr ba'ḍ al-khawāṣṣ min ahl hadhā 'l-zamān 1242 — Niz.
Ta'līq badī' wajīz — K.
(9 qaṣā'id) — ABU.

'ABD AL-QĀDIR B. AL-SHAIKH 'UTHMĀN
(Rā'iyya) — Ko.

'ABD AL-QĀDIR MO'ANNURAJO
Tawārīkh umarā' al-Islām fī arḍ Ḥausa — CAD.

ABŪ BAKR AL-'ATĪQ B. AL-SHAIKH 'UTHMĀN
Ajwiba 'an kitāb Aḥmad b. Ḥamma Lobbo — Pr. 1; ABU; Dakar.
Risāla ilā jamā'at Gwandu — ABU; (Ibadan).

AḤMAD B. AL-ḤĀJJ
Ta'rīkh Missau (akhbār aṣl Fullātā Barnū) 1928 A.D. — ABU.

AḤMAD B. SA'D
Risāla ilā 'l-wazīr Muḥammad al-Bukhārī b. Aḥmad — Pr. 1
(Ta'rīkh Gwandu) — (Ibadan)

AḤMAD AL-RUFĀ'Ī B. AL-SHAIKH 'UTHMĀN
'Alāmāt khurūj al-mahdī — ABU.
Tanbīh al-umma 'alā mā 'alaihim min al-ṭā'a li'l-a'imma 1288 — Ko; NAK.
Tanbīh al-umma fī ṭā'at Allāh 1284 — SDL; Niz; Ko.

'ALĪ B. AḤMAD (and Alkalin Waziri MUḤAMMAD)
Majmū' al-khulafā' — NAK.

ASMĀ' BINT AL-SHAIKH 'UTHMĀN

Marthiyyat Muḥammad Bello		Pr. I
Qaṣīda fī ta'rīkh Sokoto (in Fulfulde)	1256	NAK; Pr. I.
Tabshīr al-ikhwān bi'l-tawaṣṣul bi-suwar al-Qur'ān	1255	TCL.
Tabshīr al-ikhwān fī khawāṣṣ ba'ḍ suwar al-Qur'ān		Pr. I.
Tanbīh al-ghāfilīn wa-tadhkīr al-'āqilīn	1235	SDL; TCL; Niz; NAK.

GIDĀDO B. LAIMA

Ba'ḍ tanbīhāt sayyidinā Muḥammad Bello	1239	Jos.
Kashf al-ḥijāb wa-raf' al-niqāb		SDL; Niz.
al-Kashf wa'l-bayān 'an ba'ḍ aḥwāl al-sayyid Muḥammad Bello	1254	SDL; Niz; Ko; NAK.
Majmū' aṣḥab al-sayyid Muḥammad Bello		Niz; NAK.
Majmū' khiṣāl al-shaikh 'Uthmān	1254	Jos; Pr. I.
Nasab	1256	Pr. I.
Rauḍ al-jinān		K; SDL; TCL; NAK; Jos.
Waṣiyya		Pr. I

AL-ḤASAN B. AL-SHAIKH 'UTHMĀN

Tartīb al-khulafā'	1230	Ko.

ḤAYĀT B. SA'ĪD B. MUḤAMMAD BELLO

Markab al-ḥabīb ilā ḥaḍrat al-maḥbūb		Pr. I (incomplete).
Miftāḥ al-khairāt wa-mazīd al-barakāt		ABU.
Ṭibb al-i'āna ilā ahl al-mawadda		ABU.

JUNAID B. MUḤAMMAD AL-BUKHĀRĪ B. AḤMAD (historical books only)

Bughyat al-rāghibīn		Pr. I.; published, Gaskiya Corp., Zaria, 1961.

Dhikr mazār al-shaikh ʻAbdullāh b. Fūdī	1382	Pr. 1
al-Durra al-ʻaṣmā' fī qaṣā'id sayyidatinā Asmā'		Pr. 1
Ḍabṭ al-multaqaṭāt		K.
Idrāk al-amal fī'l-tanwīh bi-qaryat Degel	1382	Pr. 1.
Ifādat al-ṭālibīn fī dhikr baʻḍ qaṣā 'id amīr al-mu'minīn Muḥammad Bello		Pr. 1.
Isʻāf al-zā'irīn bi-dhikr turab al-auliyā' wa'l-ṣāliḥīn		Pr. 1.
Muthif al-ikhwān bi-mā atā fī 'l-kashf wa'l-bayān	1362	Pr. 1; printed, Kano.
Nail al-marām fī tarjamat al-imām Muḥammad Bello		Pr. 1
Nasq kitāb Saʻd ʻalā ḥurūf abjad	1380	Pr. 1.
Rawā'iḥ al-azhār min rauḍ al-jinān	1362	Pr. 1.
Ta'nīs al-aḥibbā' fī ta'rīkh umarā' Gwandu	1377	Pr. 1.
Tanshīt al-zā'irīn li-ziyārat amīr al-mu'minīn Muḥammad Bello	1378	Pr. 1; published, Gaskiya Corp., Zaria, 1960.
Tuḥfat al-ikhwān bi-baʻḍ mā li-shaikhinā ʻUthmān min al-karāmāt		Pr. 1.
al-Tuḥfat al-saniyya fī taʻrīf Ṣukkutu al-bahiyya	1377	Pr. 1.

AL-KHALĪL B. ʻABDULLĀH B. FŪDĪ

Tanbīh al-ghāfilīn fī 'l-taʻalluq bi-auliyā' Allāh al-ʻārifīn	1268	NAK; ABU.

MARIAM BINT AL-SHAIKH ʻUTHMĀN

Wathīqa ilā amīr Kano fī amr al-mahdī		ABU.

MUALLAYIDI B. 'ABD AL-QĀDIR B. AL-MUṢṬAFĀ
Nubdha yasīra tushir ilā ba'ḍ karāmāt al-shaikh — Pr. I.

MUḤAMMAD B. ṢĀLIḤ
Taqyīd al-akhbār — 1284 — Jos.

MUḤAMMAD AL-BUKHĀRĪ B. AḤMAD
Ḥikmat al-abrār 'an aqwāl al-fujjār wa'l-ashrār — TCL.
Kitāb fī-mā jarā bainī wa-bain amīr Hadijia wa-Yūsuf — NAK.
Rauḍ al-rayāḥīn fī akhbār amīr Mafara wa-amīr Anka al-darīkain — Pr. I.
Risālat al-wazīr ilā ahl al-'ilm wa'l-tadabbur — Pr. I.
Ta'nīs al-ikhwān bi-dhikr al-khulafā' al-'uẓamā' fī'l-Sūdān — NAK.

MUḤAMMAD AL-BUKHĀRĪ B. AL-SHAIKH 'UTHMĀN
(Ba'ḍ qaṣā'id) — Ko; Pr. I.
Kaff al-ikhwān fī ittibā' khaṭawāt al-shaiṭān — 1226 — Pr. I.

MUḤAMMAD JULDE B. MUḤAMMAD
Ghāyāt al-munā wa'l-amān — ABU.
Marthiyyat Gidado b. Laima — Pr. I.

MUḤAMMAD RAJI B. 'ALĪ
(Kitāb al-jawāb) — ABU.
Risāla ilā amīr Gwandu al-Khalīl — ABU; BN.

MUḤAMMAD TUKUR B. MUḤAMMAD
Ma'āwanat al-ikhwān fī mu'āsharat al-niswān — NAK.
Qirā al-aḥibbā' fī bayān sirr al-asmā' — Niz.

Ta'līm al-ikhwān		NAK.
Tanbīh al-khuṣamā' wa'l-ẓalama fī istirḍā' al-khuṣamā' wa-radd al-maẓālim		K; Jos.

SA'D B. 'ABD AL-RAḤMĀN

Tartīb al-aṣḥāb wa-tajmī' al-arbāb min aṣḥāb al-shaikh 'Abdullāh b. Fūdī		NAK.

AL-ḤĀJJ SA'ĪD

(Ta'rīkh Sokoto)		part published by Houdas, 1901; BN.

SA'ĪD B. MUḤAMMAD BELLO

Irshād al-'ābid ilā ḥaḍrat al-ma'būd		Pr.1.
Markab al-'awāmm ilā dār al-salām		Niz; NAK; Jos; printed, Zaria.

'UMAR B. ABĪ BAKR

al-Sarḥa al-warīqa fī 'ilm al-wathīqa	1294	NAK.

'UMAR B. MUḤAMMAD AL-BUKHĀRĪ B. AL-SHAIKH 'UTHMĀN

Ma'ūnat al-aḥibbā' fī 'ilm al-aṭibbā'		ABU.
al-Nubdha (fī manāqib Ibrāhīm al-Khalīl b. 'Abdullāh)		SDL; NAK.
Tanbīh al-ikhwān fī amr al-Sūdān		NAK; Pr.1.

'UMAR B. SA'ĪD AL-FŪTĪ

Rimāḥ ḥizb al-raḥīm 'alā nuḥūr ḥizb al-rajīm	1261	published, Cairo, 1345 H.
Suyūf al-sa'īd al-mu'taqid fī ahl Allāh ka'l-Tijānī 'alā raqabat al-shaqī al-ṭarīd al-muntaqid al-jānī	1252	(Ibadan)

'UTHMĀN B. ISḤĀQ		
al-Kashf wa'l-bayān	1285	CAD; Pr. I.
Sullam al-hudāt		SDL; TCL; Niz.
al-Sullam li'l-farā'iḍ		Niz; NAK.
Tanbīh al-ikhwān wa-ta'līm al-khillān	1303	SDL.
ZĀD B. MUḤAMMAD SA'D		
Khulāṣat al-qarā'iḥ 'alā 'l-sulāla wa-risālat al-naṣā'iḥ	1209	Pr. I.
(ANONYMOUS)		
Faiḍ al-qadīr		Jos.
(Kitāb fī binā' ḥiṣn al-imām)		NAK.
Tabṣirat al-nuẓẓār		NAK.
Ta'rīkh Kano (ta'rīkh arbāb Kano)		NAK.
Ta'rīkh Zakzak		NAK.
(Siyar amīr al-mu'minīn Aḥmad b. al-shaikh 'Umar al-Fūtī)		Ibadan, ms. 176.

General Works

'Abd al-Raḥmān b. 'Abdullāh al-Sa'dī, *Ta'rīkh al-Sūdān* (published and translated by O. Houdas, Paris, 1898).

'Abd al-Raḥmān b. Muḥammad Ibn Khaldūn, *Muqaddima fī 'l-ta'rīkh* (translated by F. Rosenthal, London, 1958).

Aḥmad Bābā b. Aḥmad, al-Lam' fī 'l-ishāra li-ḥukm tibgh, 1016 A.H. (1607 A.D.), Nizamiyya School Library.

Aḥmad b. 'Alī al-Qalqashandī, *Ṣubḥ al-a'shā fī ṣinā'at al-inshā'* (part III published, Algiers, 1957).

Aḥmad b. Fartuwa al-Barnāwī, *Kitāb fī shā'n sulṭān Idrīs* (published, Kano, 1932).

'Alī b. al-'Arbī Barrāda Ḥarāzim, *Jawāhir al-ma'ānī wa-bulūgh al-amānī fī faiḍ Sīdī Abī 'l-'Abbās al-Tijānī* (published, Cairo, 1345 A.H./1926–7 A.D.).

'Alī b. Muḥammad al-Māwardī, *al-Aḥkām al-sulṭāniyya* (translated by E. Fagnan, Algiers, 1915).

Maḥmūd Ka'ti b. al-Ḥājj Ka'ti, *Ta'rikh al Fattāsh* (published and translated by O. Houdas, M. Delafosse, Paris, 1913).

(ii) *Other Works*

(a) Travellers: a selected list

Allen, W.; Thomson, T. R. H., *Narrative of the Expedition into the River Niger in 1841*, (2 vols.), London, 1848

Baikie, W. B., *Narrative of an Exploring Voyage up the Rivers Kworra and Benue in 1854*, London, 1856

(Baikie, W. B.,) 'Notes of a Journey from Bida in Nupe to Kano in Hausa', *Journal, Royal Geographical Society*, XXXVII, 1867.

(Barth, H.,) 'Progress of the African Mission', *Journal, Royal Geographical Society*, XXI, 1851

Barth, H., *Travels and Discoveries in North and Central Africa* (5 vols.), 2nd edition, 1857–8.

Burdo, A. M., *Niger et Bénué*, Paris, 1880.

Cazemajou, M-C., 'Journal de Route', *Bulletin, Comité de l'Afrique Française*, 1900.

Clapperton, H., 1st journey: v. sub Denham, D., Clapperton, H.

Clapperton, H., *Journal of a Second Expedition into the Interior of Africa*, London, 1829.

Crowther, S. A.; Taylor, J. C., *The Gospel on the Banks of the Niger*, London, 1859.

Crowther, S. A., *Journal of an Expedition up the Niger and Tshadda Rivers*, London, 1855.

Denham, D.; Clapperton, H., *Narrative of Travels and Discoveries in Northern and Central Africa*, London, 1826.

Flegel, E. R., 'Expedition nach Sokoto; Reisebriefe', *Mittheilungen der Afrikanischen Gesellschaft*, III, I, 1882.

Hastings, A. C. G., *The Voyage of the Dayspring*, London, 1926.

Hornemann, F. K., *The Journal of F. Horneman's Travels*, London, 1802.

Hutchinson, T. J., *Narrative of the Niger, Tshadda and Binue Exploration*, London, 1855.

Jackson, J. G., *An Account of Timbuktoo and Hausa*, London, 1820.

Laird, M.; Oldfield, R. A. K., *Narrative of an Expedition into the Interior of Africa*, London, 1837.

Lander, R., in Clapperton, H., *Journal of a Second Expedition*, London, 1829.

(Lander, R.; Lander, J.,) *The Travels of Richard and John Lander into the Interior of Africa*, London, 1836.

Lander, R.; Lander, J., *Voyage Down the Dark River*, London, 1832.

Lyon, G. F., *A Narrative of Travels in Northern Africa in the years 1818, 1819, 1820*, London, 1820.

MacDonald, C. M., 'Exploration of the Benue and its Northern Tributary the Kebbi', *Proceedings, Royal Geographical Society*, N.S. XIII, 1891.

Mage, M. E., *Voyage dans le Soudan Occidental*, Paris, 1868.

Massari, A. M., 'Il mio Viaggio in Africa', *Nuova Antologia*, XXXI, 1.

Massari, A. M., 'La Traversée de l'Afrique', *Bulletin, Société Royale Belge de Géographie*, VII, 6, 1883.

Milum, J., 'Notes of a Journey from Lagos up the River Niger to Bida', *Proceedings, Royal Geographical Society*, N.S. III, 1881.

Mockler-Ferryman, A. F., *Up the Niger*, London, 1892.

Monteil, P. L., *De Saint-Louis à Tripoli par le lac Tchad*, Paris, 1894.

Muhammad al-Tunisi, *Voyage au Ouaday* (trans. Perron), Paris, 1851.

Nachtigal, G., *Sahara und Sudan* (3 vols.), Berlin, 1879–8.

Petermann, A. H., *An Account of the Progress of the Expedition to Central Africa*, London, 1854.

Richardson, J., *Narrative of a Mission to Central Africa (1850–1)*, London, 1853.

Robinson, C. H., *Hausaland*, London, 1896.

Rohlfs, G., *Reise durch Nord-Afrika vom Mittelandischen Meere bis zum Busen von Guinea, 1865–1867*, Gotha, 1872.

Schon, J. F.; Crowther, S. A., *Journals of the Expedition up the Niger in 1841*, London, 1842.

da Segni, P. F., 'Viaggio da Tripoli di Barbaria al Bornu nel 1850', *Bolletino della Societa Geographica Italiana*: 4, 1; 1870.

Staudinger, P., *Im Herzen der Haussa Länder*, Berlin, 1889.

Thomson, J., 'Niger and Central Sudan Sketches', *Scottish Geographical Magazine*, II, 1886.

Thomson, J., 'Sketch of a Trip to Sokoto by the River Niger', *Journal, Manchester Geographical Society*, II, 1886.

Thomson, J., 'Up the Niger to the Central Sudan', *Good Words*, 27, 1886.

dalla Vedova, 'Pellegrino di Matteucci ed il suo Diario Inedito', *Bolletino della Societa Geographica Italiana*, X, 9, 1885.
Wagner, H., *Schilderung der Reisen und Entdeckungen des Dr. Edouard Vogel in Central-Africa*, Leipsig, 1860.
Wallace, W., 'Notes on a Journey through the Sokoto Empire and Borgu in 1894', *Geographical Journal*, VIII, 1896.

(For a bibliography of early travellers' references to Sokoto Province, v. K. Kreiger, *Geschichte von Zamfara*, Berlin, 1959, pp. 9–12.)

(b) Other sources

Abadie, M., *La Colonie du Niger*, Paris, 1927.
Alkalin Gwandu Ahmad, *Tarikh Gandu*, translated by McAllister, 1909 (unpublished) Ibadan.
Arif, A. S.; Abū Hakima, A. M., *Descriptive Catalogue of Arabic Manuscripts in Nigeria*, London, 1965.
Arnett, E. J., *Gazetteer of Sokoto Province*, London, 1920.
Arnett, E. J., *The Rise of the Sokoto Fulani*, Kano, 1922.
Ba, A. H.; Daget, J., *L'Empire Peul du Macina*, Etudes Soudanaises, 3, Institut Français d'Afrique Noire, 1955 (reprinted, Paris, 1962).
Ba, A. H.; Cardaire, M., *Tierno Bokar, le Sage de Bandiagara*, Paris, 1957.
Backwell, H. F., *The Occupation of Hausaland*, Lagos, 1927.
Bello, al-haji Sir Ahmadu, *My Life*, Cambridge, 1962.
Bivar, A. D. H.; Hiskett, M., 'The Arabic Literature of Nigeria to 1804', *Bulletin, School of Oriental and African Studies*, XXV, 1962.
Bivar, A. D. H., 'Arabic Documents of Northern Nigeria', *Bulletin, School of Oriental and African Studies*, XXII, 1959.
Bivar, A. D. H., 'The Wathīqat ahl al-sudan', *Journal of African History*, II, 2, 1961.
Bjorkman, W., 'Zwei Hamburger arabische Handschriften über den Islam im Sudan' (Muḥammad Bello: Miftāḥ al-sadād; Uṣūl al-siyāsa), *Folia Ethno-Glossica*, III, 2–4, 1927.
Boyo, O. E.; Hodgkin, T.; Wilks, I., *Check List of Arabic Works from Ghana*, Legon, 1962.

Brockelmann, C., *Geschichte der Arabischen Litteratur*, Leiden, 1937–49.
Buchanan, K. M.; Pugh, J. C., *Land and People in Nigeria*, London, 1955.
Burdon, J. A., *Northern Nigeria. Historical Notes on Certain Emirates and Tribes*, London, 1909.
Burdon, J. A., Notes on Tribute in Sokoto Province. National Archives, Kaduna (Sokprof 2/2/7).
Burdon, J. A., 'Sokoto History', *Journal, African Society*, VI, 24, 1907.
Burdon, J. A., Sokoto Province: Reports. National Archives, Kaduna (SNP 15/1/60; Sokprof 2/1/1–5).
Cattenoz, H-G., *Tables de Concordance des Eres Chrétienne et Hégirienne*, 3rd edition, Rabat, 1961.
Delafosse, M., *Essai de Manuel Pratique de la Langue Mandé*, Paris, 1901.
Delafosse, M., 'Traditions musulmanes relatives à l'origine des Peuls', *Revue du Monde Musulman*, XX, 1912.
Dokaji, al-haji Abubakar, *Kano Ta Dabo Cigari*, Zaria, 1958.
Duff, F. C.; Hilton Browne, W., *Gazetteer of Kontagora Province*, London, 1920.
Dupire, M., *Peuls Nomades*, Paris, 1962.
East, R. M., *Labarun Hausawa da Makwabtansu*, Zaria, 1932.
Edgar, F., *Litafi na Tatsuniyoyi na Hausa* (3 vols.), Belfast, 1911–13.
Edgar, F., *Notebook* (unpublished), Ibadan.
El-Masri, F. H., 'The Life of Shehu Usuman dan Fodio before the jihād', *Journal, Historical Society of Nigeria*, II, 4, 1963.
Fagnan, E. (trans.), *Mawerdi: Les Statuts Gouvernmentaux*, Algiers, 1915.
Flint, J. E., *Sir George Goldie*, Oxford, 1960.
Fremantle, J. H., 'History of the region comprising the Katagum Division of Kano Province', *African Affairs: Journal, African Society*, X–XI, 39–42, 1911–12.
Gibb, H. A. R.; Bowen, H., *Islamic Society and the West*, Oxford, 1950, 1957.
Gowers, W. F., *Gazetteer of Kano Province*, London, 1921.
Greenberg, J. H., *The Influence of Islam on a Sudanese Religion*, New York, 1946.
(Grüner, Dr.), *Deutsche Kolonialzeitung*, Jun.-Okt., 1895.

Hamet, I., 'Nour el-Eulbabe de Cheikh Otmane dan Foudiou', *Revue Africaine*, Algiers 41/227; 42/228, 1897–8.

Harris, P. G., *Gazetteer of Sokoto Province*, mimeographed, 1939.

Heepe, M., 'Haussa Handschriften in der Preussischen Staatsbibliothek zu Berlin', *Mittheilungen des Seminars für Orientalische Sprachen zu Berlin*, XXXI, 1928.

Hassan; Shuaibu Naibi, *A Chronicle of Abuja*, new edition, Lagos, 1962.

Hillary, H. R. P., Sokoto Province: Reports. National Archives, Kaduna (SNP 15/1/60; Sokprof 3/27/(S.2909).

Hiskett, M., 'An Islamic tradition of reform in the Western Sudan from the 16th to the 18th century', *Bulletin, School of Oriental and African Studies*, XXV, 1962.

Hiskett, M., 'Kitāb al-Farq: a work on the Habe kingdoms attributed to Uthman dan Fodio', *Bulletin, School of Oriental and African Studies*, XXIII, 1960.

Hiskett, M., 'Material relating to the state of learning among the Fulani before their jihad', *Bulletin, School of Oriental and African Studies*, XIX, 1957.

Hiskett, M., *Tazyīn al-waraqāt*, Ibadan, 1963.

Hodgkin, T. L., *Nigerian Perspectives*, Oxford, 1960.

Hodgkin, T. L., 'Uthman dan Fodio', *The Nigerian Magazine* (special independence issue), October, 1960.

Hogben, S. J., *The Muhammedan Emirates of Nigeria*, Oxford, 1930 (new edition, with Kirk-Greene, A. H. M., 1966).

Hopen, C. E., *The Pastoral Fulbe Family in Gwandu*, Oxford, 1958.

Houdas, O. V. (ed.), *Es-Sa' di: Tarikh es-Soudan*, Paris, 1898–1900.

Houdas, O. V. (ed.), *Hadj Sa'id: Tarikh Sokoto*, in *Tedzkiret en-Nisian*, Paris, 1901.

Houdas, O. V. (ed.), *Katī: Tarikh el-Fettach*, Paris, 1913.

Hunwick, J. O., 'Arabic manuscript material bearing on the history of the Western Sudan', *Supplement, Bulletin of News, Historical Society of Nigeria*, VII, 2, 1962.

Idris b. Ibrahim, *Biography of Abubakr Yero*, translated by R. Abraham, 1926 (unpublished), National Archives, Kaduna.

Junaidu, Wazirin Sakkwato, *Tarihin Fulani*, Zaria, 1957.

Kensdale, W. E. N., *A Catalogue of Arabic Manuscripts Preserved in the University Library, Ibadan*, Ibadan, 1955–8.

Kensdale, W. E. N., 'Field notes on the Arabic literature of the

Western Sudan', *Journal, Royal Asiatic Society*, 3 and 4, 1955; 1 and 2, 1956; 1 and 2, 1958.

Kirk-Greene, A. H. M., *Adamawa, Past and Present*, Oxford, 1958.

Koelle, S. W., *African Native Literature*, London, 1854.

(Krause, G. A.), 'Haussa Handshriften in der Preussischen Staatsbibliothek zu Berlin', *Mittheilungen des Seminars für Orientalische Sprachen zu Berlin*, XXXI, 1928.

Krieger, K., *Geschichte von Zamfara*, Berlin, 1959.

Krieger, K., 'Weitere Bemerkungen zur Geschichte von Zamfara', *Baessler-Archiv* (Neue Folge), Band XII, 1964.

Last, D. M.; al-Hajj, M. A., 'Attempts at defining a Muslim in 19th century Hausaland and Bornu', *Journal, Historical Society of Nigeria*, III, 2, 1965.

Last, D. M., 'A solution to the problems of dynastic chronology in 19th century Zaria and Kano', *Journal, Historical Society of Nigeria*, III, 3, 1966.

Levy, R., *The Social Structure of Islam*, Cambridge, 1957.

De Loppinot, A., 'Souvenirs d'Agibou', *Bulletin, Comité d'Etudes Historiques et Scientifiques de l'A.O.F.*, 1919.

MacDonald, C. M., *Report of his visit as H.M.'s Commissioner to the Niger and Oil Rivers*, (Foreign Office) London, 1890.

Martin, B. G., 'Five Letters from the Tripoli Archives', *Journal, Historical Society of Nigeria*. II, 3, 1962.

Meek, C. K., *Land Tenure and Land Administration in Nigeria*, London, 1957.

Mischlich, A.; Lippert, J., 'Beitrage zur Geschichte der Haussastaaten', *Mittheilungen des Seminars für Orientalische Sprachen zu Berlin, Afrikanische Studien*, VI, 1903.

Mischlich, A., 'Uber Sitten und Gebrauche der Haussa', *M.S.O.S.*, X–XII, 1907–9.

Muffett, D. J. M., *Concerning Brave Captains*, London, 1964.

Muhammad Ali, *Religion of Islam*, Lahore, 1950.

Muhammad Bukhari, *Salsalar Toronkawa*, Zaria, 1961.

Muhammad b. Muhammad (Imam), *Tarikh Bauchi* (unpublished), National Archives, Kaduna.

Nadel, S. F., *A Black Byzantium*, Oxford, 1942.

NEDECO, *River Studies*, Amsterdam, 1959.

Nicolas, F., *Tamesna*, Paris, 1950.

Olderogge, D. A., *Zapadnyi Sudan*, Moscow, 1960.

Palmer, H. R., *Bornu Sahara and Sudan*, London, 1936.

Palmer, H. R., 'An early Fulani conception of Islam', *Journal, African Society*, XIII, 52; XIV, 53 and 54, 1914–15.

Palmer, H. R., *Gazetteer of Bornu Province*, Lagos, 1929.

Palmer, H. R., *Sudanese Memoirs* (3 vols.), Lagos, 1928.

Palmer, H. R., 'Western Sudan history: being the Raudthat'ul Afkari', *Journal, African Society*, XV, 59, 1916.

De Pedrals, D-P., *Archéologie de l'Afrique Noire*, Paris, 1950.

Perham, M., *Lugard*, London, 1960.

Perié, J., 'Notes historiques sur la région de Maradi (Niger)', *Bulletin, Institut Français d'Afrique Noire*, I, 1939.

Robinson, C. H., *Specimens of Hausa Literature*, Cambridge, 1896.

Rodd, F. R., *People of the Veil*, London, 1926.

Rosenthal, F. (transl.), *Ibn Khaldun: Muqaddimah*, London, 1958.

Ruxton, F. H., *Maliki Law*, London, 1916.

Schon, J. F., *Dictionary of the Hausa Language*, London, 1876.

Smith, H. F. C., 'Arabic manuscript material bearing on the history of the Western Sudan', *Supplement, Bulletin of News, Historical Society of Nigeria*, IV, 2, 1959.

Smith, H. F. C., 'The dynastic chronology of Fulani Zaria', *Journal, Historical Society of Nigeria*, II, 1, 1961.

Smith, H. F. C., 'The Islamic revolutions of the 19th century', *Journal, Historical Society of Nigeria*, II, 1, 1961.

Smith, H. F. C., 'Source material for the history of the Western Sudan', *Journal, Historical Society of Nigeria*, I, 3, 1958.

Smith, M. F., *Baba of Karo*, Oxford, 1954.

Smith, M. G., *Government in Zazzau*, Oxford, 1960.

Sölken, H., 'Geschichte von Ada', *Mittheilungen der Ausland-Hochschule*, Berlin, XL, XLII, 1937–9.

Sölken, H., 'Die Geschichte von Kabi nach Imam Umaru', *Mittheilungen des Instituts für Orientforschung*, VII, 1, 1959; IX, 1, 1963.

Sourdel, D., *Le Vizirat Abbaside*, Paris, 1959–60.

Stenning, D. J., *Savannah Nomads*, Oxford, 1959.

Suret-Canale, J., 'Essai sur la signification sociale et historique des hegemonies Peules', *Cahiers du Centre d'Etudes et de Recherches Marxistes*, Paris, 1964.

Tapiero, N., 'Le grand shaykh Peul 'Uthmān Ibn Fūdi', *Revue des Etudes Islamiques*, 1963.

Tauxier, L., *Mœurs et Histoire des Peuls*, Paris, 1937.

Temple, C. L., Report on the death of the Amir al-muminin Attahiru. National Archives, Kaduna (SNP 15).

Temple, O and C. L., *Notes on the Tribes, Provinces, Emirates and States of the Northern Provinces of Nigeria*, Lagos, 1922.

(Tilho), *Documents Scientifiques de la Mission Tilho* (vol. 2), Paris, 1911.

Tremearne, A. J. H., *The Ban of the Bori*, London, 1914.

Trimingham, J. S., *A History of Islam in West Africa*, Oxford, 1962.

Tyan, E., *Histoire de l'Organisation Judiciaire en pays d'Islam*, 2nd edition, Leiden, 1960.

Urvoy, Y., 'Chroniques d'Agades', *Journal, Société des Africanistes*, IV, 1934.

Urvoy, Y., 'Essai de bibliographie des populations du Soudan Central', *Bulletin, Comité d'Etudes Historiques et Scientifiques de l'Afrique Occidentale Française*, XIX, 1936.

Urvoy, Y., *Histoire de l'Empire de Bornou*, Paris, 1949.

Urvoy, Y., 'Histoire des Oullimiden de l'Est', *Bulletin, Comité d'Etudes Historiques et Scientifiques de l'A.O.F.*, XVI, 1, 1933.

Urvoy, Y., *Histoire des Populations du Soudan Central*, Paris, 1936.

Uthman b. Ibrahim, *Tarikh Kontagora* (1336 A.H.). Kontagora Div. Office (from Mr. E. J. Lannert).

Vajda, G., 'Contribution à la connaissance de la littérature arabe en Afrique Occidentale', *Journal, Société des Africanistes*, XX, 2, 1950.

Vajda, G., *Index Général des Manuscrits Arabes Musulmans de la Bibliothèque Nationale de Paris*, Paris, 1953.

Waldman, M. F., 'The Fulani jihād: a reassessment', *Journal of African History*, VI, 3, 1965.

Whitting, C. E. J. (ed.), *Bello: Infaku'l maisuri*, London, 1951.

Whitting, C. E. J., *Hausa and Fulani Proverbs*, Lagos, 1940.

Whitting, C. E. J. (trans.), *History of Sokoto*, Kano, 1949.

Index

In the alphabetical order of this index the Arabic article al- has been disregarded.

Index

Gwandu (*contd.*)
139 n, 169, 196, 204, 232; Fulani, *see* Fulani
Gwaram, 105 n, 181
Gwari, 43 n
Gwomki, Sarkin Gobir, 70, 75
Gwongazo, 71, 75
Gwongono, liii, 29 n
Gwoni Mukhtār, 56

Hadejia, 44, 55, 135, 137, 158, 186, 187, 188, 202; crisis, xxxvii, xlvi, 19 n, 88–9, 130, 136, 159, 160, 206; Emir of, 54, 186, 199, 202 n
Ḥafṣa bint al-Shaikh, 18, 19, 151
al-Ḥājj, Amīr Rafi, 133
Ḥāmid, Emir of Adar, 35, 36, 107
Ḥāmid b. al-Hindī, 215
Ḥamīd, Malam, 172
Hamma, 109
Hamma b. ʻAlī, 93
Hammada, cousin of Bello, 93
Hammada, Emir of Zaria, 160
Hamza, Dangaladima of Raba, 176
Ḥaras, 93
Hārūn, Shaikh of the Ningi, 203
al-Ḥasan b. ʻAbdullāh b. Gidado, 165
al-Ḥasan b. Abī Bakr Atiku, Sarkin Zamfara, 101 n, 122 n, 123, 127; his descendants, 102
al-Ḥasan b. Aḥmad, judge, 49
al-Ḥasan b. Dembo, 19 n
al-Ḥasan b. al-Shaikh, 151
Hāshim, Shaikh of Bornu, 202 n
Hausa: language, xxxviii, xliii, xlix, l, lii, liii, lx, 9, 51, 67, 98 n, 103 n, 112 n, 122, 149, 192, 194, 221, 222; people, lxxxii, 18, 19, 27, 36 n, 67, 69, 92, 106, 192, 229; land, states, and towns, xlviii, xlix, lv, lix, lx, (map) lxiv, lxiv–lxx, lxxiii, lxxv, lxxvi, lxxx, lxxxii, 28, 39 n, 53, 55, 60 n, 96, 112, 131 n, 138, 209 n, 219, 228; trade, xlviii, lxiv, lxx; sultans, lxxvi, 36; malams, lxxvi–lxxvii, lxxix–lxxx; titles, lv, 28 n, 92 n
Ḥawwā' bint Muḥammad (mother of the Shaikh), 4
Ḥayāt b. Saʻīd b. Bello, 122, 138, 159 n 204
Hijra of the Shaikh, xxxiv, 10, 15–16, 23–9, (map) 25, 49, 93, 109, 140–1, 151, 234 n; date of, 23 n
Hodi, Sultan of Kebbi, 34 n
al-Ḥusain, wālī al-shurṭa (chief of police), 50, 93 n

Ibn Isḥāq, *see* ʻUthmān b. Isḥāq
Ibn Jada, or Dan Jada, *see* Abū Bakr dan Jada
Ibn Jodi, 100
Ibn Māsanih, 208
Ibra, Tuareg leader, lxxv, lxxviii, 71, 110–12, 154
Ibrāhīm, Emir of Adar, 36, 107–8
Ibrāhīm, Sāʻī, 19, 51, 53
Ibrāhīm Dabo, Emir of Kano, 159 n, 161
Ibrāhīm b. Abī Bakr b. Bello, Emir of Raba, 176
Ibrāhīm b. ʻAlī, Sultan of Gobir, 124–5
Ibrāhīm b. Muḥammad Bello, 71, 77, 122; son of, *see* Abū Bakr b. Ibrāhīm
Ibrāhīm b. Muḥammad Bello, Sarkin Shano, 136 n
Ibrāhīm b. ʻUmar, Emir of Kontagora, 135
Ibrāhīm b. Yaʻqūb of Bauchi, 82
Ibrāhīm Khalilu b. ʻAbd al-Qādir, Vizier, lii, 162–3, 170, 171, 184 n, 187, 190 n, 215, 223, 225; his poetry, 221; son of, 177
Ibrāhīm Zaki, Emir of Katagum, 54, 56, 202
Illela (Washr) liii, 111
Illo, 10
Ilorin, 43, 139; Emir of (*see also* Yoruba), 92 n, 196 n, 222
Imagerem, *see* Tuareg
Imam(s), 18, 20, 21, 80, 92, 182, 184, 189
Imanan, 44
Imgad, *see* Tuareg
Iname, 23, 26, 28, 78, 94
Ineslemen, *see* Tuareg
Isa, liii, 78–9, 114, 115, 119, 126